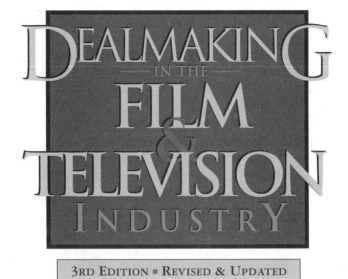

DEALMAKING IN THE FILM & TELEVISION INDUSTRY

3RD EDITION ▪ REVISED & UPDATED

Other books by Mark Litwak

Reel Power
Courtroom Crusaders
Contracts for the Film and Television Industry
Litwak's Multimedia Producer's Handbook

DEALMAKING
IN THE
FILM & TELEVISION
INDUSTRY
FROM NEGOTIATIONS TO FINAL CONTRACTS

3RD EDITION ▪ REVISED & UPDATED

BY MARK LITWAK

SILMAN-JAMES PRESS
LOS ANGELES

10 9 8 7 6 5 4 3 2

Library of Congress Cataloging-in-Publication Data

Litwak, Mark.
Dealmaking in the film & television industry :
from negotiations to final
contracts / by Mark Litwak. -- 3rd ed., rev. and updated.
p. cm.
ISBN 978-1-879505-99-5 (alk. paper)
1. Artists' contracts--United States. 2. Performing arts--Law and legislation--United States. 3. Motion pictures--Law and legislation--United
States. 4. Entertainers--Legal status, laws, etc.--United States. I.
Title. II. Title: Dealmaking in the film and television industry.
KF4290.L58 2009
344.73'099--dc22
                                                      2008055263

ISBN: 1-879505-99-5

Cover design by Heidi Frieder

Printed and bound in the United States of America

SILMAN-JAMES PRESS
1181 Angelo Drive
Beverly Hills, CA 90210

To my sons, David and Michael

DISCLAIMER

This book is designed to help readers understand legal issues frequently encountered in the entertainment industry. It will provide you with an understanding of basic legal principles, enabling you to better communicate with your attorney.

The information contained in this book is intended to provide general information and does not constitute legal advice. This book is not intended to create an attorney-client relationship between you and the author or any of his associates, and you should not act or rely on any information in this book without seeking the advice of an attorney.

The information provided is not a substitute for consulting with an experienced attorney and receiving counsel based on the facts and circumstances of a particular transaction. Many of the legal principles mentioned are subject to exceptions and qualifications that may not be noted in the text. Furthermore, case law and statutes are subject to revision and may not apply in every state. Because of the quick pace of technological change, some of the information in this book may be outdated by the time you read it. Readers should be aware that business practices, distribution methods, and legislation continue to evolve in the rapidly changing entertainment industries.

THE INFORMATION IS PROVIDED "AS IS," AND THE AUTHOR MAKES NO EXPRESS OR IMPLIED REPRESENTATIONS OR WARRANTIES, INCLUDING WARRANTIES OF PERFORMANCE,

Mark Litwak can be contacted by e-mail. However, if you communicate with him electronically or otherwise in connection with a matter for which he does not already represent you, your communication may not be treated as privileged or confidential. An attorney-client relationship can only be created with a written retainer agreement signed by both parties.

ACKNOWLEDGEMENTS

I am grateful for the assistance of Phil Hacker, Tiiu Lukk, Gary Salt, and Lon Sobel for reading and critiquing early drafts of this work, and to Shannon C. Hensley, Esq., for editing the Second Edition. Thanks also to Elizabeth Zook, Ryan Pastorek, Chrys Wu, Jessica Dubick, Cyndie Chang, Lawrence Young, and Danielle Casselman for checking case citations and facts.

My thanks to Elliott Williams at the Directors Guild of America, Grace Reiner at the Writers Guild, and Vicki Shapiro at the Screen Actors Guild, for reviewing portions of the chapters pertaining to their members and guild rules.

I am also indebted to my publishers, Gwen Feldman and Jim Fox, for their helpful suggestions.

CONTENTS

CONTRACTS

CASE SUMMARIES

PREFACE

After the publication of my book *Reel Power* in 1986, I was invited to lecture at many universities in the United States and abroad. On numerous occasions I was asked to recommend a guide to entertainment legal issues. I was not able to recommend such a guide because I did not know of one.

While there are several texts on entertainment law, most are not addressed to the general reader. Many of these books are written by entertainment lawyers for other lawyers and are confusing, if not impenetrable, for everyone else.

Eventually I resolved to write a layperson's guide to entertainment law, and this is that book. I have attempted to explain complex legal ideas as simply as possible, avoiding jargon and explaining terms of art. I have taken a practical, problem-solving approach, rather than exploring theoretical issues of interest to academicians.

Of course there is a danger in trying to simplify complex information. Important exceptions and qualifications may be overlooked. The unwary reader may be misled into thinking he knows more than he does. It is well to recall the maxim that a little knowledge can be dangerous. So I caution readers

DEALMAKING
IN THE
FILM AND
TELEVISION
INDUSTRY—
3RD EDITION

XVIII

to consult an experienced entertainment lawyer before making decisions with legal ramifications.

While this book is not a substitute for consulting an attorney, it does familiarize the reader with entertainment law and industry practice. It will impart to the neophyte some wisdom of show-biz veterans, enabling newcomers to protect themselves from exploitation as they learn to become savvy dealmakers.

Moreover, this guide can save readers thousands of dollars in legal fees. Entertainment attorneys generally charge $300 to $500 an hour for their time. Armed with this guide, laypeople won't need to ask their attorney to explain basic legal concepts and common deal structures. The lawyer and client can work more efficiently. Moreover, as the reader becomes more knowledge-able about his rights, he can take measures to prevent legal problems from arising in the first place.

I welcome comments and suggestions from readers. Additional information is available on my website, "Entertainment Law Resources." You can contact me at: Law Offices of Mark Litwak & Associates, e-mail: law2@marklitwak.com, phone (310) 859-9595, website www.marklitwak.com.

I hope this guide will prove useful to you.

Mark Litwak
January 2009

CHAPTER I

INTRODUCTION

Before delving into the details of dealmaking, it is important for the reader to understand the context in which deals are made and the motivation of the players. Shrewd dealmakers know how to structure a deal to meet the needs, often unspoken, of all the parties.

Here follows background information on the social, legal, and technological forces that have influenced, and continue to influence, the industry. Readers can gain additional insight by reading the books in the recommended reading list in the Appendix.

THE AMERICAN FILM INDUSTRY

The United States motion picture and television industry is a uniquely successful enterprise. In those countries that allow American films to be freely exhibited, they usually dominate the marketplace. Hollywood's films succeed in the world to an extent unrivaled by other American products. In 2007, for example, they earned total export revenues of $17.1 billion dollars.[1]

Yet the industry is extremely volatile, risky, and beset with problems. Managements frequently change, profits are erratic, and smaller production and distribution companies regularly go bust. A typical major studio movie now costs about $70.8 million to produce and another $35.9 million to market. Many movies

---

[1] According to the Motion Picture Association of America (MPAA).

DEALMAKING
IN THE
FILM AND
TELEVISION
INDUSTRY—
3RD EDITION

2

are expensive flops. Most television pilot programs don't become successful series or recoup their production costs.

In the last several years, American major and minor distributors have released between 460 and 600 feature films per year.[2]

Major studios distribute less than half of those films; yet earn more than 95% of all box office revenues. Upon further examination, one discovers that a relative handful of movies earn most of the revenues. In 2007, there were only 17 motion pictures that had a gross domestic box office of $100 million or more. Of any ten major theatrical films produced, on the average, six or seven are unprofitable,[3] and one will break even, according to Harold Vogel, entertainment analyst for Merrill Lynch and Co. Thus, while Hollywood dominates the world market with its product, it is hardly an efficient producer of popular entertainment.

THE MOVIE INDUSTRY THEN AND NOW

The movie industry was founded by European immigrants. They were an unsophisticated and uneducated lot. Adolph Zukor, the builder of Paramount, was a furrier from Hungary. Universal's Carl Laemmle was a clothing-store manager from Germany. These pioneers were modestly successful small businessmen who decided to invest their capital in a fledgling industry.

Business barons of the era expressed little interest in the movie industry. The public's fascination with the medium was considered a fad and the enterprise deemed risky. Besides, movies were entertainment for the unwashed masses, not for educated individuals who patronized plays and operas.

Los Angeles became the center of the industry because labor was cheap, the weather good, and the location far from the Edison Company and the Motion Picture Patents Company, which controlled the patents for moviemaking. These companies contended that producers who made movies without their permission were outlaws operating illegally.

---

[2] For 2007 there was a total of 590 releases, with 179 pictures released by the major studios (MPAA members: Walt Disney Company; Sony Pictures Entertainment, Inc.; Metro-Goldwyn-Mayer, Inc.; Paramount Pictures Corporation; 20th Century Fox Film Corp.; Universal Studios, Inc., and Warner Bros.

[3] However, many films earn substantial additional revenue from ancillary markets such as home video and cable television.

The founders of the industry became known as the "moguls." While they had a great love of movies, they were foremost tough businessmen out to make a buck. They made some high-quality pictures but mostly churned out grade-B movies like *Son of Dracula* and *Abbott & Costello Meet Frankenstein*. Fox's biggest moneymaker was Shirley Temple. Rin Tin Tin kept Warner Bros. afloat.

Unabashed tyrants, the moguls ran their studios with an iron hand. They would change the names of their stars, tell them what their next movie would be, and loan them to one another like chattel. One year David Selznick made $425,000 lending Ingrid Bergman—she received $60,000. Anyone who dared object would be suspended without pay, and no other studio would employ them.

Many of the abuses the moguls were famous for no longer exist in Hollywood. The mogul's practice of seducing actresses on "casting couches" is not acceptable behavior in the more corporate atmosphere that now prevails.[4] Writers, directors, and stars are no longer indentured servants working under long-term contracts. They have unions, agents, and attorneys to protect their interests.

Nowadays the studios are run by college-educated men and women, many of whom have MBAs or law degrees. Generally bright, hard-working, and liberal-minded, they try to make decisions rationally and have invested in state-of-the-art technology that has vastly improved picture quality. They have many types of market research to help them, and they promote films with sophisticated ads, merchandising tie-ins, slick music videos, and websites.

But observers note that today's movies are not any better—artistically or commercially—than those produced by the moguls.

THE END OF THE STUDIO SYSTEM

The motion picture industry has undergone a remarkable transformation over the past 50 years. Major changes began in 1948 when the United States Supreme Court upheld the Justice Department's antitrust suit against the studios, which divested the studios of

[4] Of course, there is plenty of sexual activity in the industry and numerous instances of sexual harassment in the workplace.

DEALMAKING
IN THE
FILM AND
TELEVISION
INDUSTRY—
3RD EDITION

4

their theater chains. In the early 1950s a fierce new competitor, television, came on the scene, drastically reducing attendance at movies. This, in turn, reduced the level of studio production and ultimately led to the end of long-term contracts and the studio system.

Eventually the studios began producing for television. They diversified into related areas such as amusement parks and music recording. Cable television and home video created new markets for films and additional sources of revenue. The studios became conglomerates or were acquired by conglomerates. A number of studios were purchased by foreign investors.

There has been a sea change in the attitude of the captains of industry. The moguls, for all their failings, were entrepreneurs. They built an industry based on gut instinct—perhaps because they lacked market research, but also because they were inclined to take chances.

"The great gamblers are dead," Steven Spielberg commented several years ago, "and I think that's the tragedy of Hollywood today. In the old days, the Thalbergs and the Zanucks and the Mayers came out of nickelodeon vaudeville, they came out of borscht-belt theater, and they came with a great deal of showmanship and esprit de corps to a little citrus grove in California. They were brave. They were gamblers. They were high-rollers.

"There is a paranoia today. People are afraid. People in high positions are unable to say 'okay' or 'not okay,' they're afraid to take the big gamble. They're looking for the odds-on-favorite. And that's very, very hard when you're making movies. All motion pictures are a gamble. Anything having to do with creating something that nobody's seen before, and showing it, and counting on 10 or 20 million people, individuals, to go into the theater to make or break that film—that's a gamble. And I just think in the old days, in the Golden Age of Hollywood, gambling was just taken for granted. Today, gambling is a no-no. And I'm sorry to see that go."[5]

The primary drive of many studio executives, as with businesspeople in much of corporate America, is risk avoidance. They try to make films they can justify to their boards of directors. If they develop a story similar to a recent hit and attach a successful director and a couple of stars, they will have

---

[5] Michael Ventura, "Spielberg on Spielberg," *L.A. Weekly*, December 9–15, 1983, p. 12.

an impressive-looking package with some "insurance." Should the picture flop, they can exclaim, "Look, I got you Brad Pitt in a project like *Titanic*, directed by the guy who made *Men in Black*." And the board of directors will be sympathetic, chalk up the loss to a fickle public, and the executive is less likely to be fired.

The desire of executives to play it safe has induced them to devise complex schemes to reduce the financial risks of moviemaking. By entering pre-sale agreements with cable and home-video companies, or by cutting deals with outside investors, a studio can eliminate much risk.

Perhaps that is why the most-prized executives are often the top dealmakers. When these executives go beyond business and financial matters, however, interjecting themselves into the creative process, problems can arise because they lack filmmaking knowledge and training. Most executives today have little hands-on filmmaking experience.

It is important to bear in mind that, in spite of the financial acumen of contemporary executives, today's studios are no more profitable than in the days of the studio system. Because the studios compete so heavily for the services of a small pool of stars and big-name directors, the price of these commodities has risen dramatically. According to the Motion Picture Association of America (MPAA), the average cost to make and market a major MPAA member company film was $106.6 million in 2007. This includes $70.8 million in negative costs and $35.9 million in marketing costs.[6]

A UNIQUE PRODUCT

Hollywood suffers from many of the same problems that plague other American industries. Professional managers have taken the reins of control. They are better-educated than their predecessors but often lack their entrepreneurial zeal and willingness to take risks.

Entrepreneurs who start businesses often don't have the desire or management skills to run a large organization. Inventors, like Steve Wozniak, may find it more satisfying to tinker in their

---

[6] www.mpaa.org/researchStatistics.asp

DEALMAKING
IN THE
FILM AND
TELEVISION
INDUSTRY—
3RD EDITION

6

garages and invent new products than attend board of directors' meetings and manage a large bureaucracy. While these entrepreneurs may function well as lone operators or in small groups, when called upon to supervise large enterprises, their shortcomings can prevent the organization from prospering. So the entrepreneurs stand aside—or are shoved aside—and the managers take over.

But the movie and television industry is different from other industries. The commodity being sold is creativity. Movies don't lend themselves to assembly-line manufacturing. It's not like making soap, where once you devise the right formula you can churn out the same product time and again. A consumer who finds a brand of soap he/she likes may stick with it for a long time. He/she doesn't want the tenth bar to be any different from the first. He/she doesn't expect the product to entertain him/her or provide a new experience.

But people don't find one movie they like and watch it repeatedly. Moviegoers always want something different. They want to be taken where they haven't been before. They want fresh situations, plots, and characters—not a rehash of last week's hit.

Consequently, the movies that do best are often those that are distinctly original. *Star Wars* was a breakthrough film because of its wonderful special effects, unusual setting, and fresh characters. Moviegoers had never seen anything like it before.

Unfortunately, the atmosphere prevalent at many major studios today is not conducive to creative filmmaking because executives are so risk-adverse. United Artists and Universal rejected *Star Wars* before Alan Ladd Jr. at 20th Century Fox decided to back it. Often filmmakers can't find a single executive willing to gamble on anything that is offbeat or unusual. It took director Oliver Stone ten years to produce *Platoon*, and then he succeeded only because an independent company provided the financing.

Many intelligent, provocative, and innovative movies—like *Crouching Tiger, Hidden Dragon*; *The Crying Game*; *Roger & Me*; *Sex, Lies, and Videotape*; *Hollywood Shuffle*; *Kiss of the Spider Woman*; and *Blood Simple*—have been made with independent financing. Some of these independently made pictures are enormously profitable, such as *The Full Monty* and *My Big Fat Greek Wedding*, and many have received Academy Award nominations for Best Picture. Such critically acclaimed films as *Juno, Crash, March of the Penguins*, and *Little Miss Sunshine* were made outside

Hollywood. The public is generally unaware of how many of the best movies are only distributed by a major studio.

Due to the risk-adverse climate in Hollywood, a common failing of studio movies today is that they are derivative of other movies. *Flashdance* spawns *Footloose*; *Animal House* is reworked into *Meatballs* and *Police Academy*. Any movie that is the least bit profitable is the basis for one or more sequels. The studios try to squeeze as much as possible from every successful property they own.

COPING WITH RISK

Because of their aversion to risk, the studios have largely withdrawn from producing films in-house. While many maintain production lots, which are rented to anyone needing a soundstage, the studios essentially function as specialized banks, lending money to produce worthy projects and then distributing the finished product.

Like banks, they evaluate proposals submitted to them but rarely initiate projects. After borrowing money from large banks or obtaining investment funds, the studios decide which producers to back. The producer and director make the movie, with oversight by the studio concerned about protecting its investment. Once the picture is complete, the studio markets it, creating an advertising campaign and duplicating and distributing prints. Finally, the studio uses its clout to collect receipts from exhibitors.

There are some exceptions to this modus operandi. At some independent production entities like Castle Rock Entertainment and Imagine Entertainment, the executives who run the company are more involved in creating product.

But most studios are run by dealmakers, not filmmakers. Many executives rise to the top based on their relationships with big-name talent and their dealmaking prowess, not because of their understanding of what makes a good script or their filmmaking ability.

Other problems have arisen because the studios have relinquished much of their creative authority. Increasingly, executives make decisions based on market research, demographic trends, and minimizing financial risks. It has become much more of a

DEALMAKING
IN THE
FILM AND
TELEVISION
INDUSTRY—
3RD EDITION

8

lawyer-agent game, with less showmanship, according to producer Martin Ransohoff (*Jagged Edge*): "Picture-making itself had a better shot under the old moguls. They were basically movie guys. Not conglomerate or bank-endorsed people."

The old studio staff producers have been replaced by creative-affairs executives. "They function as staff producers but without the public shame and responsibility that comes from having your name on the picture," says industry analyst A.D. Murphy. "They exercise authority but remain anonymous. And when you have a lot of faceless people who are not out there naked next to their films, you have a lot of copping-out and log-rolling."

Large talent agencies such as CAA and William Morris exercise considerable influence in developing and packaging projects. Agents conceive ideas for movies, discover new talent, and decide which writers, directors, and stars shall work together in the packages they create. In the old days, the studios performed these creative tasks.

MANAGING A CREATIVE ENTERPRISE

In many ways the atmosphere for creative moviemaking was better during the era of the moguls. More than 50 million Americans went to the theater every week in the days before television. Admissions reached an all-time high of four billion in 1946.[7] Because films cost less and there was no competition from television, videogames, and the like, even mediocre films stood a better chance of making a profit. Since the moguls owned the studios they ran, they were more secure in their positions and could afford to take more risks—if a picture flopped, it might hurt their pocketbook but they wouldn't lose their job.

Some studios have belatedly realized the importance of creativity in moviemaking. Burned by expensive star-studded flops based on agency packages, these studios have hired executives who can play a more creative role in filmmaking.

In 1984, after *Rhinestone* (starring Sylvester Stallone and Dolly Parton) bombed, 20th Century Fox fired Alan Hirschfield and Joe Wizan and hired Barry Diller. Diller was head of the much-vaunted Paramount team (Diller/Eisner/Katzenberg/Mancuso)

---

[7] With the advent of television the numbers dropped to approximately one billion per year. In 2001, 1.49 billion tickets were sold.

that insisted on developing projects itself rather than accepting agency packages. Disney also lured two other members of that Paramount team, Michael Eisner and Jeff Katzenberg, to replace the more business-oriented Ron Miller.[8]

In each of these instances, studios replaced executives with backgrounds in finance and dealmaking with people known for their creative abilities. But creativity can be risky. In 1994, Steven Spielberg, Jeffrey Katzenberg, and David Geffen launched Dreamworks SKG to create an artist-friendly studio. However, by 2006, after flirting with bankruptcy twice, the company was sold to Viacom, losing its independence. Likewise, independent New Line Cinema, founded in 1967, was acquired by Turner Broadcasting System in 1994, which in 1996 merged with Time Warner. The company lost its autonomy in 2008 when Time Warner absorbed it.

---

[8] Disney has generally avoided big-budget star packages, and after its release of *Dick Tracy*, which earned relatively modest returns, Katzenberg cautioned his staff to be wary of expensive star packages.

CHAPTER 2

DEALMAKING

There is more dealmaking activity in the movie business today than ever before. Late in his career, director Billy Wilder complained, "Today we spend 80% of the time making deals and 20% making pictures."[1] Indeed, most people who work in the industry devote far more time to dealmaking than filmmaking. It wasn't always this way; in the Golden Age of Hollywood, when the moguls ran the industry, the emphasis was just the reverse.

Dealmaking increased with the end of the studio system. With talent no longer tied to long-term contracts, the studios dismantled their rosters of stars and stables of writers. Nowadays, talent is hired on an ad-hoc, picture-by-picture basis, and as a result, many more deals need to be negotiated.

Imagine a football game where the players' employment must be renegotiated after every play. The referee blows the whistle and the agents and attorneys rush onto the field to consult with their clients and begin bargaining with management. This would change the game as we know it—perhaps at halftime the lawyers could march in precision drill teams to entertain the fans. Well, the process has not become quite that unwieldy in Hollywood, but you get the idea.

Dealmaking has become more complex as well. Methods of financing films have multiplied. Under the old studio system, films were funded from current revenues or bank loans. The

---

[1] *The Book of Hollywood Quotes,* compiled by Harry Herman (London/New York/Sydney/Tokyo/Cologne: Omnibus Press, 1979), p. 118.

DEALMAKING
IN THE
FILM AND
TELEVISION
INDUSTRY—
3RD EDITION

12

studios didn't rely on intricate Wall Street investment schemes, pre-sale deals, foreign co-productions, and insurance-backed financing.

Other complications have arisen as new markets developed. Today, deals must take account of revenue from cable television, home video, syndication, video on demand, electronic sell-through, Internet, wireless, merchandising, soundtrack albums and foreign sales. As studios began to share "profits" with talent, other problems arose. Studios and profit participants often disagreed on accounting methods and interpretation of contracts. To avoid ambiguity, net profit's definitions grew. One studio attaches an 18-page, single-spaced definition of the term.

Because of these industry changes, an understanding of deal-making has become vital for anyone interested in filmmaking. It is always important to remember, however, that the final product is the film. In the heat of negotiations, parties may forget that audiences don't care about the deal. Can you imagine moviegoers reviewing deal memos projected on the screen as they exclaim: "Wow, look at deal point five!" or "Isn't that an interesting definition of gross?" No, the viewer only cares about the story. Since a good deal does not necessarily produce an entertaining movie, attorneys and agents must take care not to put their clients into projects that stand little chance of success because the deals don't leave enough money to produce a quality film.

DISINCENTIVES TO GOOD FILMMAKING

The Pay-or-Play Clause

Dealmakers need to be aware of disincentives to good moviemaking. Certain deals can encourage bad moviemaking. For example, a pay-or-play deal may induce a studio to produce a poorly written screenplay.

A pay-or-play provision is often demanded by actors and directors in return for their commitment to participate in a project. Essentially, the deal guarantees talent their salary even if the movie ultimately does not get made. The desire for such a provision is reasonable for sought-after talent, although it may put a producer or studio in a bind. To understand the dynamics of such a deal, let us consider a hypothetical scenario:

You are a filmmaker with an idea for a movie. You want Julia Roberts to star in your picture. Somehow you gain access to her, tell her the idea, and she responds favorably. She will not, however, commit to the project based on a mere idea. No star in their right mind would commit to a film at this stage. So Julia tells you that if you can produce an acceptable script, she would love to star in your film.

You write a script, or hire a writer to create one, and after several rewrites incorporating Julia's suggestions, she is satisfied with the screenplay and decides she wants to be in the film. You ask her to commit to the project. She, or her agent, wants to know if this film is really going to happen. She does not want to block out three months of her summer schedule and hold herself available to make your film if it is not a sure thing.

Once Julia commits contractually to star in your movie, she must turn down other projects that may be offered to her that will shoot at the same time. She knows that there are many reasons why, despite your great efforts and talent, you may not succeed in getting the script produced. Perhaps you can't secure financing, or obtain the right co-star, or attract a studio-acceptable director. So her agent tells you that she will not commit to the project until you have all the other elements in place. The problem is that the other elements feel the same way. No one wants to commit first.

To obtain talent commitments, a pay-or-play clause, guaranteeing the talent's salary, may be needed. If the salary is large, this can be a very risky commitment to make. Suppose you are an executive who has made such a deal with a star and you cannot surmount all the obstacles to production. In the realm of feature films, perhaps one out of ten projects that are developed gets produced.[2] So as your start date rapidly approaches, you become increasingly agitated. You are faced with a terrible dilemma: Do you go forward and produce the project under less-than-ideal circumstances or should you pay off the actor with the pay-or-play commitment?

This is exactly what happened with *Villa Rides*. The studio was committed to pay Yul Brynner and Robert Mitchum regardless of whether the film was made. Let's suppose that the studio was on the hook for $1 million on pay-or-play deals, and it would

---

[2] For television movies, a much greater percentage of projects that are developed ultimately get produced.

DEALMAKING
IN THE
FILM AND
TELEVISION
INDUSTRY—
3RD EDITION

14

cost another million to make the film. In such a case it might make sense financially, if not artistically, to go forward in the hope that the movie could recoup its budget before bad word-of-mouth killed it. On the other hand, if you scrap the project, you can't possibly recoup your investment. You may also find it difficult to explain to your board of directors why you spent $1 million of their money and have nothing to show for it.

Have you ever wondered as you watched a terrible movie: "How could a studio produce this piece of dreck? Couldn't the executives discern from the script that this story was flawed? Are these executives brain-dead?" Well, the answer may be that the executives knew full well that the project was third-rate, but it may have made financial sense to go forward.

Another disincentive to good filmmaking occurs when agents push clients into making movies they shouldn't. Sometimes agents are more interested in earning their 10% commission than in furthering the client's long-range career goals. After all, if a client is making $20 million a picture, an agent has a powerful incentive to keep him/her working. The attitude of some agents is to grab as much as you can when the client is hot, because who knows if you will be representing him/her two years from now.

Overall Development Deals

Producers who enter overall development deals with studios sometimes have an incentive to make their films at other studios.

There are several types of overall development deals, including EXCLUSIVE, FIRST LOOK, and HOUSEKEEPING deals.

Studios enter overall development deals with producers to ensure a steady flow of product. Keeping the pipeline full satisfies exhibitors and helps the studio amortize certain fixed overhead expenses, such as the cost of the marketing staff.

Producers benefit in several ways from overall development deals. The producer often receives an office on the studio lot, a secretary, and perhaps a development person or two. The studio agrees to pay for development expenses, such as hiring writers to develop the producer's projects. Also, the studio pays the producer a fee for every project produced, and often provides an advance.

For a top producer, the advance may be hundreds of thousands of dollars per year. The money is paid out in monthly or weekly installments like a salary and is non-recoupable—it doesn't have to be repaid, even if the producer doesn't produce anything. Essentially, the overall development deal takes the financial risk of producing off a producer's shoulders and places it on the studio's shoulders.

When a producer enters an EXCLUSIVE development deal, he/she agrees to distribute all his/her projects through one studio. This deal may be exclusive for features or television or both, but whatever the parameters, the producer is essentially a captive of that studio and cannot produce projects elsewhere.

A FIRST-LOOK deal, on the other hand, simply gives the studio first look, or first crack, at the producer's projects. If the studio passes on a project, the producer can develop it elsewhere. Most deals allow the studio several weeks to decide if they want a project, and if no decision is made, the producer automatically has the right to take it to another studio.

A HOUSEKEEPING DEAL is one in which the producer receives an office and development expenses but no advance. Typically this deal is offered to novice producers. The studio wants to have an ongoing relationship without incurring a lot of expense. The producer gets to set up housekeeping on the studio lot and cover his/her overhead expenses. The producer may gain credibility within the industry by being able to use the studio stationery and switchboard. Agents promptly return his/her phone calls, the producer can network with others on the lot, and most importantly, he/she can take his/her parents to the commissary when they visit.

Obviously, producers prefer first-look deals. The producer likes to have alternative sources of financing and distribution available. Savvy producers also know that a first-look deal gives one leverage within the studio decision-making bureaucracy. You can force the studio to make up its mind on a project or risk losing it. On the other hand, if you have an exclusive deal, the studio knows you can't take a project elsewhere, and consequently there may be no urgency to make a decision.

Studios prefer exclusive deals. They will argue that since they are paying an advance and overhead expenses, it is only fair that the producer spend her time developing projects for the studio and not for others. Another reason studio executives

DEALMAKING
IN THE
FILM AND
TELEVISION
INDUSTRY—
3RD EDITION

16

prefer exclusive deals are to avoid the embarrassment of passing on a project on a first-look basis and later see it become a blockbuster hit for another studio. In such a case, the studio's board of directors may ask the executive, "Isn't Producer X one of ours?" And, "Why is X making films for our competitor while we pay his expenses?" The chagrined executive may be forced to admit that he/she foolishly passed on a hit project.

The problem with overall development deals is that they create disincentives. Let's say a producer has entered such a deal with Studio A. It's a three-year deal and the producer receives a $200,000 advance each year, paid out in monthly installments. This advance is against producer fees of $500,000 per picture.

After one year, the producer is about to produce his/her first project. Thus he/she is entitled to a fee of $500,000, less the $200,000 advance, or $300,000. However, if the project goes into turnaround,[3] the producer could obtain a larger producer fee from Studio B, which hasn't invested anything in the film's development or the producer. Thus the producer has a financial incentive to produce the film at a studio other than his/her home base.

Most producers realize that a bird in the hand is worth ten in the bush, and they would not purposely sabotage a deal in the hope of earning more elsewhere. But, this has been known to happen.

TYPES OF CONTRACTS

Contracts can be either WRITTEN or ORAL. Contrary to popular belief, oral contracts may be valid and binding. Most states have a law, known as the Statute of Frauds,[4] requiring that certain kinds of agreements must be in writing to be valid. For example, you cannot transfer real estate orally. Other kinds of agreements may be made orally, but oral contracts can be difficult to enforce.

Let's assume you made an oral agreement with a buyer to sell your car for $3,000. You shake hands on the deal but don't put

---

[3] A turnaround clause gives the producer the option of taking the project to a second studio if the first shelves it. The right to take the project elsewhere is often predicated on reimbursing the first studio its development expenses.

[4] See, e.g. California Civil Code § 1624.

anything in writing. One month later there is a dispute and you eventually end up in small claims court.

The buyer informs the judge that you offered to sell him/her your car. You agree. The buyer then claims you promised to tune up the car before delivery. You disagree. There are no documents or witnesses or evidence that the judge can review to figure out the terms of the agreement. In this situation, whom should the judge believe? The judge may simply throw up her hands and refuse to enforce the contract because she cannot ascertain its terms.

So while the law does not require that all contracts be in writing, it is usually advantageous to have an agreement in writing, if only for the sake of creating evidence. Otherwise, you risk ending up with an unenforceable deal.

Another way to classify contracts is as EXPRESS or IMPLIED contracts. When parties make an express contract, it is explicit that they are making an agreement. Typically, they sign a piece of paper or shake hands.

An implied contract is a contract implied from facts or from the law. It may be implied from the behavior of the parties. Let's suppose that you enter a store and pick up a candy bar. Without saying a word to anyone, you remove the wrapper and begin eating it. Then you head for the door. The proprietor says, "Hey, wait a minute, you didn't pay for the candy bar." You reply, "I never agreed to pay for it." Under these circumstances, a court would imply that an agreement exists, based on your conduct. It is understood that when a person consumes a candy bar under these circumstances, he/she has agreed to buy it.

Sometimes implied contracts are not based on behavior but are implied by law in the name of equity and fairness, or to prevent the unjust enrichment of one party at the expense of another.

CONTRACT LAW AS A REMEDY FOR STORY THEFT

The law of oral and implied contracts can provide the basis for a successful lawsuit for story theft. A basic tenet of copyright law is that ideas are not copyrightable because they are not considered an "expression of an author." As courts sometimes observe, "Ideas are as free as the air." Similarly, concepts, themes, and titles are not protected by copyright law.

DEALMAKING
IN THE
FILM AND
TELEVISION
INDUSTRY—
3RD EDITION

18

A copyright does protect embellishments upon ideas, however. So while a single word cannot be copyrighted, the particular manner in which a writer organizes words—his/her craft, his/her approach—is protected. While other writers remain free to create their own work based on the same topic, theme, or idea, they cannot copy the particular expression of another.

Since one cannot protect an idea under copyright law, a writer who pitches a story idea to another is vulnerable to theft. But there is another way to protect ideas. Ideas can be the subject of a contract. A writer can protect himself/herself by getting the recipient of the idea to agree to pay for it.

The best way for the writer to protect himself/herself would be to use a written agreement. However, it may be awkward to begin a meeting by asking a producer to sign a contract, even a short one. Such a request might offend some producers or make them uncomfortable. They might worry about liability and might want to consult a lawyer. Since writers often have difficulty getting in the door to see powerful producers, asking for a written agreement may not be practicable.

A less-threatening approach would be to make an oral agreement. The writer begins the meeting by simply saying: "Before I tell you my idea, I want to make sure you understand that I am telling you this idea with the understanding that if you decide to use it, I expect to receive reasonable compensation." The producer most likely will nod his/her head yes, or say, "Of course," in which case you have a deal. If the producer does not agree to these terms, don't pitch your story and leave.

Since this contract is oral, there might be a problem proving its existence and terms. That is why it's a good idea to have a witness or some documentation. You could bring a co-writer, agent, or associate along to the meeting, and you could send a letter after the meeting to the producer reiterating your understanding. The letter should be cordial and non-threatening. You could write: "It was really a pleasure meeting with you to discuss my story about. . . . As we agreed, if you decide to exploit this material, I will receive reasonable compensation." If the terms set forth in your letter are not disavowed by the recipient, the letter could be used as evidence of your agreement.[5]

---

[5] Since the letter has not been signed by the producer, his agreement to the terms is merely implied if he does not object. Of course, if the writer has a letter from the producer confirming these terms, that would be much better evidence.

But what if the producer listening to your pitch doesn't steal your story but repeats it to another producer who uses it? You can protect yourself against this peril by saying: "I am telling you my idea with the understanding that you will keep it confidential and will not tell it to anyone else without my permission." If the producer nods his/her head okay or says yes, you have a deal, and you can sue if he/she breaches that promise.

The following case illustrates how contract law has been applied in a story-theft dispute.

Desny v. Wilder (1956)[6]

FACTS: In 1949, Plaintiff (P), a writer, telephoned Billy Wilder's office on the Paramount lot and spoke to his secretary, saying that he wished to see Wilder. She insisted that P explain his purpose. P told her about a story based on the life of a boy, Floyd Collins, who had been trapped in a cave. The incident had been the subject of widespread news coverage for several weeks back in the 1920s.

The secretary liked the story, but when she learned of its length (sixty-five pages), she said that Wilder would not read it. She offered to send the story to the script department to be put in synopsis form. P said that he preferred to condense it himself. He did so and called back two days later. The secretary asked him to read her a three-page outline over the phone. He read the outline as she took it down shorthand. She said she would discuss it with Wilder. P then told her that he expected to be paid for the story if Wilder used it.

Later P discovers that Paramount has made a movie about the boy, including a fictionalized incident that P created. P sues.

ISSUES: Can P sue for the theft of a story based on a true story in the public domain?

Does it matter that P never directly spoke or met with Wilder or Paramount?

Can there be an implied contract between the parties?

Can P recover even though he didn't ask for compensation until the second conversation?

HOLDING: P prevails.

---

[6] 46 Cal. 2d 715, 299 P.2d 257 (1956).

DEALMAKING
IN THE
FILM AND
TELEVISION
INDUSTRY—
3RD EDITION

20

RATIONALE: Literary property can be created out of historical events in the public domain. Paramount had the right to go back to the historical record and prepare its own story. P has no hold over public-domain material or the idea of doing a screenplay about this subject. But if the defendants used P's research and work, there may be an implied agreement to compensate him.

The writer in this case didn't sue for copyright infringement because his story was largely a true historical incident in the public domain. Writers cannot gain rights to stories in the public domain. However, a writer can incorporate public-domain material into his/her own literary work, which can be copyrighted (although the public-domain material remains in the public domain).

In other words, ten different authors can draw upon public-domain material to write biographies of George Washington. Each possesses a copyright to his/her book, but the copyright is limited to the author's expression—his approach in arranging and organizing the facts. The author cannot prevent others from using the same facts in their work.

While the writer in the Wilder case may not be able to sue for copyright infringement, he may have a remedy under contract law. The court sent the case back to the trial level so a jury could decide if Paramount relied on P's synopsis in making the film. In other words, the court held that an implied contract could exist. A contract could be implied from the conversations between the writer and the secretary. Ultimately, a jury upon retrial would decide if the facts show that such an agreement did exist.

While P never spoke to Wilder or any Paramount executives, he could still successfully sue them. The secretary was considered an agent of Wilder and Paramount to the extent that she acted within the scope of her duties. A secretary has the authority to accept stories and manuscripts for her employer. If she had made commitments beyond her authority ("I'll give you a two-picture deal"), those promises would not be binding on Wilder or Paramount.

Nevertheless, how could there be a contract when the writer didn't ask to get paid until the end of the second conversation? Didn't the writer give the idea away and then ask to be paid for it?

No, said the court. The two conversations should be construed as one. Courts sometimes bend over backwards to help victims.

What should you remember from Desny v. Wilder? Although you don't have a written agreement, you may have a legal remedy. Now, consider the following case:

Blaustein v. Burton (1970)[7]

> FACTS: Plaintiff (P), a producer, conceives the idea of producing a movie based on Shakespeare's play *The Taming of the Shrew*, starring Richard Burton and Elizabeth Taylor Burton with Franco Zeffirelli as director. P approached the Burtons' agent about their availability and suggested he had something in mind for them. The agent said he would like to hear P's idea and P disclosed it. The agent liked the idea, and P later met with the Burtons, who said they would like to do the movie.
>
> Later, the Burtons made the movie with Zeffirelli but without P's participation. P sues, alleging that the circumstances surrounding the disclosure of his idea were such as would imply a contract.
>
> ISSUE: Can a contract be implied under these circumstances?
>
> HOLDING: Yes, P wins. Case remanded to trial court to decide if the circumstances created an implied-in-fact contract.

Here the P didn't have a story idea; he just had some casting ideas and a suggestion for director. Shakespeare's story is in the public domain, and the Burtons have just as much right to it as P. Moreover, there was never an explicit agreement among the parties that P would get to produce the project. P didn't tell the agent, "I'll disclose my idea if you agree that I can produce the project."

P contends that such an understanding is implied from the fact that he is a veteran producer contacting an agent for the Burtons. The court agreed that such an agreement could exist, implied from the behavior of the parties.

But what if P wasn't a veteran producer? Suppose a carpenter in the checkout line at the supermarket sees a picture of Cher on the cover of the *National Enquirer*. She writes Cher a fan letter

---

[7] 9 Cal. App. 3d 161, 88 Cal. Rptr. 319 (1970).

DEALMAKING
IN THE
FILM AND
TELEVISION
INDUSTRY—
3RD EDITION

22

suggesting that Cher star in a movie version of *Hamlet*. Cher reads the letter, thinks this is a wonderful idea, and makes the movie. Now the carpenter contacts Cher and says, "Remember me? I sent you the idea for the *Hamlet* movie. I want compensation, a producer credit, and a piece of the profits."

Is Cher obligated to pay? No, the circumstances are different. There are no facts to suggest that the carpenter submitted the idea with a reasonable expectation of receiving anything in return. It appears she was making a gift. Similarly, if a veteran producer at a social function casually mentions to Elizabeth Taylor that she would be wonderful in *The Taming of the Shrew*, no obligation would arise.

As a result of these idea submission cases, many studios and producers have adopted a policy of never accepting unsolicited material or requiring that those who submit materials sign a submission release. While such releases do not necessarily insulate them from intentional wrongdoing, they can make it much more difficult for someone who has submitted an idea or story to prevail.

In summary, if you think someone has ripped you off, don't assume you are without a legal remedy. Consult an attorney.

Let us now turn to an examination of some industry contracts.

TYPES OF DEALS

Option Contracts

Option contracts are not unique to the movie and television industry. In many enterprises they provide a useful way for parties to share risk.

Perhaps you have heard friends in the industry talk about "optioning a book" to be made into a movie. When you take an option on a literary property, you are buying the exclusive right to purchase the movie rights in the future.

Suppose you are a producer and you read a wonderful novel written by Alex. You would like to make a movie based on this book. Since a movie based on the book is considered a derivative work, and since Alex owns the copyright to his book, you cannot make a movie without his permission.

You approach Alex and offer to buy the movie rights. He, or his agent, says, "Fine, we would like $50,000 for the rights." You cannot afford to pay $50,000 at this time. Even if you could afford the expense, it would be very risky to buy the movie rights outright. What if you couldn't get a good screenplay written? Or secure the right director? Or obtain production financing? There are many obstacles to getting a movie produced, and if you buy the movie rights to Alex's book and cannot get the movie made, you have bought something you ultimately don't need.

A better way for you to approach the situation would be to offer a different kind of deal to Alex. Instead of buying the movie rights outright, you offer to take an option to purchase them.

Let's say you offer Alex $5,000 for a one-year option. During that one-year period you have the exclusive right to EXERCISE the option and buy the movie rights. Let's also suppose that the purchase price is $50,000. As a rule of thumb, options are often 10% of the full purchase price, but the amount is negotiable. Sometimes sellers are willing to give a "free" option or an option for a nominal sum (e.g., "for ten dollars"). Of course, a seller is not required to option his movie rights, and if you are dealing with the author of a best-seller, he/she may refuse to sell an option and insist on an outright sale.

The option period can be any length of time, but the initial option period is often a year. The buyer may seek certain RIGHTS OF RENEWAL, which allows him/her to extend the option upon payment of an additional sum. Let's suppose that you have taken a one-year option for $5,000 and have a right of renewal to extend the option for a second year for $6,000. The right of renewal must be exercised before the initial option period expires. The parties could agree to second and/or third renewal periods to allow the buyer to extend the option further.

Renewals let the purchaser extend an option without exercising it. Assume Alex has sold you a one-year option that is about to expire. You have commissioned a screenplay, which you are pleased with, and you have the interest of an important director. But you don't have a star attached to your project and your financing is not in place. At this time, you don't want to buy Alex's movie rights for $50,000, but you also don't want to lose the right to buy those rights in the future. If you have a right of renewal in your agreement, you can extend the option. Generally, buyers don't want to purchase movie rights until the first

DEALMAKING
IN THE
FILM AND
TELEVISION
INDUSTRY—
3RD EDITION

24

day of principal photography, when they know for sure that a movie will be produced.

Note that an option gives the buyer the exclusive right to purchase movie rights within the option period. No one else can buy the movie rights during that time. The seller can do nothing that would interfere with the buyer purchasing those rights during the option period.

Once the option expires, however, the writer retains not only the option money but all movie rights as well. Some writers have repeatedly sold options on the same property because the earlier options were never exercised. Of course, once the option is exercised, the buyer owns the movie rights outright, and the writer can't sell or option what he/she no longer owns.

The option payments, and any payments for rights of renewals, can be APPLICABLE or NON-APPLICABLE. If the payments are applicable, they count as an advance against the purchase price. If they are non-applicable, they do not apply against the purchase price. For example, if an option was for $5,000 applicable against a purchase price of $50,000, a buyer wanting to exercise the option would pay $45,000 to the writer. If the $5,000 option were non-applicable, the buyer would pay $50,000 because the $5,000 option payment would not count against the purchase price.

The most important point to remember when taking (purchasing) an option is that you must simultaneously negotiate the terms of the purchase agreement. Usually the option contract is a two- or three-page document with a literary purchase agreement attached as an exhibit. When the option is exercised, the literary purchase agreement automatically kicks in. A buyer who enters an option agreement without negotiating the underlying literary purchase agreement has purchased a WORTHLESS OPTION. All you have bought is the right to haggle with the buyer should you choose to buy the movie rights. The buyer is under no obligation to sell on the terms you propose.

For example, you purchase an option for $500 for one year but don't work out the terms of the literary purchase agreement. Nine months later you decide to exercise the option and buy the movie rights. You send a check for $10,000 to the writer, but she objects. She wants $20,000. Since the parties have not agreed to this essential term of the sale, the contract is unenforceable. You have a worthless option, and the time and money you spent developing the project may be wasted. The writer now has you over the barrel and can demand any amount she wants for the rights.

Step Deals

Producers often use step deals to hire writers. Suppose you are a producer interested in hiring Marcia, a novice writer. You have read a wonderful action/adventure script that she wrote, and now you want her to write an original comedy. Since you're a Writers Guild signatory, you must pay Marcia Writers Guild scale, $109,783 ($58,478 for a low-budget film).[8] However, you are not entirely confident that Marcia can produce an acceptable script because she has no experience in this genre. You want to reduce your financial risk. One way is to hire her on a step deal.

A step deal proceeds, step by step, with the producer having the option after each step to stop the writer's services. For the first step you agree to pay Marcia to write a treatment. If you like the treatment, you pay her an additional sum to go to the second step and write a first draft. If you like the first draft, you can pay her more for a final draft or take additional steps for rewrites and polishes. The Writers Guild sets minimums for each step, and the total paid to her will be at least the minimum she would receive if you had hired her to write a completed script from the outset.

The step deal allows the producer to bail out of his/her commitment to the writer early. If upon completion of the treatment the producer has lost confidence in the writer, or isn't happy with the direction the story has taken, he/she is not obligated to continue employing the writer. As the owner of all the work created by the writer, the producer can shelve the project or bring in a new writer. The writer retains the payments received for the work completed.

In a step deal, the producer has "reading periods," usually a couple of weeks, in which to decide whether to go to the next step. When a producer decides not to go onto the next step, or fails to make a decision within the reading period, the writer is free to accept other work. This prevents the producer from

---

[8] The WGA Minimum Basic Agreement Flat Deal for a non-original screenplay, including treatment, is $95,158 for a high-budget film for the period of 2/13/08- 5/1/09.

DEALMAKING
IN THE
FILM AND
TELEVISION
INDUSTRY—
3RD EDITION

26

endlessly stringing along the writer. During the reading period, the writer must hold himself/herself available to continue working for the producer if the producer should choose to go to the next step.

Of course, top writers may decline to be hired on a step deal, and producers cannot force them to accept such a deal. More experienced writers may be able to negotiate a deal in which the steps are guaranteed rather than at the producer's option.

Merchandising and Product Placement Deals

Movie merchandising has earned studios money and promoted their movies for a long time. Walt Disney made a fortune selling toys, Mickey Mouse ears, and other products, not to mention the enormous revenue generated from theme parks.

In the past few decades, there has been a renaissance of merchandising activity. You may recall that when the movie *E.T.* was released in 1982, it contained a scene in which the friendly alien was fed some candy by a child. That candy was Reese's Pieces, and as a result of showing that candy in the film, sales shot up 65%. This bonanza delighted the makers of Reese's Pieces, but distressed the executives at Mars, Incorporated, who had rejected Steven Spielberg's request to use their M&M's. Some marketing genius figured that having an alien eating M&M's would reflect unfavorably on the product—one of the greatest marketing blunders of all time.

This incident was widely reported in the trade press, encouraging manufacturers to place their products in films. They realized that product placement in a film could be more rewarding than television advertising, which costs a great deal and often produces meager results.

Because of this interest, a new breed of agent arose: the product-placement agent. These agents don't represent people; they represent products. One agent might represent several non-competing products: Mars Bars for candy, Dr Pepper for soda, Coors for beer, Ford for cars, and so forth.

The product-placement agent spends her time looking for scripts in which to place products. Of course, not every placement is desirable. Coca-Cola would not want their soda to be consumed by a character that then vomits and goes into convulsions. But assuming the placement is in a neutral or positive light, the manufacturer will probably be interested.

A producer does not always need a release in order to show a product in a film. Assuming you don't disparage the product, or misleadingly use its trademark in a manner that implies the manufacturer has endorsed or sponsored your film, a manufacturer would find it difficult to prevail in a lawsuit simply on the grounds that its product was shown without consent.

From a practical point of view, if a product is momentarily shown on the screen or is not identifiable, a producer may not bother to obtain a release.[9] No director who shoots a scene in a supermarket is going to obtain releases for every product in the background. Still, a release never hurts, even if not legally required. Remember that your distributor and insurance carrier may demand to see releases for every identifiable product, regardless of legal precedent.

There is little case law concerning the unauthorized use of products in motion pictures because many disputes are settled out of court. Attorneys for product manufacturers have claimed that a non-approved use of a product in a motion picture, even if non-disparaging, could be a violation of the Lanham Act or product's trademark. However, courts tend to disagree, finding that trademark law does not entitle the owner of a trademark to prevent any display of a trademark when it is communicating ideas or expressing points of view.

For example, in *Wham-O, Inc. v. Paramount Pictures Corp.*, the manufacturer of the Slip 'n Slide toy slide brought suit and sought a temporary restraining order against Paramount Pictures for its unauthorized use of the toy in the movie *Dickie Roberts: Former Child Star.*

In this movie David Spade plays a former child star seeking to reenact the childhood experiences he missed while busy working in the entertainment industry. In an amusing sequence, the character misuses the toy slide to comic effect and suffers injuries. Paramount claimed the film used the Slip 'n Slide to convey an image of childhood fun. Wham-O argued that in a world where consumers know about product placement, "the viewing public has come to expect, that trademarked products featured in movies are there because, in fact, the trademark

---

[9] You should always have a lawyer review your script before production to determine what releases may be required.

DEALMAKING
IN THE
FILM AND
TELEVISION
INDUSTRY—
3RD EDITION

28

owner is associated with or has endorsed the movie through such product-placement arrangements."[10]

The court found that Wham-O was not likely to succeed on the merits of the case because Paramount's use of the product did not create an improper association in consumers' minds between the product and the trademark.[11]

Most manufacturers, however, are pleased to have their products featured in a motion picture. To induce filmmakers to insert products in movies, the product-placement agent can offer several inducements:

1) Release: You won't have to bother writing to the manufacturer for permission.

2) Freebies: Agents can give producers cartons of candy bars, free airline tickets, or a truckload of beer. These freebies can help a producer lower production costs by eliminating the need to buy props and food. If an item is expensive, such as a car, a mink stole, or fine jewelry, often the agent will lend it for the duration of the shoot.

3) Promotion: If McDonald's agrees to distribute millions of *Men in Black* cups to its customers, and spend additional millions of dollars to advertise the promotion, the movie benefits from increased public awareness. For distributors, promotional campaigns are often the most alluring aspect of a product-placement deal.

4) Cash: Sometimes cash is part of a placement deal. Nabisco paid $100,000 to have its Baby Ruth candy bar displayed in *The Goonies*. The company also agreed to provide $1.5 million of network advertising and to give away free movie posters with the purchase of its candy from displays in 37,000 stores.

Usually manufacturers only offer multi-million-dollar cross-promotional deals and cash payments for major studio releases. However, they often will provide freebies to independent low-budget filmmakers.

---

[10] *Wham-O, Inc. v. Paramount Pictures Corp.*, United States Court of Appeals for the Ninth Circuit, Appeal No. 03-17052, Appellant's Reply Brief, May 18, 2004.
[11] Wham-O's trademark infringement and dilution claims were also rejected and its request for injunctive relief was denied *Wham-O, Inc. v. Paramount Pictures Corp.*, 286 F. Supp.2d 1254 (N.D. Cal. 2003).

There are several reasons why product placement has become widespread. With hundreds of channels now available to viewers, they easily click their remote controls and switch to another channel to avoid commercials. If they have a Digital Video Recorder (DVR) device such as TiVo, they can skip over advertising, which some experts estimate total up to 3,000 per day.[12] Manufacturers are keen to have their products placed in motion pictures because, if done carefully, their presence in a scene appears more natural and closer to a true endorsement rather than a blatant hard-sell pitch. Moreover, the growth of reality television has provided many more opportunities for product placement.[13] Shows such as *Survivor*" and *American Idol* actively partner with brands, and the entire show becomes a product-placement forum. Likewise, the growth of specialized cable networks such as the Food Channel and The Learning Channel enable their producers to deliver niche audiences of great interest to certain manufacturers.[14] The show *Trading Spaces*, for example, integrates sponsors such as The Home Depot directly into the shopping and building experiences of its stars.[15]

Digital technologies such as "virtual placements" permit film and television library owners to offer up-to-date product placements in older programs when they are rerun or syndicated to television stations, or when released as a DVD collection. Princeton Video Image, a company best known for its digital yellow "virtual first down line" in college and pro football game broadcasts, provides this "virtual placement" technology to eager advertisers.[16] This technology allows advertisers to seamlessly replace old products digitally with new ones. On a rerun of a *Seinfeld* episode, for instance, Jerry might drink a Pepsi One, even if his character originally drank a Diet Coke.

At the extreme end of the product-placement world is something referred to as product integration, a concept that automakers embrace. Unlike traditional product placement, which features a product in a movie or television show, product integration

---

[12] Lee Ann Gjertsen, "Insurers Cut Marketing, But 3 Campaigns Shine," *Am. Banker*, Mar. 11, 2004 (Vol. 169, Issue 48), at 11, available at 2004 WLNR 4062609.

[13] Amy Johannes, "TV Placements Overtake Film," *PROMO Magazine*, May 1, 2005 at 7.

[14] *Id.*

[15] Steve Rogers, "The Home Depot to Take Over the Sponsorship of TLC's *Trading Spaces* from Lowe's," *Reality TV World*, Aug. 11, 2003, at www.realitytvworld.com/index/articles/story.php?s=1548.

[16] Wayne Friedman, "Eagle-Eye Marketers Find Right Spot, Right Time," *Advertising Age*, Jan. 22, 2001 (Vol. 72, Issue 4) (Midwest Region Ed., at S2), available at 2001 WLNR 9681673.

DEALMAKING
IN THE
FILM AND
TELEVISION
INDUSTRY—
3RD EDITION

30

goes one step further by creating a movie or TV show around a product. Ford Motor Company recently signed a deal with Revolution Studios that allows Ford to write its cars and trucks into movie scripts. Ford marketing executives play an active role in the scriptwriting and approval process.[17] The producers of the film *Are We There Yet?*, starring Ice Cube and a tricked-out Lincoln Navigator, ensured Ford that the Navigator would appear in 75 percent of the film. Ford has also paid hefty sums for vehicles appearances in *Alias* and *24*, and the James Bond movie *Die Another Day*. It's estimated that in 2004, automakers made up 40 percent of all product-placement spending.[18]

As product placement, merchandising, and other forms of stealth advertising multiply, filmmakers need to carefully consider the legal issues that may arise and secure permission when needed.

DEALMAKING TIME LINE

A. DEVELOPMENT

    A) Retainer agreement with attorney and/or agent

    B) Literary acquisition agreement

    C) Writer employment agreement

B. PRE-PRODUCTION

    A) Actor, director, and crew employment agreements

    B) Completion bond agreement

    C) Errors & omissions insurance [19]

    D) Worker's compensation, negative film, and other insurance

    E) Location releases and permits

    F) Signatory agreements with Union and Guilds

    G) Financing and producing agreements

C. POST-PRODUCTION

    A) Distribution agreement, if not already obtained.

    B) Music permissions

    C) Film and tape clip permissions

    B) Distributor/exhibitor agreements

[19] Errors and Omissions Insurance covers the insured against judgments, costs, and attorneys' fees incurred as a result of a successful or unsuccessful suit involving defamation, invasion of privacy and copyright infringement. It does not cover breach of contract or intentional wrongdoing.

[17] Amy Wilson, "Ford Woos Hollywood Partners; Agreement Assures Product Placement in Revolution Studios' Films," *Automotive News*, Feb. 23, 2004, at 1.
[18] Jason Stein, "Automakers Go Hollywood," *Automotive News*, Mar. 22, 2004, at 42 (Vol. 78, Pub. No. 6085), available at 2004 WLNR 175832.

Product Placement Releases and Permissions

Almost every time a viewer can identify a brand name, logo, or product appearing in a major studio film or network television show, the manufacturer has given the producer a release or license to depict it. Sometimes companies refuse permission, or the production company neglects to obtain a release, so producers ask their prop department to create a pseudo-product that does not exist. If the footage has already been recorded, brand names can be blurred out or virtually removed from a scene.

If the product is shown in a neutral or positive light, of course, a manufacturer is unlikely to complain. Indeed, most of the time they will be thrilled to obtain such exposure. But if they are not pleased, their legal counsel will advise them that it can be difficult, if not impossible, to prove damages since the legal basis for a recovery is murky at best.

Manufacturers will usually give a release if asked, provided they are assured that their product will not be depicted in a derogatory manner. Coca-Cola is happy to have a character in a television show drink its soda, but will not be if the character goes into convulsions and vomits after drinking Coke. Some companies may attempt to negotiate restrictions on use, but the majority of manufacturers are pleased to have their product shown because it is free publicity, and much less expensive than buying a 30-second spot. Even low-budget independent producers are often able to secure permission to include products in their films.

When drafting a product placement agreement, it is important to ensure that (1) product-placement requirements do not conflict with other production contracts related to the film or television show; and (2) there are clear examples of authorized and non-authorized product uses. The more positive the light, and the greater the level of celebrity use/endorsement, the more willing the manufacturer will be to cooperate. However, attorneys also need to understand that some directors will refuse to allow insertion of products in their scripts, and stars may refuse to use such products. Robin Williams is renowned for not accommodating product placements,[20] and Pamela Anderson refuses to be shown with any fur or meat products. It is common for a

---

[20] *See* fn. 5, *supra*.

DEALMAKING
IN THE
FILM AND
TELEVISION
INDUSTRY—
3RD EDITION

32

star's employment contracts to require that promotional tie-ins and merchandising deals will be subject to the star's approval. A sample product-placement agreement can be found at the end of this chapter.

Besides product-placement deals, studios license the right to sell spin-off products to manufacturers. In most of these deals there is no risk to the studio because the licensees incur all manufacturing and distribution expenses. The studio receives an advance per product and royalty payments (often between 5% and 10% of gross revenues) from retailers (i.e., the whole-sale price). If the movie flops and the products don't sell, the manufacturer absorbs the loss.

Musicals such as *Saturday Night Fever, Grease, Flashdance,* and *Dirty Dancing* can earn substantial revenues from sound-track recordings. Moreover, a hit song can effectively promote a film. Similarly, music videos have become important market-ing tools.

Keep in mind that few films lend themselves to extensive mer-chandising. Movies that can spin off toys, posters, and similar items have the greatest potential. But with a film like *American Beauty*, there are limited merchandising possibilities.

PRODUCT RELEASE

(Date) _____

_____

_____

_____

Re: _____ (Picture)

Dear _____:

When countersigned by you, on behalf of _____ ("Company"), this letter will confirm that Company has agreed to, and hereby does grant, to _____ ("Producer") the right to use its product _____, including any related logo(s) and trademark(s) (collectively, the "Product") in the theatrical motion picture presently entitled _____ (the "Picture"). Company acknowledges that the Picture may be exhibited and exploited worldwide, in all languages and in all media now known or hereafter devised in perpetuity.

Producer agrees that the Product will not be used in a disparaging manner. Company hereby warrants and represents that it has the right and authority to grant the rights granted herein, that the consent of no other person or company is required to enable Producer to use the Product as described herein, and that such use will not violate the rights of any kind of any third parties. Company agrees to indemnify and hold harmless Producer, its officers, shareholders, assignees, and licensees, and each of their successors-in-interest from and against any and all liabilities, damages, and claims (including attorneys' fees and court costs) arising out of (i) any breach of Company's warranties, (ii) Producer's use of the Product, as provided herein, and/or (iii) the rights granted herein.

The sole remedy of Company for breach of any provision of this agreement shall be an action at law for damages, and in no event shall Company seek or be entitled to injunctive or other equitable relief by reason of any breach or threatened breach of this Product Release agreement, or for any other reason pertaining hereto, nor shall Company be entitled to seek to enjoin or restrain the exhibition, distribution, advertising, exploitation, or marketing of the Picture.

Your countersignature below will confirm this Agreement.

Sincerely,

_____

By: _____ on behalf of

_____

AGREED TO AND ACCEPTED:

"COMPANY"

_____ Date: _____

_____ on behalf of

_____

CHAPTER 3

PERMISSION TO PORTRAY PEOPLE AND PLACES

DEPICTION AND LOCATION RELEASES

PURCHASING THE RIGHTS TO A PERSON'S LIFE STORY

Do you need to buy the rights?

Before you decide to purchase the rights to a person's life story, it is worth considering what you are buying. When you buy the rights to portray someone in film or television, you are buying a bundle of rights. These rights include protection from suits based on defamation, invasion of privacy, and the right to publicity. You may also be buying the cooperation of the subject and his/her family or heirs. Perhaps you want access to diaries and letters that are not otherwise available to you.

If the subject of the life story is deceased, much of the rationale for buying these rights disappears, since defamation and invasion of privacy actions protect personal rights that do not descend to the estate.[1] In other words, people can spread lies and

---

[1] The right of publicity may or may not descend, depending on which states' laws apply.

DEALMAKING
IN THE
FILM AND
TELEVISION
INDUSTRY—
3RD EDITION

36

falsehoods about the dead, reveal their innermost secrets, and their heirs cannot sue for defamation or invasion of privacy. A writer could publish a revisionist history of George Washington, portraying our first President as a child molester and a thief, and his heirs would have no remedy. So when a subject is deceased, a producer has less need for a depiction release.

It is also important to consider whether the subject of your film is a private individual or a public official or public figure. As we will discuss later in Chapters 14 and 15, public officials and figures have opened more of their lives to public scrutiny, and consequently more of their lives can be portrayed without invading their privacy. Moreover, public officials and figures must meet a much higher burden of proof in order to establish defamation or invasion of privacy. They must prove that a defamer intentionally spread a falsehood or acted with reckless disregard of the truth.

One should also consider the possibility of fictionalizing a true story. If you change the names of the individuals involved, change the location and make other alterations so that the real-life people are not recognizable to the public, you could avoid the necessity of a depiction release.

Keep in mind, however, that the story's appeal may be predicated on the fact that it is a true story. In such a case, fictionalization is not a good alternative. Suppose you wanted to do the Jessica McClure story, describing how a Texas community rallied to the rescue of a young girl who fell down a well-hole. Here you would want to bill the movie as *The Jessica McClure Story*. That is why viewers would tune in.

Terms of the Agreement

In negotiating for life-story rights, there are a number of important issues that need to be resolved. At the outset, the parties must determine the extent of the rights granted. Does the grant include remakes, sequels, television series, merchandising, novelization, live-stage rights, and radio rights? Are the rights worldwide? Buyers will usually want as broad a grant as possible. The seller may insist on retaining certain rights.

The buyer must also consider other releases that may be needed. What about the subject's spouse, children, friends, and relatives?

Will these people consent to be portrayed? Will the subject ask his/her friends and relatives to cooperate? Can these secondary characters be fictionalized? If the producer is planning an ensemble piece about a basketball team, it makes no sense to sign up players one by one, hoping to get them all. A smart producer will gather the team in a room and purchase all of the rights or none.

Another issue is whether the rights can be assigned to a studio or production company. If the buyer is a producer, she will often need to assign such rights to a studio or network later as part of a financing/distribution agreement.

The purchase of life-story rights can be structured as either an option/purchase deal or as an outright sale, often with a reversion clause. A reversion clause provides that in the event the rights are not exploited within a certain number of years (i.e., the movie is not made), then all rights would revert to the subject. This provision protects the subject if he/she has sold rights to his/her life story to a producer who never uses them, and some time later another producer is interested in making such a film.

The agreement should recite the consideration exchanged. Consideration is a legal term of art. Consideration is that which is given in exchange for a benefit received. It is a necessary element for the existence of a contract. A contract is only binding with consideration. It is what distinguishes a contract from a gift, which may be revocable.

Consideration is usually money, but it can be anything of value. As a general principle, courts do not review the adequacy of consideration. In other words, should you be foolish enough to agree to sell your brand-new car, worth $15,000, for only $5,000, don't expect a judge to rescue you from the results of your poor judgment. Unless there was some sort of fraud or duress involved, the contract will be enforced, although it may be unfair to one party.

To ensure that a contract is binding, agreements often recite: "For ten dollars and other valuable consideration." This clause establishes that there has been an exchange of value, even if it is nominal consideration. Make sure the consideration is actually paid. It is wise to pay by check so that you will have the cancelled check as proof of payment.

DEALMAKING
IN THE
FILM AND
TELEVISION
INDUSTRY—
3RD EDITION

38

Mutually exchanged promises can be adequate consideration. For example, a producer's efforts to develop a project could be deemed adequate consideration for an option. But to be sure their contracts are enforceable, producers may want to pay some money for the option. There are some exceptional circumstances when courts will throw out a contract if the terms of the contract are unconscionable.

There are other ways to compensate a subject of a life story besides a flat fixed fee. You could give the subject points (percentage of net profits), consulting fees, and/or bonuses to be paid when the film is exploited in ancillary markets.

An important part of any depiction agreement is the "Warranties and Representations" clause. A warranty is a promise. The buyer will want the seller to promise never to sue for an invasion of his/her rights of publicity and privacy, or for defamation, even if the buyer takes some creative liberties in telling the story. The warranties must cover all conceivable situations. No one wants to buy a lawsuit.

There will also be a provision that gives the buyer the right to embellish, fictionalize, dramatize, and adapt the life story in any way he/she chooses. This is a frequent sticking point in negotiations. The subject is delighted to be asked to have her story told on the silver screen, but when you present her with a depiction release, she becomes concerned. She asks, "This document says you can change my story any way you like and I can't sue for defamation. How do I know you won't portray me as a monster?"

A producer may reply: "Trust me, trust me." Sometimes that will work. But the subject may respond: "I have no intention of trusting any of you charming Hollywood types. I want script approval. Write your script, and if I like it, I'll sign the release."

Can a producer give a subject script approval? No sane producer would. No producer is going to expend a lot of time and money developing a script only to find that the subject has changed her mind or is unreasonably withholding approval.

If the subject refuses to give the producer carte blanche, are any compromises possible? Yes. The subject could have approval over the treatment or selection of the writer. Perhaps the subject will figure that if she approves only a classy writer, her portrayal will be acceptable.

Alternatively, the producer could offer to make the subject a creative or technical consultant to the production. "You'll be right there by the director's side," says the producer, "giving him advice and suggestions to ensure that everything is authentic." The producer may not mention that the director doesn't want the subject on the set and is not required to accept her suggestions.

Another possible compromise could limit the subject matter and period portrayed. Perhaps the subject is primarily concerned that an embarrassing incident in her life not be re-enacted in Panavision. The release could say that certain incidents (e.g., a divorce) are not included in the release. Or the release could cover limited periods of the subject's life (e.g., only those incidents that occurred before 1947).

Finally, the subject might have the right to determine screen notice. She could decide if the film will be billed as a true story or a dramatized account. Alternatively, she could decide whether real names are used for the characters.

The following case illustrates the problem that can arise when portraying another without a depiction release.

Midler v. Ford Motor Company[2]

FACTS: Ford Motor Company and its ad agency designed a series of television commercials. Bette Midler (P) was asked to sing the song "Do You Want To Dance" for the advertisement. Midler had performed the song on her 1973 album.

When Midler declined to participate, the ad agency hired one of Midler's former backup singers to record the song, imitating Midler's voice and style. When the advertisements were run, many listeners thought that the song had been sung by Midler. The ad agency obtained permission to use the song from its copyright owner but did not have Midler's consent to imitate her voice.

ISSUE: Does this imitation of Midler's voice infringe upon her rights?

HOLDING: Yes.

RATIONALE: The court said that when a distinctive voice of a professional singer is widely known and is deliberately imitated in order to sell a product, a tort has been

---

[2] 849 F.2d 460 (9th Cir., 1988).

DEALMAKING
IN THE
FILM AND
TELEVISION
INDUSTRY—
3RD EDITION

40

committed in California. The court limited the holding to the facts, and cautioned that not every imitation of a voice to advertise merchandise is necessarily actionable.

A voice is not copyrightable because it is not fixed in a tangible medium of expression. The defendants didn't infringe the copyright in any of Midler's recordings because her recordings were not copied. Midler's voice was not misappropriated under California Civil Code Section 3344 because the backup singer's voice was used, not Midler's. However, the court held Midler had a common-law (i.e., not based on a statute) right to protect her identity. Here, the impersonation was deemed to be an unlawful appropriation of her identity.

Section 3344 of the California Civil Code affords damages for appropriations of another person's "name, voice, signature, photograph, or likeness" to promote a product without the subject's consent. The Midler case is interesting because it extends protection to an imitation of a voice. Thus, at least in California, this type of imitation is considered an appropriation of another's identity.

DEPICTION RELEASE CHECKLIST

A. WHAT ARE YOU PURCHASING?

    1. PROTECTION AGAINST A SUIT BASED ON RIGHT TO PUBLICITY.

    2. PROTECTION AGAINST A SUIT FOR INVASION OF PRIVACY.

    3. PROTECTION AGAINST A SUIT FOR DEFAMATION.

    4. COOPERATION OF SUBJECT AND HIS/HER FAMILY.

B. WHO ARE YOU PURCHASING THE RELEASE FROM?

    1. A PRIVATE PERSON WHO HAS DONE SOMETHING NEWSWORTHY.

    2. A CELEBRITY WHO WANTS TO PROTECT HER RIGHT OF PUBLICITY.

    3. A PUBLIC PERSON, (E.G., POLITICIAN), WHOSE ACTIVITIES MAY BE IN THE PUBLIC DOMAIN.

C. DO YOU NEED THE RIGHTS?

    1. CAN YOU FICTIONALIZE THE STORY?

    2. DO YOU NEED THE SUBJECT'S COOPERATION TO OBTAIN FACTS?

    3. HOW MUCH IS IN THE PUBLIC DOMAIN?

    4. IS THE SUBJECT DECEASED?

D. THE EXTENT OF RIGHTS OBTAINED.

    1. WHAT ABOUT REMAKES, SEQUELS, TELEVISION SERIES, MERCHANDISING, NOVELIZATION, LIVE-STAGE RIGHTS, RADIO RIGHTS? ARE RIGHTS WORLDWIDE?

    2. CAN THE RIGHTS BE ASSIGNED TO A STUDIO OR PRODUCTION COMPANY?

    3. SHOULD THE RIGHTS REVERT TO THE OWNER AT SOME FUTURE TIME?

E. DEAL STRUCTURE.

    1. OPTION

    2. OUTRIGHT PURCHASE

F. CONSIDERATION

    1. OPTION MONEY

    2. PURCHASE PRICE

    3. OTHER FORMS OF COMPENSATION: POINTS, CONSULTING FEES, BONUSES.

G. WARRANTIES AND REPRESENTATIONS.

    BROAD ALL-INCLUSIVE RELEASE OF OWNER'S RIGHTS TO PUBLICITY, INVASION OF PRIVACY, AND DEFAMATION.

    1. MUST COVER ALL STATES AND CONCEIVABLE SITUATIONS.

    2. WARRANTIES BY OWNER OF ORIGINALITY AND TRUTH.

    3. PURCHASER GIVEN RIGHT TO EMBELLISH, FICTIONALIZE, DRAMATIZE, AND ADAPT STORY.

H. OTHER CHARACTERS?

    1. RELEASES FROM OTHER PEOPLE WHO APPEAR IN STORY: WIFE, CHILDREN, FRIENDS, ETC.

I. CREATIVE APPROVAL

    1. NO SCRIPT APPROVAL.

    2. POSSIBLE CONCESSIONS:

    A) APPROVAL OF TREATMENT AND/OR WRITER.

    B) OWNER OF RIGHTS BECOMES CREATIVE CONSULTANT.

    C) LIMIT SUBJECT MATTER AND PERIOD PORTRAYED.

    D) OWNER TO DETERMINE SCREEN NOTICE: BASED ON A TRUE STORY OR DRAMATIZED ACCOUNT.

DEALMAKING
IN THE
FILM AND
TELEVISION
INDUSTRY—
3RD EDITION

42

DEPICTION RELEASE
(Outright Grant with Reversion Clause)

CONSENT AND RELEASE[3]

To: Very Big Productions, Inc., a California Corporation

I understand that you desire to use all or parts of the events of my life in order to have one or more teleplays or screenplays written, and to produce, distribute, exhibit, and exploit one or more television programs and/or motion pictures of any length in any and all media now known or hereafter devised and sound recordings in any and all media now known or hereafter devised. I have agreed to grant you certain rights in that connection. This Consent and Release confirms our agreement as follows:

1. CONSIDERATION; GRANT OF RIGHTS: In consideration of your efforts to produce my story, payment to me of $_____, upon the beginning of principal photography of a full-length feature film, and/or $_____ upon the beginning of production of a television movie, and/or $_____ upon the beginning of production of a pilot program and a royalty of $_____ for each episode, and for other valuable consideration, with full knowledge I hereby grant you, perpetually and irrevocably, the unconditional and exclusive right throughout the world to use, simulate, and portray my name, likeness, voice, personality, personal identification and personal experiences, incidents, situations, and events which heretofore occurred or hereafter occur (in whole or in part), based upon or taken from my life or otherwise in and in connection with motion pictures, sound recordings, publications, and any and all other media of any nature whatsoever, whether now known or hereafter devised. Without limiting the generality of the foregoing, it is understood and agreed that said exclusive right includes theatrical, television, dramatic stage, radio, sound recording, music, publishing, commercial tie-up, merchandising, advertising, and publicity rights in all media of every nature whatsoever, whether now known or hereafter devised. I reserve no rights with respect to such uses. (All said rights are after this called the "Granted Rights.") It is further understood and agreed that the Granted Rights may be used in any manner and by any means, whether now known or unknown, and either factually or with such fictionalization, portrayal, impersonation, simulation, and/or imitation or other modification as you, your successors, and assigns, determine in your sole discretion. I

---

[3] See page 468 for information on how to obtain the contracts in this book on computer disk.

further acknowledge that I am to receive no further payment with respect to any matter referred to herein. Any and all of the Granted Rights shall be freely assignable by you.

2. PAYMENT OF CONSIDERATION; REVERSION OF RIGHTS: I understand that you shall make the payments mentioned in Paragraph 1 only if you begin production of a feature film or television movie or television pilot. In the event that you do not begin such a production within three years of the date this agreement was executed, all rights granted by me under this agreement shall revert to me. I understand that if you do begin production within three years of the date this agreement was executed, all rights granted by me under this agreement shall be perpetual.

3. RELEASE: I agree hereby to release and discharge you, your employees, agents, licensees, successors, and assigns from any and all claims, demands, or causes of actions that I may now have or may hereafter have for libel, defamation, invasion of privacy or right of publicity, infringement of copyright, or violation of any other right arising out of or relating to any utilization of the Granted Rights or based upon any failure or omission to make use thereof.

4. NAME/PSEUDONYM: You have informed me and I agree that in exercising the Granted Rights, you, if you so elect, may refrain from using my real name and may use a pseudonym that will be dissimilar to my real name; however, such agreement does not preclude you from the use of my real name should you in your sole discretion elect and that in connection with it I shall have no claim arising out of the so-called right of privacy and/or right of publicity.

5. FURTHER DOCUMENTS: I agree to execute such further documents and instruments as you may reasonably request to effectuate the terms and intentions of this Consent and Release, and in the event I fail or am unable to execute any such documents or instruments, I hereby appoint you as my irrevocable attorney-in-fact to execute any such documents and instruments, if said documents and instruments shall not be inconsistent with the terms and conditions of this Consent and Release. Your rights under this Clause 5 constitute a power coupled with an interest and are irrevocable.

6. REMEDIES: No breach of this Consent and Release shall entitle me to terminate or rescind the rights granted to you herein, and I hereby waive the right, in the event of any such breach, to equitable relief or to enjoin, restrain, or interfere with the production, distribution, exploitation, exhibition, or use of any of the Granted Rights granted, it being my understanding

DEALMAKING
IN THE
FILM AND
TELEVISION
INDUSTRY—
3RD EDITION

that my sole remedy shall be the right to recover damages with respect to any such breach.

7. PUBLIC-DOMAIN MATERIAL: Nothing in this Consent and Release shall ever be construed to restrict, diminish, or impair the rights of either you or me to use freely, in any work or media, any story, idea, pilot, theme, sequence, scene, episode, incident, name, characterization, or dialogue which may be in the public domain from whatever source derived.

8. ENTIRE UNDERSTANDING: This Consent and Release expresses the entire understanding between you and me, and I agree that no oral understandings have been made with regard thereto. This Consent and Release may be amended only by written instrument signed by you and me. I acknowledge that in granting the Granted Rights I have not been induced to do so by any representations or assurances, whether written or oral, by you or your representatives concerning the manner in which the Granted Rights may be exercised, and I agree that you are under no obligation to exercise any of the Granted Rights and agree I have not received any promises or inducements other than as herein set forth. The provisions hereof shall be binding upon me and my heirs, executors, administrators, and successors. I acknowledge that you have explained to me that this Consent and Release has been prepared by your attorney and that you have recommended to me that I consult with my attorney concerning this Consent and Release. This Consent and Release shall be construed according to the laws of the State of California applicable to agreements which are fully signed and performed within the State of California, and I hereby waive any rights I may have, known or unknown, pursuant to Section 1542 of the California Civil Code, which provides:

"A general release does not extend to claims which the creditor does not know or suspect to exist in his favor at the time of executing the release, which if known by him must have materially affected his settlement with the debtor."

In witness hereof and in full understanding of the foregoing, I have signed this Consent and Release on this ___ day of ___, 20__.

_____

(Signature)

(Name, please print)

(Address)

AGREED:

_____

DEPICTION RELEASE
(Option to Purchase Rights Format)

(date)

Mr. John Doe

242 Beverly Hills Lane

Beverly Hills, CA

Dear John:

It was a pleasure speaking to you recently. As I mentioned, I am interested in producing a television program or feature film about your life story.

This letter is intended to set forth the basic terms of our agreement regarding acquisition of the exclusive right and option to purchase all motion picture, television and allied rights concerning your life story. Please feel free to consult an entertainment attorney or an agent before signing this document.

Our agreement is as follows:

1) In consideration of $1,000, the mutual promises contained herein, and other valuable consideration, you grant my company, Very Big Productions, Inc. ("Big"), the exclusive and irrevocable right to option the motion picture, television, and all allied, ancillary, and subsidiary rights for the period of one year from the date of the signing of this agreement. Big shall have the right to extend the initial option period for an additional year by sending notice to you before the expiration of the initial period, along with the payment of two thousand dollars ($2,000), which sum shall be applicable against the full purchase price.

2) Big promises to use its best efforts to produce a television program or feature film about your life story, and is acting in reliance upon your promises in this agreement.

3) If the option is exercised, Big shall compensate you as full and final consideration for all rights conveyed as follows:

   a) Television Movie-of-the-Week or Mini-Series: A sum of fifty thousand dollars ($50,000) for a motion picture made for television based on the material.

DEALMAKING
IN THE
FILM AND
TELEVISION
INDUSTRY—
3RD EDITION

46

b) Theatrical Motion Picture: A sum of one-hundred thousand dollars ($100,000) for a theatrical motion picture based on the material.

c) Television Series: A sum of ten thousand dollars ($10,000) for the pilot episode and the sum of two thousand dollars ($2,000) for each episode after that.

All of the consideration described in this paragraph shall be payable upon completion of principal photography.

4) Consulting Services: You agree to serve as a creative consultant concerning any production made under this agreement. You shall receive one thousand dollars ($1,000) per week for each week your services are required, not to exceed four weeks unless both parties agree otherwise. If you are required to travel more than fifty miles from your home, Big shall furnish you with first-class roundtrip transportation and accommodations. Before the time that the option is exercised, at Big's request you shall disclose, without compensation, any information in your possession or under your control relating to your life story, including newspaper and magazine clippings, photographs, transcripts, and notes, and you will consult with any writer hired by Big, and share with him your observations, recollections, opinions, and experiences concerning events and activities in your life story.

5) If the option is exercised, Big will obtain the perpetual, exclusive, and irrevocable right to depict you, whether wholly or partially factual or fictional, and to use your name or likeness and voice, and biography concerning the material and any production and the advertising and exploitation of it in any and all media. While it is Big's intention to portray your story as factually as possible, Big shall have the right to include such actual or fictional events, scenes, situations, and dialogue as it may consider desirable or necessary in its sole discretion.

6) You agree to use your best efforts to obtain for Big at no additional cost those releases Big deems necessary from individuals who are a part of your life story or depicted in any information or materials you may supply Big.

7) You understand that Big shall not be obligated under this agreement to exercise any of its rights or to initiate production.

8) Big may sell, assign, and/or license any of its rights under this agreement. You agree to execute any other assignments or other instruments necessary or expedient to carry out and effectuate the purposes and intent of this agreement. You

agree to execute a complete long-form agreement with the customary language covering grants of biographical rights and a full release which will waive any claims or actions you may have against Big arising from the exercise of any of its rights under this agreement.

9) This agreement shall be governed and controlled by the laws of the State of California. This agreement constitutes the entire agreement between the parties and cannot be modified except in writing. Neither of the parties has made any promises or warranties other than those set forth herein.

Sincerely,

_____

on behalf of Very Big Prods.

AGREED TO AND ACCEPTED

_____

John Doe

DATE: _____

DEPICTION RELEASE
(Documentary Short-Form)

MOTION PICTURE AND TELEVISION RELEASE

I hereby irrevocably agree and consent that you (Very Big Productions, Inc.), and your assigns, may use all or part of your videotaped or filmed interview of me for your documentary program about _____ ("the program").

You have the right to use my picture, silhouette, and other reproductions of my likeness and voice in connection with any motion picture or television program in which this interview may be incorporated, and in any advertising material promoting it.

You may edit my appearance as you see fit.

You shall have all right, title, and interest in any and all results and proceeds from said use or appearance.

DEALMAKING
IN THE
FILM AND
TELEVISION
INDUSTRY—
3RD EDITION

48

The rights granted you are perpetual and worldwide, and include the use of this interview in any medium now known or hereafter invented, including broadcast and cable television, and videocassettes and DVDs. All or part of the interview may be used.

This consent is given as an inducement for you to interview me and I understand you will incur substantial expense in reliance thereof.

You are not obliged to make any use of this interview or exercise any of the rights granted you by this release.

I have read and understand the meaning of this release.

_____

Signature   Date

Print Name   Phone

LOCATION RELEASE

Today, filmmakers often shoot all or part of their motion pictures off the studio lot. They may travel widely in order to incorporate the flavor and realism of actual locations in their movies. Film-makers who shoot on location without securing prior permission and the necessary releases risk legal liability. Filmmakers don't have an absolute First Amendment right to trespass on other people's property. In certain circumstances, property owners could also sue for invasion of privacy/publicity and copyright and trademark infringement.

Even if a landowner doesn't bring suit, a filmmaker should secure releases for every location. Without such documents, it may be difficult to purchase Errors and Omissions (E&O) insurance and survive the scrutiny of the legal department of a potential distributor. Location agreements should be sought from landowners or land possessors when shooting on private property, and permits should be obtained from the appropriate government entity when shooting on public property.

Make sure that the person signing the release has the authority to grant the rights.

Location agreements don't necessarily cost much. In a small community where filmmakers rarely visit, the arrival of a movie crew can generate a lot of excitement. Residents may offer their homes for little or no money. On the other hand, movie crews have worn out their welcome in many neighborhoods in Los Angeles. Residents are annoyed by the traffic congestion and noise that accompanies a shoot. Homeowners may have had their property damaged by film crews in the past. These homeowners also know what the major studios are willing to pay for locations. They will demand top dollar, which can amount to thousands of dollars a day.

LOCATION AGREEMENT

Agreement entered into this ____ day of _____, 20__, by and between _____ ("Production Company") and _____ ("Grantor").

1. IDENTITY OF FILMING LOCATION: Grantor hereby agrees to permit Production Company to use the property located at

_____

("Property") in connection with the motion picture currently entitled _____ ("Picture") for rehearsing, photographing, filming, and recording scenes and sounds for the Picture. Production Company and its licensees, sponsors, assigns, and successors may exhibit, advertise, and promote the Picture or any portion thereof, whether or not such uses contain audio and/or visual reproductions of the Property and whether or not the Property is identified, in any and all media which currently exist or which may exist in the future in all countries of the world and in perpetuity.

2. RIGHT OF ACCESS: Production Company shall have the right to bring personnel and equipment (including props and temporary sets) onto the Property and to remove same after completion of its use of the Property hereunder. Production Company shall have the right but not the obligation to photograph, film, and use in the Picture the actual name, if any, connected with the Property or to use any other name for the Property. If Production Company depicts the interior(s) of any structures located on the Property, Grantor agrees that Production Company shall not be required to depict such interior(s) in any particular manner in the Picture.

DEALMAKING
IN THE
FILM AND
TELEVISION
INDUSTRY—
3RD EDITION

50

3. TIME OF ACCESS: The permission granted hereunder shall be for the period commencing on or about _____ and continuing until _____. The period may be extended by Production Company if there are changes in the production schedule or delays due to weather conditions. The within permission shall also apply to future retakes and/or added scenes.

4. PAYMENT: For each day the Production Company uses the location, it shall pay Grantor the sum of _____ in consideration for the foregoing.

5. ALTERATIONS TO LOCATION: Production Company agrees that (with Grantor's permission) if it becomes necessary to change, alter, or rearrange any equipment on the Property belonging to Grantor, Production Company shall return and restore said equipment to its original place and condition, or repair it, if necessary. Production Company agrees to indemnify and hold harmless Grantor from and against any and all liabilities, damages, and claims of third parties arising from Production Company's use hereunder of the Property (unless such liabilities, damages, or claims arise from breach of Grantor's warranty as set forth in the immediately following sentence) (and from any physical damage to the Property proximately caused by Production Company, or any of its representatives, employees, or agents). Grantor warrants that it has the right and authority to enter this Agreement and to grant the rights granted by it herein. Grantor agrees to indemnify and hold harmless Production Company from and against any and all claims relating to breach of its aforesaid warranty.

6. NO KICKBACKS FOR USE: Grantor affirms that neither it nor anyone acting for it gave or agreed to give anything of value to any member of the production staff, anyone associated with the Picture, or any representative of Production Company, or any television station or network for mentioning or displaying the name of Grantor as a shooting location on the Property (except the use of the Property, which was furnished for use solely on or in connection with the Picture).

7. BILLING CREDIT: Grantor acknowledges that any identification of the Property which Production Company may furnish shall be at Production Company's sole discretion and in no event shall said identification be beyond that which is reasonably related to the content of the Picture.

8. RELEASE: Grantor releases and discharges Production Company, its employees, agents, licensees, successors, and assigns from any and all claims, demands, or causes of actions that Grantor may now have or may from now on have for

libel, defamation, invasion of privacy or right of publicity, infringement of copyright, or violation of any other right arising out of or relating to any utilization of the rights granted herein.

The undersigned represents that he/she is empowered to execute this Agreement for Grantor.

IN WITNESS WHEREOF, the parties have hereunto set their names and signatures:

_____

Production Company

By: _____

_____

Grantor (Name)

By: _____

Questions and Answers

1. I recently read a magazine article about a bank robbery. The story would make a wonderful movie. I tried to buy the rights from the author of the magazine article, but she declined to sell. Do I need to buy those rights? And do I need to buy the life story rights of the individuals portrayed in the article?

Answer: If you want to use the magazine writer's approach to the material, her expression, you will need to buy the rights from her. She owns the copyright to the story she wrote. She does not own, however, the rights to the underlying facts and historical incidents, and you are free to use them without her permission. So, if you don't base your movie on her article, but work off the underlying true story, using your own approach to the material, you don't need to buy the rights to her article.

You may need to buy life-story rights from the individuals involved, unless the entire story is deemed to be in the public domain. In determining whether a release is needed, one must consider whether without a release the subject would have a viable cause of action for defamation, invasion of privacy, copyright infringement and other causes of action. Alternatively, you might be able to avoid buying a release if you fictionalize the

DEALMAKING
IN THE
FILM AND
TELEVISION
INDUSTRY—
3RD EDITION

52

story so that the actual individuals involved are not identifiable to the public by name or circumstances.

2. What if I have permission to enter a location on which I am shooting and my camera captures the image of a nearby location that I do not have permission to use?

Answer: If the other location is not specifically identifiable, most producers would not bother obtaining a release. A non-identifiable building would be an ordinary non-descript one that cannot be distinguished from many others. Although architectural works are copyrightable, the copyright does not prevent film-makers from filming a building that is ordinarily visible from a public place.

3. Will I be liable if I shoot a scene in an art gallery with per-mission of the owner, but without the permission of the artists whose work appears in the film?

Answer: If the artworks are identifiable, a release should be obtained from each artist. Although the gallery owner may own a copy of an artist's work, that does not mean that he/she owns the underlying copyright to it.

CHAPTER 4

CLEARANCE OF RIGHTS

You wouldn't buy a car from someone unless you were sure that person was its legitimate owner. Similarly, you wouldn't want to buy a literary property from someone who does not have clear title. How can you protect yourself?

COPYRIGHT SEARCH

First, you or your attorney should conduct a copyright search. If the literary property you desire is registered with the Copyright Office, a copyright report may reveal a transfer of the copyright, or the licensing of some rights. If the copyright report shows that the purported owner of the literary property is not the copyright holder, or if the copyright has been sold to another, you will not want to proceed with the purchase.

Anyone with Internet access can conduct their own search of the copyright office database.[1] The online database contains approximately 20 million records for works registered and documents recorded with the Copyright Office since 1978. From the Copyright Office's website, one can download Circular 22, which explains how to research the copyright status of a work.

---

[1] One can also conduct a search in person by reviewing the Copyright Card Catalog, which is located on the fourth floor (LM-459) of the James Madison Memorial Building of the Library of Congress.

DEALMAKING
IN THE
FILM AND
TELEVISION
INDUSTRY—
3RD EDITION

54

One may request that the Copyright Office conduct a search of their records for an hourly fee. A researcher will search and provide a factual, non-interpretive report. These searches may be initiated by consulting the bibliographer on duty, using the online Search Request Estimate form on the Copyright Office website at www.copyright.gov/foms/search_estimate.html, or writing to the Office.[2]

Private research companies can check additional sources of information for potential copyright, title, and trademark conflicts. These companies may review catalogs and reference works that list publications, movies, sound recordings, and products. Note that the reports supplied by the Copyright Office and from some private research companies do not offer a conclusion as to ownership of a copyright. These reports merely supply the information needed to determine the status of a copyright. Often, the opinion of an experienced attorney will be needed. Also remember that copyright owners are not required to register their work, so a review of copyright records may prove inconclusive.

CLEARANCE OF RIGHTS CHECKLIST

1. OBTAIN A COPYRIGHT REPORT.

2. PURCHASE ERRORS & OMISSIONS INSURANCE (E&O INSURANCE).

3. CLEARANCE OF TITLE.
   A) TITLES ARE NOT COPYRIGHTABLE
   B) OBTAIN TITLE REPORT
   C) CONSIDER MPAA REGISTRATION.

4. IDENTIFIABLE PRODUCTS, LOCATIONS, CHARACTERS & NAMES.
   OBTAIN RELEASE OR CHANGE NAME.

5. FILM CLIPS
   PERMISSION FROM
   A) COPYRIGHT OWNERS
   B) GUILDS AND UNIONS
   C) EVERY PERSON IN A CLIP
   D) MUSICIANS AND RIGHTS TO UNDERLYING MUSICAL COMPOSITIONS.

---

[2] Library of Congress, Copyright Office Records Research & Certification Section, 101 Independence Avenue SE, Washington, DC 20559-6000. Fax: (202) 252-3485; Tel: (202) 707-6850.

ERRORS & OMISSIONS INSURANCE

Errors & Omissions Insurance (E&O Insurance) protects the policyholder from claims for defamation, invasion of privacy, trademark, and copyright infringement. Let's say a producer (the policy holder) carelessly infringed on the copyrighted material of another in the course of producing a movie. The producer didn't intend to violate another's rights, but it is nevertheless liable for damages. E&O insurance will pay for any liability incurred as well as defense costs. Like other insurance policies, there is a deductible, typically $10,000 or more. A typical policy is for three years with coverage of one million dollars per claim and three million in the aggregate. E&O insurance does not cover intentional wrongdoing. The insurance carrier will assume liability for negligent (careless) acts but not for intentional fraud. Producers typically have their attorney review a script before production to avoid any potential liability. The insurance carrier often requires that the applicant's attorney review and approve the script before a policy will be issued.

The insurer will want to review all necessary releases and permissions before issuing a policy. Also, a copyright report and title report will be needed, and all employment agreements must be in writing. If music is going to be used, synchronization, performance, and master use licenses may be needed.

If the script is original, its origins must be determined to ensure that everything in it is original and none of it has been copied from another work. When the film is based on a true story, the screenplay should be derived from primary sources (e.g., court transcripts, interviews with witnesses), and not secondary sources (e.g., another author's work product), unless permission has been obtained to use such secondary sources.

Insurance companies usually ask applicants to disclose the name of their production attorney and will frequently contact that attorney to ensure that all necessary releases and licenses have been secured. It is best to employ an attorney before production starts so that appropriate contracts are used during production. If paperwork needs to be re-done after production has been completed, it can be difficult to locate actors, crew, and vendors to get them to sign revised agreements. It can be very expensive to have to re-edit a motion picture because required documents cannot be secured. Most companies that distribute in North America will not distribute a picture without E&O insurance.

DEALMAKING
IN THE
FILM AND
TELEVISION
INDUSTRY—
3RD EDITION

56

SCREENPLAY CHECKLIST

1) IF THE SCREENPLAY IS BASED ON ANOTHER WORK, A COPYRIGHT REPORT WILL NEED TO BE OBTAINED TO MAKE SURE ALL REQUIRED RIGHTS HAVE BEEN SECURED.

2) THERE MUST BE A WRITTEN AGREEMENT BETWEEN THE CREATOR(S) OF ALL MATERIALS, INCLUDING QUOTATIONS FROM COPYRIGHTED WORK, GRANTING PERMISSION TO USE THE MATERIAL IN THE PRODUCTION.

3) WRITTEN RELEASES ARE REQUIRED FROM ALL PERSONS WHO ARE RECOGNIZABLE OR WHOSE NAME, IMAGE, OR LIKENESS IS USED, AND IF SUCH A PERSON IS A MINOR, THE RELEASE MUST BE BINDING. IF A SUBJECT IS DECEASED, A RELEASE MAY BE NEEDED IN SOME CIRCUMSTANCES. RELEASES MAY NOT BE NEEDED IF THE PERSON IS PART OF A CROWD OR BACKGROUND SHOT AND IS NOT SHOWN FOR MORE THAN A FEW SECONDS OR GIVEN SPECIAL EMPHASIS.

4) WHERE WORK IS FICTIONAL, NAMES OF ALL CHARACTERS MUST GENERALLY BE FICTIONAL. TAKE CARE TO ENSURE THAT THE NAMES OF FICTIONAL CHARACTERS DO NOT RESEMBLE THE NAMES OF IDENTIFIABLE LIVING INDIVIDUALS.

5) WHERE PARTICULAR BUSINESSES, PERSONAL PROPERTY, OR IDENTI-FIABLE PRODUCTS ARE DEPICTED, WRITTEN RELEASES SHOULD BE OBTAINED. RELEASES MAY NOT BE NECESSARY IF PROPERTY IS A NON-DISTINCTIVE BACKGROUND.

6) ALL RELEASES MUST:
   A) GIVE RIGHT TO EDIT AND MODIFY MATERIAL,
   B) RIGHT TO FICTIONALIZE PEOPLE PORTRAYED,
   C) RIGHT TO MARKET PRODUCTION IN ALL MEDIA AND MARKETS.

7) TITLE REPORT SHOULD BE OBTAINED, SHOWING PRIOR USES OF TITLE.

8) APPLICANTS FOR INSURANCE MUST DISCLOSE RECEIPT OF SUBMIS-SIONS OF ANY SIMILAR MATERIAL.

9) WORK MAY NOT CONTAIN ANY MATERIAL THAT CONSTITUTES DEFAMATION, INVASION OF PRIVACY, OR INVASION OF THE RIGHT TO PUBLICITY.

PROTECTION OF TITLES

Like ideas and themes, titles are not eligible for copyright protection. If you cannot copyright a title, how can you protect it?

Suppose there is a producer who made an awful low-budget dinosaur movie that flopped at the box office. Now Steven Spielberg comes along with his hit *Jurassic Park*. The low-budget producer has an inspiration, perhaps his/her one and only creative thought. He/she decides to re-title his/her picture *Jurassic Park II*. As a result, some moviegoers purchase tickets to view him/her film and they are greatly disappointed. Since the title *Jurassic Park* is not copyrightable, how can Steven Spielberg prevent others from using it?

While titles are not copyrightable, they may be protected under the laws of unfair competition. The gist of an unfair competition claim is mislabeling or misdesignating a product (or service) in such a way as to cause confusion to consumers as to the origin of its manufacture. In other words, once the title *Jurassic Park* comes to be associated in the public mind with the work of Steven Spielberg,[3] it acquires what is known as a "secondary meaning." By titling his/her work *Jurassic Park II*, this producer is confusing the public as to the origin of his/her movie. That is because people associate *Jurassic Park* with the work of Steven Spielberg, and Spielberg had nothing to do with this other picture.

The major limitation on an action for unfair competition is that you cannot bring a successful action until your film has acquired a secondary meaning. What if you spent three years working on a television series, invested thousands of dollars, and the day before your program airs, another producer releases a program with the same or similar title? Since your program hasn't been released, it has not yet acquired a secondary meaning.

For some works in a series, you may be able to protect yourself against this danger by registering the title of your work for trademark protection. Because of recent changes in federal trademark law, one can now prospectively register a trademark before it is used in interstate commerce.[4] Thus, once a producer has chosen

---

[3] Obviously, the work is also associated in the public's mind with author Michael Crichton.

[4] Before the 1988 revisions to the trademark law, you could not register a trademark until you were actually using the mark on a product in interstate commerce. Thus, manufacturers would sometimes attach a mark to a product which they distributed in a token manner in order to try to protect themselves. Token use is no longer sufficient to obtain federal trademark protection.

DEALMAKING
IN THE
FILM AND
TELEVISION
INDUSTRY—
3RD EDITION

58

a title, she may be able to register it as a trademark.[5] She could reserve that mark for a limited period.[6] If she does not use the mark, she will lose all rights to it. Otherwise, she can obtain a trademark for 10 years, renewable for 10-year terms for as long as she is using the mark on her product.

The Motion Picture Association of America (MPAA), a trade group that represents the major studios, offers another way to protect a title. The MPAA allows its members, and independent producers, to register a title with it. The first party to register a title has the right to use it. You can imagine the confusion and problems that would arise if Fox and Paramount simultaneously released pictures with similar titles. Both films might suffer if moviegoers were confused.

The primary shortcoming of the MPAA Title Registration Bureau is that it only protects producers against other producers who have signed the agreement. In other words, the MPAA protects titles by contract. All the major studios are parties to the deal, and some independents have chosen to join. But the MPAA scheme offers no protection against a producer who is not a signatory to the agreement. There is a $300 fee per year to subscribe to the MPAA service. There is a $200 charge to register ten titles. Registration is good for one year and can be renewed.[7] Independent producers should carefully weigh the risks and benefits of registration. If you register a title that is similar to one registered by a studio, the studio can contest your title and you can end up in a protracted and expensive legal dispute.

One final method to protect oneself against title conflicts deserves mention. One can order a title report that may disclose other products or services that have used the same or similar title. If someone has used the title you want on a similar product or service that is offered in the same geographical area, you should not use the title unless it has been abandoned or you have obtained a release from the prior user.

In creating a title, a highly fanciful or original one is preferred because it will be least likely to infringe others. Such a title will also help the creator protect his/her title from subsequent infringers.

---

[5] Titles of individual entertainment works have not been granted federal trademark registration on the ground that the title is merely descriptive of the work. However, titles of a series of works, such as a television series or magazine, may be registered, and movie titles used on merchandise may be protected.
[6] Extensions can be obtained.
[7] For more information, contact Mitchell Schwartz, Director of Title Registration, at (818) 995-6600.

ANNOTATING A SCRIPT

SCREENWRITERS SHOULD ANNOTATE THEIR SCRIPTS TO DOCUMENT THE SOURCE OF THEIR WORK. A CAREFUL ANNOTATION WILL HELP A SCREENWRITER DEFEND AGAINST DEFAMATION AND INVASION OF PRIVACY LAWSUITS BY DEMONSTRATING THAT THE WRITER ACTED CAREFULLY. WHEN A PUBLIC FIGURE OR PUBLIC OFFICIAL SUES FOR DEFAMATION, THEY MUST PROVE THAT THE DEFENDANT ACTED WITH "ACTUAL MALICE."

ANNOTATIONS SHOULD SPECIFY THE SOURCE OF ALL SCRIPT ELEMENTS EXCEPT THOSE ELEMENTS THAT ARE COMPLETELY FICTIONAL AND ARISE WHOLLY FROM THE WRITER'S IMAGINATION. SCRIPT ELEMENTS INCLUDE CHARACTERS, EVENTS, SETTINGS, AND DIALOGUE. ANNOTATIONS SHOULD INCLUDE THE FOLLOWING INFORMATION:

1. CHARACTER LIST: FOR EACH CHARACTER PROVIDE THE FOLLOWING INFORMATION:
   (A) WHETHER THE CHARACTER IS A REAL PERSON, A FICTIONAL OR A COMPOSITE CHARACTER.
   (B) FOR REAL CHARACTERS, WHETHER THE ACTUAL PERSON IS LIVING OR DEAD.
   (C) FOR COMPOSITE CHARACTERS, THE NAME(S) OF ACTUAL PERSON(S) ON WHOM THE COMPOSITE CHARACTER IS BASED, AND WHAT CHARACTERISTICS CAN BE ATTRIBUTED TO SUCH ACTUAL PERSON(S).

2. SCENE-BY-SCENE NOTATIONS: INDICATE WHETHER THE SCRIPT ELEMENT PRESENTS OR POR-TRAYS FACT OR FICTION.
   (A) IF FACT OR INFERENCE FROM FACT, DESCRIBE SOURCE MATERIAL FOR SCRIPT ELEMENTS, INCLUDING THE FOLLOWING:
   (I) FOR BOOKS: TITLE, AUTHOR, AND PAGE(S).
   (II) FOR NEWSPAPER OR MAGAZINE ARTICLES: DATE, PAGE, AND COLUMN.
   (III) FOR INTERVIEWS: WHETHER NOTES OR TAPES EXIST AND, IF SO, A PAGE OR TAPE REFERENCE, AND THE TRANSCRIPT PAGE NUMBER.
   (IV) FOR TRIAL OR DEPOSITION TRANSCRIPTS: THE COURT OR OTHER FORUM, DATE, PERSON TESTIFYING, AND TRANSCRIPT PAGE NUMBER.
   (V) TO THE EXTENT POSSIBLE, MULTIPLE SOURCES SHOULD BE IDENTIFIED FOR EACH SCRIPT ELEMENT.
   (B) IF PARTLY FACT AND PARTLY FICTION, INDICATE WHICH PARTS ARE FACT AND WHICH PARTS ARE FICTION. FOR FACTUAL PARTS, DESCRIBE SOURCE MATERIAL AS SPECIFIED IN PARAGRAPH 2(A) ABOVE.
   (C) IF WHOLLY FICTION, NOTATION NOT REQUIRED.

3. GENERAL:
   (A) COPIES OF ALL MATERIALS REFERENCED IN SOURCE ANNOTATIONS SHOULD BE RETAINED FOR NO LESS THAN FIVE YEARS AND CROSS-INDEXED BY REFERENCE TO SCRIPT PAGE AND SCENE NUMBERS.
   (B) IF ANNOTATIONS IN THE MARGINS ARE COPIED TO AVOID REPEATED LENGTHY REFER-ENCES, A KEY TO SUCH CODING SHOULD BE PROVIDED.

DEALMAKING
IN THE
FILM AND
TELEVISION
INDUSTRY—
3RD EDITION

60

IDENTIFIABLE PRODUCTS, LOCATIONS, AND PERSONS

As mentioned in the discussion of merchandising deals in Chapter 2, producers should obtain releases for the depiction of any identifiable products shown in a film. Similarly, producers may need to obtain releases for identifiable locations and for any character names that resemble living individuals.[8]

You should not assume that a thinly disguised portrayal of a living person immunizes you from liability. If the person is recognizable from the circumstances, you could be liable. A disclaimer (e.g., "Any resemblance to people living or dead is purely coincidental. . .") does not provide absolute protection. What if you wrote a novel about supposedly fictional events in the life of a widow of an American President who was assassinated in Dallas? The widow later marries a Greek shipping tycoon. Call the character what you will, but readers may assume you are writing about Jackie Kennedy. She may be able to bring a successful suit if she is defamed or her privacy is invaded.[9]

Depiction releases should allow the producer to edit, modify, and embellish the story. If a minor has given consent, the consent must be legally binding, which may require court approval.

END OF FILM NOTICE

THE CHARACTERS AND EVENTS PORTRAYED AND THE NAMES USED HEREIN ARE FICTITIOUS, AND ANY SIMILARITY IN THE NAME, CHARACTER, OR HISTORY OF THESE PERSONS IS ENTIRELY INCIDENTAL AND COINCIDENTAL.

THIS MOTION PICTURE PHOTOPLAY IS PROTECTED PURSUANT TO THE PROVISION OF THE LAWS OF THE UNITED STATES OF AMERICA AND OTHER COUNTRIES. ANY UNAUTHORIZED DUPLICATION AND/OR DISTRIBUTION OF THIS PHOTOPLAY MAY RESULT IN CIVIL LIABILITY AND CRIMINAL PROSECUTION.

THIS MOTION PICTURE IS PROTECTED BY COPYRIGHT AND OTHER APPLICABLE LAWS AND ANY UNAUTHORIZED DUPLICATION, DISTRIBUTION, OR EXHIBITION OF THIS MOTION PICTURE COULD RESULT IN CRIMINAL PROSECUTION AS WELL AS CIVIL LIABILITY.

COPYRIGHT BIG TIME PRODUCTIONS, INC. 2009. ALL RIGHTS RESERVED.

---

[8] It may be easier to choose another name.
[9] Of course, now that Jackie is deceased, such actions can no longer be brought because these rights are personal and do not descend to her heirs.

FILM CLIPS

Special problems arise if you want to incorporate film clips from other motion pictures into your production. Permission may need to be obtained from the copyright owner of the film, from various unions and guilds,[10] from every person who appears in the clip, and, if music is used, from the musicians and the owners of the underlying musical composition. Usually, it is simpler and less expensive to shoot original footage than to incorporate existing footage.

Film footage can be purchased from stock footage suppliers. Additional releases may be required to use the footage. The National Archives has a library of public-domain footage available for the cost of duplication.

If film footage is bought from a studio or stock footage supplier, they will often supply a release. Here are sample releases for a still photo or artwork:

PHOTO RELEASE

_____ Corporation

Owner: _____

Fee: $____

Subject hereby grants to _____ Corporation ("Company") the exclusive right to use the photograph(s) depicting subject listed in Exhibit A, attached hereto, for all merchandising purposes. Subject acknowledges that the depiction of him/her in the Photo may be duplicated and distributed in any and all manner and media throughout the world in perpetuity.

Subject grants Company the exclusive right, license, and privilege to utilize the names, characters, artist's portrayal of characters, likeness, and visual representations in the Photo in connection with the manufacture, advertising, distribution, and sale of any articles or products. Such granted rights include the unconditional and exclusive right throughout the world to use, simulate, and portray subject's likeness, voice, personality, personal identification, and personal experiences, incidents,

---

[10] WGA, SAG, DGA, and AFM.

DEALMAKING
IN THE
FILM AND
TELEVISION
INDUSTRY—
3RD EDITION

62

situations, and events which heretofore occurred or hereafter occur (in whole or in part) in any and all other media of any nature whatsoever, whether now known or hereafter devised. Subject agrees that Company may elect to refrain from using subject's real name and may use a pseudonym.

Subject hereby releases and discharges Company, its employees, agents, licensees, successors, and assigns from any and all claims, demands, or causes of actions that it may have or may hereafter have for libel, defamation, invasion of privacy or right of publicity, infringement of copyright or trademark, or violation of any other right arising out of or relating to any utilization of the rights granted under this agreement.

Subject warrants and represents that Subject possesses all rights necessary for the grant of this license and will indemnify and hold Company, its licensees, and assigns harmless from and against any and all claims, damages, liabilities, costs, and expenses arising out of a breach of the foregoing warranty.

Subject agrees that Company shall have the unlimited right to vary, change, alter, modify, add to and/or delete from his/her depiction in the Photo, and to rearrange and/or transpose his/her depiction, and to use a portion or portions of his/her depiction or character in conjunction with any other literary, dramatic, or other material of any kind.

Subject has not committed or omitted to perform any act by which such rights could or will be encumbered, diminished, or impaired. Subject further represents and warrants that no attempt shall be made hereafter to encumber, diminish, or impair any of the rights granted herein and that all appropriate protection of such rights will continue to be maintained by Subject.

All rights, licenses, and privileges herein granted to Company are irrevocable and not subject to rescission, restraint, or injunction under any circumstances.

Nothing herein shall be construed to obligate Company to produce, distribute, or utilize any of the rights granted herein.

This agreement shall be construed in accordance with the laws of the State of California applicable to agreements that are executed and fully performed within said State.

This agreement contains the entire understanding of the parties relating to the subject matter, and this agreement cannot be changed except by written agreement executed by the party to be bound.

IN WITNESS WHEREOF, the parties hereto have signed this Agreement as of _____, 20__.

("Subject")

For _____ Corporation ("Company")

STATE OF   )

) ss.:

COUNTY OF   )

On the ____ day of _____, 20__, before me personally came
_____ to me known and known to be
the individual described in and who executed the foregoing
instrument, and he/she did duly acknowledge to me that he/
she executed the same.

Notary Public

POSTER/ARTWORK
CLEARANCE AND RELEASE

(Date)

_____

_____

_____

Dear Owner:

By signing below you hereby agree to the following terms
and conditions relating to the release of your Poster/Artwork,
(collectively "Material" as described at the end of this agreement),
for use in the production "_____" ("Production"), and
its advertising and any and all ancillary uses thereof.

Owner acknowledges and agrees that Producer and their
successors, licensees, and/or assigns shall have the right to
release, exhibit, and broadcast the Material in any and all
media throughout the world in perpetuity and in any and all
advertising, publicizing, promotion, and exploitation thereof.

Owner warrants that the Material is either original to Owner
or is fully cleared by Owner, and that neither the Material
nor Producer's use of the Material as contemplated by this
Agreement will infringe or violate any rights of any person
or entity. Owner will indemnify and hold Producer, its
successors, assigns, and licensees harmless from and against

DEALMAKING
IN THE
FILM AND
TELEVISION
INDUSTRY—
3RD EDITION

64

any and all claims, damages, liabilities, costs, and expenses (including reasonable attorneys' fees) arising out of breach of the foregoing warranty. Moreover, Owner hereby releases, discharges, and holds Producer harmless from any liability by virtue of any blurring, distortion, alteration, optical illusion, or use in composite form, whether intentional or otherwise, that may occur or be produced in the duplication of said Material or in any subsequent processing thereof, as well as any publication thereof.

Owner hereby waives any right that he/she/it may have to inspect or approve the finished motion picture, or the advertising copy or printed matter that may be used in connection therewith, or the use to which it may be applied.

It is agreed that no payments, residuals, reuse fees, or otherwise shall be made to Owner or any other affiliated company with respect to Producer's use of the Material herein. The undersigned parties warrant that they have the authority to enter into this agreement and grant the rights granted herein and that the consent of no other party is necessary to effectuate the full and complete satisfaction of the provisions contained herein.

In the event of a dispute arising from this release, I hereby agree that the laws of the State of California shall govern and that venue for the resolution of any dispute shall be in the State of California.

Owner hereby warrants that Owner is of full age and has every right to contract in Owner's own name in the above regard. Owner has read the above authorization, release, and agreement, prior to its execution, and that Owner is fully familiar with the contents thereof. If the Owner is signing as an agent or employee of a firm or corporation, the undersigned warrants that Owner is fully authorized to do so. This release shall be binding upon Owner and Owner's heirs, legal representatives, successors, and assigns.

Please indicate your agreement and consent to the foregoing by signing in the space provided below.

Sincerely,

Producer

AGREED TO AND ACCEPTED: Producer

Owner

By: _____

Its: _____

Date: _____

Description of Material

1.

2.

3.

4.

Questions and Answers

1. What is an E&O insurance policy, and why is this important in a screenplay contract negotiation?

Answer: E&O (Errors & Omissions) Insurance is akin to a malpractice insurance policy for writers and filmmakers. It protects them should they inadvertently infringe another party's copyright, defame a person, invade someone's privacy, or otherwise infringe their rights. It does not cover a writer or filmmaker if he/she knowingly engages in wrongful behavior. In other words, if a filmmaker is careless and infringes another's rights, he/she is covered, but if he/she intentionally plagiarizes a script, he/she would not be covered by the insurance policy.

The insurance covers the named insured, and you can add additional named insureds to the policy for a nominal charge. If you are a member of the Writers Guild of America, then by virtue of their collective bargaining agreement, the writer is supposed to be included on the employer's policy. However, even with E&O coverage in place, the insured may be liable for the deductible, which can be $10,000 or more.

The policy covers both any damages assessed against the writer/filmmaker, and the legal fees incurred to pay for a defense.

E&O is often required by U.S. distributors before they will license a film for distribution. They want the right to distribute the film but they do not want to buy a lawsuit.

DEALMAKING
IN THE
FILM AND
TELEVISION
INDUSTRY—
3RD EDITION

A writer and filmmaker can be liable for copyright infringement even if they don't intend to infringe another's copyrighted material. For instance, if a filmmaker licensed a piece of music for his/her film, and it turned out that, unbeknownst to the filmmaker, the musician who sold him/her the music didn't own all the rights to it, then the filmmaker could be liable even though the filmmaker was an innocent infringer.

2. If one has a script registered with the WGA and the U.S. Copyright Office but later changes its title, must one resubmit the revised/retitled script? Also, what protections are available for movie titles?

Answer: It is not necessary to re-register a script if the only change is the title. The copyright office will accept an application for Supplementary Registration, which will accomplish this purpose. The form for supplementary registration is Form CA. The information in the Supplementary Registration does not replace that contained in the original registration, but rather augments it.

Regarding titles, copyright law does not protect titles. Titles can sometimes be protected under the law of unfair competition and trademark infringement. Moreover, one can also secure limited protection against other registrants by registering a title at the Motion Picture Association of America Title Registration Bureau. The MPAA registration bureau can be reached at (818) 995-6600.

However, titles of individual products like a movie are generally not eligible for trademark protection. Only a series of products from a single source, such as sequels or a television series, such as *Bonanza*, can be protected under trademark law. However, for a one-shot project like a movie, the title would not be protected. The title, however, could possibly be protected under the laws of unfair competition once the title has acquired a secondary meaning. A movie cannot have a secondary meaning with the public before it is released. Thus, after George Lucas had produced and distributed *Star Wars*, another filmmaker could not distribute a movie called *Star Wars II*, and trade on the goodwill and name recognition of the original. This would be unfair competition, and would violate various federal and state laws. Whether the use of a name on a product or service violates the trademark rights, or violates various unfair competition laws, may be a difficult call.

Trademark rights are often restricted to a geographical area or type of product. For example, if you operate the Acme Hardware Store in Los Angeles, it would not necessarily prevent someone else from opening an Acme Hardware Store in Brooklyn, a location where you do not do business. Likewise, the fact that you operate a Hardware Store under the mark "Acme" would not prevent someone from setting up the Acme Supermarket because people do not associate hardware and food together. In other words, there is little likelihood of confusion.

Another way to protect titles is with registration with the MPAA. This is protection by contract law, through an arrangement between the MPAA companies and any independent producers who choose to join. It is a contract wherein all parties agree not to infringe each other's titles. There are some limitations because the deal is only binding on those people who choose to sign it. If you wish to contact the MPAA Title Registration Bureau, their number is (818) 995-6600.

CHAPTER 5

LITERARY ACQUISITION AGREEMENTS

A literary acquisition contract is an agreement to acquire all or some rights in a literary property such as a book or a play. Producers typically use it to buy a screenplay or movie rights to a book.

Buyers (e.g., producers) will want owners (e.g., writers) to warrant that they own all the rights they are selling, free and clear of any other obligations (encumbrances). Owners will disclose their copyright registration number so that buyers can check the copyright records and review the chain of title to be sure that they are getting all the rights they want.

Each agreement needs to define the extent of the rights being sold. Sometimes all rights, the entire copyright, are sold. Other times, limited rights, on either an exclusive or non-exclusive basis, are licensed. As explained in Chapter 12, copyrights are bundles of rights that owners can divide any number of ways.

If movie rights are sold, the buyer typically will have the right to adapt the work into a motion picture and release it in ancillary markets such as home video. The buyer may also obtain sequel and remake rights, although an additional payment may be due when and if these rights are used.

DEALMAKING
IN THE
FILM AND
TELEVISION
INDUSTRY—
3RD EDITION

70

The buyer is routinely granted the right to excerpt up to 7,500 words from the book for advertising and promotion purposes, although I can't recall an instance where a movie studio or network used such a large excerpt to promote a movie. Publicity is usually centered on stars and directors.

Writers will want to reserve certain rights. A writer who allows adaptation of his/her work into film might want to retain book rights, stage rights, radio rights, and the right to use his/her characters in a new plot.[1]

Sometimes the buyer will agree to let the writer retain certain rights, provided the writer gives the buyer first shot at purchasing the rights should he/she later decide to sell them.

For example, let's say that Writer A has sold the movie rights to his book to Warner Bros. (WB). The writer has retained all dramatic (play) rights. WB obtains a "Right of First Negotiation," giving it first opportunity to purchase the play rights if the Writer should choose to sell them. WB thinks it is only fair for it to have such a right. It is investing millions of dollars in turning the writer's book into a movie, making the underlying property and all its derivative forms more valuable. The Right of First Negotiation only requires that the writer negotiate in good faith with WB first. If no agreement is reached within a set time (e.g., 30 days), the Writer could negotiate and sell the play rights to a third party.

Another provision that may be used with, or as an alternative to, the Right of First Negotiation is the Right of Last Refusal. Here the buyer has the right to acquire the reserved right under the same terms and conditions as any offer made by a third party. If WB had a Right of Last Refusal, then the Writer would be free to offer the play rights to another buyer. Before closing the deal, however, the writer would have to offer to sell WB the rights on the same terms as the best offer received by the Writer.

As a practical matter, when a writer has given a studio a Right of Last Refusal, it can be difficult to interest third parties in buying a reserved right. Why should Universal Pictures spend time negotiating the terms of a sale with the writer, only to have the deal supplanted at the last moment by WB? Thus, the Right of Last Refusal discourages third-party offers.

---

[1] This should be distinguished from movie sequel rights, which provide the buyer with the right to use the characters in sequel motion pictures. What the writer is reserving is the right to use his/her characters in another book.

Another point important to the buyer will be the unlimited right to make changes to the work when adapting it. Paramount Pictures is not going to invest large sums of money to develop a screenplay only to find itself in a vulnerable position, unable to change a line of dialogue without the author's permission. Suppose the movie is in the midst of production and the author cannot be located? What if the author unreasonably withholds consent? No studio is going to let a writer hold a gun to its head by withholding permission to make changes.

On the other hand, authors frequently complain that studios and directors ruin their work. They are embarrassed when a studio releases a movie inferior to the original work. Some countries, such as France, grant artists so-called moral rights ("le droit moral"), which may prevent buyers from desecrating or changing artists' work without their permission.[2] The United States does not expressly recognize the doctrine of moral rights in regard to motion pictures.[3] Moreover, the buyer is going to ask the seller to waive these rights.

Writers who can't stand to see their work changed should write books and plays, where they have a larger measure of control over their work. A stage director, for example, cannot change a word of a Neil Simon play without the writer's permission. Screenwriters, however, must accept the possibility that their work will be significantly changed. Indeed, you may not even recognize your work when all the rewrites and revisions are complete. You wrote a novel about a farmer in Iowa, and now the story is set on a U-Boat in the North Atlantic.

One consolation is the money earned from the sale of movie rights and for screenwriting. Movie rights to bestselling novels can fetch a million dollars or more. Accomplished screenwriters often earn six-figure fees for their services. The Writers Guild minimum for screenwriters is as much as $109,783, which is much more than what many beginning novelists receive in book royalties.

In a literary acquisition agreement, buyers will also want sellers to make certain warranties, or promises. For example, the writer will often warrant that the work does not defame or invade anyone's privacy, or infringe on another's copyright. Buyers

---

[2] Moral rights in France, however, are limited for collaborative works.
[3] Various state and federal laws, however, accomplish much the same result through other doctrines, such as the law of unfair competition and defamation. Moreover, the federal Visual Artists Rights Act of 1990 protects the moral rights of artists who create fine art (not including motion pictures): Pub. L. No. 101-650, 104 Stat. 5128 (1990).

DEALMAKING
IN THE
FILM AND
TELEVISION
INDUSTRY—
3RD EDITION

72

usually want the warranties to be absolute, while writers want the warranties based on the best of the writer's knowledge and belief. The difference is this: If the writer unknowingly defames another, he/she would be liable under an absolute warranty but not necessarily under one to the best of his/her knowledge and belief. In other words, if the writer in good faith believed he/she had not defamed anyone, he/she wouldn't be liable.

Buyers also want writers to stand behind their warranties and indemnify buyers in the event a warranty is breached. When a writer indemnifies the buyer, the writer agrees to reimburse the buyer for any litigation costs and judgment that may arise because the writer breached his/her warranties.

Let's say a novelist invents a character named John West who lives in Ann Arbor, Michigan, where he is a bartender who moonlights as a criminal. The novel becomes a bestseller and a studio makes a movie based on it. One day a person by the name of John West who lives in Ann Arbor and tends bar sees the movie. He is shocked to see a character with his name portrayed as a criminal. He brings suit against the studio for defamation. The studio seeks indemnification (i.e. reimbursement) from the writer. The writer may be liable, even though he/she didn't intend to defame anyone.

Of course, an indemnity is only worth as much as the person standing behind it. It would be a waste of time for a studio to seek reimbursement from an impoverished writer. To protect themselves from potential liability, producers and studios can purchase Errors & Omissions (E&O) insurance. The studio's lawyers, as well as the insurance company's lawyers, may review proposed scripts before production to try to avoid any liability. In this example, a studio lawyer might telephone directory information for Ann Arbor and see if there is anyone by the name of John West living there. If so, it might make sense to change the name of the character or the location of the story.

Attorneys and agents representing writers often ask that the writer be added as a named insured on the E&O policy. This may add a few hundred dollars to the premium but will ensure that the insurance company defends the writer as well as the studio and bears any litigation expenses. It would cost the writer much more to buy an insurance policy on his/her own.

Another provision found in literary purchase agreements requires that the seller not let the property fall into the public domain. Under the old copyright law (effective before 1978), a copyright lasted for 28 years and could be renewed for an additional 28-year term. Consequently, the buyer wanted to make sure the writer would renew the copyright when it came up for renewal at the end of the first term. For works created since 1978, authors are given a copyright for their lifetimes plus 70 years.[4] There are no renewal terms for these works.

Credit is another topic that needs to be addressed. The buyer wants the right to use the name and likeness of the author to promote the picture, although the writer is rarely featured in advertising. As for billing credit, the Writers Guild agreement will usually determine who receives writing credit (assuming the Writer is in the guild and the production company is a guild signatory). The producer cannot arbitrarily assign credit. In case of a dispute over credits, the Writers Guild will impanel a group of impartial writers to arbitrate. They will read drafts of the script and allocate credit. The rules used to determine credit allocation are available from the Writers Guild (www.wga.org/subpage_writersresources.aspx?id=167).

The literary purchase agreement will also contain an explicit provision stating that the producer is under no obligation to actually produce a movie. The producer wants the right to make a movie but not the obligation to do so. This prevents the writer from forcing the producer into production.

If the writer has a reversion clause, all rights to the script can revert to him/her if production is not commenced within a set time (e.g., five years from the date the movie rights were bought). Thus the writer will regain rights to the property and has a chance to set it up elsewhere.

Another provision found in literary purchase agreements is the assignment clause. This permits the buyer to assign his/her rights to another. A producer will want the ability to assign rights because a distributor or financier may insist upon an assignment as a condition of participating in the project. If the writer is concerned where the project may end up, he/she may try to limit the assignment to major studios and networks. The writer could also ask that no assignments be permitted unless he/she gives his/her approval, which he/she may agree will not be unreasonably withheld. The writer may want the assignment

---

[4] Anonymous works and work made for hire have a different term.

DEALMAKING
IN THE
FILM AND
TELEVISION
INDUSTRY—
3RD EDITION

74

to state that any assignee must assume all the obligations owed the writer, and perhaps the assignor will remain liable as well.

Finally, the literary purchase agreement will often require the writer to refrain from engaging in any publicity activities unless they are with the consent of the buyer. The studio wants to make sure it can orchestrate a publicity campaign without worrying about the writer giving interviews on his/her own.

The following case illustrates the kind of problems that can arise from a poorly worded acquisition agreement.

SAMPLE CLAUSES

RIGHT OF FIRST NEGOTIATION: THE TERM "RIGHT OF FIRST NEGOTIATION" MEANS THAT IF, AFTER THE EXPIRATION OF AN APPLICABLE TIME LIMITATION, SELLER DESIRES TO DISPOSE OF OR EXERCISE A PARTICULAR RIGHT RESERVED TO SELLER HEREIN ("RESERVED RIGHT"), WHETHER DIRECTLY OR INDIRECTLY, THEN SELLER SHALL NOTIFY BUYER IN WRITING AND IMMEDIATELY NEGOTIATE WITH BUYER REGARDING SUCH RESERVED RIGHT. IF, AFTER THE EXPIRATION OF 30 DAYS FOLLOWING THE RECEIPT OF SUCH NOTICE, NO AGREEMENT HAS BEEN REACHED, THEN SELLER MAY NEGOTIATE WITH THIRD PARTIES REGARDING SUCH RESERVED RIGHT.

RIGHT OF LAST REFUSAL: THE TERM "RIGHT OF LAST REFUSAL" MEANS THAT IF BUYER AND SELLER FAIL TO REACH AN AGREEMENT PURSUANT TO BUYER'S RIGHT OF FIRST NEGOTIATION, AND SELLER MAKES AND/OR RECEIVES ANY BONA FIDE OFFER TO LICENSE, LEASE, AND/OR PURCHASE THE PARTICULAR RESERVED RIGHT OR ANY INTEREST THEREIN ("THIRD-PARTY OFFER"), AND IF THE PROPOSED PURCHASE PRICE AND OTHER MATERIAL TERMS OF A THIRD PARTY OFFER ARE NO MORE FAVORABLE TO SELLER THAN THE TERMS WHICH WERE ACCEPTABLE TO BUYER DURING THE FIRST NEGOTIATION PERIOD, SELLER SHALL NOTIFY BUYER (BY REGISTERED MAIL OR TELEGRAM), IF SELLER PROPOSES TO ACCEPT SUCH THIRD-PARTY OFFER, AND DISCLOSE THE NAME OF THE OFFERER, THE PROPOSED PURCHASE PRICE, AND OTHER TERMS OF SUCH THIRD-PARTY OFFER. DURING THE PERIOD OF 30 DAYS AFTER BUYER'S RECEIPT OF SUCH NOTICE, BUYER SHALL HAVE THE EXCLUSIVE OPTION TO LICENSE, LEASE, AND/OR PURCHASE, AS THE CASE MAY BE, THE PARTICULAR RESERVED RIGHT OR INTEREST REFERRED TO IN SUCH THIRD-PARTY OFFER, AT THE SAME PURCHASE PRICE AND UPON THE SAME TERMS AND CONDITIONS AS SET FORTH IN SUCH NOTICE. IF BUYER ELECTS TO EXERCISE THEREOF BY REGISTERED MAIL OR TELEGRAM WITHIN SUCH 30-DAY PERIOD, FAILING WHICH SELLER SHALL BE FREE TO ACCEPT SUCH THIRD-PARTY OFFER; PROVIDED THAT IF ANY SUCH PROPOSED LICENSE, LEASE, AND/OR SALE IS NOT CONSUMMATED WITH A THIRD PARTY WITHIN 30 DAYS FOLLOWING THE EXPIRATION OF THE AFORESAID 30-DAY PERIOD, BUYER'S RIGHT OF LAST REFUSAL SHALL REVIVE AND SHALL APPLY TO EACH AND EVERY FURTHER OFFER OR OFFERS AT ANY TIME RECEIVED BY SELLER RELATING TO THE PARTICULAR RESERVED RIGHT OR ANY INTEREST THEREIN; PROVIDED, FURTHER, THAT BUYER'S OPTION SHALL CONTINUE IN FULL FORCE AND EFFECT, UPON ALL OF THE TERMS AND CONDITIONS OF THIS PARAGRAPH, SO LONG AS SELLER RETAINS AY RIGHTS, TITLE, OR INTERESTS IN OR TO THE PARTICULAR RESERVED RIGHT. BUYER'S RIGHT OF LAST REFUSAL SHALL INURE TO THE BENEFIT OF BUYER, ITS SUCCESSORS, AND ASSIGNS, AND SHALL BIND SELLER AND SELLER'S HEIRS, SUCCESSORS, AND ASSIGNS.

Warner Bros. v. Columbia Broadcasting (1954)[5]

FACTS: Warner Bros., P, acquired the movie rights to Dashiell Hammett's book *The Maltese Falcon*, which featured the character, detective Sam Spade. Later Hammett wrote additional stories featuring Spade and granted the television, radio, and movie rights in those stories to Columbia Broadcasting (CBS). CBS began a series of radio programs featuring Sam Spade. Warner Bros. brought suit, claiming that Hammett could not sell these additional stories to CBS because Warner owned characters in them.

ISSUE: Does the sale of movie rights to a book include the rights to characters in the book?

HOLDING: Not necessarily. Decision for Hammett and CBS.

RATIONALE: The contract did not specifically say that Hammett was granting Warner exclusive rights to the characters. Warner drew up the contract and any ambiguity should be construed against it. Although Warner owns the copyright to *The Maltese Falcon*, that does not prevent the author from using the characters in other stories. "The characters were vehicles for the story told, and the vehicles did not go with the sale of the story."

Hammett sold *The Maltese Falcon* to Buyer One (Warner Bros.), then invented new stories with the same characters and sold them to buyer Two (CBS). The contract never addressed the issue of whether Warner obtained all rights to the characters when it bought *The Maltese Falcon*. Since the contract

MAJOR PROVISIONS: LITERARY ACQUISITION AGREEMENT

1) WARRANTY OF OWNERSHIP

2) EXTENT OF RIGHTS CONVEYED

3) RIGHTS RESERVED
   A) RIGHT OF FIRST NEGOTIATION
   B) RIGHT OF LAST REFUSAL

4) RIGHT TO MAKE CHANGES ("DROIT MORAL")

5) CONSIDERATION

6) INDEMNIFICATION

7) PROTECTION OF COPYRIGHT

8) CREDIT
   A) RIGHT TO USE NAME TO PROMOTE
   B) BILLING CREDIT

9) NO OBLIGATION TO PRODUCE

10) ASSIGNMENT

11) RESTRICT PUBLICITY

---

[5] 216 F.2d 945 (1954).

DEALMAKING
IN THE
FILM AND
TELEVISION
INDUSTRY—
3RD EDITION

76

was ambiguous, and since Warner drafted the contract, the ambiguity was construed against it. Consequently, Hammett and CBS won.

As a general principal of contract law, ambiguous contracts are construed against the drafter. This type of problem rarely arises today because attorneys are careful to delineate precisely which rights the writer is granting and which are retained. The writer typically retains the right to use characters in a new plot.

Readers should note that in the New York case of Burnett v. Warner Bros. Pictures,[6] the court came to a different conclusion on facts similar to the Sam Spade case. In Burnett, plaintiffs wrote the play *Everyone Comes to Rick's*, which was sold to Warner Bros. for $20,000 and became the basis for the film *Casablanca*. The agreement gave Warner Bros. "all now or hereafter existing rights of every kind and character whatsoever pertaining to said work, whether or not such rights are now known, recognized, or contemplated . . ."

Warner Bros. subsequently produced a television series based on the play and movie. Plaintiffs sued, claiming that Warner had no right to use the characters in the television series. The court concluded that the language of the contract should be interpreted to mean that plaintiffs gave up all their rights to the work, even though the language didn't specifically mention character rights. Once again, this illustrates the importance of a carefully worded contract.

Questions and Answers

1. I'm interested in acquiring the movie rights to a screenplay. Do the "movie rights" typically include the right to make sequels?

Answer: Often the rights acquired by the purchaser include the right to make one or more motion picture sequels and/or remakes. Sellers may reserve such rights, however. If the purchaser obtains sequel or remake rights, the agreement usually provides that, in the event a sequel or remake is made, the author of the screenplay is entitled to additional compensation.

---

[6] *Burnett v. Warner Bros. Pictures,* 493 N.Y.S.2d (N.Y. App. Div., 1985).

2. Can a novelist who sells the movie rights to a book write a sequel novel?

Answer: It depends on the terms of the agreement. Often the purchaser (producer/studio) has the right to make sequel films, but the author reserves the right to write sequel books. The purchaser may want to obtain a right of first negotiation or last refusal on the movie rights to a sequel novel.

3. What is a reversion clause?

Answer: A reversion clause states that certain rights revert at some future time or under some condition. In the movie industry, the author of a book who sells movie rights might ask for a reversion clause that provides that if the buyer of the rights doesn't make a movie within five years from the date of purchase, then all rights revert to the author. Thus, if the buyer (producer) is unable to make a film, the author regains those rights eventually and can try to set up the project elsewhere.

OPTION & LITERARY PURCHASE AGREEMENT

THIS AGREEMENT, made and entered into as of _____ (date), by and between _____ (name and address of seller) ("Seller") and _____ (name and address of buyer) ("Buyer").

1. SELLER'S REPRESENTATIONS AND WARRANTIES:

(a) Sole Proprietor: Seller represents and warrants to Buyer that Seller is the sole and exclusive proprietor, throughout the world of that certain original literary material written by _____ entitled _____ (the "Literary Property" or "Property").

(b) Facts: Seller represents and warrants to Buyer that the following statements are true and correct in all respects with respect to said literary material:

(i) Seller is the sole author of the Literary Property.

(ii) The Literary Property was first published on (date) by _____, under the title _____, and was registered for

DEALMAKING
IN THE
FILM AND
TELEVISION
INDUSTRY—
3RD EDITION

78

copyright in the name of _____, under copyright registration number _____, in the Office of the United States Register of Copyrights, Washington, D.C.

No Motion Picture or dramatic version of the Literary Property, or any part of it, has been manufactured, produced, presented, or authorized; no radio or television development, presentation or program based on the Literary Property, or any part of it, has been manufactured, produced, presented, broadcast, or authorized; and no written or oral agreements or commitments at all with respect to the Literary Property, or with respect to any right therein, have previously been made or entered by or on behalf of Seller (except with respect to the publication of the Literary Property as set forth above).

(c) No Infringement or Violation of Third Party Rights: Seller represents and warrants to Buyer that Seller has not adapted the Literary Property from any other literary, dramatic, or other material of any kind, nature, or description, nor, excepting for material which is in the public domain, has Seller copied or used in the Literary Property the plot, scenes, sequence, or story of any other literary, dramatic, or other material; that the Literary Property does not infringe upon any common law or statutory rights in any other literary, dramatic, or other material; that as far as Seller has knowledge, no material in the Literary Property is libelous or violative of the right of privacy of any person and the full use of the rights in the Literary Property which are covered by the within option would not violate any rights of any person, firm, or corporation; and that the Literary Property is not in the public domain in any country in the world where copyright protection is available.

(d) No Impairment of Rights: Seller represents and warrants to Buyer that Seller is the exclusive proprietor, throughout the world, of the rights in the Literary Property which are covered by the within option; that Seller has not assigned, licensed, nor in any manner encumbered, diminished, or impaired these rights; that Seller has not committed nor omitted to perform any act by which these rights could or will be encumbered, diminished, or impaired; and that there is no outstanding claim or litigation pending against or involving the title, ownership, and/or copyright in the Literary Property, or in any part of it, or in the rights which are covered by the within option. Seller further represents and warrants that no attempt hereafter will be made to encumber, diminish, or impair any of the rights herein granted and that all appropriate protections of such rights will continue to be maintained by Seller.

Without limiting any other rights Buyer may have in the Literary Property, Seller agrees that if there is any claim and/ or litigation involving any breach or alleged breach of any such representations and warranties of Seller, the option period granted hereunder and any periods within which Buyer may, pursuant to the provisions of Clause 3 hereof, extend the option, shall automatically be extended until no claim and/or litigation involving any breach or alleged breach of any such representation and warranties of seller is outstanding, but in any event not for a period more than one (1) additional year. Any time after the occurrence of such a claim and/or litigation until the expiration of the option period, as extended, Buyer may, besides any other rights and remedies Buyer may have in the Literary Property, rescind this agreement and in such event, despite anything else to the contrary contained herein, Seller agrees to repay Buyer any monies paid by Buyer to Seller hereunder concerning the Property and any reasonable amounts expended by Buyer in developing or exploiting the Property. Without limiting the generality of the foregoing, Seller agrees that Seller will not, any time during the option period, exercise or authorize or permit the exercise by others of any of the rights covered by the option or any of the rights reserved by Seller under the provisions of Exhibit A which are not to be exercised or licensed to others during any period therein specified.

2. CONSIDERATION FOR OPTION: In consideration of the payment to Seller of the sum of $_____, receipt of which is hereby acknowledged, Seller agrees to and does hereby give and grant to Buyer the exclusive and irrevocable option to purchase from Seller the rights in the Property as described in Exhibit A for the total purchase price specified and payable as provided in Exhibit A, provided that any sums paid under this Clause 2 or any other provision of this agreement with respect to the option shall be credited against the first sums payable on account of such purchase price. If Buyer shall fail to exercise this option, then the sums paid to Seller hereunder with respect to the option shall be and remain the sole property of Seller.

3. OPTION PERIOD: The within option shall be effective during the period commencing on the date hereof and ending _____ ("the Initial Option Period"). The Initial Option Period may be extended for an additional _____ months by the payment of $_____ on or before the expiration date specified above ("the Second Option Period").

4. EXERCISE OF OPTION:

(a) Notice of Exercise: If Buyer elects to exercise the within option, Buyer (any time during the Option Period) shall serve upon Seller written notice of the exercise of it by addressing such notice to seller at his/her address as specified in Exhibit A and by depositing such notice, so addressed by certified

DEALMAKING
IN THE
FILM AND
TELEVISION
INDUSTRY—
3RD EDITION

80

mail, return receipt requested with postage prepaid, in the United States mail. The deposit of such notice in the United States mail as herein specified shall constitute service of it, and the date of such deposit shall be deemed to be the date of service of such notice.

(b) The purchase price shall be paid to Seller according to Exhibit A.

(c) The option may be exercised only by notice in writing as aforesaid; no conduct or oral statement by Buyer or his/her agents, representatives, or employees shall constitute an exercise of the option.

(d) Additional Documents: If Buyer exercises the within option, Seller, without cost to Buyer (other than the consideration provided for herein or in Exhibit A), shall execute, acknowledge, and deliver to Buyer, or shall cause the execution, acknowledgement, and delivery to Buyer of such further instruments as Buyer may reasonably require to confirm unto Buyer the rights, licenses, privileges, and property which are the subject of the within option. If Seller shall fail to execute and deliver or to cause the execution and delivery to Buyer of any such instruments, Buyer is hereby irrevocably granted the power coupled with an interest to execute such instruments and to take such other steps and proceedings as may be necessary concerning it in the name and on behalf of Seller and as Seller's attorney-in-fact. Seller shall supply all supporting agreements and documentation requested by Buyer.

(e) Failure to Execute Documents: If Seller shall fail to execute, acknowledge, or deliver to Buyer any agreements, assignments, or other instruments to be executed, acknowledged and delivered by Seller hereunder, then Buyer is hereby irrevocably appointed Seller's attorney-in-fact with full right, power, and authority to execute, acknowledge, and deliver the same in the name of and on behalf of Seller, Seller acknowledging that the authority and agency given Buyer is a power coupled with an interest. If the property has not been published or registered for copyright in the United States Copyright Office, and as a result thereof Exhibits A, B, and C, attached hereto, have not been completed with respect to the publication and copyright data and other data, then Buyer is authorized and instructed by Seller to insert the correct publication and copyright data in the appropriate blanks in Exhibits A, B, and C or after the property has been published and registered for copyright, and in this connection Seller agrees to notify Buyer promptly in writing of the publication and registration of the Property for copyright, specifying in such notice the name of the publisher, the date and place of publication, the name of the copyright proprietor, and the date and entry number of the copyright registration in the United States Copyright Office, all of which information may be inserted by Buyer in the appropriate blanks in such documents.

5. EFFECTIVENESS OF EXHIBITS A, B, AND C: Concurrently with the execution of this agreement, Seller has executed Exhibits A (Literary Purchase Agreement), B (Short-Form Option Agreement for Recordation), and C (Assignment of the Copyright), which are undated, and it is agreed that if Buyer shall exercise the option (but not otherwise), then the signature of Seller to Exhibits A, B, and C shall be deemed to be effective, and these Exhibits shall constitute valid and binding agreements and assignment effective as of the date of exercise of such option, and Buyer is hereby authorized and empowered to date such instruments accordingly. If Buyer shall fail to exercise the option, then the signature of Seller to Exhibits A, B, and C shall be void and of no further force or effect whatever, and Buyer shall not be deemed to have acquired any rights in or to the Property other than the option hereinabove provided for. If Buyer exercises the option, Buyer will execute and deliver to Seller copies of Exhibit A, dated as of the date of the exercise of the option, and Seller will, if so requested by Buyer, execute and deliver to Buyer additional copies of Exhibits A, B, and C. Notwithstanding the failure or omission of either party to execute and/or deliver such additional documents, it is agreed that upon the exercise of the option by Buyer, all rights in and to the Property agreed to be transferred to Buyer pursuant to the provisions of Exhibit A shall be deemed vested in Buyer, effective as of the date of exercise of the option, which rights shall be irrevocable.

6. RIGHT TO ENGAGE IN PRE-PRODUCTION: Seller acknowledges that Buyer may, at its own expense, during the option period, undertake pre-production activities in connection with any of the rights to be acquired hereunder including, without limitation, the preparation and submission of treatments and/or screenplays based on the Property.

7. RESTRICTIONS: During the Option Period, Seller shall not exercise or otherwise use any of the rights herein granted to Buyer and as more particularly described in Exhibit A hereof nor the rights reserved to Seller pursuant to Clause 2 (Rights Reserved) of Exhibit A, nor shall Seller permit the use of nor shall Seller use any other right Seller has reserved in a way that would in any manner or for any purpose unfairly compete

DEALMAKING
IN THE
FILM AND
TELEVISION
INDUSTRY—
3RD EDITION

82

with, interfere with, or conflict with the full and unrestricted use of the rights herein granted to Buyer and as described in Exhibit A.

8. ASSIGNMENT: This Option Agreement and the rights granted hereunder may be assigned by Buyer to any other person, firm, or corporation.

9. OPTION REVERSION AND TURNAROUND RIGHT:

(a) If the Buyer does not timely exercise the option during its original or extended term and timely pay the purchase price, the option shall end and all rights in the Literary Property shall immediately revert to the seller. The seller shall retain all sums therefore paid. Buyer shall immediately execute and deliver to seller any assignments and documents required to effectuate the Reversion. If Buyer shall fail or be unable to do so, Buyer hereby grants seller a power coupled with an interest to execute and deliver such documents as Buyer's attorney-in-fact.

(b) If the option is timely exercised and the purchase price paid and if a motion picture (based on the Literary Property) is not produced within _____ years from purchase of the Literary Property, seller shall have a turnaround right to reacquire and set up the Literary Property elsewhere, and upon obtaining such other commitment, to reimburse the Buyer or Motion Picture company for its actual direct out-of-pocket development costs in connection with the Literary Property, such as fees to scriptwriters, but excluding payments to seller and any payments to Buyer not directly related to scripting services.

(c) In addition, if Buyer decides not to exercise the option in Clause 2, above, any time before the expiration of the Option Period, or decides not to extend such option for _____, Buyer agrees to notify Seller of such decision as soon as reasonably possible, but in no event later than the applicable option or extension deadline. When such notice is given, the option granted hereunder to Buyer shall automatically revert to Seller.

10. FORCE MAJEURE: "Force Majeure" means any fire, flood, earthquake, or public disaster; strike, labor dispute, or unrest; embargo, riot, war, insurrection, or civil unrest; any act of God, any act of legally constituted authority; or any other cause beyond the buyer's control which would excuse buyer's performance as a matter of law. If, because of force majeure, buyer's performance hereunder is delayed or prevented, then the option period provided herein shall be extended for the time of such delay or prevention.

11. SECTION HEADINGS: The headings of paragraphs, sections and other subdivisions of this agreement are for convenient reference only. They shall not be used in any way to govern, limit, modify, or construe this agreement or any part or provision of it.

12. ARBITRATION: Any dispute under this Agreement will be resolved by final and binding arbitration under the Independent Film & Television Alliance Rules for International Arbitration in effect as of the effective date of this Agreement ("IFTA Rules"). Each Party waives any right to adjudicate any dispute in any other court or forum, *except* that a Party may seek interim relief before the start of arbitration as allowed by the IFTA Rules. The arbitration will be held in the Forum designated in the Agreement, or, if none is designated, as determined by the IFTA Rules. The Parties will abide by any decision in the arbitration and any court having jurisdiction may enforce it. The Parties submit to the jurisdiction of the courts in the Forum to compel arbitration or to confirm an arbitration award. The Parties agree to accept service of process in accordance with the IFTA Rules. The prevailing party shall be entitled to reimbursement of its reasonable attorney fees and costs.

13. ENTIRE AGREEMENT: This agreement, including the Exhibits attached hereto, contains the complete understanding and agreement between the parties with respect to the within subject matter, and supersedes all other agreements between the parties, whether written or oral relating thereto, and may not be modified or amended except by written instrument executed by both of the parties hereto. This agreement shall in all respects be subject to the laws of the State of _____ applicable to agreements executed and wholly performed within such State. All the rights, licenses, privileges, and property herein granted to Buyer are irrevocable and not subject to rescission, restraint, or injunction under any or all circumstances.

IN WITNESS WHEREOF, the parties hereto have signed this Option Agreement as of the day and year first hereinabove written.

SELLER: _____

BUYER: _____

DEALMAKING
IN THE
FILM AND
TELEVISION
INDUSTRY—
3RD EDITION

84

Exhibit A

This Agreement made on _____ (date) by and between _____ (hereinafter "Seller") and _____ (hereinafter "BUYER").

WITNESSETH

WHEREAS, Seller is the sole and exclusive seller throughout the world of all rights in and to the literary work entitled: _____, written by _____, which work has been filed in the United States Copyright Office under Copyright Registration Number _____; this work including all adaptations and/or versions, the titles, characters, plots, themes, and storyline is collectively called the "Property"; and

WHEREAS, Buyer wants to acquire certain rights of the Seller in consideration for the purchase price provided herein and in reliance upon the Seller's representations and warranties;

NOW, THEREFORE, the parties agree to as follows:

1. RIGHTS GRANTED: Seller hereby sells, grants, conveys, and assigns to Buyer, its successors, licensees, and assigns exclusively and forever, all motion picture rights (including all silent, sound dialogue, and musical motion picture rights), all television motion picture and other television rights, with limited radio broadcasting rights and 7,500-word publication rights for advertisement, publicity, and exploitation purposes, and certain incidental and allied rights, throughout the world, in and to the Property and in and to the copyright of it and all renewals and extensions of copyright. Included among the rights granted to Buyer hereunder (without in any way limiting the grant of rights hereinabove made) are the following sole and exclusive rights throughout the world:

(a) To make, produce, adapt, and copyright one or more motion picture adaptations or versions, whether fixed on film, tape, disc, wire, audio-visual cartridge, cassette, DVD, or through any other technical process whether now known or from now on devised, based in whole or in part on the Property, of every size, gauge, color, or type, including, but not limited to, musical motion pictures and remakes of and sequels to any motion picture produced hereunder and motion pictures in series or serial form, and for such purposes to record and reproduce and license others to record and reproduce, in synchronization with such motion pictures, spoken words taken from or based upon the text or theme of the Property and any kinds of music, musical accompaniments, and/or lyrics to be performed or sung by the performers in any such motion picture and any other kinds of sound and sound effects.

(b) To exhibit, perform, rent, lease, and generally deal in and with any motion picture produced hereunder:

(i) by all means or technical processes whatsoever, whether now known or from now on devised, including, by way of example only, film, tape, disc, wire, audio-visual cartridge, cassette, DVD, or television (including commercially sponsored, sustaining, and subscription or pay-per-view television, or any derivative of it); and

(ii) anywhere whatsoever, including homes, theaters, and elsewhere, and whether a fee is charged, directly or indirectly, for viewing any such motion picture.

(c) To broadcast, transmit, or reproduce the Property or any adaptation or version of it (including, without limitations to, any motion picture produced hereunder and/or any script or other material based on or using the Property or any of the characters, themes, or plots of it), by means of television or any process analogous thereto, whether now known or from now on devised (including commercially sponsored, sustaining, and subscription or pay-per-view television, Internet, and Video on Demand), by motion pictures produced on films or by means of magnetic tape, wire, disc, audio-visual cartridge, DVD, or any other device now known or from now on devised and including such television productions presented in series or serial form, and the exclusive right generally to exercise for television purposes all the rights granted to Buyer hereunder for motion picture purposes.

(d) Without limiting any other rights granted Buyer, to broadcast and/or transmit by television or radio or any process analogous thereto, whether now known or from now on devised, all or any part of the Property or any adaptation or version of it, including any motion picture or any other version or versions of it, and announcements about said motion picture or other version or versions, for advertising, publicizing, or exploiting such motion picture or other version or versions, which broadcasts or transmissions may be accomplished with living actors performing simultaneously with such broadcast or transmission or by any other method or means including the use of motion pictures (including trailers) reproduced on film or by means of magnetic tape or wire or through other recordings or transcriptions.

(e) To publish and copyright or cause to be published and copyrighted in the name of Buyer or its nominee in

DEALMAKING
IN THE
FILM AND
TELEVISION
INDUSTRY—
3RD EDITION

any languages throughout the world, in any form or media, synopses, novelizations, serializations, dramatizations, abridged and/or revised versions of the Property, not exceeding 7,500 words each, adapted from the Property or from any motion picture and/or other version of the Property for advertising, publicizing, and/or exploiting any such motion picture and/or other version.

(f) For the foregoing purposes to use all or any part of the Property and any of the characters, plots, themes, and/or ideas contained therein, and the title of the Property and any title or subtitle of any component of the Property, and to use said titles or subtitles for any motion picture or other version of adaptation whether the same is based on or adapted from the Property and/or as the title of any musical composition contained in any such motion picture or other version or adaptation.

(g) To use and exploit commercial or merchandise tie-ups and recordings of any sort and nature arising out of or connected with the Property and/or its motion picture or other versions and/or the title or titles of it and/or the characters of it and/or their names or characteristics.

All rights, licenses, privileges, and property herein granted Buyer shall be cumulative and Buyer may exercise or use any or all said rights, licenses, privileges, or property simultaneously with or in connection with or separately and apart from the exercise of any other of said rights, licenses, privileges, and property. If Seller from now on makes or publishes or permits to be made or published any revision, adaptation, sequel, translation, or dramatization or other versions of the Property, then Buyer shall have and Seller hereby grants to Buyer without payment therefore all of the same rights therein as are herein granted Buyer. The terms "Picture" and "Pictures" as used herein shall be deemed to mean or include any present or future kind of motion picture production based upon the Property, with or without sound recorded and reproduced synchronously with it, whether the same is produced on film or digitally or by any other method or means now or from now on used for the production, exhibition, and/or transmission of any kind of motion picture productions.

2. RIGHTS RESERVED: The following rights are reserved to Seller for Seller's use and disposition, subject, however, to the provisions of this agreement:

(a) Publication Rights: The right to publish and distribute printed versions of the Property owned or controlled by Seller in book form, whether hardcover or softcover, and in magazine or other periodicals, whether in installments or otherwise subject to Buyer's rights as provided for in Clause 1 supra.

(b) Stage Rights: The right to perform the Property or adaptations of it on the spoken stage with actors appearing in person in the immediate presence of the audience, provided no broadcast, telecast, recording, photography, or other reproduction of such performance is made. Seller agrees not to exercise, or permit any other person to exercise, said stage rights earlier than _____ years after the first general release or telecast, if earlier, of the first Picture produced hereunder, or _____ years after the date of exercise of the buyer's option to acquire the property, whichever is earlier.

(c) Radio Rights: The right to broadcast the Property by sound (as distinguished from visually) by radio, subject, however, to Buyer's right always to: (i) exercise its radio rights provided in Clause 1 supra for advertising and exploitation purposes by living actors or otherwise, by using excerpts from or condensations of the Property or any Picture produced hereunder; and (ii) in any event to broadcast any Picture produced hereunder by radio. Seller agrees not to exercise, or permit any other person to exercise, Seller's radio rights earlier than _____ years after the first general release or initial telecast, if earlier, of the first Picture produced hereunder or _____ years after the date of exercise of buyer's option to acquire the property, whichever is earlier.

(d) Author-Written Sequel: A literary property (story, novel, drama, or otherwise), whether written before or after the Property and whether written by Seller or by a successor in interest of Seller, using one or more of the characters appearing in the Property, participating in different events from those found in the Property, and whose plot is substantially different from that of the Property. Seller shall have the right to exercise publication rights (i.e., in book or magazine form) any time. Seller agrees not to exercise, or permit any other person to exercise, any other rights (including but not limited to motion picture or allied rights) of any kind in or to any author-written sequel earlier than _____ years after the first general release of the first Picture produced hereunder, or _____ years after the date of exercise of buyer's option to acquire the property, whichever is earlier, provided such restriction on Seller's exercise of said author-written sequel rights shall be extended to any period during which there is in effect, in any particular country or territory, a network television broadcasting agreement for a television motion picture, (i) based upon the Property, or (ii) based upon any Picture produced in the exercise of rights assigned herein, or (iii) using a character or

DEALMAKING
IN THE
FILM AND
TELEVISION
INDUSTRY—
3RD EDITION

88

characters of the Property, plus one (1) year, which shall also be a restricted period in such country or territory, whether such period occurs wholly or partly during or entirely after the _____ year period first referred to in this clause. Any disposition of motion picture or allied rights in an author-written sequel made to any person or company other than Buyer shall be made subject to the following limitations and restrictions:

(e) Since the characters of the Property are included in the exclusive grant of motion picture rights to Buyer, no sequel rights or television series rights to the Property may be granted, but such characters from the Property which are contained in the author-written sequel may be used in a motion picture and remakes of it whose plot is based substantially on the plot of the respective author-written sequel.

It is expressly agreed that Seller's reserved rights under this subclause relate only to material written or authorized by Seller and not to any revision, adaptation, sequel, translation, or dramatization written or authorized by Buyer, although the same may contain characters or other elements contained in the Property.

3. RIGHT TO MAKE CHANGES: Seller agrees that Buyer shall have the unlimited right to vary, change, alter, modify, add to and/or delete from the Property, and to rearrange and/or transpose the Property and change the sequence of it and the characters and descriptions of the characters contained in the Property, and to use a portion or portions of the property or the characters, plots, or theme of it with any other literary, dramatic, or other material of any kind. Seller hereby waives the benefits of any provisions of law known as the "droit moral" or any similar law in any country of the world and agrees not to permit or prosecute any action or lawsuit on the ground that any Picture or other version of the Property produced or exhibited by Buyer, its assignees, or licensees, in any way constitutes an infringement of any of the Seller's droit moral or is in any way a defamation or mutilation of the Property or any part of it or contains unauthorized variations, alterations, modifications, changes, or translations.

4. DURATION AND EXTENT OF RIGHTS GRANTED: Buyer shall enjoy, solely and exclusively, all the rights, licenses, privileges, and property granted hereunder throughout the world, in perpetuity, as long as any rights in the Property are recognized in law or equity, except as far as such period of perpetuity may be shortened due to any now existing or future copyright by Seller of the Property and/or any adaptations

of it, in which case Buyer shall enjoy its sole and exclusive rights, licenses, privileges, and property hereunder to the fullest extent permissible under and for the full duration of such copyright or copyrights, whether common law or statutory, and any renewals and/or extensions of it, and shall after that enjoy all such rights, licenses, privileges, and property non-exclusively in perpetuity throughout the world. The rights granted herein are in addition to and shall not be construed in derogation of any rights which Buyer may have as a member of the public or pursuant to any other agreement. All rights, licenses, privileges, and property granted herein to Buyer are irrevocable and not subject to rescission, restraint, or injunction under any circumstances.

(a) All rights granted or agreed to be granted to Purchaser under this Agreement shall be irrevocably vested in Purchaser and shall not be subject to rescission by Owner or any other party for any cause, nor shall said rights be subject to termination or reversion by operation of law or otherwise, except to the extent, if any, that the provisions of any copyright law or similar law relating to the right to terminate grants of, or recapture rights in, literary property may apply. If, pursuant to any such copyright law or similar law, Owner or any successor or any other legally designated party (all herein referred to as the "terminating party") becomes entitled to exercise any right to reversion, recapture, or termination (the "termination right") with respect to all or any part of the rights granted or to be granted under this Agreement, and if the terminating party exercises said termination right with respect to all or part of said rights (the "recaptured rights"), then from and after the date on which the terminating party has the right to transfer to a third party all or part of the recaptured rights, Purchaser shall have the first right to purchase and acquire the recaptured rights from the terminating party. If the terminating party is prepared to accept a bona fide offer from a third party with respect to all or part of the recaptured rights, then in each such instance the terminating party shall notify Purchaser of such offer which the terminating party is prepared to accept and the name of the third party who made the offer to the terminating party, and the terminating party shall offer Purchaser the right to enter into an agreement with the terminating party with respect to the recaptured rights on the aforesaid terms and conditions. Purchaser shall have thirty (30) days from the date of its receipt of such written offer within which to notify the terminating party of its acceptance of such offer. If Purchaser shall acquire from the terminating party all or part of the recaptured rights, then the terminating party agrees to enter into appropriate written agreements with

DEALMAKING
IN THE
FILM AND
TELEVISION
INDUSTRY—
3RD EDITION

90

Purchaser covering said acquisition. If Purchaser shall elect not to purchase the recaptured rights from the terminating party, then the terminating party may dispose of said recaptured rights, but only to the aforesaid third party and only upon the terms and conditions specified in the aforesaid written notice given by the terminating party to Purchaser, it being understood and agreed that the terminating party may not dispose of said recaptured rights either to: (i) any other proposed transferee; or (ii) upon terms and conditions which are more favorable to any transferee than the terms and conditions previously offered to Purchaser hereunder, without again offering to enter into an agreement with Purchaser on: (A) the terms offered to such other transferee; or (B) such more favorable terms and conditions offered to said proposed transferee, whichever of (A) or (B) shall apply. Any such required offer made to Purchaser by the terminating party shall be governed by the procedure set forth in the preceding four sentences of this Paragraph. The unenforceability of any portion of this Paragraph shall not invalidate or affect the remaining portions of this Paragraph or this Agreement.

5. CONSIDERATION: As consideration for all rights granted and assigned to Buyer and for seller's representations and warranties, Buyer agrees to pay to Seller, and Seller agrees to accept:

(a) For a theatrical or television motion picture $_____ besides any sums paid in connection with the option periods so payable upon exercise of the option to acquire the Property.

(b) For any mini-series, $_____ per hour, pro-rated for part hours.

(c) For any sequel or remake of a theatrical or television motion picture based on the Property, one-half (½) and one-third (⅓), respectively, of the amount paid for the initial motion picture, payable upon commencement of principal photography of the subsequent production.

(d) For any television series produced, based on the Property, Buyer will pay the following royalties per initial production upon completion of production of each program: up to thirty (30) minutes $_____; over thirty (30), but not more than sixty (60), minutes $_____; over sixty (60) minutes $_____; and in addition to the foregoing, as a buy-out of all royalty obligations, one-hundred percent (100%) of the applicable initial royalty amount, in equal installments over five (5) reruns, payable within thirty (30) days after each such rerun.

As and for contingent compensation, _____ percent of one-hundred percent (100%) of the net profits (including allied and ancillary rights) of each motion picture and television program or series based on the Property, in whole or in part, with profits defined according to the same definition obtained by Buyer; provided, however, that Seller's percentage shall not be subject to any reductions or preconditions whatsoever.

6. REPRESENTATIONS AND WARRANTIES:

(a) Sole Proprietor: Seller represents and warrants to Buyer that Seller is the sole and exclusive proprietor, throughout the universe, of that certain original literary material written by Seller entitled "_____."

(b) Facts: Seller represents and warrants to Buyer as follows:

(i) Seller is the sole author and creator of the Property.

(ii) The Property was first published in 20____ by _____ (publisher) under the title _____, and was registered for copyright in the name of _____, under copyright registration number _____, in the Office of the United States Register of Copyrights, Washington, D.C.

(iii) No motion picture or dramatic version of the Property, or any part of it, has been manufactured, produced, presented, or authorized; no radio or television development, presentation, or program based on the Property, or any part of it, has been manufactured, produced, presented, broadcast, or authorized; and no written or oral agreements or commitments at all with respect to the Property, or with respect to any rights therein, have been made or entered by or on behalf of Seller (except with respect to the Publication of the Property as set forth above).

(iv) None of the rights herein granted and assigned to Buyer have been granted and/or assigned to any person, firm, or corporation other than Buyer.

(c) No Infringement or Violation of Third-Party Rights: Seller represents and warrants to Buyer that Seller has not adapted the Property from any other literary, dramatic, or other material of any kind, nature, or description, nor, except material which is in the public domain, has Seller copied or used in the Property the plot, scenes, sequence, or story of any other literary, dramatic, or other material; that the Property does not infringe upon any common law or statutory rights in any other literary, dramatic, or other material; that no material contained in the Property is libelous or violative of the right of privacy of any

DEALMAKING
IN THE
FILM AND
TELEVISION
INDUSTRY—
3RD EDITION

92

person; that the full utilization of any and all rights in and to the Property granted by Seller pursuant to this Agreement will not violate the rights of any person, firm, or corporation; and that the Property is not in the public domain in any country in the world where copyright protection is available.

(d) No Impairment of Rights: Seller represents and warrants to Buyer that Seller is the exclusive proprietor, throughout the universe, of all rights in and to the Property granted herein to Buyer; that Seller has not assigned, licensed, or in any manner encumbered, diminished, or impaired any such rights; that Seller has not committed or omitted to perform any act by which such rights could or will be encumbered, diminished, or impaired; and that there is no outstanding claim or litigation pending against or involving the title, ownership, and/or copyright in the Property, or in any part thereof, or in any rights granted herein to Buyer. Seller further represents and warrants that no attempt shall be made hereafter to encumber, diminish, or impair any of the rights granted herein and that all appropriate protection of such rights will continue to be maintained by Seller.

7. INDEMNIFICATION:

(a) Seller agrees to indemnify Buyer against all judgments, liability, damages, penalties, losses, and expense (including reasonable attorneys' fees) which may be suffered or assumed by or obtained against Buyer by reason of any breach or failure of any warranty or agreement herein made by Seller.

(b) Buyer shall not be liable to Seller for damages of any kind in connection with any Picture it may produce, distribute, or exhibit, or for damages for any breach of this agreement (except failure to pay the money consideration herein specified) occurring or accruing before Buyer has had reasonable notice and opportunity to adjust or correct such matters.

(c) All rights, licenses, and privileges herein granted to Buyer are irrevocable and not subject to rescission, restraint, or injunction under any circumstances.

8. PROTECTION OF RIGHTS GRANTED: Seller hereby grants to Buyer the free and unrestricted right, but at Buyer's own cost and expense, to institute in the name and on behalf of Seller, or Seller and Buyer jointly, any and all suits and proceedings at law or in equity, to enjoin and restrain any infringements of the rights herein granted, and hereby assigns and sets over to Buyer any and all causes of action relative to or based upon any such infringement, as well as any and all recoveries obtained thereon. Seller will not compromise, settle, or in any

manner interfere with such litigation if brought; and Buyer agrees to indemnify and hold Seller harmless from any costs, expenses, or damages which Seller may suffer as a result of any such suit or proceeding.

9. COPYRIGHT: Regarding the copyright in and to the Property, Seller agrees that:

(a) Seller will prevent the Property and any arrangements, revisions, translations, novelizations, dramatizations, or new versions thereof, whether published or unpublished and whether copyrighted or not copyrighted, from vesting in the public domain, and will take or cause to be taken any and all steps and proceedings required for copyright or similar protection in any and all countries in which the same may be published or offered for sale, insofar as such countries now or hereafter provide for copyright or similar protection. Any contract or agreement entered into by Seller authorizing or permitting the publication of the Property or any arrangements, revisions, translations, novelizations, dramatizations, or new versions thereof in any country will contain appropriate provisions requiring such publisher to comply with all the provisions of this clause.

(b) Without limiting the generality of the foregoing, if the Property or any arrangement, revision, translation, novelization, dramatization, or new version thereof is published in the United States or in any other country in which registration is required for copyright or similar protection in accordance with the laws and regulations of such country, and Seller further agrees to affix or cause to be affixed to each copy of the Property or any arrangement, revision, translation, novelization, dramatization, or new version thereof which is published or offered for sale such notice or notices as may be required for copyright or similar protection in any country in which such publication or sale occurs.

(c) At least _____ months prior to the expiration of any copyright required by this provision for the protection of the Property, Seller will renew (or cause to be renewed) such copyright, as permitted by applicable law, and any and all rights granted Buyer hereunder shall be deemed granted to Buyer throughout the full period of such renewed copyright, without the payment of any additional consideration, it being agreed that the consideration payable to Seller under this agreement shall be deemed to include full consideration for the grant of such rights to Buyer throughout the period of such renewed copyright.

(d) If the Property, or any arrangement, revision, translation,

DEALMAKING
IN THE
FILM AND
TELEVISION
INDUSTRY—
3RD EDITION

94

novelization, dramatization, or new version thereof, shall ever enter the public domain, then nothing contained in this agreement shall impair any rights or privileges that the Buyer might be entitled to as a member of the public; thus, the Buyer may exercise any and all such rights and privileges as though this agreement were not in existence. The rights granted herein by Seller to Buyer, and the representations, warranties, undertakings, and agreements made hereunder by Seller, shall endure in perpetuity and shall be in addition to any rights, licenses, privileges, or property of Buyer referred to in this subclause (d).

10. CREDIT OBLIGATIONS: Buyer shall have the right to publish, advertise, announce, and use in any manner or medium the name, biography, and photographs or likenesses of Seller in connection with any exercise by Buyer of its rights hereunder, provided such use shall not constitute an endorsement of any product or service.

During the term of the Writers Guild of America Minimum Basic Agreement ("WGA Agreement"), as it may be amended, the credit provisions of the WGA Agreement shall govern the determination of credits, if any, which the Buyer shall accord the Seller hereunder in connection with photoplays.

Subject to the foregoing, Seller shall be accorded the following credit on a single card on screen and in paid ads controlled by Buyer and in which any other writer is accorded credit, and in size of type (as to height, width, thickness, and boldness) equal to the largest size of type in which any other writer is accorded credit:

(a) If the title of the Picture is the same as the title of the Property "_____"; or

(b) If the title of the Picture differs from the title of the Work, "_____."

Additionally, if Buyer shall exploit any other rights in and to the Property, then Buyer agrees to give appropriate source material credit to the Property, to the extent that such source material credits are customarily given in connection with the exploitation of such rights.

No casual or inadvertent failure to comply with any of the provisions of this clause shall be deemed a breach of this agreement by the Buyer. Seller hereby expressly acknowledges that in the event of a failure or omission constituting a breach of the provisions of this paragraph, the damage (if any) caused Seller thereby is not irreparable or sufficient to entitle Seller to injunctive or other equitable relief. Consequently, Seller's rights and remedies in the event of such breach shall be limited to the right to recover damages in an action at law. Buyer agrees to provide in its contracts with distributors of the Picture that such distributors shall honor Buyer's contractual credit commitments and agrees to inform such distributors of the credit provisions herein.

11. RIGHT OF FIRST NEGOTIATION: The term "Right of First Negotiation" means that if, after the expiration of an applicable time limitation, Seller desires to dispose of or exercise a particular right reserved to Seller herein ("Reserved Right"), whether directly or indirectly, then Seller shall notify Buyer in writing and immediately negotiate with Buyer regarding such Reserved Right. If, after the expiration of _____ days following the receipt of such notice, no agreement has been reached, then Seller may negotiate with third parties regarding such Reserved Right subject to Clause 12 infra.

12. RIGHT OF LAST REFUSAL: The term "Right of Last Refusal" means that if Buyer and Seller fail to reach an agreement pursuant to Buyer's right of first negotiation, and Seller makes and/or receives any bona fide offer to license, lease, and/or purchase the particular Reserved Right or any interest therein ("Third-Party Offer"), and if the proposed purchase price and other material terms of a Third-Party Offer are no more favorable to Seller than the terms which were acceptable to Buyer during the first negotiation period, Seller shall notify Buyer, by registered mail or telegram, if Seller proposes to accept such Third-Party Offer, the name of the offerer, the proposed purchase price, and other terms of such Third-Party Offer. During the period of _____ days after Buyer's receipt of such notice, Buyer shall have the exclusive option to license, lease, and/or purchase, as the case may be, the particular Reserved Right or interest referred to in such Third-Party Offer, at the same purchase price and upon the same terms and conditions as set forth in such notice. If Buyer elects to exercise thereof by registered mail or telegram within such _____ day period, failing which Seller shall be free to accept such Third-Party Offer; provided that if any such proposed license, lease, and/or sale is not consummated with a third party within _____ days following the expiration of the aforesaid _____ day period, Buyer's Right of Last Refusal shall revive and shall apply to each and every further offer or offers at any time received by Seller relating to the particular Reserved Right or any interest therein; provided, further, that Buyer's option shall continue in full force and effect, upon all of the terms and conditions of this paragraph, so long as

DEALMAKING
IN THE
FILM AND
TELEVISION
INDUSTRY—
3RD EDITION

96

Seller retains any rights, title, or interests in or to the particular Reserved Right. Buyer's Right of Last Refusal shall inure to the benefit of Buyer, its successors, and assigns, and shall bind Seller and Seller's heirs, successors, and assigns.

13. NO OBLIGATION TO PRODUCE: Nothing herein shall be construed to obligate Buyer to produce, distribute, release, perform, or exhibit any motion picture, television, theatrical, or other production based upon, adapted from, or suggested by the Property, in whole or in part, or otherwise to exercise, exploit, or make any use of any rights, licenses, privileges, or property granted herein to Buyer.

14. ASSIGNMENT: Buyer may assign and transfer this agreement or all or any part of its rights hereunder to any person, firm, or corporation without limitation, and this agreement shall be binding upon and inure to the benefit of the parties hereto and their successors, representatives, and assigns forever.

15. NO PUBLICITY: Seller will not, without Buyer's prior written consent in each instance, issue or authorize the issuance or publication of any news story or publicity relating to (i) this Agreement, (ii) the subject matter or terms hereof, or to any use by Buyer, its successors, licensees, and assigns, and (iii) any of the rights granted Buyer hereunder.

16. AGENT COMMISSIONS: Buyer shall not be liable for any compensation or fee to any agent of Seller in connection with this Agreement.

17. ADDITIONAL DOCUMENTATION: Seller agrees to execute and procure any other and further instruments necessary to transfer, convey, assign, and copyright all rights in the Property granted herein by Seller to Buyer in any country throughout the world. If it shall be necessary under the laws of any country that copyright registration be acquired in the name of Seller, Buyer is hereby authorized by Seller to apply for said copyright registration thereof; and, in such event, Seller shall and does hereby assign and transfer the same unto Buyer, subject to the rights in the Property reserved hereunder by Seller. Seller further agrees, upon request, to duly execute, acknowledge, procure, and deliver to Buyer such short-form assignments as may be requested by Buyer for the purpose of copyright recordation in any country, or otherwise. If Seller shall fail to so execute and deliver, or cause to be executed and delivered, the assignments or other instruments herein referred to, Buyer is hereby irrevocably granted the power coupled with an interest to execute such assignments and instruments in the name of Seller and as Seller's attorney-in-fact.

18. NOTICES: All notices to Buyer under this agreement shall be sent by United States registered mail, postage prepaid, or by telegram addressed to Buyer at _____ _____ (address) with a courtesy copy to _____ (Buyer's attorney), and all notices to Seller under this agreement shall be sent by United States registered mail, postage prepaid, or by telegram addressed to at _____ (address) seller with a courtesy copy to _____ (Seller's attorney). The deposit of such notice in the United States mail or the delivery of the telegram message to the telegraph office shall constitute service thereof, and the date of such deposit shall be deemed to be the date of service of such notice.

19. ARBITRATION: Any dispute under this Agreement will be resolved by final and binding arbitration under the Independent Film & Television Alliance Rules for International Arbitration in effect as of the effective date of this Agreement ("IFTA Rules"). Each Party waives any right to adjudicate any dispute in any other court or forum, *except* that a Party may seek interim relief before the start of arbitration as allowed by the IFTA Rules. The arbitration will be held in the Forum designated in the Agreement, or, if none is designated, as determined by the IFTA Rules. The Parties will abide by any decision in the arbitration and any court having jurisdiction may enforce it. The Parties submit to the jurisdiction of the courts in the Forum to compel arbitration or to confirm an arbitration award. The Parties agree to accept service of process in accordance with the IFTA Rules. The prevailing party shall be entitled to reimbursement of its reasonable attorney fees and costs.

20. MISCELLANEOUS:

(a) Relationship: This agreement between the parties does not constitute a joint venture or partnership of any kind.

(b) Cumulative Rights and Remedies: All rights, remedies, licenses, undertakings, obligations, covenants, privileges, and other property granted herein shall be cumulative, and Buyer may exercise or use any of them separately or in conjunction with any one or more of the others.

(c) Waiver: A waiver by either party of any term or condition of this agreement in any instance shall not be deemed or construed to be a waiver of such term or condition for the future, or any subsequent breach thereof.

(d) Severability: If any provision of this agreement as applied to either party or any circumstances shall be adjudged by a court to be void and unenforceable, such shall in no way

DEALMAKING
IN THE
FILM AND
TELEVISION
INDUSTRY—
3RD EDITION

98

affect any other provision of this agreement, the application of such provision in any other circumstance, or the validity or enforceability of this agreement.

(e) Governing Law: This agreement shall be construed in accordance with the laws of the State of _____ applicable to agreements which are executed and fully performed within said State.

(f) Captions: Captions are inserted for reference and convenience only and in no way define, limit, or describe the scope of this agreement or intent of any provision.

(g) Entire Understanding: This agreement contains the entire understanding of the parties relating to the subject matter, and this agreement cannot be changed except by written agreement executed by the party to be bound.

IN WITNESS WHEREOF, the parties hereto have signed this Agreement as of the day and year first above written.

_____

("Seller")

_____

("Buyer")

Exhibit B

OPTION AGREEMENT
(Short Form for Recordation at U.S. Copyright Office)

For good and valuable consideration, receipt of which is hereby acknowledged, the undersigned hereby grants to _____ (the "BUYER"), its successors, and assigns, the sole and exclusive option to purchase all motion picture and certain allied rights, in the original literary and/or dramatic work (the "Work") described as follows:

Title:

Author:

Publisher:

Date of Publication:

Copyright Registration:

The Work includes but is not limited to: (i) all contents; (ii) all present and future adaptations and versions; (iii) the title, characters, and theme; and (iv) the copyright and all renewals and extensions of copyright.

This instrument is executed in accordance with and is subject to the agreement (the "Option Agreement") between the undersigned and the Buyer dated as of _____ (date) relating to the option granted to the Buyer to purchase the above-mentioned rights in the Work, which rights are more fully described in the Purchase Agreement, attached to the Option Agreement.

Date: _____

Attest _____   _____

      (name of witness)   (name of seller)

Exhibit C
(Short-Form Copyright Assignment)

KNOW ALL MEN BY THESE PRESENTS that, in consideration of One Dollar ($1.00) and other good and valuable consideration, receipt of which is hereby acknowledged, the undersigned _____ ("Assignor") do(es) hereby sell, grant, convey, and assign unto _____ ("Assignee"), its successors, assigns, and licensees forever, all right, title, and interest including, but not limited to, the exclusive worldwide Motion Picture and allied rights of Assignor in and to that certain literary work to wit: that certain original screenplay written by _____ entitled _____ ("Literary Property"), and all drafts, revisions, arrangements, adaptations, dramatizations, translations, sequels, and other versions of the Literary Property which may heretofore have been written or which may hereafter be written with the sanction of Assignor.

Dated this _____ day of _____, 20__.

_____

("Assignor")

AGREED TO:

_____

("Assignee")

DEALMAKING
IN THE
FILM AND
TELEVISION
INDUSTRY—
3RD EDITION

100

Acknowledgment

STATE OF   )

) ss.:

COUNTY OF   )

On the ___ day of ____, 20__, before me personally came _____ to me known and known to be the individual described in and who executed the foregoing instrument, and he/she did duly acknowledge to me that he/she executed the same.

_____

Notary Public

Questions and Answers

1. Do I sign the option and the purchase agreement together?

Answer: Yes, they are one contract. Usually the way these deals are structured is that there is an option contract that runs a few pages, and attached to it as an exhibit is a purchase agreement that automatically kicks in if the option is exercised (see the sample contract above).

2. Do I have any leverage if the producer asks for a free sixth-month option?

Answer: You can always refuse to option your work. Whether that is a wise decision depends on the circumstances. If the option is not exercised, then all the purchaser's rights expire. Whether you should give an indie producer a free six-month option depends upon your assessment of whether or not this producer has the ability to get your screenplay into production, and whether you have other opportunities that you would have to forego if you grant the option.

3. How much do options cost in relation to the actual purchase of the book rights?

Answer: As a general rule of thumb, options are often 10% of the purchase price. However, options are negotiable and it is not uncommon today for authors with little clout to grant options for a nominal amount of money in the hope a producer will succeed in turning their book into a film. The purchase price will depend greatly on the demand for the work. A John Grisham novel will go for millions, and the author may refuse to option it at all, insisting on an outright sale. Probably the best source for the type of information you want is an experienced literary agent who actively buys and sells book rights.

4. As a first-time screenwriter, am I entitled to a percentage of net profits if my script is licensed?

Answer: It is not unusual for a first-time writer to be able to negotiate for a percentage of net profits. Typically, the amount is tied to how much that writer contributed to the final draft of the script. They might receive 5% of 100% of the net profits if they receive sole screen writing credit or 2.5% of 100% if they receive shared credit, but no profit participation if they are so extensively rewritten that they are not entitled to screen credit. Note that *how* profits are defined can be more important than the amount of profit participation. There is no standard definition of net profits, and there are many different types of profit participation.

CHAPTER 6

EMPLOYMENT CONTRACTS

LOAN-OUT COMPANIES

Writers, directors, and actors often incorporate themselves by setting up loan-out companies. At one time there were significant tax advantages to setting up such companies. Most of these benefits have now been abolished, although some pension and health-plan benefits remain. Also, a loan-out corporation on a fiscal-year basis could spread out income to its owner over two personal calendar tax years, placing income in lower tax brackets.[1]

In a loan-out deal, the studio (employer) does not contract directly with the talent (e.g., the writer). The employer contracts with the talent's company, a company that is typically owned 100% by the talent or the talent's family.

The company is called a "loan-out" company because it loans out the talent's services first to Studio A, then to Studio B, and so on. All the money earned from the talent's services is paid to

---

[1] That is, by timing the payouts of salary, and having a corporate tax year that runs from June to May, for example (instead of the usual calendar year of January to December), the corporation can spread income over two personal tax years. This may keep more of an individual's income in lower tax brackets.

DEALMAKING
IN THE
FILM AND
TELEVISION
INDUSTRY—
3RD EDITION

104

the company. The loan-out company pays the talent's business expenses and a salary.

Studios don't object to paying talent through their loan-out companies if the studio's interests are protected. The studio usually wants the talent to sign an "Inducement Agreement." This is a contract between the studio and the talent guaranteeing that the talent will abide by the agreement between the studio and the loan-out company. Otherwise, if the loan-out company breaches the contract, the studio can only sue the company. The company may not have any assets and cannot perform itself (i.e., corporations cannot act, write, direct—only people can).

Therefore, when talent requests that the deal be structured as a loan-out deal, three agreements are made. First is the employment contract between the studio and the loan-out company. Second is the agreement between the studio and the talent, the inducement agreement. And third is the employment agreement between the loan-out company and the talent.

Employing talent through a loan-out agreement is not much different from employing talent directly. You can immediately spot a loan-out deal because it refers to one party as the "Lender." The "Lender" is the loan-out company, not a bank.

WRITERS

Writers can create screenplays on their own and sell them to a studio (or a producer). As discussed in Chapter 12 on Copyright, the screenplay is a form of intellectual property, and it can be sold by the owner like any other property. We have already reviewed option agreements and literary purchase agreements, which are contracts for the sale of a writer's rights in a literary property.

Another method studios use to acquire screenplays entails hiring someone to write one for them. The idea for the screenplay may be proposed by the writer in a pitch meeting, or it may be suggested by the studio.[2]

The advantage to the writer of being employed is that the employer takes the risk of the project not turning out well. A writer who spends six months creating a screenplay that he/she

---

[2] The idea could be an original one or one based on another work, such as play, magazine article, or book that the studio wants to adapt as a movie.

cannot sell does not earn any income for his/her efforts. The writer working as an employee, however, receives a guaranteed payment for his/her labor, even if the script never gets produced. And if the script is produced, the writer may receive additional compensation in the form of a bonus or percentage of profits.

Producers use employment contracts to hire writers. As a "work for hire," the employer owns the copyright. The writer gets the money; the producer gets the script. Since the producer owns the work, it can shelve the project or hire someone else to rewrite it at any time.

As you will see, many provisions found in a writer's employment agreement are also present in actor and director employment agreements. The methods of structuring compensation, force majeure conditions, and credit provisions are similar.

A producer can hire a writer on a step deal or flat deal basis. In a step deal, the employer has the right to end the writer's services after each step. Step deals are often used when an employer is hiring a novice writer or a writer whose ability is uncertain. The employer reduces his/her financial risk by proceeding in a series of steps instead of hiring the writer to write a first draft of a script.

Let's say you are a producer interested in hiring Writer A to create a romantic comedy for you, based on your own idea. Writer A has never written a romantic comedy before. You are uncertain whether he/she has the ability to write what you want. You don't want to risk $110,000 (the approximate WGA scale for a feature) to hire that writer. So you propose a step deal.

The steps could be:

a) treatment/outline

b) first draft screenplay

c) second draft

d) rewrite

e) polish

After each step, you will have the option of whether to proceed to the next step. After any step you can decide to shelve the project or bring in another writer. As the employer, you own all of the writer's work. The writer gets to keep the money for the work he/she completes, even if he/she does not complete all steps.

DEALMAKING
IN THE
FILM AND
TELEVISION
INDUSTRY—
3RD EDITION

106

The Writers Guild sets minimums for each step, and the total compensation paid for the steps will be no less than the minimum scale payment for a flat deal for a complete screenplay. The scale of minimums is available on the WGA website at www .wga.org/minimums/index.html.

A step deal will set forth "reading periods." These are periods, usually a couple of weeks, in which the producer has the opportunity to decide whether he/she wants to go to the next step. If the producer does not exercise his/her right to proceed within the reading period, he/she risks losing the writer. During the reading period the writer cannot accept other assignments that might prevent him/her from completing the remaining steps.

The writer's employment agreement will also set out the time requirements when various items are due. Usually the writer gets one to three months to complete a first draft.

There are different ways that writers receive compensation. Fixed compensation is a guaranteed payment. Typically, producers pay half up front and half when the work is delivered. If the writer doesn't do the work in a craftsman-like manner, the producer is not obliged to pay for it. But the producer is obliged to pay fixed compensation regardless of whether the producer likes the writer's work or whether the script gets produced. Thus, the employer takes the risk of the script turning out poorly.

The Writers Guild prohibits its members from working on speculation without a guarantee of fixed compensation. The amount of fixed compensation is often minimum WGA scale for a first-time writer. For more experienced writers, the amount is often a modest increase over their last deal. Of course, if the writer wins an Academy Award or a movie of his/hers becomes a blockbuster hit, the writer's price will multiply.

Bonus compensation is another form of payment. Let's say you are a producer and a writer asks to be paid $200,000. You can't afford that amount up front, so you counter by offering $100,000 fixed compensation and another $100,000 as bonus compensation. Bonus compensation is not guaranteed. Payment is contingent on a certain event, such as the script going into production. So if the script doesn't get produced, the bonus need not be paid. Thus, bonus compensation is more uncertain than fixed compensation.

Deferred compensation is more uncertain than bonus compensation. Deferments are often used in low-budget films when the producer can't afford to pay the cast and crew their usual wages. Perhaps he/she offers to hire everyone at $250 a week and to defer the rest of the salary they would normally earn. Deferments are usually not payable unless the script gets produced, the movie is released, and revenue is received. Deferments can be payable before or after investors recoup their investment. The employment agreement may provide that some deferment holders be paid first or everyone share in revenues equally (in pari passu).

The most uncertain kind of payment is contingent compensation, or net profits (points). Here the employee will receive payment only if the script is produced, released, and it generates revenue. And the revenue must be substantial enough that after recoupment of all costs and expenses, including distribution fees and marketing costs, there is something left. It is rare that net profit participants receive anything. Artists often complain that studios use creative accounting to deny them their share of profits. This topic is addressed in Chapter 11.

Writers typically receive between 1% and 5% of 100% of net profits. Why do we state the writer's share in terms of a percent of 100%? So, that there won't be any ambiguity as to the size of the writer's portion of net profits. If we simply said the writer gets 5% of net profits, it would be unclear whether she gets 5% of all the net profits or 5% of the producer's share of net profits.

Typically, the studio and the producer split net profits 50/50. The producer, however, often must give a writer, a director, and a star a piece of his/her net profits. These profit participants take from the producer's half of net profits. Nevertheless, the custom in the industry is to express net profits in terms of the whole (all profits) so that there is no ambiguity. Instead of saying a writer gets 5% of 100% of net profits, one could say he/she gets 10% of 50%. It would be the same size slice of the pie.

Another form of payment is known as "additional" compensation. Producers make these payments if they make a sequel, remake, or television spin-off series based on the original work. Writers often receive 50% of what they were paid for the original movie for a sequel and 33% for a remake. For a television spin-off series the writer usually gets a royalty for every episode. An example of a successful spin-off series would be *M*A*S*H*. The television series was based upon a successful movie written by

DEALMAKING
IN THE
FILM AND
TELEVISION
INDUSTRY—
3RD EDITION

108

Richard Hooker and Ring Lardner, Jr. Since the series was so successful, the writers may have earned more in royalties from the series than they were paid for writing the film.

The series royalty is a passive one. That means the writer is not obliged to do any work on the series. The payment is due the writer because of his/her work on the original. The writer is entitled to the royalty even if he/she is not involved in the series. Of course, if the writer works on the series, he/she would be entitled to additional payment.

The writer's employment agreement will also contain a credit clause. For a WGA writer and a signatory company, the WGA credit determination rules apply. Consequently, the producer does not have the discretion to allocate writing credits any way he/she may choose. After the "Notice of Tentative Credits" is given, all writers on the project have an opportunity to object and request credit arbitration.

Credit is important for reasons besides ego and professional stature. The determination of credit can have financial repercussions. Often the amount of points a writer receives will vary depending on whether he/she receives sole, shared, or no credit.

Writers sometimes complain about directors who have their writer friends needlessly rewrite a script, thereby forcing the first writer to share credit and profits with another. The Writers Guild credit

MAJOR PROVISIONS: WRITER EMPLOYMENT AGREEMENT

1) TYPE OF DEAL
   FLAT DEAL OR STEP DEAL

2) TIME DEADLINE

3 READING PERIODS

4) COMPENSATION
   FIXED
   BONUSES
   DEFERRED
   CONTINGENT
   ADDITIONAL

5) CREDIT

6) PERFORMANCE STANDARDS

7) FORCE MAJEURE

8) SUPERSEDING EFFECT OF WGA

guidelines give a strong preference to the first writer. The second writer will only obtain credit if his/her contribution is 50% or more of the completed script. Of course, this encourages the second writer to extensively revise the first and may induce this second writer to revise good material.[3]

Performance standards will also be addressed in the employment agreement. The writer is required to perform diligently and efficiently, to follow the suggestions and instructions of the company, and to devote all time exclusively to the project during the term of the agreement.

A force majeure clause is another common provision. Force majeure means superior force, and it refers to certain events beyond control of the production company that may force suspension of the contract. Such forces could be a fire, earthquake, strike, act of God, war, new law, closing of most theaters in the country, and death or illness of a principal member of the cast or director.

In the event one of these events causes a suspension of work, the company does not have to pay the writer any compensation during the suspension. Usually, if the suspension lasts more than five weeks, for example, the production company and the writer each have the right to terminate the contract.

Finally, contracts with WGA writers will provide that, should anything in the agreement conflict with the WGA's collective-bargaining agreement, the terms of the latter agreement will prevail. This is to prevent the employer from negotiating a deal with a writer that is more favorable than the minimums set forth in the agreement reached through collective bargaining.

---

[3] The WGA credit rules are available on the WGA website at www.wga.org/subpage
_writersresources.aspx?id=167

DEALMAKING
IN THE
FILM AND
TELEVISION
INDUSTRY—
3RD EDITION

110

Below is a sample writer employment agreement. It was used to employ a writer who worked as part of a writing team, and it is structured as a loan-out agreement.

WRITER EMPLOYMENT AGREEMENT

Agreement dated _____ 20___, between The Writer's Co., a New York Corporation ("Lender") with Federal I.D. # _____, regarding the services of Jim Writer ("Writer") and Big Films ("Production Company").

1. EMPLOYMENT: Production Company agrees to borrow from Lender and Lender agrees to lend to Production Company the writing services of Writer, upon the terms and conditions herein specified, for the proposed Theatrical Motion Picture currently entitled "_____" ("Picture"), based upon a screenplay of the same name supplied by Production Company ("Basic Property"). Lender represents and warrants that it is a New York Corporation that Lender has entered into a written contract with Writer which is now in full force and effect, and that pursuant to such contract Lender has the right and authority to lend to Production Company the services of Writer upon the terms and conditions herein specified. Lender and Writer shall perform such writing services in collaboration with _____ pursuant to the Employment Agreement dated _____ 20__, between _____ and Production Company ("Agreement"). Writer and _____ are hereinafter collectively referred to as the "Writer's Team."

2. THE PRODUCT AGREEMENT WITH OPTIONS: The completed results of Writer's services hereunder shall be deemed collectively the "Product" and individually the "Product Form," and shall be created as follows:

First Draft screenplay with option for one Revision/Draft thereof and dependent option for one polish.

3. COMMENCEMENT OF SERVICES: Lender shall cause Writer to commence services in writing the first draft of the screenplay upon execution of this agreement and Production Company becoming a signatory of the Writers Guild of America. Lender shall cause Writer to commence writing each subsequent Product Form on a date to be designated by Production Company, which date may be earlier, but shall not be later than the first business day after expiration of the then current Reading Period or Option Period, as the case may be, described in Clause 4.

4. TIME REQUIREMENTS: Writer's services shall be rendered pursuant to the following time requirements:

(a) Delivery Periods: Lender shall cause Writer to deliver each Product Form within the period ("Delivery Period") which commences on the date Writer is obligated to commence writing each designated Product Form and which ends upon expiration of the applicable time period listed in Clause 4(e).

(b) Reading Periods: Each time Writer delivers any Product Form, if Writer's engagement herein requires additional writing services, Production Company shall have a period ("Reading Period"), which commences on the first business day following the delivery of such Product Form and which continues for the length of time listed in Clause 4(e) opposite the description of the Product Form delivered within which to read such Product Form and advise Lender to cause Writer to commence writing the next Product Form.

(c) Postponement of Services: If Production Company does not exercise within the applicable Reading Period its right to require Lender to cause Writer to commence writing either the first set of revisions or the polish, Production Company may nonetheless require Lender to cause Writer to render such services at any time within the one (1) year period commencing upon delivery of the immediately preceding Product Form, subject to Writer's availability and provided: 1) Writer's services are to be rendered during the one year period, and 2) Production Company shall furnish Lender with thirty (30) days' prior written notice of the date designated for the commencement of such services, and 3) that Production Company has paid Lender in a timely manner for the postponed product forms as those services were timely rendered.

(d) Option Periods: Each Option, if any, under Clause 4(e), shall be exercised if at all in writing within the period ("Option Period") which commences on the first business day following the delivery of the Product Form immediately preceding that for which an Option may be exercised, or upon the expiration of the Delivery Period applicable to such Product Form, whichever is later, and which continues for the length of time listed in Clause 4(e) opposite the description of the Product Form delivered.

(e) Length of Periods: Delivery, Reading, and Option Periods shall be the following lengths:

Product Form	Delivery Period	Reading/Option Period
First-Draft Screenplay	8 weeks	2 weeks

DEALMAKING
IN THE
FILM AND
TELEVISION
INDUSTRY—
3RD EDITION

112

First Revision/ Second-Draft Screenplay	4 weeks	2 weeks
Polish of Screenplay	2 weeks	2 weeks

5. DELIVERY: TIME OF THE ESSENCE:

(a) Effective Delivery: Delivery of Product Form to any person other than _____ shall not constitute delivery of such Product Form as required by this Agreement.

(b) Time of the Essence: Lender shall cause Writer to write and deliver each Product Form for which Writer is engaged as soon as reasonably possible after commencement of Writer's services thereon, but not later than the date upon which the applicable Delivery Period expires. Time of delivery is of the essence.

(c) Revisions: For each Product Form which is in the nature of a Revision, Writer's services shall include the writing and delivery of such changes as may be required by Production Company within a reasonable time prior to the expiration of the Delivery Period applicable to such Product Form.

6. COMPENSATION:

(a) Fixed Compensation: Production Company shall pay Lender as set forth below for Writer's services and all rights granted by Lender:

(i) For First-Draft Screenplay: $_____, payable half upon commencement, half upon delivery.

(ii) For First Revision/Second-Draft Screenplay: $_____, payable half upon commencement, half upon delivery.

(iii) For Polish of Screenplay: $_____, payable half upon commencement, half upon delivery.

(b) Payment: Production Company shall have no obligation to pay Lender any compensation with respect to any Product Form for which Production Company has failed to exercise its Option under Clause 4.

(c) Bonus Compensation: Subject to the production and release of the Picture, and to the Lender and Writer not being in material default hereunder, in addition to the Fixed Compensation set forth above, Lender shall be entitled to be paid the following:

(i) If Writer receives sole or shared screenplay credit pursuant to final Writers Guild of America ("WGA") credit determination with respect to the Picture, Lender shall be entitled to receive as Bonus Compensation the sum of $25,000 over the compensation provided by Clause 6(a), less the aggregate of all sums paid to Lender pursuant to Clause 6(a) above, which shall be payable upon commencement of principal photography.

(ii) If the production budget is above $700,000, the bonus payment shall escalate $2,500 per $100,000 increase. Alternatively, if the production budget exceeds $1 million, the production bonus will be $50,000. The sums payable under this section shall be less the aggregate of all sums (not already deducted) paid to Lender pursuant to Clause 6(a) and 6(c) above and shall be payable 60 days after completion of principal photography.

(iii) Repayment: If Bonus Compensation set forth in Clause 6(c) above is paid to Lender as set forth hereinabove, and if Writer receives neither sole screenplay credit nor shared screenplay credit pursuant to final WGA credit determination for the Picture, Lender shall repay to Production Company such sum so paid to Writer within five (5) days of such determination.

(d) Contingent Compensation: Subject to the production and release of the Picture and subject to Lender and Writer not being in default of their obligations hereunder, in addition to the Fixed Compensation and Bonus Compensation set forth above, Lender shall be entitled to be paid the following:

(i) Sole Screenplay Credit: If the Writer's Team receives sole screenplay credit pursuant to final WGA credit determination for the Picture, Lender shall be entitled to receive as Contingent Compensation an amount equal to two and one-half percent (2½%) of one-hundred percent (100%) of the Net Profits of the Picture.

(ii) Shared Screenplay Credit: If the Writer's Team receives shared screenplay credit pursuant to final WGA credit determination for the Picture, Lender shall be entitled to receive as Contingent Compensation an amount equal to one and one-quarter percent (1¼%) of one-hundred percent (100%) of the Net Profits of the Picture.

(e) For purposes of this Agreement, "Net Profits" shall be computed, determined, and paid in accordance with definition of net profits defined in the production/distribution agreement between Production Company and the distributor of the Picture,

DEALMAKING
IN THE
FILM AND
TELEVISION
INDUSTRY—
3RD EDITION

114

provided that Lender's definition shall be as favorable as any other net-profit participant.

(f) Additional payments to Lender for Sequel, Remake, and Television Use of the Work; Right of First Negotiation: Subject to the provisions of Clauses 6(g) and 6(h) below, and subject to the production and release of the Picture and the performance of all obligations of Lender and Writer hereunder:

(i) Theatrical Sequel Motion Picture: If the Writer's Team receives sole/shared screenplay credit, then for each Theatrical Sequel Motion Picture based on the Picture produced and released, Lender shall be entitled to be paid an amount equal to fifty percent (50%) of one-hundred percent (100%) of the sum paid to Lender as Compensation pursuant to Clause 6(a) and 6(c) above, and a percentage participation in the Net Profits of such Theatrical Sequel Motion Picture in an amount equal to fifty percent (50%) of one hundred percent (100%) of the rate of percentage participation in Net Profits of the Picture payable to Lender as Contingent Compensation pursuant to Clauses 6(d)(i) or 6(d)(ii) above, if any.

(ii) Theatrical Remakes: If the Writer's Team receives sole/shared screenplay credit, then for each Theatrical Remake of the Picture produced and released, Lender shall be entitled to be paid an amount equal to thirty-three percent (33%) of one-hundred percent (100%) of the sum paid to Writer as Compensation pursuant to Clause 6(a) and 6(c) above, and thirty-three percent (33%) of one-hundred percent (100%) of the percentage participation in Net Profits of the Picture payable to Lender as Contingent Compensation pursuant to Clauses 6(d)(i) or 6(d)(ii) above, if any.

(iii) Television Sequels and Television Remakes:

(A) Pilot and Series: If Writer is accorded sole or shared screenplay credit with respect to the Picture, then for each Television Sequel Motion Picture based upon the Picture and/or Television Remake of the Picture which is produced and licensed for exhibition by Production Company and which is a Pilot or an episode of an episodic or anthology television series (collectively "TV Program"), Lender shall be entitled to receive the following royalties:

(1) $_____ for each TV Program of not more than thirty (30) minutes in length.

(2) $_____ for each TV Program in excess of thirty (30) minutes but not more than sixty (60) minutes in length.

(3) $_____ for each TV Program in excess of sixty (60) minutes in length.

(4) If any TV Program is rerun, Lender shall be paid twenty percent (20%) of the applicable sum initially paid Lender pursuant to Subclauses (1), (2) or (3) above for the second run, third run, fourth run, fifth run, and sixth run respectively. No further rerun payments shall be due or payable for any rerun after the sixth run.

(B) Movies-of-the-Week and Mini-Series: If Writer is accorded sole or shared screenplay credit for the Picture, then for each Television Sequel Motion Picture or Television Remake of the Picture which is produced and licensed for exhibition by Production Company and which is a so-called "Movie-of-the-Week" or so-called "Mini-Series," Lender shall be entitled to receive the following royalties, which sum shall constitute full payment for all rerun use and/or other exploitation thereof:

(1) $_____ for the first two (2) hours of running time of each such Movie-of-the-Week and/or each such Mini-Series.

(2) $_____ for every hour of running time, if any, exceeding the first two (2) hours of running time of such Movie-of-the Week and/or such Mini-Series up to a maximum of $_____.

(iv) Definitions—The following terms, as utilized in connection with this Agreement, shall be defined as set forth below:

(A) "Television Remake": A remake primarily intended to be initially distributed for free-television exhibition.

(B) "Television Sequel": A sequel motion picture primarily intended to be initially distributed for free-television exhibition.

(C) "Theatrical Remake": A remake primarily intended to be initially distributed for theatrical exhibition.

(D) "Theatrical Sequel": A studio sequel motion picture primarily intended to be initially distributed for theatrical exhibition.

(E) WGA Agreement: All sums payable to Lender pursuant to this Agreement shall be in lieu of, and not in addition to, any similar payment to which Lender may be entitled pursuant to the current Writers Guild of America Theatrical and Television Agreement ("WGA Agreement").

7. CONDITIONS AFFECTING OR RELATED TO COMPENSATION:

DEALMAKING
IN THE
FILM AND
TELEVISION
INDUSTRY—
3RD EDITION

116

(a) Method of Payment: All compensation which shall become due to Lender hereunder shall be sent to Lender at the address provided in Clause 26. Such address may be changed to such other address as Lender may hereafter notify Production Company in accordance with Clause 26.

(b) Performance: Production Company's obligation to pay compensation or otherwise perform hereunder shall be conditioned upon Lender and Writer not being in default of their obligations under the Agreement. No compensation shall accrue to Lender during Lender or Writer's inability, failure, or refusal to perform, according to the terms and conditions of this Agreement, the services contracted for herein, nor shall compensation accrue during any period of Force Majeure, Suspension, or upon Termination except as otherwise herein provided.

(c) Governmental Limitation: No withholding, deduction, reduction, or limitation of compensation by Production Company which is required or authorized by law ("Governmental Limitation") shall be a breach of this Agreement by Production Company or relieve Lender and Writer from Lender's and Writer's obligations hereunder. Payment of compensation as permitted pursuant to the Governmental Limitation shall continue while such Governmental Limitation is in effect and shall be deemed to constitute full performance by Production Company of its obligation to pay compensation hereunder.

(d) Garnishment/Attachment: If Production Company is required, because of the service of any garnishment, writ of execution or lien, or by the terms of any contract or assignment executed by Lender to withhold, or to pay all or any portion of the compensation due Lender hereunder to any other person, firm or corporation, the withholding or payment of such compensation or portion thereof, pursuant to the requirements of any such garnishment, writ of execution, lien, contract, or assignment, shall not be construed as a breach by Production Company of this Agreement.

(e) Overpayment/Offset: If Production Company makes any overpayment to Lender hereunder for any reason or if Lender and/or Writer is indebted to Production Company for any reason, Lender or Writer shall pay Production Company such overpayment or indebtedness on demand, or at the election of Production Company may deduct and retain for its own account an amount equal to all or any part of such overpayment or indebtedness from any sums that may be due or become due or payable by Production Company to Lender or for the account of Lender and such deduction or retention shall not be deemed a breach of this Agreement.

(f) Pay or Play: Production Company shall not be obligated to use Writer's services for the Picture, nor shall Production Company be obligated to produce, release, distribute, advertise, exploit, or otherwise make use of the results and proceeds of Writer's services if such services are used. Production Company may elect to terminate Writer's services at any time without legal justification or excuse provided that the Fixed Compensation provided in Clause 6(a), which shall have been earned and accrued prior to such termination shall be paid to Lender. In the event of such termination, all other rights of Lender and Writer herein shall be deemed void ab initio except such rights as may have accrued to Lender/Writer in accordance with the terms of Clauses 21 (relating to Guilds and Unions), 22 (relating to Credits), and 6(c) (relating to bonus compensation).

8. PERFORMANCE STANDARDS: Writer's services hereunder shall be rendered promptly and in collaboration with _____ in a diligent, conscientious, artistic, and efficient manner to Writer's best ability. Writer shall devote all of Writer's time and shall render Writer's services exclusively (during writing periods only) to Production Company in performing the writing services contemplated hereunder, and shall not render services for any other party during the period of Writer's engagement. Writer's services shall be rendered in such manner as Production Company may direct pursuant to the instructions, suggestions, and ideas of and under the control of and at the times and places required by Production Company's authorized representatives. Lender shall cause Writer, as and when requested by Production Company, to consult with Production Company's daily authorized representatives and shall be available for conferences in person or by telephone with such representatives for such purposes at such times during Writer's engagement as may be required by such representatives.

9. RESULTS AND PROCEEDS OF SERVICES:

(a) Ownership: Production Company shall solely and exclusively own the Product, each Product Form, and all of the results and proceeds thereof, in whatever stage of completion as may exist from time to time (including but not limited to all rights of whatever kind and character, throughout the world, in perpetuity, in any and all languages of copyright, trademark, patent, production, manufacture, recordation, reproduction, transcription, performance, broadcast, and exhibition by any art, method, or device, now known or hereafter devised, including without limitation radio broadcast, theatrical and non-theatrical exhibition, and television exhibition or otherwise), whether such results and proceeds consist of literary, dramatic,

DEALMAKING
IN THE
FILM AND
TELEVISION
INDUSTRY—
3RD EDITION

118

musical, motion picture, mechanical, or any other form or works, themes, ideas, compositions, creations, or products. Production Company's acquisition hereunder shall also include all rights generally known in the field of literary and musical endeavor as the "moral rights of authors" in and/or to the Product, each Product Form, and any musical and literary proceeds of Writer's services. Production Company shall have the right but not the obligation, with respect to the Product, each Product Form, the results and proceeds thereof, to add to, subtract from, change, arrange, revise, adapt, rearrange, make variations, and to translate the same into any and all languages, change the sequence, change the characters and the descriptions thereof contained therein, change the title of the same, record and photograph the same with or without sound (including spoken words, dialogue, and music synchronously recorded), use said title or any of its components in connection with works or motion pictures wholly or partially independent thereof, to sell, copy, and publish the same as Production Company may desire, and to use all or any part thereof in new versions, adaptations, and sequels in any and all languages and to obtain copyright therein throughout the world. Lender/Writer hereby expressly waives any and all rights which Lender or Writer may have, either in law, in equity, or otherwise, which Writer may have or claim to have as a result of any alleged infringements of Lender's or Writer's so-called "moral rights of authors." Lender acknowledges that the results and proceeds of Writer's services are works specially ordered by Production Company for use as part of a motion picture and the results and proceeds of Writer's services shall be considered to be works made for hire for Production Company, and, therefore, Production Company shall be the author and copyright owner of the results and proceeds of Writer's services.

(b) Assignment and Vesting of Rights: All rights granted or agreed to be granted to Production Company hereunder shall vest in Production Company immediately and shall remain vested whether this Agreement expires in normal course or is terminated for any cause or reason, or whether Writer executes the Certificate of Authorship required infra. All material created, composed, submitted, added, or interpolated by Writer hereunder shall automatically become Production Company's property, and Production Company, for this purpose, shall be deemed author thereof with Writer acting entirely as Production Company's employee. Lender and Writer do hereby assign and transfer to Production Company all of the foregoing without reservation, condition, or limitation, and no right of any kind, nature, or description is reserved by Lender or Writer. The said assignment and transfer to Production Company by Lender and

Writer are subject to the limitations contained in the current Writers Guild of America Theatrical and Television Film Basic Agreement ("WGA Agreement").

(c) Execution of Other Documents:

(i) Certificate of Authorship: Lender further agrees, if Production Company requests Lender to do so, to cause Writer to execute and deliver to Production Company, in connection with all material written by writer hereunder, a Certificate of Authorship in substantially the following form:

I hereby certify that I wrote the manuscript hereto attached, entitled "The Big Story" based upon a screenplay of the same name written by Jane Doe, as an employee of Big Films, which furnished my services pursuant to an employment Agreement between The Writer's Co., a New York Corporation, and Big Films dated _____, in performance of my duties thereunder and in the regular course of my employment, and that Big Films is the author thereof and entitled to the copyright therein and thereto, with the right to make such changes therein and such uses thereof as it may from time to time determine as such author.

IN WITNESS WHEREOF, I have hereto set my hand this _____ (date).

If Production Company desires to secure separate assignments or Certificates of Authorship of or for any of the foregoing, Lender agrees to have Writer execute such certificate upon Production Company's request therefore. Lender and Writer irrevocably grant(s) Production Company the power coupled with an interest to execute such separate assignments or Certificates of Authorship in Lender's/Writer's name and as Lender's/Writer's attorney-in-fact.

(ii) Lender recognizes that the provisions in Clause 9(c) (iii) dealing with any other documents to be signed by Lender are not to be construed in derogation of Production Company's rights arising from the employer-employee relationship but are included because in certain jurisdictions and in special circumstances the rights in and to the material which flow from the employer-employee relationship may not be sufficient in and of themselves to vest ownership in Production Company.

(iii) If Production Company desires to secure further documents covering, quitclaiming, or assigning all or any of the results and proceeds of Writer's services, or all or any rights in and to the same, then Lender/Writer agrees to execute and

DEALMAKING
IN THE
FILM AND
TELEVISION
INDUSTRY—
3RD EDITION

120

deliver to Production Company any such documents at any time and from time to time upon Production Company's request, and in such form as may be prescribed by Production Company, without limiting the generality of the foregoing Lender/Writer agrees to execute and deliver to Production Company upon Production Company's request therefore an assignment of all rights, it being agreed that all of the representations, warranties, and agreements made and to be made by Lender/Writer under this Exhibit shall be deemed made by Lender/Writer as part of this agreement. If Lender/Writer shall fail or refuse to execute and deliver the certificate above described and/or any such documents within ten (10) business days of a written request, Lender/Writer hereby irrevocably grants Production Company the power coupled with an interest to execute this certificate and/or documents in Lender's/Writer's name and as Lender's/ Writer's attorney-in-fact. Lender's/Writer's failure to execute this certificate and/or documents shall not affect or limit any of Production Company's rights in and to the results and proceeds of Writer's services.

(iv) Separation of Rights: Since Writer has been assigned material, he/she is not entitled to separation of rights under the WGA Agreement. Notwithstanding anything to the contrary contained herein, Production Company shall have the right to publish and copyright, or cause to be published and copyrighted, screenplays, teleplays, and scripts adapted from or based upon the Product and the novelization of screenplays, teleplays, and scripts adapted from or based upon the Product or any Product Form created hereunder.

10. LENDER'S/WRITER'S WARRANTIES:

Subject to Article 28 of the WGA Basic Agreement, Lender/ Writer warrants:

(a) that, except as provided in the next sentence hereof, all material composed and/or submitted by Writer for or to Production Company shall be wholly original with Writer and shall not infringe upon or violate the right of privacy of, nor constitute a libel or slander against, nor violate any common-law rights or any other rights of any person, firm, or corporation. The same agreements and warranties are made by Lender and Writer regarding any and all material, incidents, treatments, characters, and action which Writer may add to or interpolate in any material assigned by Production Company to Writer for preparation, but are not made regarding violations or infringements contained in the material so assigned by Production Company to Writer. The said agreements and warranties on Lender's/Writer's part are subject to the limitations contained in the WGA Agreement.

(b) Further Warranties: Lender and Writer hereby warrant that Writer is under no obligation or disability, created by law or otherwise, which would in any manner or to any extent prevent or restrict Lender and Writer from entering into and fully performing this Agreement, and Lender and Writer hereby accept the obligations hereunder. Lender and Writer warrant that Lender/Writer has not entered into any agreement or commitment that would prevent their fulfilling its commitments with Production Company hereunder and that Lender and Writer will not enter into any such agreement or commitment without Production Company's specific approval. Lender and Writer hereby agree that Writer shall devote his/her entire time and attention and best talents and ability exclusively to Production Company as specified herein and observe and be governed by the rules of conduct established by Production Company for the conduct of its employees.

(c) Indemnification: Lender and Writer agree to indemnify Production Company, its successors, assigns, licensees, officers, directors, and employees, and hold them harmless from and against any and all claims, liability, losses, damages, costs, expenses (including but not limited to attorneys' fees), judgments, and penalties arising out of Lender's and Writer's breach of warranties under this Agreement. Production Company agrees to indemnify Lender, its successors, assigns, licensees, and employees, and hold them harmless from and against any and all claims, liability, losses, damages, costs, expenses (including but not limited to attorneys' fees), judgments, and penalties arising out of any suit against Lender/Writer (arising from Lender's employment under this agreement) not based on Lender's/Writer's breach of his/her warranties under this Agreement.

11.   NAME AND LIKENESS: Production Company shall always have the right to use and display Writer's name and likeness for advertising, publicizing, and exploiting the Picture or the Product. However, such advertising may not include the direct endorsement of any product (other than the Picture) without Writer's prior written consent. Exhibition, advertising, publicizing, or exploiting the Picture by any media, even through a part of or in connection with a product or a commercially sponsored program, shall not be deemed an endorsement of any nature.

12. PUBLICITY RESTRICTIONS: Lender or Writer shall not, individually or jointly, or by any means of press agents or publicity or advertising agencies or others, employed or paid by Lender or Writer or otherwise, circulate, publish, or otherwise disseminate any news stories or articles, books,

DEALMAKING
IN THE
FILM AND
TELEVISION
INDUSTRY—
3RD EDITION

122

or other publicity, containing Writer's name relating directly or indirectly to Lender's/Writer's employment by Production Company, the subject matter of this Agreement, the Picture, or the services to be rendered by Lender or Writer or others for the Picture, unless first approved by Production Company. Lender/Writer shall not transfer or attempt to transfer any right, privilege, title, or interest in or to any of the aforestated things, nor shall Lender/Writer willingly permit any infringement upon the exclusive rights granted to Production Company. Lender and Writer authorizes Production Company, at Production Company's expense, in Lender's or Writer's name or otherwise, to institute any proper legal proceedings to prevent such infringement.

13. REMEDIES:

(a) Remedies Cumulative: All remedies of Production Company or Lender shall be cumulative, and no one such remedy shall be exclusive of any other. Without waiving any rights or remedies under this Agreement or otherwise, Production Company may from time to time recover, by action, any damages arising out of any breach of this Agreement by Lender and/or Writer and may institute and maintain subsequent actions for additional damages which may arise from the same or other breaches. The commencement or maintaining of any such action or actions by Production Company shall not constitute or result in the termination of Lender's/Writer's engagement hereunder unless Production Company shall expressly so elect by written notice to Lender. The pursuit by Production Company or Lender of any remedy under this Agreement or otherwise shall not be deemed to waive any other or different remedy which may be available under this Agreement or otherwise.

(b) Services Unique: Lender and Writer acknowledge that Writer's services to be furnished hereunder and the rights herein granted are of a special, unique, unusual, extraordinary, and intellectual character which gives them a peculiar value, the loss of which cannot be reasonably or adequately compensated in damages in an action at law, and that Lender's or Writer's Default will cause Production Company irreparable injury and damage. Lender and Writer agree that Production Company shall be entitled to injunctive and other equitable relief to prevent default by Lender or Writer. In addition to such equitable relief, Production Company shall be entitled to such other remedies as may be available at law, including damages.

14. FORCE MAJEURE:

(a) Suspension: If, (i) by reason of fire, earthquake, labor dispute or strike, act of God or public enemy, any municipal ordinance, any state or federal law, governmental order or regulation, or other cause beyond Production Company's control, Production Company is prevented from or hampered in the production of the Picture, or if, (ii) by reason of the closing of substantially all the theaters in the United States for any of the aforesaid or other causes which would excuse Production Company's performance as a matter of law, Production Company's production of the Picture is postponed or suspended, or if, (iii) by reason of any of the aforesaid contingencies or any other cause or occurrence not within Production Company's control, including but not limited to the death, illness or incapacity of any principal member of the cast of the Picture or the director or individual producer, the preparation, commencement, production, or completion of the Picture is hampered, interrupted, or interfered with, and/ or if, (iv) Production Company's normal business operations are hampered or otherwise interfered with by virtue of any disruptive events which are beyond Production Company's control ("Production Company Disability"), then Production Company may postpone the commencement of or suspend the rendition of Writer's services and the running of time hereunder for such time as the Production Company Disability continues; and no compensation shall accrue or become payable to Lender hereunder during such suspension. Such suspension shall end upon the cessation of the cause thereof.

(b) Termination:

(i) Production Company Termination Right: If a Production Company Disability continues for a period of eight (8) weeks, Production Company may terminate this Agreement upon written notice to Lender.

(ii) Lender's Termination Right: If a Production Company Disability results in the payment of compensation being suspended hereunder for a period exceeding eight (8) weeks, Lender may terminate this Agreement upon written notice to Production Company.

(iii) Production Company Re-Establishment Right: Despite Lender's election to terminate this Agreement, within five (5) business days after Production Company's actual receipt of such written notice from Lender, Production Company may elect to reestablish the operation of this Agreement.

15. WRITER'S INCAPACITY: If, by reason of mental or physical disability, Writer shall be incapacitated from performing or complying with any of the terms or conditions hereof ("Writer's Incapacity") for a consecutive period exceeding fifteen (15) days during the performance of Writer's services, then:

DEALMAKING
IN THE
FILM AND
TELEVISION
INDUSTRY—
3RD EDITION

124

(a) Suspension: Production Company may suspend the rendition of services by Writer and the running of time hereunder so long as Writer's Incapacity shall continue.

(b) Termination: Production Company may terminate this Agreement and all of Production Company's obligations and liabilities hereunder upon written notice to Lender.

(c) Right of Examination: If any claim of mental or physical disability is made by Writer or on Writer's behalf, the Production Company may have Writer examined by such physicians as Production Company may designate. Writer's physician may be present at such examination, and shall not interfere therewith. Any tests performed on Writer shall be related to and be customary for the treatment, diagnosis, or examination to be performed in connection with Writer's claim.

16. LENDER/WRITER DEFAULT: If Lender or Writer fails or refuses to write, complete, and deliver to Production Company the Product Form provided for herein within the respective periods specified or if Lender or Writer otherwise fails or refuses to perform or comply with any of the terms or conditions hereof (other than by reason of Writer's Incapacity) ("Lender/ Writer Default"), then:

(a) Suspension: Production Company may suspend the rendition of services by Writer and the running of time hereunder as long as the Lender/Writer Default shall continue.

(b) Termination: Production Company may terminate this Agreement and all of Production Company's obligations and liabilities hereunder upon written notice to Lender.

(c) Lender/Writer Default shall not include any failure or refusal of Writer to perform or comply with the material terms of this Agreement by reason of a breach or action by Production Company which makes the performance by Writer of his/her services impossible.

(d) Prior to termination of this Agreement by Production Company based upon Lender/Writer Default, Production Company shall notify Lender and Writer specifying the nature of the Lender/Writer Default and Lender/Writer shall have a period of seventy-two (72) hours after giving of such notice to cure the Default. If the Lender/Writer Default is not cured within said period, Production Company may terminate this Agreement forthwith.

17. EFFECT OF TERMINATION: Termination of this Agreement, whether by lapse of time, mutual consent, operation of law, exercise of right of termination, or otherwise shall:

(a) Compensation: Terminate Production Company's obligation to pay Lender any further compensation. Nevertheless, if the termination is not for Lender/Writer Default, Production Company shall pay Lender any compensation due and unpaid prior to termination.

(b) Refund/Delivery: If termination occurs pursuant to Clauses 14, 15, or 16, prior to Writer's delivery to Production Company of the Product Form on which Writer is then currently working, then Lender or Writer (or in the event of Writer's death, Writer's estate) shall, as Production Company requests, either forthwith refund to Production Company the compensation which may have been paid to Lender as of that time for such Product Form, or immediately deliver to Production Company all of the Product then completed or in progress, in whatever stage of completion it may be.

18. EFFECT OF SUSPENSION: No compensation shall accrue to Lender during any suspension. During any period of suspension hereunder, Lender shall not permit Writer to render services for any party other than Production Company. However, Writer shall have the right to render services to third parties during any period of suspension based upon a Production Company Disability subject, however, to Production Company's right to require Writer to resume the rendition of services hereunder upon three (3) days' prior notice. Production Company shall have the right (exercisable at any time) to extend the period of services of Writer hereunder for a period equal to the period of such suspension. If Production Company shall have paid compensation to Lender during any period of Writer's Incapacity or Lender/Writer Default, then Production Company shall have the right (exercisable at any time) to require Writer to render services hereunder without compensation for a period equal to that period of Writer's Incapacity or Lender/Writer Default.

19. LENDER'S RIGHT TO CURE: Any Writer's Incapacity or Lender/Writer Default shall be deemed to continue until Production Company's receipt of written notice from Lender specifying that Writer is ready, willing, and able to perform the services required hereunder; provided that any such notice from Lender to Production Company shall not preclude Production Company from exercising any rights or remedies Production Company may have hereunder or at law or in equity by reason of Writer's Incapacity or Lender/Writer Default.

20. TEAM OF WRITERS: The obligations of the Writer's Team under this Agreement shall be joint and several, and references in this Agreement to Writer shall be deemed to refer to the Team of Writers jointly and severally. Should any right of termination

DEALMAKING
IN THE
FILM AND
TELEVISION
INDUSTRY—
3RD EDITION

126

arise as a result of the Incapacity or Default of any one of the Team of Writers, the remedies of the Production Company may be exercised either as to such Writer or as to the Team of Writers or as to Lender, at Production Company's election. Should Production Company elect to exercise its remedies only as to the Writer affected, the engagement of the other Writer or Lender shall continue and such remaining Lender/Writer shall receive only his/her share of the compensation provided herein.

21. GUILDS AND UNIONS:

(a) Membership: During Writer's engagement hereunder, as Production Company may lawfully require, Lender at Lender's sole cost and expense (and at Production Company's request) shall remain or become and remain a member in good standing of the then properly designated labor organization or organizations (as defined and determined under the then applicable law) representing persons performing services of the type and character required to be performed by Writer hereunder.

(b) Superseding Effect of Guild Arrangements: Nothing contained in this Agreement shall be construed so as to require the violation of the applicable WGA Agreement, which by its terms is controlling with respect to this Agreement; and whenever there is any conflict between any provision of this Agreement and any such WGA Agreement, the latter shall prevail. In such event the provisions of this Agreement shall be curtailed and limited only to the extent necessary to permit compliance with such WGA Agreement.

22. CREDITS:

(a) Billing: Provided that Lender and Writer fully perform all of Lender's/Writer's obligations hereunder and the Picture is completed and distributed, Production Company agrees that credits for authorship by Writer shall be determined and accorded pursuant to the provisions of the WGA Agreement in effect at the time of such determination.

(b) Inadvertent Non-Compliance: Subject to the foregoing provisions, Production Company shall determine, in Production Company's discretion, the manner of presenting such credits. No casual or inadvertent failure to comply with the provisions of this clause, nor any failure of any other person, firm, or corporation to comply with its agreements with Production Company relating to such credits, shall constitute a breach by Production Company of Production Company's obligations under this clause. Lender and Writer hereby agree that, if through inadvertence Production Company breaches its obligations pursuant to this Paragraph, the damages (if any) caused Lender or Writer by Production Company are not irreparable or sufficient to entitle Lender/Writer to injunctive or other equitable relief. Consequently, Lender's and/or Writer's rights and remedies in such event shall be limited to Lender's/ Writer's rights, if any, to recover damages in an action at law, and Lender and Writer shall not be entitled to rescind this Agreement or any of the rights granted to Production Company hereunder, or to enjoin or restrain the distribution or exhibition of the Picture or any other rights granted to Production Company. Production Company agrees, upon receipt of notice from Writer of Production Company's failure to comply with the provisions of this Paragraph, to take such steps as are reasonably practicable to cure such failure on future prints and advertisements.

23. INSURANCE: Production Company may secure life, health, accident, cast, or other insurance covering Writer, the cost of which shall be included as a direct charge of the Picture. Such insurance shall be for Production Company's sole benefit and Production Company shall be the beneficiary thereof, and Lender/Writer shall have no interest in the proceeds thereof. Lender and Writer shall assist in procuring such insurance by submitting to required examinations and tests and by preparing, signing, and delivering such applications and other documents as may be reasonably required. Lender and Writer shall, to the best of their ability, observe all terms and conditions of such insurance of which Production Company notifies Lender as necessary for continuing such insurance in effect.

24. EMPLOYMENT OF OTHERS: Lender and Writer agree not to employ any person to serve in any capacity, nor contract for the purchase or renting of any article or material, nor make any agreement committing Production Company to pay any sum of money for any reason whatsoever in connection with the Picture or services to be rendered by Writer or provided by Lender hereunder, or otherwise, without written approval first being had and obtained from Production Company.

25. ASSIGNMENT AND LENDING:

(a) Assignability: This Agreement is non-assignable by Lender and Writer. Production Company and any subsequent assignee may freely assign this Agreement and grant its rights hereunder, in whole or in part to any person, firm, or corporation, provided that such party assumes and agrees in writing to keep and perform all of the executory obligations of Production Company hereunder. Upon such assumption, Production Company is hereby released from all further obligations to Lender and Writer hereunder, except that unless the assignee or borrower

DEALMAKING
IN THE
FILM AND
TELEVISION
INDUSTRY—
3RD EDITION

128

is a so-called major motion picture company, or mini-major, Production Company shall remain secondarily liable under this agreement.

(b) Right to Lend to Others: Lender understands and acknowledges that the actual production entity of a motion picture to be made from the Product may be a party other than Production Company. In such event, Writer's services shall be rendered hereunder for the actual production entity but without releasing Production Company from its obligations hereunder.

26. NOTICES:

(a) Lender's Address: All notices from Production Company to Writer, in connection with this Agreement, may be given in writing by addressing the same to Lender c/o _____. Production Company may deliver such notice to Lender or Writer personally, either orally or in writing. A courtesy copy shall be given to _____ at the address above. If such notice is sent by mail, the date of mailing shall be deemed to be the date of service of such notice.

(b) Writing Requirement: Any oral notice given in respect to any right of termination, suspension, or extension under this Agreement shall be confirmed in writing. If any notice is delivered to Lender personally, a copy of such notice shall be sent to Lender at the above address.

(c) Producer's Address: All notices from Lender to Production Company hereunder shall be given in writing addressed to Production Company as follows: _____ and by depositing the same, so addressed, postage prepaid, in the mail. A courtesy copy shall be given to _____, Attorney at Law _____. Unless otherwise expressly provided, the date of mailing shall be deemed to be the date of service of such notice.

27. TRANSPORTATION AND EXPENSES: When Writer's services are required by Production Company to be rendered hereunder at a place more than fifty (50) miles from Writer's domicile, Production Company shall furnish Writer transportation to and from such places and meals and lodging accommodations while Writer is on location to render Writer's services.

28. GOVERNING LAW: This Agreement shall be construed in accordance with the laws of the State of _____ applicable to agreements which are executed and fully performed within said State.

29. CAPTIONS: The captions used in connection with the clauses and subclauses of this Agreement are inserted only for the purpose

of reference. Such captions shall not be deemed to govern, limit, modify, or in any other manner affect the scope, meaning, or intent of the provisions of this Agreement or any part thereof; nor shall such captions otherwise be given any legal effect.

30. SERVICE OF PROCESS: In any action or proceeding commenced in any court in the State of _____ for the purpose of enforcing this Agreement or any right granted herein or growing out hereof, or any order or decree predicated thereon, any summons, order to show cause, writ, judgment, decree, or other process, issued by such court, may be delivered to Lender or Writer personally without the State of _____; and when so delivered, Lender and Writer shall be subject to the jurisdiction of such court as though the same had been served within the State of _____, but outside the county in which such action or proceeding is pending.

31. ILLEGALITY: Nothing contained herein shall require the commission of any act or the payment of any compensation which is contrary to an express provision of law or contrary to the policy of express law. If there shall exist any conflict between any provision contained herein and any such law or policy, the latter shall prevail; and the provision or provisions herein affected shall be curtailed, limited, or eliminated to the extent (but only to the extent) necessary to remove such conflict; and as so modified the remaining provisions of this Agreement shall continue in full force and effect.

32. EMPLOYMENT ELIGIBILITY: All of Production Company's obligations herein are expressly conditioned upon Writer's completion, to Production Company's satisfaction, of the I-9 Form (Employee Eligibility Verification Form) and upon Writer's submission to Production Company of original documents satisfactory to demonstrate to Production Company Writer's employment eligibility.

33. ENTIRE AGREEMENT: This Agreement contains the entire agreement of the parties and all previous agreements, warranties, and representations, if any, are merged herein.

By signing in the spaces provided below, Lender and Production Company accept and agree to all of the terms and conditions of this Agreement.

The Writer's Co.   Date:
("Lender")

Big Films
("Production Company")

By: _____, its President

Date: _____

DEALMAKING
IN THE
FILM AND
TELEVISION
INDUSTRY—
3RD EDITION

130

CERTIFICATE OF AUTHORSHIP

Each of the undersigned does hereby certify that pursuant to a loan-out agreement between _____ (loan-out company) ("Lender") f/s/o _____ (name of writer) ("Writer") and _____ (name of production company), Lender, for good and valuable consideration, loaned Production Company the services of Writer and that pursuant to said loan-out agreement, all literary material (the "Material") submitted and to be submitted by Writer, other than the "Assigned Material" (as defined in the Agreement between Lender and Production Company), in connection with a motion picture tentatively entitled "_____" (name of picture), was written and will be written by Writer as a work-made-for-hire specially ordered or commissioned by Production Company for use as part of a motion picture, with Production Company being deemed the author of the Material and entitled to the copyrights (and all extensions and renewals of copyrights) therein and thereto, with the right to make such changes therein and such uses thereof as Production Company may from time to time determine as such author. Subject only to Article 28 of the applicable Writers Guild of America, West, Inc., Theatrical and Television Basic Agreement, each of the undersigned hereby warrants that other than Assigned Material, the Material is original with Writer, does not to the best of Writer's knowledge defame, infringe upon, or violate the rights of privacy or other rights of any person, firm, or corporation, and is not the subject of any litigation or claim that might give rise to litigation and the undersigned does hereby agree to indemnify Production Company, its assignees, and licensees against any breach of any of the aforesaid warranties and undertake to execute such documents and do such other acts and deeds as may be required by Production Company or its assignees or licensees to further evidence or effectuate its rights hereunder. Production Company's rights in the Material may be freely assigned and licensed and its rights shall be binding upon the undersigned and inure to the benefit of such assignees and licensees.

IN WITNESS WHEREOF the parties hereto have caused this document to be executed this _____ day of _____, 20___.

_____
(Lender)

By: _____

Its: _____

INDUCEMENT AGREEMENT

Big Films

22 Fantasy Lane

Hollywood, CA

Re: "The Big Story"

Reference is made to the Agreement dated _____ ("Lending Agreement"), being executed concurrently herewith, between (The Writer's Co.), a New York Corporation ("Lender"), and Big Films ("Borrower"), covering the loan of the services of the undersigned The Writer's Co. ("Artist").

1.   CONCURRENT EMPLOYMENT AGREEMENT: Artist has heretofore entered into an agreement ("Employment Agreement") with Lender covering the rendition of Artist's services for Lender for a period not less than the period Lender provides Artist's services under the Lending Agreement and Lender has the right to enter into the Lending Agreement and to furnish the Artist's services and to grant the rights granted pursuant to the terms and conditions therein specified.

2. RATIFICATION OF LENDING AGREEMENT: Artist is familiar with the terms and conditions of the Lending Agreement and consents to the signing thereof; Artist shall perform and comply with all of the terms and conditions of the Lending Agreement requiring performance or compliance by Artist even if the Employment Agreement should hereafter be terminated, suspended, or become ineffective; Artist shall render to Borrower all of the services provided to be rendered by Artist under the Lending Agreement; all notices served upon Lender in accordance with the Lending Agreement shall be deemed notices to Artist of the contents thereof with the same effect as if served upon Artist personally. Artist hereby expressly agrees that all of the results and product of all services to be performed by Artist pursuant to the Lending Agreement are results considered a work-made-for-hire for Borrower and that Borrower shall be the author and copyright owner of such results and product.

3. NO RESTRICTIONS: Artist is under no obligation or disability, by law or otherwise, which would interfere with Artist's full performance and compliance with all of the terms and conditions of the Lending Agreement which require performance or compliance by Artist.

4. REMUNERATION SOLE RESPONSIBILITY OF LENDER: Except as may otherwise be provided in the Lending Agreement, Artist shall look solely to Lender for all compensation and other

DEALMAKING
IN THE
FILM AND
TELEVISION
INDUSTRY—
3RD EDITION

132

remuneration for any and all rights and services which Artist and/or Lender may grant and render to Borrower under the Lending Agreement.

5. BREACH: Artist's services are unique and extraordinary and the breach of this Inducement Agreement and/or of any of the terms of the Lending Agreement which require performance or compliance by Artist will cause irreparable damage to Borrower. Therefore, in the event of breach or threatened breach by Artist of this Inducement Agreement, Borrower shall be entitled to legal or equitable relief by way of injunction or otherwise, against Artist or against Lender or against both, at the discretion of Borrower, to restrain, enjoin, and/or prevent such breach by Artist, Lender, or both. All of the foregoing shall be to the same extent and with the same force and effect as if Artist was a direct party to the Lending Agreement in the first instance, and as if in the Lending Agreement, Artist had personally agreed to render the services therein provided to be rendered by Artist and to perform and observe each and all of the terms and conditions of the Lending Agreement requiring performance or compliance on the part of Artist, Lender, or both.

6. SUBSTITUTION FOR LENDER: If Lender should be dissolved or should otherwise cease to exist or for any reason whatsoever should fail, neglect, refuse, or be unable to perform and observe each and all of the terms or conditions of the Lending Agreement requiring performance or compliance by Lender, Artist shall, at the election of Borrower, be deemed substituted as a direct party to said Lending Agreement in the place and stead of Lender.

7. GOVERNING LAW: This Inducement Agreement shall be governed and construed by the laws of the State of _____.

Very truly yours,

_____
Artist

WGA CREDIT ARBITRATION

Producers do not have the unfettered power to award writing credits in their sole discretion. The Writers Guild contract provides that a production company must send each writer a copy of the final shooting script and a "Notice of Tentative Credits." If a writer agrees with the tentative credits, he/she does nothing. If he/she disagrees, he/she must protest within the time specified in the notice. Writers may meet on their own and try to agree how credit should be allocated. If they cannot agree, the matter will be resolved through arbitration.

Writers have the right to challenge a reasonable number of arbiters. Three arbiters are selected from those remaining on the list. Identities remain confidential. At the request of any participating writer, the identities of the writers are not revealed to the arbitrators. Each writer may submit a written statement of his/her position to the arbiters.

As a writer, you should protect your rights by saving copies of every draft. Each draft should be dated and have your name on it. If you make suggestions in story conferences which do not appear in the script, document your contribution by sending a dated memorandum to the producer. If scripts are similar, arbiters will assume that a subsequent writer had access to prior drafts.

If you are collaborating with another writer, the Guild assumes the collaboration is a 50/50 partnership unless there is evidence to the contrary. If that is not your understanding, you should document your agreement in writing.

According to WGA credit rules,[4] a writer whose work represents 33% of a screenplay is entitled to a screenplay credit. However, for original screenplays, subsequent writers must contribute 50% to the final screenplay to receive a credit. The Guild guarantees the writer of an original screenplay a minimum credit ("irreducible story minimum") of a shared story credit.

---

[4] The WGA screen credits manual is at www.wga.org/subpage_writersresources .aspx?id=167

DEALMAKING
IN THE
FILM AND
TELEVISION
INDUSTRY—
3RD EDITION

134

DIRECTORS

The director is the person primarily responsible for supervising the creation of a film or television program. She must be enough of an artist to satisfy critics and viewers and enough of a business-person to satisfy the financiers. From the studio's point of view, hiring a director is critical because she is the person charged with keeping the production on budget and on schedule.

Director employment agreements share many provisions found in writer employment agreements. The agreement may be structured as direct employment or through a loan-out arrangement. In the latter case, the director's company is called the "Lender."

Directors are hired for the period of principal photography as well as the time needed beforehand to prepare for filming (pre-production) and time after to supervise editing (post-production). The director may also work with the writer during development.

Often the director is hired on a flat fee basis that covers all these phases. Payments are made in installments with most of the fee paid during principal photography. A director is typically hired on an exclusive basis, preventing her from accepting outside employment and working on more than one film at a time.

The agreement is frequently a "pay or play" deal, which means that if the studio does not use the director's services, or replaces her, the director is still entitled to her fixed compensation. The director may also receive bonus, deferred, contingent, and additional compensation, although these payments may not vest until and unless the person is entitled to a director credit.

Usually the director does not have the right of "final cut," which is the power to determine the composition of the final edited version of the picture. Studios may insist on reserving this right to protect their investment and make sure that the director does not create an artistic masterpiece that is a commercial flop. Also, the agreement will specify that the film be a certain length (e.g., within 90 to 120 minutes). Directors may be required to produce two versions of the film: one for theatrical release and another for television broadcast.

The director may have the right to select key personnel such as the Director of Photography, Production Manager, and Editor. A veteran director with clout could have the power to hire certain cast and crew members without studio approval.

DIRECTOR EMPLOYMENT AGREEMENT

Agreement

Agreement dated _____ between _____ ("Director") and _____ ("Production Company").

1. EMPLOYMENT: Production Company agrees to employ Director to perform and Director agrees to perform, upon the terms and conditions herein specified, directing services in connection with the Theatrical Motion Picture currently entitled _____ ("Picture").

2. TERM: The Term of this agreement shall commence on _____ and shall continue until the completion of all of Director's required services on the Picture.

3. SERVICES:

(a) Pre-Production: Director shall be available and undertake a location search on or about _____.

(b) Photography: Director's exclusive services for the Picture shall commence _____ weeks prior to the start of principal photography and shall be rendered exclusively after that until completion of all photography. The start date of principal photography shall be mutually approved by Production Company and Director. The scheduled start date of principal photography is _____.

(c) Post-Production: Director's post-production services shall be rendered on a non-exclusive but first-call basis, if Production Company so requires in order to work during the post-production period with the editor until completion of the final corrected answer print. Director's other undertakings shall not interfere with Director's post-production services hereunder.

(1) Cooperation with Editor: Director hereby warrants and agrees that Director will do nothing to hinder or delay the assemblage of film by the editor during the photography of the Picture so that the assembled sequences will be completed immediately following the completion of principal photography.

(2) Post-Production Schedule: Attached hereto marked Exhibit S and by this reference incorporated herein is a schedule for the post-production work on the Picture which has been agreed to by Director and Production Company. Director agrees that this schedule will be followed by Director.

(3) Final Cutting Authority: _____ is designated as the

DEALMAKING
IN THE
FILM AND
TELEVISION
INDUSTRY—
3RD EDITION

136

Production Company Executive with final cutting authority over the Picture. The foregoing shall be subject to applicable guild and union requirements, if any.

(d) Dailies: Production Company shall have the right to view the dailies during the production of the Picture, the rough cut, and all subsequent cuts of the Picture.

(e) Television Cover Shots: Director shall furnish Production Company with protective cover shots necessary for the release of the Picture on television, based on network continuity standards in existence at the time of commencement of principal photography.

(f) Additional Post-Production Services: If after the completion of principal photography, Production Company requires retakes, changes, dubbing, transparencies, added scenes, further photography, trailers, sound track, process shots, or other-language versions (herein collectively called "retakes, etc.") for the Picture, Director shall report to Production Company for such retakes, etc., at such place or places and on such consecutive or nonconsecutive days as Production Company may designate. Subject to Director's professional availability, Director shall cooperate to make such services available to Production Company at the earliest possible date.

4. COMPENSATION: As full and complete consideration for Director's services and Director's undertakings hereunder and for all rights granted to Production Company hereunder, and subject to Director's full compliance with the terms and conditions of this Agreement, Production Company agrees to pay Director as follows:

(a) Fixed Compensation:

(1) The total sum of $_____ payable:

(A) $_____ upon approval of the Budgeted Negative Cost for production of the Picture.

(B) $_____ prorated weekly commencing ____ weeks prior to the start of principal photography of the Picture.

(C) $_____ payable in equal weekly installments over the scheduled period of principal photography.

(D) $_____ upon delivery of the director's cut.

(E) $_____ upon the completion of the final answer print of the Picture.

(2) Flat-Fee Basis: Production Company and Director hereby mutually acknowledge that the Fixed Compensation

as herein above specified is a "flat fee" and Director shall not be entitled to any additional and/or so-called "overage" compensation for any services rendered by Director during the development, pre-production, production, or post-production phases, or for additional post-production services rendered by Director. Without limiting the generality of the foregoing, no additional compensation shall be payable to Director under Clause 4(a)(1)(C) above if the actual principal photography period for the Picture neither exceeds the scheduled principal photography period, nor for any services rendered pursuant to Clause 3(f).

(b) Deferred Compensation: In addition to the Fixed Compensation payable under Clause 4(a), subject to the production and release of the Picture and subject to the performance of all obligations of Director hereunder, Director shall be entitled to receive the sum of $_____, which shall be deferred and paid pro rata with all similar deferments of compensation payable _____ at the point just preceding the payment of percentage participations in the Net Profits of the Picture.

(c) Contingent Compensation: In addition to the Fixed Compensation payable under Clause 4(a), and any Deferred Compensation payable under Clause 4(b), subject to the production and release of the Picture and subject to the performance of Director's obligations hereunder, Director shall be entitled to receive as Contingent Compensation an amount equal to _____ percent of the Net Profits of the Picture, if any.

(d) Net Profits Definition: Net Profits shall be computed, determined, and paid in accordance with Exhibit ___ attached hereto and by this reference incorporated herein.

(e) Conditions Related to Compensation: Notwithstanding anything to the contrary contained in any of the above compensation provisions:

(1) Performance: No compensation shall accrue or become payable to Director during Director's inability, failure, or refusal to perform the services contracted for herein according to the terms and conditions of this Agreement.

(2) Pay or Play: Production Company shall not be obligated to use Director's services on the Picture, nor shall Production Company be obligated to produce, release, distribute, advertise, exploit, or otherwise make use of the Picture; provided, however, that the full amount of the Fixed Compensation hereinabove specified shall be paid to Director should Production Company

DEALMAKING
IN THE
FILM AND
TELEVISION
INDUSTRY—
3RD EDITION

138

without legal justification or excuse (as provided elsewhere in this Agreement or by operation of law), elect not to utilize Director's services.

(f) Vesting: The Fixed Compensation and Contingent Compensation hereinabove specified shall be deemed fully vested if, notwithstanding the termination of Director's services due to Producer Disability or Director's incapacity or Director default, Director shall be entitled to receive "Directed by" credit pursuant to the Directors Guild of America Basic Agreement of 1993, as same may be amended from time to time ("Basic Agreement").

If the services of Director are terminated by Production Company due to Production Disability or Director's Incapacity or Director Default, as defined below, and Director is not entitled to receive credit pursuant to the Basic Agreement, then the Fixed Compensation shall vest and accrue in the same manner as set forth herein and the Contingent Compensation shall accrue and vest in the same ratio that the number of linear feet in the completed Picture as released, which was directed by Director, bears to the total number of linear feet in the completed Picture as released. Notwithstanding the foregoing, if principal photography has not commenced on the scheduled start date as set forth in Clause 3(b) hereof, then the total Fixed Compensation shall vest and accrue on the aforesaid scheduled start date and production of the Picture is thereafter terminated prior to completion of principal photography and/or delivery of the final answer print to Production Company, then that portion of the Fixed Compensation not theretofore accrued shall fully vest and accrue on the date of such termination. If Production Company terminates this Agreement by reason of a Director Default, notwithstanding any vesting of Fixed Compensation and/or Contingent Compensation as set forth above, such vesting shall be subject to any and all the rights accorded to Production Company at law and in equity.

(g) Mitigation: If Production Company elects to exercise its pay-or-play right as set forth above and/or fails to produce the Picture; Director shall have no obligation to mitigate damages.

5. CREDITS:

(a) Credit: Subject to the production and release of the Picture and provided Director performs his/her material obligations hereunder, then Production Company shall accord Director credit in connection with the Picture in accordance with the requirements of the Directors Guild of America, Inc., Basic Agreement of 1993 immediately after the main title, which shall be fifty percent (50%) of the size of the title on a separate card.

(b) Artwork Title Exception: If both a regular (or repeat) title and an artwork title are used, the position and percentage requirements above, as they relate to the title of the Picture, shall relate to the regular (or repeat) title. If only an artwork title is used, the percentage requirements above, as they relate to the title, shall be not less than fifteen percent (15%) of the average size of the letters used in the artwork title.

(c) Credit Limitation: Production Company agrees that no other individual and/or entity (other than members of the cast receiving "starring" billing before or after the title of the Picture or the company distributing and/or financing the Picture) shall receive credit larger than that used to display the credit accorded to Director.

(d) Inadvertent Non-Compliance: No casual or inadvertent failure to comply with the provisions of this Paragraph shall be deemed to be a breach of this Agreement by Production Company. Director hereby recognizes and confirms that in the event of a failure or omission by Production Company constituting a breach of Production Company obligations under this Paragraph, the damages, if any, caused Director by Production Company are not irreparable or sufficient to entitle Director to injunctive or other equitable relief. Consequently, Director's rights and remedies hereunder shall be limited to the right, if any, to obtain damages at law, and Director shall have no right in such event to rescind this Agreement or any of the rights assigned to Production Company hereunder or to enjoin or restrain the distribution or exhibition of the Picture. Production Company agrees to advise its assignees and licensees of the credit requirements herein. If Production Company shall learn of such failure of a third party to give such credit, Production Company shall notify such party of such failure and Production Company may, but shall not be obligated to, take action to cause such party to prospectively cure such failure.

6. TRANSPORTATION AND EXPENSES: If Director's services are required at Production Company's request to be rendered on location more than (e.g., fifty (50)) miles from the City of Los Angeles, Production Company shall furnish Director first-class round-trip transportation for one (1), and Production Company shall reimburse Director for Director's living expenses in the amount of $_____ per week. If Director can demonstrate to Production Company's satisfaction that said living expense allowance is insufficient for any particular location, Production

DEALMAKING
IN THE
FILM AND
TELEVISION
INDUSTRY—
3RD EDITION

140

Company shall, at such time, give good-faith consideration to an increase. For any period week which is less than one (1) week, said reimbursement shall be upon the pro rata basis that one (1) day is equal to one-seventh ($^1/_7$) of one (1) week. Director shall furnish Production Company with itemized detailed accountings of such living expenses, including vouchers, bills, receipts, and statements satisfactory to meet the requirements and regulations of the Internal Revenue Service.

7. PERFORMANCE STANDARDS: Except as specifically provided to the contrary herein, during the Term of this Agreement, Director shall render his/her directive services exclusively to Production Company and, to such extent as Production Company may require, in otherwise assisting in the production of the Picture. Said services shall be rendered either alone or in collaboration with another or other artists in such manner as Production Company may direct, pursuant to the instructions, controls, and schedules established by Production Company, and at the times, places, and in the manner required by Production Company. Such manners, instructions, directions, and controls shall be exercised by Production Company in accordance with standards of reasonableness and also with what is customary practice in the Motion Picture industry. Such services shall be rendered in an artistic, conscientious, efficient, and punctual manner, to the best of Director's ability and with full regard to the careful, efficient, economical, and expeditious production of the Picture within the budget and shooting schedule established by Production Company immediately prior to the commencement of principal photography. It is further understood that the production of motion pictures by Production Company involves matters of discretion to be exercised by Production Company with respect to art and taste, and Director's services and the manner of rendition thereof is to be governed entirely by Production Company.

8. UNIQUE SERVICES: Except as specifically provided to the contrary hereinabove, Director's services shall be rendered exclusively to Production Company until expiration of the Term of this Agreement, it being mutually understood that said services are extraordinary, unique, and not replaceable, and that there is no adequate remedy at law for breach of this contract by Director, and that Production Company, in the event of such breach by Director, shall be entitled to equitable relief by way of injunction or otherwise to prevent default by Director.

9. RESULTS AND PROCEEDS OF SERVICES: Production Company shall be entitled to and shall solely and exclusively own, in addition to Director's services hereunder, all results and proceeds

thereof (including but not limited to all rights, throughout the world, of copyright, trademark, patent, production, manufacture, recordation, reproduction, transcription, performance, broadcast, and exhibition of any art or method now known or hereafter devised, including radio broadcasting, theatrical and non-theatrical exhibition, and exhibition by the medium of television or otherwise), whether such results and proceeds consist of literary, dramatic, musical, motion picture, mechanical, or any other forms of works, themes, ideas, compositions, creations, or production, together with the rights generally known in the field of literary and musical endeavor as the "moral rights of authors" in and any musical and/or literary proceeds of Director's services, including but not limited to the right to add to, subtract from, arrange, revise, adapt, rearrange, make variations of the property, and to translate the same into any and all languages, change the sequence, change the characters and the descriptions thereof contained in the property, change the title of the same, record and photocopy the same with or without sound (including spoken words, dialogue, and music synchronously recorded), use this title or any of its components in connection with works or motion pictures wholly or partially independent of said property, and to use all or any part of the property in new versions, adaptations, and sequels in any and all languages, and to obtain copyright therein throughout the world. Director does assign and transfer to Production Company all the foregoing without reservation, condition, or limitations, and no right of any kind, nature, or description is reserved by Director. If Production Company shall desire separate assignments or other documents to implement the foregoing, Director shall execute the same upon Production Company's request, and if Director fails or refuses to execute and deliver any such separate assignments or other documents, Production Company shall have and is granted the right and authority to execute the same in Director's name and as Director's attorney-in-fact. Production Company shall supply Director with a copy of any document so executed.

10. WARRANTIES RELATED TO CREATED MATERIAL: Director hereby warrants and agrees that all material, works, writings, idea, "gags," or dialogue written, composed, prepared, submitted, or interpolated by Director in connection with the Picture or its preparation or production shall be wholly original with Director and shall not be copied in whole or in part from any other work, except that submitted to Director by Production Company as a basis for such material. Director further warrants that neither the said material nor any part thereof will to the best of Director's knowledge violate the rights of privacy or constitute a libel or slander against any

DEALMAKING
IN THE
FILM AND
TELEVISION
INDUSTRY—
3RD EDITION

142

person, firm, or corporation, and that the material will not infringe upon the copyright, literary, dramatic, or photoplay rights of any person. Director further warrants and agrees to hold Production Company and its successors, licensees, and assigns harmless against all liability or loss which they or any of them may suffer by reason of the breach of any of the terms or warranties of this Clause.

11. VESTING OF PRODUCTION COMPANY'S RIGHTS: All rights granted or agreed to be granted to Production Company hereunder shall vest in Production Company immediately and shall remain so vested whether this Agreement expires in normal course or is terminated for any cause or reason.

12. NAME AND LIKENESS: Production Company shall always have the right to use and display Director's name and likeness for advertising, publicizing, and exploiting the picture. However, such advertising may not include the direct endorsement of any product (other than the Picture) without Director's consent. Exhibition, advertising, publicizing, or exploiting the Picture by any media, even though a part of or in connection with a product or a commercially sponsored program, shall not be deemed an endorsement of any nature.

13. PUBLICITY RESTRICTIONS: Director shall not individually or by means of press agents or publicity or advertising agencies or others, employed or paid by Director or otherwise, circulate, publish, or otherwise disseminate any news stories or articles, books, or other publicity, containing Director's name relating to Director's employment by Production Company, the subject matter of this contract, the Picture, or the services to be rendered by Director or others in connection with the Picture unless first approved by Production Company. Director shall not transfer any right, privilege, title, or interest in or to any of the things above specified, nor shall Director authorize or willingly permit infringement upon the exclusive rights granted to Production Company, and Director authorizes Production Company, at Production Company's expense, in Director's name or otherwise, to institute any proper legal proceedings to prevent any infringement.

14. FORCE MAJEURE:

(a) Suspension: If, by reason of fire, earthquake, labor dispute or strike, act of God or public enemy, any municipal ordinance, any state or federal law, governmental order or regulation, or other cause beyond Production Company's control which would excuse Production Company's performance as a matter of law, Production Company is prevented from or hampered in the production of the Picture, or if, by reason of the closing of substantially all theaters in the United States, which would excuse Production Company's performance as a matter of law, Production Company's production of the Picture is postponed or suspended, or if, by reason of any of the aforesaid contingencies or any other cause or occurrence not within Production Company's control, including but not limited to the death, illness, or incapability of any principal member of the cast of the Picture, the preparation or production of the Picture is interrupted or delayed and/or, if Production Company's normal business operations are interrupted or otherwise interfered with by virtue of any disruptive events that are beyond Production Company's control ("Production Company Disability"), then Production Company may postpone the commencement of or suspend the rendition of services by Director and the running of time hereunder for such time as the Production Company Disability shall continue; and no compensation shall accrue or become payable to Director hereunder during the period of such suspension. Such suspension shall end upon the cessation of the cause thereof.

(b) Termination:

(1) Production Company Termination Right: If a Production Company Disability continues for a period in excess of six (6) weeks, Production Company shall have the right to terminate this Agreement upon written notice to Director.

(2) Director's Termination Right: If a Production Company Disability results in compensation being suspended hereunder for a period in excess of six (6) weeks, Director shall have the right to terminate this Agreement upon written notice to Production Company.

(3) Production Company Re-Establishment Right: Despite Director's election to terminate this Agreement, within _____ days after Production Company's actual receipt of such written notice from Director, Production Company shall have the right to elect to re-establish the operation of this Agreement.

15. DIRECTOR'S INCAPACITY:

(a) Effect of Director's Incapacity: If, by reason of mental or physical disability, Director is incapacitated from performing or complying with any of the terms of conditions hereof ("Director's Incapacity") for a consecutive period in excess of seven (7) days or aggregate period in excess of ten (10) days, then Production Company shall have the right to terminate this Agreement upon written notice to Director.

(b) Right of Examination: If any claim of mental or physical

DEALMAKING
IN THE
FILM AND
TELEVISION
INDUSTRY—
3RD EDITION

144

disability is made by Director or on Director's behalf, Production Company shall have the right to have Director examined by such physicians as Production Company may designate. Director's physician may be present at such examination but shall not interfere therewith. Any tests performed on Director shall be related to and customary for the treatment, diagnosis, or examination to be performed in connection with Director's claim.

16. DIRECTOR'S DEFAULT: If Director fails or refuses to perform or comply with any of the material terms or conditions hereof (other than by reason of Director's Incapacity) ("Director's Default"), then Production Company may terminate this Agreement upon written notice to Director. Director Default shall not include any failure or refusal of Director to perform or comply with the material terms of this Agreement due to a breach or action by Production Company which makes the performance by Director of his/her services impossible. Prior to termination of this Agreement by Production Company based upon Director Default, Production Company shall notify Director specifying the nature of the Director Default and Director shall have a period of forty-eight (48) hours to cure the Director Default. If the Director Default is not cured within said forty-eight (48) hour period, Production Company may terminate this Agreement forthwith.

17. EFFECT OF TERMINATION: Termination of this Agreement, whether by lapse of time, mutual consent, operation of law, exercise of a right of termination or otherwise, shall:

(a) Terminate Production Company's obligation to pay Director any further compensation. Nevertheless, if the termination is not for Director's Default, Production Company shall pay Director any compensation due and unpaid prior to the termination, and;

(b) Production Company shall not be deemed to have waived any other rights it may have or alter Production Company's rights or any of Director's agreements or warranties relating to the rendition of Director's services prior to termination.

18. PRODUCTION COMPANY RIGHT TO SUSPEND: In the event of Director's Incapacity or Director's Default, Production Company may postpone upon written notice the commencement of or suspend the rendition of services by Director and the running of time hereunder so long as any Director's Disability or Director's Default shall continue; and no compensation shall accrue or become payable to Director during the period of such suspension.

(a) Director's Right to Cure: Any Director's Incapacity or Director's Default shall be deemed to continue until Production Company's receipt of written notice from Director specifying that Director is ready, willing, and able to perform the services required hereunder; provided that any such notice from Director to Production Company shall not preclude Production Company from exercising any rights or remedies Production Company may have hereunder or at law or in equity by reason of Director's Incapacity or Director's Default.

(b) Alternative Services Restricted: During any period of suspension hereunder, Director shall not render services for any person, firm, or corporation other than Production Company. However, Director shall have the right to render services to third parties during any period of suspension based upon a Production Company Disability, subject, however, to Production Company's right to require Director to resume the rendition of services hereunder upon twenty-four (24) hours' prior notice.

(c) Production Company Right to Extend: If Production Company elects to suspend the rendition of services by Director as herein specified, then Production Company shall have the right (exercisable at any time) to extend the period of services of Director hereunder for a period equal to the period of such suspension.

(d) Additional Services: If Production Company shall have paid compensation to Director during any period of Director's Incapacity or Director's Default, then Production Company shall have the right (exercisable at any time) to require Director to render services hereunder without compensation for a period equal to the period for which Production Company shall have paid compensation to Director during such Director's Incapacity or Director's Default.

19. FURTHER WARRANTIES: Director hereby warrants that Director is not under any obligation or disability, created by law or otherwise, which would in any manner or to any extent prevent or restrict Director from entering into and fully performing this Agreement; Director warrants that Director has not entered into any agreement or commitment that would prevent Director from fulfilling Director's commitments with Production Company hereunder and that Director will not enter into any such agreement or commitment without Production Company's specific approval; and Director hereby accepts the obligation hereunder and agrees to devote Director's entire time and attention and best talents and abilities exclusively to Production Company as specified herein, and to observe and to be governed by the rules of conduct established by Production Company for the conduct of its employees.

DEALMAKING
IN THE
FILM AND
TELEVISION
INDUSTRY—
3RD EDITION

146

(a) Indemnity: Director shall at all times indemnify Production Company, its successors, assignees, and licensees, from and against any and all costs, expenses, losses, damages, judgments, and attorneys' fees arising out of or connected with or resulting from any claims, demands, or causes of action by any person or entity which is inconsistent with any of Director's representations, warranties, or agreements hereunder. Director will reimburse Production Company on demand for any payment made by Production Company at any time after the date hereof in respect of any liability, loss, damage, cost, or expense to which the foregoing indemnity relates.

20. REMEDIES: All remedies accorded herein or otherwise available to either Production Company or Director shall be cumulative, and no one such remedy shall be exclusive of any other. Without waiving any rights or remedies under this Agreement or otherwise, Production Company may from time to time recover, by action, any damages arising out of any breach of this Agreement by Director, and may institute and maintain subsequent actions for additional damages which may arise from the same or other breaches. The commencement or maintenance of any such action or actions by Production Company shall not constitute an election on Production Company's part to terminate this Agreement nor constitute or result in termination of Director's services hereunder unless Production Company shall expressly so elect by written notice to Director. The pursuit by either Production Company or Director of any remedy under this Agreement or otherwise shall not be deemed to waive any other or different remedy which may be available under this Agreement or otherwise, either at law or in equity.

21. INSURANCE: Production Company may secure life, health, accident, cast, or other insurance covering Director, the cost of which shall be included as a Direct Charge of the Picture. Such insurance shall be for Production Company's sole benefit and Production Company shall be the beneficiary thereof, and Director shall have no interest in the proceeds thereof. Director shall assist in procuring such insurance by submitting to required examinations and tests and by preparing, signing, and delivering such applications and other documents as may be reasonably required. Director shall, to the best of Director's ability, observe all terms and conditions of such insurance of which Production Company notifies Director as necessary for continuing such insurance in effect.

If Production Company is unable to obtain pre-production or cast insurance covering Director at prevailing standard rates and without any exclusions, restrictions, conditions, or exceptions of any kind, Director shall have the right to pay any premium in excess of the prevailing standard rate in order for Production Company to obtain such insurance. If Director fails or refuses to pay such excess premium, or if, Production Company having obtained such insurance, Director fails to observe all terms and conditions necessary to maintain such insurance in effect, Production Company shall have the right to terminate this Agreement without any obligation to Director by giving Director written notice of termination.

22. EMPLOYMENT OF OTHERS: Director agrees not to employ any person to serve in any capacity, nor contract for the purchase or renting of any article or material, nor make any agreement committing Production Company to pay any sum of money for any reason whatsoever in connection with the Picture or services to be rendered by Director hereunder or otherwise, without written approval first being had and obtained from Production Company.

23. ASSIGNMENT: This Agreement, at the election of Production Company, shall inure to the benefit of Production Company's administrators, successors, assigns, licensees, grantees, and associated, affiliated, and subsidiary companies, and Director agrees that Production Company and any subsequent assignee may freely assign this Agreement and grant its rights hereunder, in whole or in part, to any person, firm, or corporation, provided that such person, firm, or corporation assumes and agrees in writing to keep and perform all of the executory obligations of Production Company hereunder.

24. ARBITRATION: Any controversy or claim arising out of or relating to this agreement or any breach thereof shall be settled by arbitration pursuant to the Directors Guild of America 2008 Basic Agreement, Article 2.

Signed and agreed to by the undersigned as of _____ 20__.

_____

John Doe on behalf of

Big Productions Inc.

("Production Company")

_____

Henry Smith

("Director")

EXHIBIT ____

Net Profits Definition

DEALMAKING
IN THE
FILM AND
TELEVISION
INDUSTRY—
3RD EDITION

148

ACTORS

Actor employment agreements contain many provisions also found in writer and director agreements. Agreements often refer to the employer as the "Producer" and the employee as the "Player."

The actor's employment agreement will grant the producer the right to use the name and likeness of the actor in the film. The producer may also obtain the right to use the actor's name and likeness for merchandising, in which case the actor will be entitled to a percentage participation of the revenues received by the producer.

Typically, the producer will supply any costumes required for a role. However, if a contemporary story is being filmed, the producer may ask the player to provide his/her own clothing. In this case, the actor should receive a cleaning allowance.

Employment of child actors raises special concerns because minors can disaffirm contracts.[5] A producer cannot enforce a disaffirmed contract. However, California law provides that when a minor is employed as an entertainer, he/she cannot disaffirm a contract if that contract has been approved by the Superior Court beforehand. The minor or the employer must petition the Superior Court to determine if the contract is fair to the minor. State law now requires that 15% of the minor's earnings be set aside in a trust fund for him/her.

In hiring a minor, the employer must also comply with provisions of his/her state's Labor Code and regulations of its Labor Commission. For example, a California employer must obtain a work permit from the Division of Labor Standards Enforcement.[6] Minors cannot perform work that is hazardous or detrimental to their health, safety, morals, or education.[7] Working hours are limited, and minors of school age must attend three hours of schooling per day during the school year.[8] Minors under 16 years of age must have a parent or guardian present on the set.[9]

Actor employment agreements may contain a "morals" clause that requires the actor to conduct himself/herself so as not to violate public conventions or subject himself/herself to public

---

[5] See California Civil Code § 6710.
[6] California Administrative Code Title 8, §11751.
[7] California Administrative Code Title 8, §11751(b).
[8] California Education Code, §48224.
[9] California Administrative Code Title 8, §11757.

hatred, contempt, or ridicule. If the actor violates this clause, the employer has the right to terminate the agreement.

The employer may want to purchase life, accident, or health insurance covering the actor. The actor is typically required to submit to a medical examination to obtain this coverage. If the employer is unable to obtain insurance at standard rates, the employer may have the right to terminate the employment agreement. If the actor fails the medical exam or insurance coverage is denied, the employer may be required to give prompt notice to the actor.

A producer who hires an actor for a television series will want to have an option on that actor's services for five to seven years. The actor may have to refuse attractive offers that conflict with this commitment. Before an actor enters an exclusive agreement, he/she also needs to consider whether it will restrict him/her from performing in such related fields as theatrical motion pictures, the legitimate stage, and commercials.

Negotiators sometimes try to resolve issues quickly by agreeing to a "favored nations" clause. Such a provision guarantees that no other actor on the picture will obtain more advantageous terms. If another actor negotiates better terms, the terms of the deal for the actor with a favored nations clause must be upgraded to the same extent. It makes sense for a fledgling actor to accept a favored nations clause because, if an actor with more clout gets better terms, the fledgling actor will benefit.

When a novice signs a series deal, he/she has little bargaining power. The agreement will set the amount of compensation due in future years. If the series becomes a hit, the actor may become a star, and he/she may chafe under the terms of an agreement that he/she now thinks does not compensate him/her fairly. With such newfound clout, he/she might try to renegotiate the deal and achieve more favorable terms. Sometimes the star will refuse to work or become uncooperative or "sick" to pressure the employer to sweeten the deal. The employer may threaten to sue, but often a compromise is reached as neither party wants to kill the golden goose.

DEALMAKING
IN THE
FILM AND
TELEVISION
INDUSTRY—
3RD EDITION

150

ACTOR EMPLOYMENT AGREEMENT
(SAG Theatrical Release)

Continuous Employment

Weekly Basis

Weekly Salary

One Week

Minimum Employment

THIS AGREEMENT, made this _____ day of _____, 20___,
between _____, hereafter called "Producer," and
_____, hereafter called "Player."

1. PHOTOPLAY, ROLE, SALARY, AND GUARANTEE: Producer
hereby engages Player to render services as such in the role
of _____, in a photoplay, the working title of which is
now "_____," at the salary of $_____ per "studio
week." (Schedule B Players must receive an additional overtime
payment of four (4) hours at straight-time rate for each overnight
location Saturday.) Player accepts such engagement upon the
terms herein specified. Producer guarantees that it will furnish
Player not less than _____ weeks' employment (if this blank
is not filled in, the guarantee shall be one week). Player shall
be paid pro rata for each additional day beyond guarantee
until dismissal.

2. TERM: The term of employment hereunder shall begin on
or about _____ and shall continue thereafter until the
completion of the photography and recordation of said role.

3. BASIC CONTRACT: All provisions of the collective-bargaining
agreement between Screen Actors Guild, Inc., and Producer,
relating to theatrical motion pictures, which are applicable
to the employment of the Player hereunder, shall be deemed
incorporated herein.

4. PLAYER'S ADDRESS: All notices which the Producer is
required or may desire to give to the Player may be given either
by mailing the same addressed to the Player at _____,
or such notice may be given to the Player personally, either
orally or in writing.

5. PLAYER'S TELEPHONE: The Player must keep the Producer's
casting office or the assistant director of said photoplay advised
as to where the Player may be reached by telephone without
unreasonable delay. The current telephone number of the
Player is _____.

6. MOTION PICTURE RELIEF FUND: The Player does hereby authorize the Producer to deduct from the compensation hereinabove specified an amount equal to _____ percent of each installment of compensation due the Player hereunder, and to pay the amount so deducted to the Motion Picture and Television Relief Fund of America, Inc.

7. FURNISHING OF WARDROBE: The Player agrees to furnish all modern wardrobe and wearing apparel reasonably necessary for the portrayal of said role; it being agreed, however, that should so-called "character" or "period" costumes be required, the Producer shall supply the same. When Player furnishes any wardrobe, Player shall receive the cleaning allowance and reimbursement, if any, specified in the basic contract.

Number of outfits furnished by Player:

(formal) _____ @ $_____

8. ARBITRATION OF DISPUTES: Should any dispute or controversy arise between the parties hereto with reference to this contract, or the employment herein provided for, such dispute or controversy shall be settled and determined by conciliation and arbitration in accordance with the conciliation and arbitration provisions of the collective bargaining agreement between the Producer and Screen Actors Guild relating to theatrical motion pictures, and such provisions are hereby referred to and by such reference incorporated herein and made a part of this Agreement with the same effect as though the same were set forth herein in detail.

9. NEXT STARTING DATE: The starting date of Player's next engagement is: _____.

10.   The Player may not waive any provision of this contract without the written consent of the Screen Actors Guild, Inc.

11. Producer makes the material representation that either it is presently a signatory to the Screen Actors Guild collective-bargaining agreement covering the employment contracted for herein, or that the above-referred-to photoplay is covered by such collective-bargaining agreement under the Independent Production provisions of the General Provisions of the Producer-Screen Actors Guild Codified Basic Agreement of 2001 as the same may be supplemented and/or amended.

12. Producer shall have the exclusive right to make one or more promotional films of thirty (30) minutes or less and to utilize the results and proceeds of Player's services therein upon all

DEALMAKING
IN THE
FILM AND
TELEVISION
INDUSTRY—
3RD EDITION

152

of the terms and provisions set forth in the SAG Agreement. Player agrees to render such services for said promotional films during the term of his/her employment hereunder as Producer may request and Player further agrees to use by Producer of film clips and behind-the-scenes shots in which Player appears in such promotional films. Provided Player appears therein, Producer shall pay to Player the sum specified by the SAG Agreement of _____ within ten (10) days after the first use of each such promotional film on television or before a paying audience.

13. Producer shall have the exclusive right to use and to license the use of Player's name, sobriquet, photograph, likeness, voice, and/or caricature and shall have the right to simulate Player's voice, signature, and appearance by any means in and in connection with the film and the advertising, publicizing, exhibition, and/or other exploitation thereof in any manner and by any means and in connection with commercial advertising and publicity tie-ups.

14. Producer is also granted the further exclusive right and license, but only in connection with the role portrayed by Player in the film, to use and to license the use of Player's name, sobriquet, photograph, likeness, caricature, and/or signature (collectively referred to herein as "name and likeness") in connection with any merchandising and/or publishing undertakings. In consideration therefore, Producer shall pay Player a pro rata share (payable among all players whose name, etc., is used) of two-and-one-half percent (2½%) of the gross monies actually derived by Producer after deducting therefrom a distribution fee of fifty percent (50%) and a sum equal to all Producer's actual out-of-pocket expenses in connection therewith, for the use of such name or likeness on merchandising and publishing items which utilize Player's name and likeness, other than in a listing of cast credits.

15. Producer is also granted the further and exclusive right to use and to license the use of and to advertise and publicize the use of Player's voice from the soundtrack of the film on commercial phonograph records and albums and the exclusive right to use Player's name and likeness on jackets and labels of such commercial phonograph records and albums. If Producer issues or authorizes the issuance of such record or album using Player's voice, Producer shall pay to Player a sum equal to applicable AFTRA scale.

16. EMPLOYMENT ELIGIBILITY: All of Production Company's obligation herein are expressly conditioned upon Performer's completion, to Production Company's satisfaction, of the

I-9 Form (Employee Eligibility Verification Form), and upon Performer's submission to Production Company of original documents satisfactory to demonstrate to Production Company Performer's employment eligibility.

IN WITNESS WHEREOF, the parties have executed this agreement on the day and year first above written.

Producer _____

By _____

Player _____

Social Security No. _____

LOW BUDGET NON-UNION DAY PLAYER AGREEMENT

THIS AGREEMENT is made and entered into as of the _____ day of _____, 20__, by and between Big Deal Entertainment, Inc., a California corporation (hereinafter "Producer"), and _____ (hereinafter "Player").

A. Producer intends to produce a theatrical motion picture (hereinafter the "Picture") based upon that certain screenplay tentatively entitled "_____" (hereinafter the "Screenplay") which Picture is intended for initial theatrical exhibition.

B. Producer wishes to utilize the services of Player in connection with the Picture upon the terms and conditions herein contained, including the attached rider.

ACCORDINGLY, IT IS AGREED AS FOLLOWS:

1. PHOTOPLAY, ROLE, SALARY, AND GUARANTEE: Producer hereby engages Player to render services as such in the role of _____, in the screenplay, at the salary of $_____ per day. Player accepts such engagement upon the terms herein specified. Producer guarantees that it will furnish Player not less than _____ days' employment.

2. TERM: The term of employment hereunder shall begin on or about _____, 20__ (the "Start Date"), and continue until _____, 20__, or until the completion of the photography and recordation of said role.

DEALMAKING
IN THE
FILM AND
TELEVISION
INDUSTRY—
3RD EDITION

154

3. PLAYER'S ADDRESS: All notices which the Producer is required or may desire to give to the Player may be given either by mailing the same addressed to the Player at the address listed at the end of this agreement, or such notice may be given to the Player personally, either orally or in writing.

4. PLAYER'S TELEPHONE: The Player must keep the Producer's casting office or the assistant director of said photoplay advised as to where the Player may be reached by telephone without unreasonable delay. The current telephone number of the Player is listed at the end of this agreement.

5. FURNISHING OF WARDROBE: The Player agrees to furnish all modern wardrobe and wearing apparel reasonably necessary for the portrayal of said role; it being agreed, however, that should so-called "character" or "period" costumes be required, the Producer shall supply the same. When Player furnishes any wardrobe, Player shall receive a reasonable cleaning allowance and reimbursement for any soiled or damaged clothes.

Number of outfits furnished by Player:

_____ @ $_____

_____ @ $_____

6. NEXT STARTING DATE: The starting date of Player's next engagement _____.

7. NON-UNION PICTURE: Producer makes the material representation that it is not a signatory to the Screen Actors Guild collective-bargaining agreement or any other union or guild agreement. Player warrants that Player is not a member of any union or guild, memberships in which would prevent Player from working in this picture.

8. PROMOTIONAL FILM: Producer shall have the exclusive right to make one or more promotional films of thirty (30) minutes or less and to utilize the results and proceeds of Player's services therein. Player agrees to render such services for said promotional films during the term of his/her employment hereunder as Producer may request and Player further agrees to use by Producer of film clips and behind-the-scenes shots in which Player appears in such promotional films. Provided Player appears therein, Producer shall pay to Player the sum of one hundred dollars ($100) within ten (10) days after the first use of each such promotional film on television or before a paying audience.

9. NAME AND LIKENESS: Producer shall have the exclusive right to use and to license the use of Player's name, sobriquet,

photograph, likeness, voice, and/or caricature and shall have the right to simulate Player's voice, signature, and appearance by any means in and in connection with the film and the advertising, publicizing, exhibition, and/or other exploitation thereof in any manner and by any means and in connection with commercial advertising and publicity tie-ups.

10. MERCHANDISING: Producer is also granted the further exclusive right and license, but only in connection with the role portrayed by Player in the film, to use and to license the use of Player's name, sobriquet, photograph, likeness, caricature, and/or signature (collectively referred to herein as "name and likeness") in connection with any merchandising and/or publishing undertakings. In consideration therefore, Producer shall pay Player a pro rata share (payable among all players whose name, etc., is used) of two-and-one-half percent (2½%) of the gross monies actually derived by Producer after deducting therefrom a distribution fee of fifty percent (50%) thereof and a sum equal to all Producer's actual out-of-pocket expenses in connection therewith, for the use of such name or likeness on merchandising and publishing items which utilize Player's name and likeness, other than in a listing of cast credits.

11. TRAVEL EXPENSES: Any right of Player to transportation and expenses pursuant to this Agreement shall be effective when and only when Player is required by Producer to render services more than seventy-five (75) miles from Player's principal place of residence. Any weekly expense allowance provided Employee under this Agreement shall be prorated at one-seventh ($\frac{1}{7}$) thereof per day. Player shall be reimbursed at the rate of $_____ per mile for use of Player's car to travel to distant locations.

12. INCLUSIVE PAYMENTS: All payments to Player hereunder shall be deemed to be equitable and inclusive remuneration for all services rendered by Player in connection with the Picture and to be paid by way of a complete buyout of all rights granted to Producer hereunder and no further sums shall be payable to Player by Producer by reason of the exploitation of the Picture and all results and proceeds of Player's services hereunder in any and all media throughout the universe pursuant to any collective-bargaining agreement, if any, or otherwise, by way of residuals, repeat fees, pension contributions, or any other monies whatsoever.

13. ARBITRATION: Any dispute under this Agreement will be resolved by final and binding arbitration under the Independent Film & Television Alliance Rules for International Arbitration in

DEALMAKING
IN THE
FILM AND
TELEVISION
INDUSTRY—
3RD EDITION

156

effect as of the effective date of this Agreement ("IFTA Rules"). Each Party waives any right to adjudicate any dispute in any other court or forum, *except* that a Party may seek interim relief before the start of arbitration as allowed by the IFTA Rules. The arbitration will be held in the Forum designated in the Agreement, or, if none is designated, as determined by the IFTA Rules. The Parties will abide by any decision in the arbitration and any court having jurisdiction may enforce it. The Parties submit to the jurisdiction of the courts in the Forum to compel arbitration or to confirm an arbitration award. The Parties agree to accept service of process in accordance with the IFTA Rules. The prevailing party shall be entitled to reimbursement of its reasonable attorney fees and costs.

14. EMPLOYMENT ELIGIBILITY: All of Producer's obligation herein are expressly conditioned upon Performer's completion, to Producer's satisfaction, of the I-9 Form (Employee Eligibility Verification Form), and upon Performer's submission to Producer of original documents satisfactory to demonstrate to Producer Performer's employment eligibility.

IN WITNESS WHEREOF, the parties have executed this agreement on the day and year first above written.

AGREED TO AND ACCEPTED:

_____

(signature)

_____

"Player" (print name)

Player address: _____

Player Phone number: _____

Player Social Security #_____

AGREED TO AND ACCEPTED:

Big Deal Entertainment, Inc.,

By: _____

Pat Producer, its President

RIDER TO DAY-PLAYER AGREEMENT
BIG DEAL ENTERTAINMENT

1. SERVICES/TERM: Producer engages Player as an actor in the Role set forth in the Principal Agreement and shall cause Player to render all services customarily rendered by actors in feature-length motion pictures at such times and places designated by Producer and in full compliance with Producer's instructions in all matters. Without limiting the foregoing, Player's services shall be in accordance with the following:

(a) Start Date: Principal Photography of the Picture shall commence on or about _____, 20__ but no later than _____, 20__. The Start Date shall be automatically extended without notice for a period equal to the duration of any default, disability, and/or force majeure (as such terms are defined below and regardless of whether Player's services are suspended therefore), or due to any location requirements, director and/or cast availability, weather conditions, and/or other similar contingencies.

(b) Exclusivity: Player's services hereunder shall be non-exclusive first priority during the Pre-Production, exclusive during Production Periods, non-exclusive, but on a first-priority basis, during the Post-Production Period.

(c) Retakes and Other Additional Services: During and after the Term, Player shall render such services as Producer may desire in making retakes, added scenes, transparencies, close-ups, soundtrack (including dubbing and looping), process shots, trick shots, trailers, and changes for foreign versions of the Picture. Compensation for such additional services shall be payable pursuant to Paragraph 1 of the principal agreement; provided, however, that no compensation shall be payable for such additional services to the extent they are rendered during any period for which Producer is otherwise obligated to pay or has paid Player compensation, or is entitled to Player's services without compensation.

(d) Nights, Weekends, Holidays, Work Time: No increased or additional compensation shall accrue or be payable to Player for services rendered by Player at night or on weekends or holidays, or after the expiration of any number of hours of service in any period.

2. CREDIT: There shall be no obligation to accord Player credit in paid advertising and/or publicity, although Producer may from time to time elect, in its sole discretion, to accord Player such credit. Producer shall accord Player customary shared screen credit.

DEALMAKING
IN THE
FILM AND
TELEVISION
INDUSTRY—
3RD EDITION

158

3. RIGHTS: Player grants, and Producer shall have, the perpetual and universal right to photograph and re-photograph Player (still and moving) and to record and re-record, double, and dub Player's voice and performances, by any present or future methods or means and to use and authorize others to use Player's name, voice, and likeness for and in connection with the Picture, the soundtrack (including a soundtrack album), trailers, and documentary and/or "making of" pictures, and all advertising (including Player's name and likeness on sleeves, jackets, and other packaging for soundtrack albums, video cassettes, videodiscs, written publications, and the like), merchandising, commercial tie-ups, publicity, and other means of exploitation of any and all rights pertaining to the Picture and any element thereof. Producer shall own all results and proceeds of Player's services hereunder, including the copyrights thereof, and as such owner shall have the right (among all other rights of ownership): (i) to include such results and proceeds in the Picture and in advertising and publicity relating to the Picture, (ii) to reproduce such results and proceeds by any present or future means, (iii) to combine such results and proceeds with photographs and recordings made by others for use in the Picture, (iv) to exhibit and perform such results and proceeds in theaters, on the radio and television, and in or by any other present or future media, for profit and otherwise, and for commercial or noncommercial purposes and purposes of trade, and (v) to license and assign its rights to any other person or producer. Without in any way limiting the foregoing, the results and proceeds of Player's services hereunder include any and all material, words, writings, ideas, "gags," dialogue, melody, and lyrics composed, submitted, or interpolated by Player in connection with the preparation or production of the Picture (hereinafter referred to as "material"). All said material, the copyright therein, and all renewals, extensions, or reversions of copyright now or hereafter provided, shall automatically become the property of Producer, which shall be deemed the author thereof, it being agreed and acknowledged that all of the results and proceeds of Player's services hereunder are a specially ordered and commissioned "work made for hire" within the meaning of the 1976 Copyright Act for the compensation provided in the Principal Agreement. Player hereby expressly waives and relinquishes any moral rights or "droit morale" in and to any material created by or contributed to the Picture by Player including all of Player's performance.

4. FORCE MAJEURE: As used herein, the term "force majeure" means epidemic, act of God, strike, lockout, labor condition, unavailability of materials, transportation, power or other commodity, delay of common carrier, civil disturbance, riot,

war or armed conflict (whether or not there has been an official declaration of war), the enactment of any law, the issuance of any executive or judicial order or decree, breach of contract by, or disability of, the Producer, Director, other principal cast member, breach of contract by a financier or completion guarantor, or other similar occurrence beyond the control of Producer, which causes an interruption of or materially hampers or materially interferes with the production of the Picture.

5. INSURANCE: Player warrants that, to the best of Player's knowledge, Player is in good health and has no condition which would prevent Producer from obtaining life, health, accident, cast, or other insurance covering Player at premium rates normal to Player's age and sex, without any unusual exclusion or limitation of liability on the part of the insurer.

6. WITHHOLDING: Producer may deduct and withhold from any monies otherwise payable under this Agreement such amounts as Producer may reasonably believe it is legally required to deduct and withhold.

7. ASSIGNMENT: Producer shall have the right to assign this Agreement and any of the rights granted herein, in whole or in part, to any person, firm, corporation, or entity, and nothing contained herein shall imply anything to the contrary. Upon the assignee's assumption of the obligations of Producer with respect to the rights so assigned, Producer shall be relieved of all such obligations. Producer shall also have the right to lend the services of Player to any person, firm, or corporation which is a subsidiary, parent, or affiliate of Producer or the successor to Producer by a merger or by a transfer of substantially all of Producer's assets hereunder. In the event of any such lending, Player agrees to render his/her services to the best of his/her ability to the person, firm, or corporation to whom his services are loaned hereunder.

AGREED TO AND ACCEPTED:

_____

Player

DEALMAKING
IN THE
FILM AND
TELEVISION
INDUSTRY—
3RD EDITION

160

EXTRA AGREEMENT

Producer:

MOTION PICTURE:

EMPLOYEE EMPLOYMENT DATE(S): _____

ROLE: _____

EMPLOYEE NAME: _____

ADDRESS: _____

PHONE:

    Home: _____

    Work: _____

SOCIAL SECURITY # _____

RATE: $_____

OTHER TERMS: _____

TERMS AND CONDITIONS OF EMPLOYMENT

1. Payment of Wages: Wages shall be paid to all employees no later than Friday following the week in which services were performed. Pay date may be delayed by reason of an intervening federal or state holiday. Employee is responsible for submitting her/his time card at the end of the work week to insure timely payment. No employee will be paid without fully completing these forms.

2. Employee shall not be beneficiary of additional overtime, turnaround, or other hourly payments except as expressly provided in this deal memo.

3. Nights, Weekends, Holidays Work Time: Unless expressly provided elsewhere in this deal memo, no increased or additional compensation shall accrue or be payable to employee for the rendering of services at night or on weekends or holidays, or after the expiration of any particular number of hours of service in any period.

4. The Producer will provide meal breaks and/or food service at approximately six (6) hour intervals.

5. Immigration Reform and Control Act of 1986 (IRCA): Employment (or the engagement of services) hereunder is subject to employee providing the requisite documents required by IRCA and completing and signing the required Form I9 pursuant to

IRCA. Employee shall comply with the immigration verification employment eligibility provisions required by law.

6. Use of alcohol or drugs during hours of employment will result in employee's immediate termination.

7. Employee's services are on an exclusive basis to the production of the motion picture (the "Picture") referred to in this deal memo for such period of time as required unless otherwise specified in this deal memo.

8. Screen credit is at Producer's discretion subject to employee's performing all services required through completion of term.

9. Unless expressly provided elsewhere in this agreement, employee's employment hereunder shall not be for a "run of the show" or for any guaranteed period of employment. Production reserves the right to discharge employee at any time, subject only to the obligation to pay the balance of any guaranteed compensation due. Producer will attempt to notify employees a minimum of twenty-four (24) hours in advance of layoff. This agreement is subject to immediate suspension and/or termination (at Production's election) without further obligation on the part of Production in the event of any incapacity or default of employee or in the case of any suspension, postponement, or interference with the production by reason of labor controversy, strike, earthquake, act of God, governmental action, regulation, or decree or for any other customary force majeure reason.

10. The terms and conditions of this deal memo and the attached extra release are binding on Producer and employee and shall not be waived or altered by any method.

11. Producer shall be the owner of all of the results and proceeds of employee's services as a work-made-for-hire and shall have the right to use employee's name, voice, picture, and likeness in connection with the Picture, the advertising and publicizing thereof, and any promotional films or clips respecting the Picture without additional compensation therefore.

12. Any dispute under this Agreement will be resolved by final and binding arbitration under the Independent Film & Television Alliance Rules for International Arbitration in effect as of the effective date of this Agreement ("IFTA Rules"). Each Party waives any right to adjudicate any dispute in any other court or forum, *except* that a Party may seek interim relief before the start of arbitration as allowed by the IFTA Rules. The arbitration will be held in the Forum designated in the Agreement, or, if none is designated, as determined

DEALMAKING
IN THE
FILM AND
TELEVISION
INDUSTRY—
3RD EDITION

162

by the IFTA Rules. The Parties will abide by any decision in the arbitration and any court having jurisdiction may enforce it. The Parties submit to the jurisdiction of the courts in the Forum to compel arbitration or to confirm an arbitration award. The Parties agree to accept service of process in accordance with the IFTA Rules. The prevailing party shall be entitled to reimbursement of its reasonable attorney fees and costs.

EMPLOYEE ACCEPTS ALL CONDITIONS OF EMPLOYMENT AS DESCRIBED ABOVE.

AGREED TO AND ACCEPTED:

EMPLOYEE SIGNATURE: _____

DATE: _____

PRODUCER SIGNATURE: _____

DATE: _____

ATTACHMENT

EXTRA RELEASE

For ten dollars ($10) and other good and valuable consideration, receipt of which is hereby acknowledged, I grant to Big Deal Entertainment, Inc. ("Producer"), and to its licensees, assignees, and other successors-in-interest all rights of every kind and character whatsoever in perpetuity worldwide in and to my performance, appearance, name, and/or voice and the results and proceeds thereof (the "Performance") in connection with the motion picture currently entitled "_____" ("The Picture"), and I hereby authorize Producer to photograph and record (on film, tape, or otherwise) the Performance; to edit same at its discretion and to include it with the performance of others and with sound effects, special effects, and music; to incorporate same into Picture or other program or not; to use and to license others to use such recordings and photographs in any manner or media whatsoever, including without limitation unrestricted use for purposes of publicity, advertising, and sales promotion; and to use my name, likeness, voice, biographic, or other information concerning me in connection with the Picture, commercial tie-ups, merchandising, and for any other purpose. I agree that Producer owns all rights and proceeds of my services rendered in connection herewith as a work made for hire.

AGREED TO AND ACCEPTED:

_____ DATE: _____

Extra Player

PRODUCERS

Producers are not as powerful as they used to be. In the studio era, producers working for a studio could exercise a great deal of authority over stars and directors employed under long-term contracts. Today, however, producers, directors, and stars operate as independent freelancers. Studios often value their relationships with stars and directors more than their affiliation with producers. If there is a clash between a producer and director, a studio may find it less costly and disruptive to remove a producer than a director. Moreover, some stars and directors have established their own production companies and hire producers to work for them. Obviously, these producers can exercise little authority over their employers.

Producers are often referred to as "independent producers." While they may not be tied exclusively to one studio, most are hardly independent. They may rely heavily upon studios for financing and distribution of their pictures.

A producer's role varies a great deal depending on his/her skills and background, the strengths and weaknesses of his/her collaborators, and whether a film is being made for a studio or is financed independently. A producer like Steven Spielberg with substantial experience as a filmmaker is often much more involved in the creative aspects of producing than a producer with a background in finance or distribution. A veteran producer working with a novice director will play a larger role than a novice producer working with a veteran director. A producer who raises his/her own financing has more power and control over a production than a producer working on a studio film.

Films today often contain numerous producing credits. I have seen movies with a couple of "Executive Producers," several "Producers," "Co-Producers," and "Associate Producers," and an "Executive in Charge of Production" or two. Why have producer credits proliferated?

The Producers Guild[10] is not recognized as a union or a guild by the studios. They consider producers part of management and have refused to enter into a collective-bargaining agreement that would restrict the studio's ability to grant credits. Unlike the agreements reached with the DGA and WGA, which severely

---

[10] www.producersguild.org/pg/

DEALMAKING
IN THE
FILM AND
TELEVISION
INDUSTRY—
3RD EDITION

164

restrict the studio's ability to allocate credit for directors and writers, studios can assign producer credits as they please. Thus, studios can give producing credits away as perks to persons who have not earned them. A personal manager, for instance, might receive an "Executive Producer" credit for bringing a client into a project, even though the manager doesn't perform any producing function. The proliferation of producer credits has devalued their worth.

The producer function is often divided into "Executive Producer" and "Line Producer." The "Executive Producer" is the dealmaker, the financier. He/she may be producing several projects at once. He/she will often hire a "Line Producer" to work for him/her. The line producer is the person in charge of logistics for the shoot. He/she will hire crew, order supplies and equipment, and make sure that everything the director needs to make the film is available when needed. During production, a line producer will only be able to handle one project at a time.

Producer deals vary a great deal in their compensation and terms. Here is a sample line producer contract for a low-budget feature film.

LINE PRODUCER EMPLOYMENT AGREEMENT

THIS AGREEMENT is made and entered into as of the _____ day of _____, 20__, by and between _____ Entertainment, Inc., a California corporation (hereinafter "Production Company"), and _____ (hereinafter "Employee").

This Agreement is entered into with reference to the following facts:

A. Production Company intends to produce a theatrical motion picture (hereinafter the "Picture") based upon that certain screenplay tentatively entitled "_____" (hereinafter the "Screenplay"), which Picture is intended for initial theatrical exhibition.

B. Production Company wishes to utilize the services of Employee as line producer in connection with the production and delivery of the Picture upon the terms and conditions herein contained.

ACCORDINGLY, IT IS AGREED AS FOLLOWS:

1. Engagement: Subject to events of force majeure, default, or the disability or death of Employee, Production Company hereby engages the services of Employee on a "pay or play" basis, and Employee agrees to render exclusive services as line producer, in connection with the production of the Picture upon the terms and conditions herein contained. Subject to Production Company's final approval, Employee shall supervise and be responsible for the preparation of the budget and the production schedule of the Picture, the testing of persons proposed for the cast, scouting for shooting locations, assembling the crew, the supervision of the photography of the Picture, the supervision of the editing, and sound mixing, assisting in the selection of music, the supervision of the final dubbing and scoring, the supervision of all other post-production requirements of the Picture, the delivery of the final answer print and all other customary delivery items to Production Company and its principal distributors, foreign and domestic, and perform such other services as are reasonably required by Production Company and are usually and customarily performed by producers in the motion picture industry. Employee will report to such place(s) as are reasonably designated by Production Company and will be available at all times and for such periods of time as are reasonably designated by Production Company. Employee will advise Production Company of Employee's whereabouts so that Employee may be reached at any reasonable hour of the night or day. During the term of employment, Employee will render his/her services at all places and at all times reasonably required by Production Company, including nights, Saturdays, Sundays, and holidays.

In addition, Employee shall assist in the preparation and delivery to Production Company of a fully detailed and comprehensive preliminary and final below-the-line budget ("Budget") for the Picture, which Budget shall not exceed the sum of $_____, exclusive of contingency, completion-bond fee, insurance, and any "above the line costs." Employee shall also consult with and assist Production Company, as and when requested by Production Company, in connection with Production Company's negotiations for the services of the production personnel and cast for the Picture.

2. Term: Employee shall render the services required of him/her as set forth in Paragraph 1 hereof during the period commencing on _____, 20__, and continuing thereafter for such time as preproduction, principal photography, and customary post-production and delivery of the Picture as required by Production Company. It is contemplated that principal photography of the

DEALMAKING
IN THE
FILM AND
TELEVISION
INDUSTRY—
3RD EDITION

166

Picture will commence approximately on _____, 20__, and subject to extension for events beyond Production Company's control and other events of force majeure, Employee's exclusive services shall not be required beyond _____, 20__, but he/she shall nevertheless supervise the delivery of the Picture hereunder.

3. Compensation: In consideration for all of the services to be rendered by Employee hereunder and for all of the rights granted by Employee to Production Company, and on condition that Employee is not in default hereunder, and subject to the terms and conditions specified herein, Production Company agrees to pay Employee, and Employee agrees to accept $_____ dollars as a flat fee, and contingent compensation as described in subparagraph (a) below. Payment of the flat fee shall be prorated over the term of this agreement with the first payment made within ten (10) days of execution of this agreement.

(a) Contingent Compensation: If employee is entitled to a line producer credit in accordance with Paragraph 9 of this agreement, Production Company shall pay employee five percent of one-hundred percent (5% of 100%) of the "Net Profits" in accordance with Production Company's agreement with distributors of the Picture. Notwithstanding the foregoing, "Net Profits" shall be the monies remaining, if any, after all customary deductions, including, but not limited to, all production expenses, interest, overhead, debts, deferred expenses and the cost of prints, advertising, and marketing are deducted in accordance with Production Company's distribution agreement. Production Company shall only be obliged to pay Producer his/her share of "Net Profits" upon receipt of same from the distributor(s). Disbursements of contingent compensation shall be on a semiannual basis, beginning no later than six months after completion of the picture.

4. Services: At all times during the term of Employee's services hereunder, Employee will promptly and faithfully comply with all of Production Company's reasonable instructions, directions, requests, rules, and regulations. Employee will perform his/her services conscientiously and to the full limit of his talents and capabilities when wherever reasonably required or desired by Production Company and in accordance with Production Company's reasonable instructions and directions in all matters, including those involving artistic taste and judgment. Employee will perform such service as Production Company may reasonably require of him/her, and as customarily and usually rendered by and required of producers employed to produce low-budget theatrical motion pictures in the motion-picture industry.

5. Insurance: Employee agrees that Production Company may at any time or times, either in Production Company's name or otherwise, but at Production Company's expense and for, Production Company's own benefit, apply for, and take out, life, health, accident, and other insurance covering Employee whether independently or together with others in any reasonable amount which Production Company may deem necessary to protect Production Company's interests hereunder. Production Company shall own all rights in and to such insurance and in the cash values and proceeds thereof and Employee shall not have any right, title, or interest therein. Employee agrees to the customary examinations and correctly preparing, signing, and delivering such applications and other documents as may be reasonably required.

6. Control: Production Company shall have complete control of the production of the Picture including, but not limited to, all artistic controls and the right to cut, edit, add to, subtract from, arrange, rearrange, and revise the Picture in any manner. Production Company shall not be obligated to make any actual use of Employee's services or to produce or to release or to continue the distribution or release of the Picture once released.

7. Rights: In addition to Employee's services as a line producer, Production Company shall be entitled to and shall own as a work-made-for-hire all of the results and proceeds thereof throughout the world in perpetuity (including, but not limited to, all rights throughout the world of production, public performance, manufacture, television, recordation, and reproduction by any art or method, whether now known or hereafter devised, copyright, trademark, and patent), whether such results and proceeds consist of literary, dramatic, musical, motion picture, mechanical, or any other form of works, ideas, themes, compositions, creations, or products and without obligation to pay any fees, royalties, or other amounts except those expressly provided for in this Agreement. Specifically, but without in any way limiting the generality of the foregoing, Production Company shall own all rights of every kind and character in and to any and all acts, poses, plays, and appearances of any and all kinds which Employee may write, suggest, direct, or produce during the term hereof. In the event that Production Company shall desire to secure separate assignments of any of the foregoing, Employee agrees to execute them upon Production Company's request therefore. All rights granted or agreed to be granted to Production Company hereunder shall vest in Production Company immediately and shall remain vested in Production Company and Production Company's

DEALMAKING
IN THE
FILM AND
TELEVISION
INDUSTRY—
3RD EDITION

168

successors and assigns whether this Agreement expires in normal course or whether Employee's engagement hereunder is sooner terminated for any cause or reason. Production Company shall have the right to use and authorize others to use the name, voice, and likeness of Employee, and any results and proceeds of his/her services hereunder, to advertise and publicize the Picture, including, but not limited to, the right to use the same in the credits of the Picture, in trailers, in commercial tie-ups, and in all other forms and media of advertising and publicity, including merchandising, publications, records, and commercial advertising and publicity tie-ups derived from or relating to the Picture.

8. Representations, Warranties and Indemnity:

(a) Employee represents and warrants that all material of every kind authored, written, prepared, composed, and/or submitted by Employee hereunder for or to Production Company shall be wholly original with him/her, and shall not infringe or violate the right of privacy of, or constitute libel against, or violate any copyright, common-law right, or any other right of any person, firm, or corporation. The foregoing warranties shall not apply to any material not authored, written, prepared, composed, or submitted by Employee, but shall apply to all material, incidents, and characterizations which Employee may add to or incorporate in or cause to be added to or incorporated in such material. Employee further represents and warrants that Employee is free to enter into this Agreement and to render the required services hereunder and that Employee is not subject to any obligations or disability which will or might interfere with Employee's fully complying with this Agreement; that Employee has not made, and will not make, any grant or assignment which might interfere with the complete enjoyment of the rights granted to Production Company hereunder; and that Employee will not at any time render any services or do any acts which shall derogate from the value of Employee's services rendered pursuant to this Agreement or which shall interfere with the performance of any of Employee's covenants or obligations pursuant to this Agreement. Employee hereby indemnifies Production Company, its successors, assigns, licensees, officers, and employees, and hold it harmless from and against any and all liability losses, damages, and expenses (including attorneys' fees) arising out of (i) the use of any materials furnished by Employee for the Picture, or (ii) any breach by Employee of any warranty or agreement made by Employee hereunder.

(b) Production Company represents and warrants that Production Company has the right to enter into this Agreement, and to render the required obligations hereunder, and that Production Company is not subject to any other obligations or disabilities which will or might interfere with Production Company's fully complying with this Agreement; that Production Company has not made, and will not make, any grant or assignment which might interfere with the complete enjoyment of the compensation granted to Employee hereunder; that Production Company has secured all necessary financing to make all payments hereunder, and complete the Picture as budgeted; and that Production Company will not at any time render any services or do any acts which shall derogate from the value of Production Company's obligations pursuant to this Agreement, or which shall interfere with the performance of any of Production Company's covenants or obligations pursuant to this Agreement. Production Company hereby indemnifies Employee and his/her successors and assigns, and holds them harmless from and against any and all liability, losses, damages, and expenses (including reasonable attorneys' fees) arising out of any breach by Production Company of any warranty or agreement made by Production Company hereunder.

9. Credit: Provided that Employee shall fully and completely keep and perform all of his/her obligations and agreements hereunder, and if the Picture has been produced substantially with the use of Employee's services hereunder, Employee shall receive a line producing credit on the positive prints and/or tape for the Picture in the main titles thereof and in all paid advertisements in which any other producer receives a credit (subject to customary distributor exclusions). Production Company shall determine in its sole discretion the manner of presenting and the size of such credits. No casual or inadvertent failure to comply with the provisions of this paragraph or failure of any third party to comply with same shall be deemed to be a breach of this Agreement by Production Company. In the event of a failure or omission by Production Company constituting a breach of its credit obligations under this Agreement, Employee's rights shall be limited to the right, if any, to seek damages at law, and Employee shall not have any right in such event to rescind this Agreement or any of the rights granted to Production Company hereunder, or to enjoin the distribution, exhibition, or other exploitation of the Picture or the advertising or publicizing thereof. Production Company shall, however, upon receipt of written notice of any such breach of its credit obligations, cure such breach on a prospective basis on materials to be created in the future.

10. Contingencies: If Employee shall become incapacitated or prevented from fully performing his/her services hereunder

DEALMAKING
IN THE
FILM AND
TELEVISION
INDUSTRY—
3RD EDITION

170

by reason of illness, accident, or mental and physical disability, and/or if the production of the Picture is hampered or interrupted or interfered with for any event or reason beyond the control of Production Company or any other event of force majeure (hereinafter collectively referred to as "incapacity"), Production Company shall have the right to suspend Employee's services and the compensation payable to Employee during the continuance of any such incapacity. In the event any such incapacity continues for a period of seven (7) consecutive days or for an aggregate period of twenty-one (21) days, Production Company shall have the right to terminate Employee's engagement hereunder. In the event that Employee should fail, refuse, or neglect, other than because of incapacity, to perform any of his/her required services hereunder, Production Company shall have the right at any time to suspend Employee's services and the compensation payable to Employee during the continuance of such default, and Production Company shall have the right at any time to terminate Employee's engagement hereunder by reason of such default.

11. No Right to Contract: Employee acknowledges and agrees that he/she has no right or authority to and will not employ any person to serve in any capacity, nor contract for the purchase or rental of any article or material, nor make any commitment or agreement whereby Production Company shall be required to pay any monies or other consideration or which shall otherwise obligate Production Company, without Production Company's express prior written consent.

12. Travel and Expenses: If Production Company shall require Employee to render his/her services on location at any place(s) more than fifty (50) miles from his/her residence, Production Company shall furnish Employee with transportation from his residence to such place(s) and return, or reimburse employee __ cents per mile if employee uses his/her own means of transportation. Production Company shall also furnish Employee with or reimburse Employee for actual reasonable expenses for each day Production Company requires Employee to render services away from Employee's residence on a no-less-favorable basis than the expense allowance accorded the director. All transportation expenditures shall require the prior approval in writing by Production Company or its designee. Any miscellaneous expenses that Employee incurs relating to his/her employment shall be reimbursed by Production Company within seven days after receipts are submitted to Production Company.

13. Assignment: Production Company may transfer and assign

this Agreement or all or any of its rights hereunder to any person, firm, or corporation, but no such assignment or transfer shall relieve Production Company of its executory obligations hereunder. This Agreement shall inure to the benefit of Production Company's successors, licensees, and assigns. Employee shall not assign or transfer this Agreement or any of his/her rights or obligations hereunder, it being understood that the obligations and duties of Employee are personal to Employee, and any purported assignment shall be void. Employee may, however, assign his/her right to receive any monies hereunder.

14. Limitation of Remedy: All rights assigned by this Agreement shall be irrevocable under all or any circumstances and shall not be subject to reversion, rescission, termination, or injunction. Employee agrees that he/she shall not have the right to enjoin the exhibition, distribution, or exploitation of any motion picture produced hereunder or to enjoin, rescind, or terminate any rights granted to Production Company hereunder. Employee further agrees that Employee's sole remedy in the event of any default by Production Company hereunder, including the failure by Production Company to pay Employee any consideration payable to Employee pursuant hereto, or to accord Employee credit (to the extent that Production Company is obligated to accord Employee such credit) pursuant hereto, shall be an action at law for damages and/or for an accounting (if applicable). At all times, the Production Company shall have all rights and remedies which it has at law or in equity, pursuant hereto or otherwise.

15. Production Budget and Schedule: Employee represents and warrants that Employee has read the Screenplay for the Picture, and based upon Employee's substantial experience in the production of motion pictures, Employee has advised Production Company that based upon the current Screenplay, and an anticipated _____ week schedule for principal photography, the Picture can be produced for a below-the-line cost of $_____, excluding any contingencies, completion-bond fees, insurance, events of force majeure, and all "above-the-line" costs. It is the essence of this Agreement that Employee produce the Picture in accordance with the approved production schedule and for a below-the-line cost not exceeding _____ thousand dollars ($_____). Employee agrees to timely notify Production Company of any potential over-budget situations and further agrees not to proceed with any production cost overages without the prior written consent of Production Company. If, after such notification, the below-the-line cost of the Picture exceeds _____ dollars ($_____), or the

DEALMAKING
IN THE
FILM AND
TELEVISION
INDUSTRY—
3RD EDITION

172

approved production schedule through no fault of Employee, then Production Company shall be solely responsible for said cost overruns. If, however, Employee fails to give such timely notification, and/or proceeds with production cost overages without the written consent of Production Company, and as a result it reasonably appears, based upon Production Company's good-faith judgment, that the below-the-line cost of the Picture will exceed $_____, or the approved production schedule by five percent (5%), then Production Company may, in addition to any other rights or remedies which Production Company may have at law or in equity, terminate this Agreement, and any further payments or other obligations due Employee hereunder. Under no circumstances will the employee be personally liable for any cost overruns.

16. Further Documents: Employee agrees to execute any and all additional and further documents and instruments required by Production Company to further the intents and purposes of this Agreement and to vest in Production Company all right, title, and interest in and to the Picture. In the event Employee fails or refuses to execute such document or instrument, Employee hereby irrevocably appoints Production Company his/her attorney-in-fact (such appointment being coupled with an interest) to execute such documents or instruments on behalf of Employee.

17. Notices: All notices or payments which Production Company may be required to give or make to Employee hereunder may be delivered personally or sent by certified or registered mail or telegraph, or by fax to Employee at _____.

All notices that Employee may wish to give to Production Company hereunder may be delivered personally or sent by certified or registered mail or telegraph, or fax, to Production Company at _____.

The date of delivery, or attempted delivery, as the case may be, of any notice or payment hereunder shall be deemed to be the date of service of such notice or payment.

18. Section Headings: The headings of paragraphs, sections, or other subdivisions of this Agreement are for convenience in reference only. They will not be used in any way to govern, limit, modify, construe, or otherwise be given any legal effect.

19. Arbitration: Any dispute under this Agreement will be resolved by final and binding arbitration under the Independent Film & Television Alliance Rules for International Arbitration in effect as of the effective date of this Agreement ("IFTA Rules"). Each Party waives any right to adjudicate any dispute in any

other court or forum, *except* that a Party may seek interim relief before the start of arbitration as allowed by the IFTA Rules. The arbitration will be held in the Forum designated in the Agreement, or, if none is designated, as determined by the IFTA Rules. The Parties will abide by any decision in the arbitration and any court having jurisdiction may enforce it. The Parties submit to the jurisdiction of the courts in the Forum to compel arbitration or to confirm an arbitration award. The Parties agree to accept service of process in accordance with the IFTA Rules. The prevailing party shall be entitled to reimbursement of its reasonable attorney fees and costs.

20. Entire Agreement: This Agreement represents the entire understanding between the parties hereto with respect to the subject matter hereof, and this Agreement supersedes all previous representations, understandings, or agreements, oral or written, between the parties with respect to the subject matter hereof, and cannot be modified except by written instrument signed by the parties hereto. This Agreement shall be governed by and construed in accordance with the laws of the State of California, and the exclusive venue for resolution of any dispute arising out of, or in connection with, this Agreement shall be in Los Angeles, California.

AGREED TO AND ACCEPTED:

_____

"Employee"

AGREED TO AND ACCEPTED:

_____ Entertainment, Inc.

By: _____

President

Questions and Answers

1. I am in negotiation with a production company to write a script for hire, but they have deferred payment until the film is complete. What should I be aware of in making this deal?

Answer: You are working on spec. You should write the script on your own without any obligation to them, because, after all, they aren't making any commitment to you. Thus, if you choose

DEALMAKING
IN THE
FILM AND
TELEVISION
INDUSTRY—
3RD EDITION

174

to proceed, you should retain all rights to your script and be free to take it elsewhere later.

2. Is a letter of intent a binding agreement for an actor who is interested in a role?

Answer: No, the letter of intent merely states that the actor intends to do the film if various conditions are met: the rehearsal and shoot are convenient for their schedule, you reach terms on compensation, etc. It is not a binding contract and will only impress unsophisticated investors.

3. I am going to shoot a no-budget feature using my friends as actors. Two or three (out of ten or twelve) are members of SAG with no major credits. Do I need to become a SAG signatory?

Answer: If you are not a signatory to SAG, and you hire SAG actors, the actors may get in trouble with their union. Since you haven't signed with SAG, you have not violated or breached any contract with SAG. The major danger to you is having the actors run off in the middle of a shoot because a SAG representative shows up. Note that under some SAG agreements you are not required to hire SAG members as background actors.

4. If an assistant to a producer develops a project which gets licensed, does the assistant share in the profits? Does he or she get a credit?

Answer: An assistant to a producer is probably an employee, and other than whatever salary the employee is entitled to, he/she would usually not have any ownership interest in projects developed for the producer. Of course, if your agreement with the producer promises otherwise, then you need to look to those terms. As for a producer credit, that could range from anything that is merely honorary to a credit that represents what you actually did on the production. Notwithstanding all of the forgoing, if your job working for the producer does not involve developing projects, (i.e., this project was outside the scope of your employment), then you should be treated no differently from any outsider who has submitted a project to this producer.

CHAPTER 7

ADVICE FOR WRITERS, DIRECTORS, AND ACTORS

Writers, directors, and actors are often vulnerable to exploitation by producers and studios. Here are some specific suggestions and strategies for protection:

WRITERS

Most industry insiders believe that the script is the single most important element in the success of a movie. That is because the screenplay is the foundation on which everyone else's efforts rest. Mediocre direction and mundane acting may not ruin a great script. But a terrible script can't be saved with brilliant direction and exceptional performances.

Since the script is the most important element of any package, one would think that writers would be the most highly sought-after talent in Hollywood. That is not the case. Top writers are not paid anywhere near as much as leading directors or stars. Nor are writers accorded the respect and credit given directors. Writers exercise little influence and power and are often treated like second-class citizens.

DEALMAKING
IN THE
FILM AND
TELEVISION
INDUSTRY—
3RD EDITION

176

Writers lack clout because their contributions are made during development, not production. Studios own the copyright to writers' work and can change it without their permission. Few of the many scripts written are ever produced, and when a studio executive wants to produce a script, pleasing the writer is not a high priority. The executive is usually more concerned with attracting a director or star to the project. Without these elements, the movie can't get made.

When a director or star comes aboard, they often want to change the script. A power struggle may ensue with the writer's intent on protecting his/her work. Although non-writers may have little writing ability, they often think they can improve a screenplay. Scripts are not accorded the respect given other art forms.

Consider, for example, a producer who spends $100,000 to buy a Picasso painting. Can you imagine that producer looking at this masterpiece and saying to his/her spouse, "You know honey, I think the picture could use some more blue. Where are the paints? It will just take me a moment to fix this." Or would a producer spend $100,000 on a piece of sculpture, bring it home and say to his spouse: "You know the nose looks a little big. Where's the chisel?" Of course, no producer in his right mind would buy a $100,000 piece of fine art and change it. But it is not uncommon for a producer to spend $100,000 or more on a script and promptly rewrite it.

Since the writer has already provided his/her services, he/she can't withhold them as a bargaining chip. Nobody cares if the writer threatens to lock himself/herself in his/her Winnebago. Indeed, he/she usually doesn't get a Winnebago, and he/she may not even be welcome on the set.

Thus, scripts are often changed, and sometimes ruined, by those with more clout. Imagine, if you will, a top star who tells the studio executive that he will only participate in a project if his pet dog stars opposite him. When the writer hears this suggestion, he goes ballistic: "You can't turn the romantic interest into a dog. That changes the entire story!" But the star insists: "I promised Fluffy that he would be in my next movie. Either Fluffy gets the part, or I'm history."

The studio executive is faced with a dilemma. Without a star, the project doesn't get made and a lot of development expenses may have to be written off. On the other hand, the worst that happens if the writer is alienated is that he refuses to work for the executive again.

Aware of their lack of power, seasoned writers use diplomacy to protect their work. One veteran screenwriter advises novice writers not to be disagreeable with studio executives, no matter how silly their suggestions. If *Jaws* was last week's hit, the executive may suggest that you add a shark to your story. It doesn't matter that you've written a Western with no water in sight.

If you argue, you get a reputation for being obstreperous, and will be replaced with a more malleable writer. Better to take copious notes, and if the suggestions are moronic, ignore them. Often the executive will forget what he suggested at the last meeting. If he asks, simply say, "I tried the shark. It was a good idea, but it just didn't work."

HOW WRITERS ARE EXPLOITED

There are many ways that writers are exploited. The methods are only limited by the imaginations of unscrupulous producers—and in this regard writers concede that producers are a creative force to be reckoned with.

Some of the more common abuses are:

1. BAIT: Producers may hire a prestigious writer to help attract an important director or star to a project. The writer's script is later rewritten and ruined.

2. IDEA THEFT: Producers may steal a writer's story idea. As explained in Chapter 12, one cannot copyright an idea. The writer pitches his idea to the producer. He responds: "Oh, my gosh. Just this morning in the shower I had the same thought. What a coincidence. I guess brilliant minds think alike. See you around." If the writer is not represented by an attorney or an agent, and doesn't know how to protect himself/herself by contract law, he is especially vulnerable.

There are several strategies writers can employ to foil idea thieves. First, don't talk about your story until you put it in writing. Remember that old Navy saying: "Loose lips sink ships." Don't tell anyone about your brilliant idea. The listener may forget he was told it in confidence, or he may inadvertently let

DEALMAKING
IN THE
FILM AND
TELEVISION
INDUSTRY—
3RD EDITION

178

it slip out. Since ideas are as free as the air, anyone who hears it can legally use it as the basis for his own screenplay.

While ideas cannot be copyrighted, a treatment or screenplay can be. The embellishment upon the idea is what copyright law protects. Thus, the more you write out and express your story, the more protection you will obtain.

As soon as you write your story, register it with the Writers Guild, or even better, register it with the Copyright office. Registration with the WGA does not grant the writer any additional legal rights. It does, however, create some great evidence that can be used in the event of a plagiarism dispute. The outcome of such a lawsuit may turn on which party can convince the jury that they created the story first. The first writer will be presumed to be the creator of the original, while the second will be presumed to be a copier.[1]

How do you prove that you came up with the story first? You could bring your spouse into court to testify as a witness that he/she read an early version of the manuscript. Or you could mail a copy of the manuscript to yourself, registered mail, in a postmarked and sealed envelope. But spouses are not impartial witnesses, and envelopes can be steamed open and their contents changed. The best evidence is a signed declaration by a neutral third-party custodian who swears that he received your manuscript on a certain date and has kept it in seclusion ever since. This is what registration with the Writers Guild accomplishes. Registration with the copyright office also establishes a record of your claim and entitles you to statutory damages and reimbursement of attorney fees.

Another way to protect oneself from story theft is to establish an implied or oral contract between the producer and the writer. While ideas cannot be copyrighted, they have value and can be the subject of a contract. As described in Chapter 2, a writer can make a binding oral contract before disclosing his idea.

It is also advisable to put a copyright notice on your work before you publish it. Typically, scripts are not published, and under the new copyright law, notice is optional anyway. Nevertheless, copyright notice can protect you from anyone claiming that they

---

[1] If the second writer can prove that he/she independently created the same story, without copying the first writer, he/she will be entitled to the copyright to the second story just as the first writer will have the copyright to the first story. Thus both writers will own the copyright to their own work, notwithstanding their similarities. Of course, if two stories are very similar, it is highly unlikely that one writer didn't copy from the other.

innocently infringed your copyright.[2] Innocent infringers may still be liable, though for less damages than willful infringers.

Idea theft will be deterred if you are represented by an agent or entertainment attorney. A studio executive will think twice before ripping off a client of a powerful agency. Foul play may jeopardize his access to other agency clients.

I believe most idea theft occurs between fringe producers and novice writers. Sometimes the theft is inadvertent and done by lower-level staffers who don't understand the fine points of copyright law. I don't think most successful producers regularly steal ideas—it doesn't make any sense. There is little reason for Steven Spielberg to rip off a writer. The best writers are anxious to work with him and their fees comprise a small part of a production budget. Besides, Spielberg can make so much money legitimately that it would be foolish for him to steal a story. No one wants to become enmeshed in expensive and lengthy litigation, not to mention the bad publicity and harm to reputation that such a lawsuit can generate.

Writers are well advised to try to deal only with reputable producers. Find out who the sleazy operators are and avoid them. In my experience, most producers who have bad reputations have earned them.

Although writers should be careful, they shouldn't become so paralyzed with fear that they refrain from submitting their work to potential buyers. I have found that those writers who most fear story theft are novices who have the least to worry about. Many of their scripts are so bad they couldn't be given away.

3. FREE CONSULTING SERVICE: Another industry abuse involves veteran writers who are brought in to consult on a project on the pretext that they are being considered for a rewrite. Let's say you have a producer who has commissioned and received a first draft of a screenplay. He likes the script but there are certain problems. Despite the producer's and writer's efforts, they cannot fix the script. So the producer calls the agents of several veteran writers and says, "I'm thinking of hiring your client to rewrite my script. I'd like to send him a copy of the first draft and have him come in to discuss with me how he would rewrite it, if I hired him."

---

[2] See Chapter 12 for adding a proper copyright notice.

DEALMAKING
IN THE
FILM AND
TELEVISION
INDUSTRY—
3RD EDITION

180

The writers dutifully come in and offer their suggestions, but the producer doesn't hire any of them. He uses their suggestions, however, to rewrite the script. The producer has essentially used these writers as a free consulting service. Novice writers need not worry about this abuse, as producers don't value their suggestions enough to steal them.

4. SHOPPING: Shopping refers to the practice of producers pitching a story that they do not own or have an option on. Let's say you are a writer. You go in to see a producer and pitch your project. The producer says, "Interesting. Let me think about it for a few days and get back to you." After you depart, the producer calls his buddy, an executive at ABC, and pitches your story without your knowledge. If there is interest, the producer takes an option on your project. If there is no interest, he passes. He never tells you that he pitched your story behind your back to ABC and it was rejected.

You go on your merry way and pitch your story to a more ethical buyer. Let's call him producer Bob. He takes an option on your story before pitching it. When he goes in to ABC, they inform him that they already heard your story and passed on it. Producer Bob is unhappy that you did not mention this fact to him.

Shopping is a widespread practice. Producers who do not risk any money on an option tend to hastily package and pitch a project. The tendency is to throw the project up against the wall to see if it will stick. A more careful approach could produce better results. Shopping can tarnish a project. Once ABC has heard and passed on your story, it is unlikely that they will reconsider, even if the second pitch is better.[3]

A writer may choose to let a producer pitch a property without taking an option. Essentially, the writer is giving the producer a free option. The writer may feel that the project will get its best shot if an experienced producer pitches it rather than a novice writer. Perhaps the writer doesn't have the stature or contacts needed to arrange a pitch meeting himself/herself. As long as the writer gives the producer permission to pitch the project, there is no abuse.

---

[3] See Chapter 3 as to how to deter unauthorized presentation of your project by establishing an agreement that your story be kept in confidence.

The Writers Guild Minimum Basic Agreement (MBA) provides some protection for its members. For theatrical motion pictures, a writer may restrict, in writing, the extent to which a company may shop material to third parties. In television, shopping is not permitted unless the writer gives written permission. Violations are punishable by a fine of $750 for an unauthorized submission. The Guild also prohibits companies from distributing their critiques or script coverage of material it has not optioned or acquired to persons outside the company unless the writer consents.[4]

ADVICE
FOR
WRITERS,
DIRECTORS &
ACTORS

181

5. WRITING ON SPEC: Writing on speculation, which is writing on the promise that you will be paid subject to some contingency (e.g., the producer likes the script or can obtain financing), is strictly prohibited by the Writers Guild. Writers must receive the minimum fixed compensation as set forth in the Guild's schedule. Additional payments above and beyond the minimum may be predicated on a contingency (i.e., bonus, deferred, contingent, and additional compensation).

Although writers naturally resist working on only a promise of payment, clever producers may persuade them otherwise. Let's say you are called in to see a producer who has read your script. The producer gushes with praise of your work, saying he loves your characters, the first act is brilliant, and the second is even better. After raving about your creation, he tells you that he has just one reservation: "That third act just doesn't work for me." He claims that if you had written it differently, he would have bought it. Well, you can read between the lines. You run home and spend two months revising the script. You submit it to him and he turns it down again. The producer has essentially induced you to work for free.

6. STIFFING THE WRITER: Sometimes writers are not paid for their work despite their contract with a producer. Agreements typically provide that the writer receives half her fixed compensation when she begins writing and half when she turns in the completed work. Suppose she turns in the finished manuscript and the producer refuses to pay the balance due. The producer professes dissatisfaction with the script. His disappointment,

---

[4] The MBA makes an exception for those individuals with whom the company has a business relationship, such as a development deal or production deal. See 1988 MBA, article 60.

DEALMAKING
IN THE
FILM AND
TELEVISION
INDUSTRY—
3RD EDITION

182

however, is not a valid excuse because the producer bears the risk of the script not turning out well.

What remedy does the writer have? If the amount owed is $5,000 or less, the writer might be able to sue in California's small claims court. However, if the amount owed is more than $5,000, but not enough to justify hiring a lawyer to litigate, the writer is caught in a bind.[5]

If the writer is a member of the Writers Guild, and the producer a signatory, the Guild will attempt to secure payment for the writer. Ultimately, the Guild can threaten to put the production company on the Unfair or Strike Lists.[6] This means that all WGA members are prohibited from working for the production company. This would appear to be a crushing blow to any production entity.

But what if the producer dissolves his company, incorporates a new legal entity, and signs another agreement with the WGA? Then he goes his merry way, exploiting a new crop of writers. The WGA is now trying to crack down on unethical producers who attempt this ruse. The Guild keeps a cross-reference of producer names and companies. Producers who dissolve and re-incorporate must satisfy all prior obligations to WGA members before a new agreement is signed.

7. UNNECESSARY REWRITES: Writers' scripts may be rewritten for extraneous reasons. Not all rewrites are bad; some may improve the work. But often the maxim "Too many cooks spoil the broth" reflects what can happen when a script is rewritten too many times. Such scripts may lose their distinctive point of view and become homogenized, limp stories.

Rewrites cannot only ruin the writer's work but can have significant impact on compensation. As discussed in Chapter 6, the amount of a writer's bonus and contingent compensation may be tied to whether he/she receives sole or shared screenplay credit.

---

[5] This is when it is great to have an arbitration clause in your agreement. See Chapter 17, Remedies, for more information on binding arbitration.
[6] The Unfair List is for producers whom the Guild has determined are unreliable as to payment or are financially insolvent. The Strike List is comprised of producers who refuse to bargain or sign the basic agreement after hiring a WGA member.

CASES

ADVICE
FOR
WRITERS,
DIRECTORS &
ACTORS

183

Rossner v. CBS, Inc.[7]

FACTS: Rossner (P) wrote a novel entitled *Looking for Mr. Goodbar* about a young woman who was picked up in a singles' bar and murdered. The novel was loosely based on a true story that was widely reported in the press.

Rossner's novel became a bestseller. She sold the movie rights to Paramount, which produced a movie titled *Looking for Mr. Goodbar*. Rossner first conceived of the term "Goodbar" to identify a fictional character in her book.

After Rossner's novel was published, but before Paramount's movie was released, a newspaper reporter who covered the murder wrote several magazine articles titled "Finding Mr. Goodbar" and "Finding the Real Mr. Goodbar." The journalist subsequently wrote a book, *Closing Time: The True Story of the "Goodbar" Murder*. The publications were widely disseminated. While Rossner was aware of these publications and the use of the word "Goodbar" in their titles, she didn't bring any legal action.

As a result of the publicity surrounding the murder, and the various publications and movie, the public began to associate the word "Goodbar" with the murder and with the singles' scene or a dangerous pickup.

CBS subsequently made a television movie entitled *Trackdown: Finding the Goodbar Killer* based on the true story of the murder investigation. Rossner objected to the use of the term "Goodbar" in the title, claiming that viewers were likely to believe CBS's movie was based upon Rossner's work. CBS claimed the term "Goodbar Killer" was in the public domain.

ISSUE: Can CBS use the term "Goodbar" in the title of their movie without Rossner's permission?

HOLDING: Yes, although the court directed that CBS must broadcast a disclaimer in the credits informing viewers that the CBS movie is not based on Rossner's novel.

RATIONALE: Rossner claimed the term "Goodbar" had become associated in the public mind with her work. Having thus acquired a "secondary meaning," it became her trademark, and CBS's use of the term was unfair competition. The court said that while the term was associated

---

[7] 612 F. Supp. 334 (1985).

DEALMAKING
IN THE
FILM AND
TELEVISION
INDUSTRY—
3RD EDITION

184

with Rossner when her novel was first published, the strength of her trademark was diminished by the later use of the mark by others.

In other words, Rossner's failure to police the mark, and prevent others from using it, caused the mark to lose its association with her. It lost its secondary meaning. The court did require, however, that a disclaimer be included in the broadcast to prevent any viewer confusion about the origin of the television movie.

Rogers v. Grimaldi[8]

FACTS: Federico Fellini conceived, co-wrote, and directed a film entitled *Federico Fellini's Ginger & Fred*. The movie was a fictional work about two retired dancers. The dancers used to make a living in Italian cabarets imitating Fred Astaire and Ginger Rogers, thus earning the nickname "Ginger and Fred." The story was a satire about the world of television. According to Fellini, the characters did not resemble or portray Fred Astaire and Ginger Rogers. Ginger Rogers (P) brought suit, claiming that Fellini violated her rights of privacy and publicity.

ISSUE: Have Rogers' rights been violated?

HOLDING: No.

RATIONALE: Fellini's movie is a work protected by the First Amendment. The work is protected expression rather than a use for a purely commercial purpose.

Sometimes a person's right to protect their privacy and personality come into conflict with another's rights under the First Amendment. The courts draw a distinction between "commercial speech," which entails the use of someone's name or likeness on a product or in an advertisement, from artistic expression, which is protected by the First Amendment. In this case, the court determined that Fellini's rights under the First Amendment outweighed any infringement of Rogers' rights.

---

[8] 875 F.2d 994 (1989).

ADVICE
FOR
WRITERS,
DIRECTORS &
ACTORS

185

REGISTERING A SCRIPT WITH THE WGA[9]

WHAT CAN BE REGISTERED: LITERARY PROPERTIES WRITTEN FOR MOTION PICTURES AND TELEVISION AS CONCEPTS, TREATMENTS, AND SCRIPTS.

WHAT CANNOT BE REGISTERED: BOOK MANUSCRIPTS OR STAGEPLAYS.

PROCEDURE: THROUGH THE MAIL, IN PERSON, OR ONLINE.

MAIL:
SUBMIT ONE 8½ x 11-INCH UNBOUND COPY, A COVER SHEET LISTING THE TITLE OF THE MATERIAL, ALL WRITERS' FULL LEGAL NAMES; AND THE SOCIAL SECURITY NUMBER, RETURN ADDRESS, AND PHONE NUMBER OF AT LEAST ONE WRITER, AND A CHECK FOR $20.00 (NON-MEMBERS), $15.00 (STUDENTS), OR $10.00 (MEMBERS).

DURATION OF REGISTRATION: FIVE YEARS, BUT IT IS RENEWABLE.

MAILING ADDRESS: WGAW REGISTRY, 7000 W. 3RD ST., LOS ANGELES, CA 90048. PHONE: (323) 782-4500.

PRE-RECORDED INFORMATION TAPE: L.A. (323) 782-4500; NEW YORK: (212) 757-4360.

IN PERSON:
COMPLETE THE STEPS FOR MAILING ABOVE AND DELIVER IN-PERSON TO THE MAILING ADDRESS ABOVE (7000 W. 3RD ST. IN LOS ANGELES). REGISTRATION HOURS ARE FROM 9:30AM TO 5:30PM MONDAY THROUGH FRIDAY; HOWEVER, A 24-HOUR DROP BOX EXISTS FOR AFTER-HOURS DELIVERY IN THE MAIN LOBBY OF THE WGA.

ONLINE:
VISIT WWW.WGAWREGISTRY.ORG/WEBRSS/REGINSTRUCT.HTML AND FOLLOW THE DIRECTIONS PROVIDED, THEN CLICK THROUGH TO THE ACTUAL REGISTRATION FORM. THE ONLINE FORM ESSEN-TIALLY REQUIRES THE SAME INFORMATION REQUIRED FOR MAILING ABOVE; HOWEVER, THE REGISTRATION IS DONE VIA THE INTER-NET, PROCESSED, AND REGISTERED IMMEDIATELY.[10]

---

[9] Note that registration with the Copyright Office also provides legal evidence of the Owner's claim and is usually preferable to WGA registration. Timely registration of one's copyright may entitle the owner to statutory damages and reimbursement of legal fees, which is not a benefit of WGA registration.
[10] Go to www.wga.org/subpage_register.aspx?id=1189 for a list of answers to frequently asked questions.

DEALMAKING
IN THE
FILM AND
TELEVISION
INDUSTRY—
3RD EDITION

186

ADMISSION REQUIREMENTS TO THE WRITERS GUILD

YOU NEED **24** CREDITS FOR ADMISSION, ACCUMULATED WITHIN THE PRECEDING THREE YEARS.

CREDITS ARE ALLOCATED AS FOLLOWS:

2 UNITS: FOR EACH WEEK OF EMPLOYMENT ON A WEEK-TO-WEEK OR TERM BASIS.

3 UNITS: FOR A STORY FOR A RADIO OR TELEVISION PROGRAM LESS THAN 30 MINUTES (PRORATED IN INCREMENTS OF 10 MINUTES OR LESS).

4 UNITS: FOR A STORY FOR A THEATRICAL SHORT OF ANY LENGTH; OR RADIO OR TELEVISION PROGRAM OR BREAKDOWN FOR A NON-PRIME-TIME SERIAL 30 TO 60 MINUTES.

6 UNITS: FOR A "CREATED BY" CREDIT; OR A TELEPLAY OR RADIO PLAY LESS THAN 30 MINUTES (PRORATED IN 5 MINUTE INCREMENTS); OR A TELEVISION FORMAT FOR A NEW SERIAL OR SERIES.

8 UNITS: FOR A STORY FOR A RADIO PLAY OR TV PROGRAM OR BREAKDOWN FOR A NON-PRIME-TIME SERIAL MORE THAN 60 MINUTES AND LESS THAN 90 MINUTES; OR SCREENPLAY FOR A SHORT-SUBJECT THEATRICAL MOTION PICTURE OR FOR A RADIO PLAY OR TELEPLAY 30 MINUTES THROUGH 60 MINUTES.

12 UNITS: FOR A STORY FOR A RADIO OR TELEVISION PROGRAM 90 MINUTES OR LONGER; OR STORY FOR A FEATURE-LENGTH THEATRICAL MOTION PICTURE; OR BREAKDOWN FOR A NON-PRIME-TIME SERIAL 90 MINUTES OR LONGER; OR FOR A RADIO PLAY OR TELEPLAY MORE THAN 60 MINUTES AND LESS THAN 90 MINUTES.

24 UNITS: FOR A SCREENPLAY FOR A FEATURE-LENGTH THEATRICAL MOTION PICTURE; RADIO PLAY OR TELEPLAY 90 MINUTES OR LONGER; OR BIBLE FOR ANY TELEVISION SERIAL OR PRIME-TIME MINI-SERIES OF AT LEAST 4 HOURS; OR LONG-TERM STORY PROJECTION WHICH IS DEFINED FOR THIS PURPOSE AS A BIBLE, FOR A SPECIFIED TERM, ON AN EXISTING, 5-TIMES-PER-WEEK, NON-PRIME-TIME SERIAL.

REWRITE: ½ THE NUMBER OF UNITS ALLOTTED TO THE APPLICABLE CATEGORY OF WORK.

POLISH: ¼ THE NUMBER OF UNITS ALLOTTED TO THE APPLICABLE CATEGORY OF WORK.

INITIATION FEE: $2,500.

CALL THE WRITERS GUILD AT (323) 782-4500 FOR ADDITIONAL INFORMATION.

RIGHTS OF WRITERS GUILD MEMBERS

ADVICE
FOR
WRITERS,
DIRECTORS &
ACTORS

187

The Writers Guild agreement, also known as the Minimum Basic Agreement (MBA),[11] sets the minimum terms for options and purchases of material from professional writers and the minimum terms for the employment of writers for feature films and television programs. The agreement is more than 400 pages long, and its terms are incorporated by reference in every WGA writer's contract.

The MBA only binds signatory companies. Smaller production companies and some producers may not be signatories to the agreement. Guild members are prohibited from writing for non-signatory companies, and are encouraged to contact the Guild to ensure that any production company seeking to hire them is a signatory. Furthermore, members cannot work for less than minimum-scale compensation and can never write on spec, which is an agreement between a writer and a producer whereby the writer's payment is contingent upon acceptance or approval of the work product. All agreements between writers and producers must be in writing, and a writer may not work without a contract.

Although the MBA sets forth the minimum terms that producers must grant Guild writers, the Guild encourages writers to negotiate more favorable terms. Such agreements are known as "overscale" deals.

SUMMARY OF WGA BASIC AGREEMENT

Coverage

The WGA Basic Agreement applies to both writer-employment agreements and acquisition of literary material from "professional" writers that is unpublished and unexploited. A professional writer is one who has a theatrical motion picture or television credit or has had at least 13 weeks of prior employment, or has a credit for a produced play or published novel.

A signatory company must pay guild minimums to non-professional writers and non-guild members if employing them. The

---

[11] The Writer's Guild also has a public television agreement that covers certain public television stations and producers for a three-year period, beginning November 13, 2005.

DEALMAKING
IN THE
FILM AND
TELEVISION
INDUSTRY—
3RD EDITION

188

minimums do not apply, however, if the company merely buys a literary property unless a writer is a "professional" writer and the material has not been previously exploited. In other words, the MBA does not cover contracts for purchase of literary properties that have been published or exploited in any medium, or contracts to buy literary material from nonprofessional writers.

As of the 2008 MBA, new media (such as Internet or cellular technology) is now included under the agreement.

The WGA has a number of publications relating to guild rules that are available at no charge. Call the Guild at (323) 951-4000, or toll free (800) 548-4532, or check the WGA website, www.wga.org.

Compensation

Unless the writer defaults or fails to deliver the work, minimum compensation is guaranteed. Producers cannot withhold payment because they do not like the material, can't secure financing, or any other condition. Overscale payments may be tied to conditions.

For literary purchases, the minimum payments are the same as for a flat deal. The MBA provides that in no event may the week-to-week or term writer receive less for the material than he would have received had he worked on a freelance basis at minimum compensation.

Writers are entitled to other payments. The producer must furnish first-class transportation, board, and accommodations if the writer works on location. A signatory must contribute 6% of gross compensation to the Pension plan and 8.5%[12] to the Health Fund. Producers have to make payments on amounts paid to purchase literary material if in conjunction with employment, but not on residuals, certain additional compensation, supplemental payments, and compensation in excess of $225,000 for a single feature film.

For writers who work through a loan-out company, the production company is responsible for these contributions.

---

[12] However, the rate is 8% from 10/01/08 to 3/31/09.

Credits

ADVICE
FOR
WRITERS,
DIRECTORS &
ACTORS

189

Upon completion of principal photography, the producer must file with the Guild a "Notice of Tentative Writing Credits" and send a copy to each writer. If any writer protests, the guild arbitrates.

Credit must be given in a form authorized by the MBA. The agreement requires credit be given in most publicity and advertising when credit is given a producer or director.

Sometimes a writer may choose to use a pseudonym. For a feature, a writer who receives compensation of $200,000 or less has the right to use a pseudonym. In television, a writer may use pseudonyms if paid less than three times the minimum.[13]

Revisions

Generally, when a producer hires a writer to write a story for television, the company has the right to request one revision. The request must be made within 14 days of the first submission. When a producer pays for a teleplay, the producer gets two sets of revisions if requested in the allocated time.

The writer of an original screenplay or teleplay who grants an option to a producer has the right to do the first rewrite during the option period. After acquisition, the producer usually must offer the writer the first rewrite.[14]

Residuals

Residuals are payments for reruns, foreign telecasts, and certain other uses, such as when theatrical movies are exhibited on television or home video media. For example, when there is a foreign theatrical exhibition of a television movie, additional compensation is due the writer. If there is a domestic theatrical exhibition, additional compensation of 150% of the applicable television minimum or the minimum scale for a feature, whichever is greater, is payable.

---

[13] The writer must promptly request a pseudonym, however. For features the request must be made within five business days after the credits are final. (Credits become final after expiration of the deadline for protesting tentative credits that the company specifies in the "Notice of Tentative Writing Credits" sent to each writer at the end of principal photography or at the conclusion of credit arbitration.)

[14] See MBA, Article 16.A.3.c and 16.B.3.h.

DEALMAKING
IN THE
FILM AND
TELEVISION
INDUSTRY—
3RD EDITION

190

The company and writer may agree by contract that any portion of the compensation paid to the writer beyond twice the applicable initial minimum may be applied against amounts due for theatrical exhibition.

As of May 2, 2001, the credited writer(s) of a theatrical motion picture receive a one-time $5,000 payment as a DVD script publication fee, regardless of whether the producer actually publishes the script on DVD.

The WGA, as well as SAG and the DGA, have collective-bargaining agreements that require independent producers to have their distributors sign assumption agreements when the producers secure distribution. The assumption agreement provides that the distributor will assume the obligation to pay residuals directly to the unions. The unions want the distributor to agree to assume the residual obligation, because some producers have failed to pay the unions the residuals due their members. Since the unions are not a party to the distribution agreement, they cannot directly enforce the residual obligation against distributors. Some distributors simply refuse to sign assumption agreements. However, the unions convinced Congress to enact as part of the Digital Millennium Copyright Act of 1998 (DMCA)[15] a provision that imposes on distributors the obligation to make these residual payments. Therefore, if distribution rights to a film are transferred, the assignment is deemed to include the obligation to make residual the payments.[16]

---

[15] Public Pub. L. No. 105-304, 112 Stat. 2860 (Oct. 28, 1998)

[16] The actual language states:

§4001. Assumption of contractual obligations related to transfers of rights in motion pictures.

(a) Assumption of Obligations. (1) In the case of a transfer of copyright ownership under United States law in a motion picture (as the terms "transfer of copyright ownership" and "motion picture" are defined in section 101 of title 17) that is produced subject to 1 or more collective-bargaining agreements negotiated under the laws of the United States, if the transfer is executed on or after the effective date of this chapter and is not limited to public performance rights, the transfer instrument shall be deemed to incorporate the assumption agreements applicable to the copyright ownership being transferred that are required by the applicable collective-bargaining agreement, and the transferee shall be subject to the obligations under each such assumption agreement to make residual payments and provide related notices, accruing after the effective date of the transfer and applicable to the exploitation of the rights transferred, and any remedies under each such assumption agreement for breach of those obligations, as those obligations and remedies are set forth in the applicable collective bargaining agreement, if

(A) the transferee knows or has reason to know at the time of the transfer that such collective-bargaining agreement was or will be applicable to the motion picture; or

(B) in the event of a court order confirming an arbitration award against the transferor under the collective-bargaining agreement, the transferor does not have the financial ability to satisfy the award within 90 days after the order is issued.

Separation of Rights

ADVICE
FOR
WRITERS,
DIRECTORS &
ACTORS

191

An unusual aspect of the MBA is that signatory companies are required to grant WGA members certain rights although the writer, as an employee for hire, doesn't own the copyright to the material. These rights are granted to a credited writer who originates material as follows:

FEATURES

Publication rights: The writer has a license that he cannot exercise until six months after the general release of the picture or three years from the date of the employment agreement or purchase of the material, whichever is earlier. The producer retains a limited right of publication for publicity purposes.

Dramatic rights: If a producer fails to exploit these rights within two years after general release, these rights revert to the writer. In any event, the writer is entitled to royalty payments if a stage show is produced.

Sequel payments: The writer doesn't have sequel rights but a right to payment upon production of a sequel. For a feature sequel, a writer receives 25% of initial fixed compensation. If the sequel is a television series or program, the writer receives (subject to offsets) the sequel payments provided in the MBA.

TELEVISION

Writers entitled to separation of rights retain all rights other than television film and television sequel rights. The production company owns exclusive film television rights for 30 months from delivery of the material if the material is not in active development, or four years from delivery if the material is in active development, or four years if the material is more than 60 minutes and is not topical. After that, the company and the writer own these rights non-exclusively.

Sequel rights: Company has the exclusive right for a limited time. Then rights revert to the writer if they are not exercised.

DEALMAKING
IN THE
FILM AND
TELEVISION
INDUSTRY—
3RD EDITION

192

The rights reserved to the writer include legitimate stage rights, theatrical motion picture rights, publication rights, merchandising rights, radio rights, live television rights, and interactive rights. Some of these rights are subject to holdback periods, during which the writer cannot exploit them.

Two-Meeting Rule

In no event may there be a third meeting between the writer and a company regarding an assignment unless a firm commitment has been made or is made in the third interview.

If in the first interview the writer proposes a story, then a second meeting at the request of the company entitles the writer to a story commitment at minimum compensation.

Warranties and Indemnification

The company must indemnify the writer against claims or actions respecting material assigned to the writer, and the writer must be named an additional insured on the Errors & Omissions policy.

ADVICE
FOR
WRITERS,
DIRECTORS &
ACTORS

193

TERMS & DEFINITIONS

TREATMENT: The adaptation of a story or literary material as a basis for a screenplay.

ORIGINAL TREATMENT: An original story written as the basis for a screenplay.

SCREENPLAY: Final script with scenes, dialogue, and camera setups. Scripts written for television are called "teleplays."

FIRST DRAFT SCREENPLAY: First complete draft of any script in continuity form, including full dialogue.

REWRITE: Significant changes in plot, storyline, or interrelationship of characters in a screenplay.

POLISH: Changes in dialogue, narration, or action, but not including a rewrite.

FORMAT: The framework within which the central running characters will operate and be repeated in each episode, including detailed characters, and the setting, theme, premise, or general storyline of the proposed series.

BIBLE: Format for a mini-series but more detailed.

MERCHANDISING RIGHTS (THEATRICAL): Under the MBA, the right to sell objects described in literary material provided such objects are fully described and are unique and original. For features, a writer has no merchandising rights but is entitled to 5% of absolute gross of monies remitted by the manufacturer. This applies even to writers not entitled to Separation of Rights.

DRAMATIC RIGHTS: Essentially "play" rights.

SEQUEL: New film with the same characters as first film but in a new plot.

WGA LOW-BUDGET AGREEMENT: costs less than $1.2 million.

WGA BASIC AGREEMENT—LOW-BUDGET FEATURE: costs $1.2-$5 million.

WGA BASIC AGREEMENT—HIGH-BUDGET FEATURE: costs $5 million or more.

PILOT SCRIPT: Story and/or teleplay for a proposed episodic series.

BACK-UP SCRIPT: Story and/or teleplay for a proposed episodic series other than a pilot script.

SINGLE UNIT: A television program intended for broadcast as a single show and not a part of a series.

UNIT SERIES: A series of programs with a complete story without characters in common but held together by the same title (i.e., anthology) or trade name or mark.

EPISODIC SERIES: A series of programs each with a separate complete story but characters in common.

ASSIGNED MATERIAL: Story material given the writer. In other words, the writer didn't create the work from scratch; the producer gave him/her assigned material (e.g., characters, story outline) from which to work.

FLAT DEALS: Opposite of week-to-week or term employment. The writer is hired to write a certain type of work (e.g., treatment or screenplay), and compensation is tied to the type of work, length of program, and whether it is high-budget or low-budget. Producers must pay the writer in installments according to Guild standards.

DEALMAKING
IN THE
FILM AND
TELEVISION
INDUSTRY—
3RD EDITION

194

COLLABORATING WITH OTHERS

Writing can be a lonely profession. The writer has to sequester himself/herself for long periods and possess the self-discipline to work unsupervised. Some writers find it helpful to collaborate with others.

I think it is very difficult to find a good writing partner. Personalities must mesh, and both parties need to be willing to put their egos aside and do what is best for the project. Moreover, for a collaboration to last, each party must bring something valuable to the partnership that the other lacks.

Many writers embark upon a collaborative endeavor with high hopes, only to discover later that the partnership is not working. Not only has time been wasted, but difficult questions may arise as to ownership of the work that has been created. Antagonism between the parties may make it difficult to resolve outstanding issues. If ownership of the embryonic story is unclear, neither party may safely use it. Thus, writers are well advised to enter a collaboration agreement beforehand.

The collaboration agreement is useful because it forces the parties to deal with important issues before a lot of time and effort have been invested in the venture. If the relationship is not going to work, it is best to know at the outset.

Here is a sample agreement for writers collaborating on a book project.

COLLABORATION AGREEMENT

This Agreement between _____ (Writer A), residing at _____, City of _____, State of _____ (herein called Writer A), and _____ (Writer B), residing at _____, City of _____, State of _____ (herein called Writer B).

WITNESSETH

The parties desire to collaborate in the writing of a book on the terms hereinafter set forth.

NOW THEREFORE, in consideration of the promises, and of the mutual undertakings herein contained, and for other good and valuable considerations, the parties agree as follows:

ADVICE
FOR
WRITERS,
DIRECTORS &
ACTORS

195

1. The parties hereby undertake to collaborate in the writing of a certain nonfiction book (herein called the "Book"), dealing with _____, and provisionally entitled "_____."

2. They have agreed on a tentative outline, a copy of which is annexed. In the outline, the name of Writer A has been placed opposite the titles of certain proposed chapters; and the name of Writer B has been placed opposite the titles of certain other chapters. It is the intention of the parties that the first draft of each chapter shall be prepared by the party whose name it bears, and shall be submitted to the other party for comments and suggestions. The final drafts shall be worked out by the parties together.

3. The parties contemplate that they will complete the manuscript of the Book by _____, 20__. If they fail to do so, they may by mutual agreement extend the time for completion. In the absence of any such extension, they shall endeavor to fix by negotiation their respective rights in the material theretofore gathered and written, and in the project itself (i.e., whether one or the other of them shall have the right to complete the Book alone or in collaboration with someone else, and on what terms). Their understanding as to these matters shall thereupon be embodied in a settlement agreement. If they are unable to agree, their respective rights and the terms pertaining thereto shall be fixed by arbitration. In either event, this agreement shall cease when the rights of the parties have been fixed as aforesaid; and thereafter they shall have only such rights and obligations as will be set forth in the settlement agreement or the arbitration award, as the case may be.

4. If the manuscript of the Book is completed, the parties shall endeavor to secure a publisher. Each shall have the right to negotiate for this purpose, but they shall keep each other fully informed with reference thereto. No agreement for the publication of the Book or for the disposition of any of the subsidiary rights therein shall be valid without the signature of both parties. However, either party may grant a written power of attorney to the other, setting forth the specific conditions under which the power may be exercised. For services rendered under such power of attorney, no agency fee or extra compensation shall be paid to the attorney-in-fact.

5. The copyright in the Book shall be recorded in the names of both parties, and shall be held jointly by them.

6. The parties shall receive equal authorship credit on the same line and in type of equal size, except that the name of Writer A shall precede that of Writer B.

DEALMAKING
IN THE
FILM AND
TELEVISION
INDUSTRY—
3RD EDITION

196

7. All receipts and returns from the publication of the Book and from the disposition of any subsidiary rights therein shall be divided equally between the parties. All agreements for publication and for the sale of subsidiary rights shall provide that each party's one-half (½) share shall be paid directly to him/her.

8. If the parties by mutual agreement select an agent to handle the publication rights in the Book or the disposition of the subsidiary rights therein, and if the agent is authorized to make collection for the parties' account, such agent shall remit each party's one-half (½) share directly to him/her.

9. After the completion of the manuscript of the Book, no change or alteration shall be made therein by either party without the other's consent. However, such consent shall not be unreasonably withheld. No written consent to make a particular revision shall be deemed authority for a general revision.

10. If either party (herein called the First Party) desires to transfer his one-half (½) share in the Book or in the subsidiary rights thereof to a third person, he shall give written notice by registered mail to the other party (herein called the Second Party) of his intention to do so.

(a) In such case the Second Party shall have an option for a period of _____ days to purchase the First Party's share at a price and upon such terms indicated in the written notice.

(b) If the Second Party fails to exercise his option in writing within the aforesaid period of ____ days, or if, having exercised it, he fails to complete the purchase upon the terms stated in the notice, the First Party may transfer his rights to the third person at the price and upon the identical terms stated in the notice; and he shall forthwith send to the Second Party a copy of the contract of sale of such rights, with a statement that the transfer has been made.

(c) If the First Party fails for any reason to make such transfer to the third person, and if he desires to make a subsequent transfer to someone else, the Second Party's option shall apply to such proposed subsequent transfer.

11. All expenses which may reasonably be incurred in connection with the Book shall be subject to mutual agreement in advance, and shall be shared equally by the parties.

12. Nothing herein contained shall be construed to create a general partnership between the parties. Their relation shall be one of collaboration on a single work.

13. If the Book is published, this agreement shall continue for the life of the copyright therein. Otherwise, the duration hereof shall be governed by the provisions of Clause 3.

14. If either party dies before the completion of the manuscript, the survivor shall have the right to complete the same, to make changes in the text previously prepared, to negotiate and contract for publication and for the disposition of any of the subsidiary rights, and generally to act with regard thereto as though he were the sole author, except that (a) the name of the decedent shall always appear as coauthor; and (b) the survivor shall cause the decedent's one-half (½) share of the proceeds to be paid to his estate, and shall furnish to the estate true copies of all contracts made by the survivor pertaining to the Book.

15. If either party dies after the completion of the manuscript, the survivor shall have the right to negotiate and contract for publication (if not theretofore published) and for the disposition of any of the subsidiary rights, to make revisions in any subsequent editions, and generally to act with regard thereto as if he were the sole author, subject only to the conditions set forth in subdivisions (a) and (b) of Clause 14.

16. Any dispute under this Agreement will be resolved by final and binding arbitration under the Independent Film & Television Alliance Rules for International Arbitration in effect as of the effective date of this Agreement ("IFTA Rules"). Each Party waives any right to adjudicate any dispute in any other court or forum, *except* that a Party may seek interim relief before the start of arbitration as allowed by the IFTA Rules. The arbitration will be held in the Forum designated in the Agreement, or, if none is designated, as determined by the IFTA Rules. The Parties will abide by any decision in the arbitration and any court having jurisdiction may enforce it. The Parties submit to the jurisdiction of the courts in the Forum to compel arbitration or to confirm an arbitration award. The Parties agree to accept service of process in accordance with the IFTA Rules. The prevailing party shall be entitled to reimbursement of its reasonable attorney fees and costs.

17. This agreement shall inure to the benefit of, and shall be binding upon, the executors, administrators, and assigns of the parties.

18. This agreement constitutes the entire understanding of the parties.

IN WITNESS WHEREOF, the parties hereunto set their respective hand and seal this _____ day of _____, 20__.

_____
Writer A

_____
Writer B

ADVICE
FOR
WRITERS,
DIRECTORS &
ACTORS

197

DEALMAKING
IN THE
FILM AND
TELEVISION
INDUSTRY—
3RD EDITION

198

DIRECTORS

Before directing a motion picture, a director usually must persuade investors and/or studio executives to let him/her direct. For the first-timer, this is a difficult task, for there is scant reason to hire an inexperienced director when so many veterans are available. First-time directorial candidates can exert leverage by threatening to withhold some other valuable commodity. For example, a star may refuse to accept a role unless he is also permitted to direct the film. A writer may refuse to sell a script unless she can direct it.

Once in the director's chair, the novice must have expertise in four areas to succeed. First, she must understand the basic principles of good storytelling. The director need not be a writer, but she better be able to distinguish good writing from bad. A director who chooses material poorly will never shine. A poorly told story will not involve an audience no matter how impressive the camera work or performances.

Second, the director must have a good visual sense. She must understand the basics of cutting, editing, and cinematography. Pictures with crowd scenes, stunts, and special effects require special expertise.

Third, the director must be able to manage a large endeavor. She must be well-organized, decisive, and able to communicate well with her collaborators. The cast and the crew look to her for guidance, and if she is indecisive or unable to express her vision, the moviemaking machinery will grind to a halt.

Fourth, the director must understand the art of acting. The director need not be an actor, but she must know how to talk to actors in their language. Actors need to understand the story and their character's motivation. Speaking to them about the size of the camera lens does not impart useful information.

Many directors believe that achieving a good performance is largely a function of casting the right person for the role. The best directors create a supportive atmosphere on the set that encourages the actors to take chances in an effort to give their best possible performance.

Directors share writers' concerns about liability for story theft and obscenity. Directors are also concerned that they not be penalized if the production goes over budget through no fault of their own. Directors' contracts may contain an Eat-In Clause, which provides that if a production goes over budget, the director's fees and profit participation may be eaten into (reduced). On the other hand, directors can ask that their contract provide that they share in any savings obtained if the production comes in under budget.

To gain admission to the Directors Guild, directors need to direct a feature for a signatory company.

ADVICE
FOR
WRITERS,
DIRECTORS &
ACTORS

199

RIGHTS OF DIRECTORS GUILD MEMBERS[17]

The Directors Guild Basic Agreement of 2008 guarantees DGA directors certain creative rights. The agreement acknowledges that the director contributes to all creative elements in the making of a motion picture. With few exceptions, a producer may assign only one director to a film at a time.

CREATIVE DECISIONS

As soon as the director is hired, she is entitled to participate in all decisions concerning the selection of cast and other creative personnel. The director needs to be consulted on any creative decisions regarding preparation, production, and post-production, and the director's advice and suggestions need to be considered in good faith. No director may be discriminated against or be subjected to retaliation because she asserts her creative rights.

DISCLOSURE

Before a director is assigned to a film, the producer must give her:
1) a list of creative personnel already employed,
2) a description of any existing film footage contemplated to be used,
3) a report of any rights of script or cast approval held by someone other than the employer or individual producer,
4) a copy of the motion picture's budget top sheet,
5) the story and script, if any, and
6) an explanation of all other creative commitments.

---

[17] A more detailed summary of Director's Creative Rights is available from the DGA and on the DGA website at www.dga.org/dga_members/ag_crh.php3

DEALMAKING
IN THE
FILM AND
TELEVISION
INDUSTRY—
3RD EDITION

200

DEAL MEMO

Deal memos must designate the person with final-cutting author-ity over the motion picture. Also, the intended post-production locale must be mentioned.

HIRING CREW

The employer must consult with the director about the selec-tion of the Unit Production Manager for any theatrical motion picture and selection of the Second Unit Director. A director has the right to select the First Assistant Director on any theatrical motion picture and any non-series television motion picture that is 90 minutes or longer.

CASTING SESSIONS

Casting sessions are open only to persons who have a reason-able purpose for being there and are invited by the director, individual producer, or employer.

FACILITIES

The director must be provided a private office at the studio. The office must be large enough for two people, have a door that shuts, and possess a telephone, desk, chair, and good lighting. Employers must use their best efforts to provide reasonable parking at no cost to the director.

STUNTS

The employer may not increase the difficulty of stunts or add a stunt to the script, unless the director consents.

DAILIES

The director must be permitted to see the dailies at a reasonable time. Before departing for a distant location, the director has the right to request interlocking sound and picture projection facilities for viewing of dailies on location. The studio must ship these dailies to the location within 24 hours of synchronization.

POST-PRODUCTION

A studio cannot replace a director who directs 100% of the scheduled principal photography except if the director has engaged in gross willful misconduct. A director must be given the opportunity to direct additional photography and retakes. If a director directs 90% to 99% of scheduled principal photography, the director is entitled to all post-production creative rights, provided that the director was not primarily responsible for the motion picture going over budget.

These creative rights include the right to be present at all times and to be consulted throughout the entire post-production period. The director must have a reasonable opportunity to discuss the last version of the film before negative cutting or dubbing, whichever is first.

DIRECTOR'S CUT

The director supervises the editing of the first cut following completion of the editor's assembly. The director has the right to instruct the editor and to make whatever changes the director deems necessary in preparing his cut. No one may interfere with the editing during the period of the director's cut. Directors have the following time to complete their cut:

Theatrical Motion Picture: Ten weeks, or one day of editing for every two days of scheduled photography, whichever is longer. For low-budget films, six weeks or one day of editing for every two days of scheduled photography, whichever is longer.

Television Motion Picture

a) Thirty minutes or less: within one day plus time, which is not to exceed one more day, to make changes if necessary.

b) Thirty to sixty minutes: four days

DEALMAKING
IN THE
FILM AND
TELEVISION
INDUSTRY—
3RD EDITION

202

c) Sixty to ninety minutes: fifteen days

d) Ninety minutes to two hours: twenty days

e) Each additional hour: five days

PROTECTION AGAINST FALSE STORY-THEFT CLAIMS

Writers, directors, and actors need to protect themselves from idea thieves. They also need to protect themselves from people who may falsely accuse them of theft. Generally, one is free to borrow ideas, concepts, themes, and historical facts from others without paying compensation because these items are not copyrightable. However, if you agree to compensate another for such material, you may be liable under contract law.

What if someone sends you unsolicited material? Are you obligated to compensate the sender? The following case illustrates the issue:

CASE

Yadkoe v. Fields (1944)[18]

FACTS: In 1938, Yadkoe (P) wrote W.C. Fields (D) a letter in which he provided Fields with material for use as an entertainer. Fields replied by letter, accepting the material and inviting Yadkoe to submit additional material without compensation. Fields stated that if he were able to use the material, he "might" enter into a contract with Yadkoe. Yadkoe sent additional material to Fields, including scenes and dialogue for the movie *You Can't Cheat an Honest Man*. Fields used these materials but didn't compensate Yadkoe. A jury awarded Yadkoe judgment for $8,000 for breach of contract. Fields appealed.

ISSUE: Is an obligation incurred by the unsolicited submissions of ideas?

HOLDING: No. But once such ideas are solicited, this may give rise to an implied contract. Judgment affirmed.

To avoid liability to persons who submit unsolicited ideas, studios use release forms. Writers, directors, and actors can use

[18] 66 Cal. App. 2d 150, 141 P.2d 906 (1944).

the same form to protect themselves when accepting material from others. While this form does not protect the writer/director/actor if he intentionally steals another's work, it will make it more difficult for someone to successfully pursue a frivolous claim.

ADVICE
FOR
WRITERS,
DIRECTORS &
ACTORS

203

SUBMISSION RELEASE

Dan Director
1219 LaVine Ave.
Hollywood, CA 90088

Dear Mr. Director:

I am submitting the enclosed material ("said material") to you:

_____, an original screenplay. WGA REGISTRATION NO. _____. Copyright Registration No. _____.

The material is submitted on the following conditions:

1. I acknowledge that because of your position in the entertainment industry you receive numerous unsolicited submissions of ideas, formats, stories, suggestions, and the like and that many such submissions received by you are similar to or identical to those developed by you or your employees or otherwise available to you. I agree that I will not be entitled to any compensation because of the use by you of any such similar or identical material.

2. I further understand that you would refuse to accept and evaluate said material in the absence of my acceptance of each and all of the provisions of this agreement. I shall retain all rights to submit this or similar material to persons other than you. I acknowledge that no fiduciary or confidential relationship now exists between you and me, and I further acknowledge that no such relationships are established between you and me by reason of this agreement or by reason of my submission to you of said material.

3. I request that you read and evaluate said material with a view to deciding whether you will undertake to acquire it.

4. I represent and warrant that I am the author of said material, having acquired said material as the employer-for-hire of all

DEALMAKING
IN THE
FILM AND
TELEVISION
INDUSTRY—
3RD EDITION

204

writers thereof; that I am the present and sole owner of all right, title, and interest in and to said material; that I have the exclusive, unconditional right and authority to submit and/or convey said material to you upon the terms and conditions set forth herein; that no third party is entitled to any payment or other consideration as a condition of the exploitation of said material.

5. I agree to indemnify you from and against any and all claims, expenses, losses, or liabilities (including, without limitation, reasonable attorneys' fees and punitive damages) that may be asserted against you or incurred by you at any time in connection with said material, or any use thereof, including without limitation those arising from any breach of the warranties and promises given by me herein.

6. You may use without any obligation or payment to me any of said material which is not protectable as literary property under the laws of plagiarism, or which a third person would be free to use if the material had not been submitted to him/her or had not been the subject of any agreement with him/her, or which is in the public domain. Any of said material which, in accordance with the preceding sentence, you are entitled to use without obligation to me is hereinafter referred to as "unprotected material." If all or any part of said material does not fall in the category of unprotected material, it is hereinafter referred to as "protected material."

7. You agree that if you use or cause to be used any protected material, provided it has not been obtained from, or independently created by, another source, you will pay or cause to be paid to me an amount that is comparable to the compensation customarily paid for similar material.

8. I agree to give you written notice by registered mail of any claim arising in connection with said material or arising in connection with this agreement, within 60 calendar days after I acquire knowledge of such claim, or of your breach or failure to perform the provisions of this agreement, or if it be sooner, within 60 calendar days after I acquire knowledge of facts sufficient to put me on notice of any such claim, or breach or failure to perform; my failure to so give you written notice will be deemed an irrevocable waiver of any rights I might otherwise have with respect to such claim, breach, or failure to perform. You shall have 60 calendar days after receipt of said notice to attempt to cure any alleged breach or failure to perform prior to the time that I may file a Demand for Arbitration.

9. Any dispute under this Agreement will be resolved by final and binding arbitration under the Independent Film &

Television Alliance Rules for International Arbitration in effect as of the effective date of this Agreement ("IFTA Rules"). Each Party waives any right to adjudicate any dispute in any other court or forum, *except* that a Party may seek interim relief before the start of arbitration as allowed by the IFTA Rules. The arbitration will be held in the Forum designated in the Agreement, or, if none is designated, as determined by the IFTA Rules. The Parties will abide by any decision in the arbitration and any court having jurisdiction may enforce it. The Parties submit to the jurisdiction of the courts in the Forum to compel arbitration or to confirm an arbitration award. The Parties agree to accept service of process in accordance with the IFTA Rules. The prevailing party shall be entitled to reimbursement of its reasonable attorney fees and costs.

10. I have retained at least one copy of said material, and I release you from any and all liability for loss or other damage to the copies of said material submitted to you hereunder.

11. Either party to this agreement may assign or license its or their rights hereunder, but such assignment or license shall not relieve such party of its or their obligations hereunder. This agreement shall inure to the benefit of the parties hereto and their heirs, successors, representatives, assigns, and licensees, and any such heir, successor, representative, assign, or licensee shall be deemed a third-party beneficiary under this agreement.

12. I hereby acknowledge and agree that there are no prior or contemporaneous oral agreements in effect between you and me pertaining to said material, or pertaining to any material (including, but not limited to, agreements pertaining to the submission by me of any ideas, formats, plots, characters, or the like). I further agree that no other obligations exist or shall exist or be deemed to exist unless and until a formal written agreement has been prepared and entered into by both you and me, and then your and my rights and obligations shall be only such as are expressed in said formal written agreement.

13. I understand that whenever the word "you" or "your" is used above, it refers to (1) you, (2) any company affiliated with you by way of common-stock ownership or otherwise, (3) your subsidiaries, (4) subsidiaries of such affiliated companies, (5) any firm, person, or corporation to whom you are leasing production facilities, (6) clients of any subsidiary or affiliated company of yours, and (7) the officers, agents, servants, employees, stockholders, clients, successors, and assigns of you, and of all such persons, corporations referred to in (1) through (6) hereof. If said material is submitted by more than

DEALMAKING
IN THE
FILM AND
TELEVISION
INDUSTRY—
3RD EDITION

206

one person, the word "I" shall be deemed changed to "we," and this agreement will be binding jointly and severally upon all the persons so submitting said material.

14. Should any provision or part of any provision be void or unenforceable, such provision or part thereof shall be deemed omitted, and this agreement with such provision or part thereof omitted shall remain in full force and effect.

15. This agreement shall be governed by the laws of the state of California applicable to agreements executed and to be fully performed therein.

16. I have read and I understand this agreement, and no oral representations of any kind have been made to me and this agreement states our entire understanding with reference to the subject matter hereof. Any modification or waiver of any of the provisions of this agreement must be in writing and signed by both of us.

Sincerely,

_____

Signature

_____

Wally Writer

_____

Address

_____

Telephone Number

ACCEPTED AND AGREED TO:

_____

By Dan Director

STATE OF   )

) ss.:

COUNTY OF   )

On the ____ day of _____, 20__, before me personally came _____ to me known and known to be the individual described in and who executed the foregoing instrument, and he did duly acknowledge to me that he executed the same.

_____

Notary Public

OBSCENITY

ADVICE
FOR
WRITERS,
DIRECTORS &
ACTORS

207

The First Amendment does not protect obscene works. The difficulty that creators, judges, and everyone else confronts is understanding what is obscene. It is difficult, perhaps impossible, to articulate a useful definition. Here is the three-part test as set forth in Miller v. California:[19]

1) Whether the average person, applying contemporary community standards, would find that the work, taken as a whole, appeals to prurient interest;

2) Whether the work depicts or describes, in a patently offensive way, sexual conduct specifically defined by the applicable state law; and

3) Whether the work, taken as a whole, lacks serious literary, artistic, political, or scientific value.

ACTORS

In the creative community, actors have the worst lot. It is often said that they are always waiting to be invited to the party. They cannot perform their craft unless a director casts them in a role. They have little control over their careers.

Novices pursuing an acting career must be prepared for a long and difficult struggle with no assurance of success. Gaining admission to the Screen Actors Guild (SAG) is important because even "non-union" low-budget producers often hire SAG actors or become signatories to the SAG agreement.

ADMISSION TO SAG

A performer is eligible to join SAG under either of the following conditions:

1) Proof of SAG Employment. This can be either as:

a) Principal Performer: upon proof of employment or prospective employment in a principal role in a film, videotape, television program, or commercial for a SAG signatory company.

b) Extra Player: upon proof of employment as a SAG-

---

[19] 413 U.S. 15, 93 S. Ct. 2607, 37 L.Ed.2d 419 (1973).

DEALMAKING
IN THE
FILM AND
TELEVISION
INDUSTRY—
3RD EDITION

208

covered background player at full SAG rates and conditions for a minimum of three work days after March 25, 1990. Employment must be with a signatory company to the SAG Background Players Agreement.

2) Employment by a sister union. You must have been a paid-up member of an affiliated performer's union (AFTRA, AEA, AGVA, or AGMA) for at least one year and worked at least once as a principal performer in that union's jurisdiction.

INITIATION FEE: Currently $2,277 plus semi-annual dues of $58.

ACTOR CAREER CHECKLIST

1. PROJECT ENERGY AND SELF-CONFIDENCE AT INTERVIEWS AND AUDITIONS. BE PERSONABLE AND FRIENDLY. DON'T OVERSTAY YOUR WELCOME. LEARN TO HANDLE REJECTION.

2. PREPARE YOURSELF FOR THE LONG HAUL. STORIES OF OVERNIGHT SUCCESS ARE MYTHS. GET A NIGHT JOB OR EMPLOYMENT THAT PERMITS YOU TO TAKE OFF TIME FOR AUDITIONS. BE PREPARED TO INVEST FIVE TO TEN YEARS BEFORE YOU EXPECT TO EARN A LIVING FROM ACTING. EVEN THEN, THERE ARE NO GUARANTEES.

3. OBTAIN AN ANSWERING MACHINE OR MESSAGE SERVICE TO TAKE MESSAGES. YOU BETTER KNOW WHEN YOUR LUCKY BREAK ARRIVES.

4. GET A GOOD HEAD SHOT AND POSSIBLY A COMPOSITE SHOT. THE PHOTO SHOULD BE BLACK AND WHITE, PORTRAY YOUR APPEARANCE ACCURATELY, AND HAVE YOUR NAME AND PHONE NUMBER ON IT.

5. PREPARE A NEAT AND PROFESSIONAL-LOOKING RÉSUMÉ LISTING YOUR CREDITS, THE GUILDS YOU BELONG TO, YOUR TRAINING, AND ANY SPECIAL ABILITIES OR SKILLS YOU HAVE (E.G., HORSEBACK RIDING, PIANO). LIMIT IT TO ONE PAGE, DON'T LIE, AND DON'T CLUTTER UP THE RÉSUMÉ WITH IRRELEVANT WORK OR EDUCATIONAL BACKGROUND. LIST YOUR AGENT'S NUMBER IF YOU HAVE ONE. STAPLE RÉSUMÉ, BACK TO BACK, TO YOUR PHOTOS. ALWAYS HAVE SOME OF THESE HANDY WHEN YOU GO TO AN AUDITION OR AN INDUSTRY FUNCTION. KEEP SOME EXTRAS IN YOUR CAR.

6. BUILD UP YOUR CREDENTIALS: PERFORM IN SHOWCASE PLAYS [(EQUITY WAIVER (L.A.), OFF-OFF BROADWAY (NEW YORK)] OR NON-EQUITY PLAYS IF YOU ARE NOT A MEMBER OF EQUITY. IN SMALLER CITIES PERFORM IN COMMUNITY AND LITTLE THEATER, OR IF YOU ARE A STUDENT, PARTICIPATE IN UNIVERSITY PRODUCTIONS.

7. WHEN YOU OBTAIN A PART, INVITE AGENTS TO SEE YOU PERFORM. MOST THEATERS WILL ALLOW THEM TO ATTEND FREE. LET AGENTS KNOW YOU ARE SEEKING REPRESENTATION. HAVE PHOTOS AND RÉSUMÉS ON HAND IN YOUR DRESSING ROOM. INVITE PRODUCERS AND OTHER INDUSTRY FOLK YOU KNOW TO ATTEND YOUR PERFORMANCES.

8. CONSIDER WORKING IN NON-UNION PRODUCTIONS. READ ALL CONTRACTS CAREFULLY AND RECOGNIZE THAT YOU RISK EXPLOITATION. BUT IF YOU CAN OBTAIN A GOOD REVIEW OF YOUR PERFORMANCE, IT MAY BE WORTH THE RISK.

9. PREPARE A VIDEOTAPE COMPILATION OF YOUR WORK. IF YOU HAVE APPEARED ON TELEVISION OR IN FILMS, OBTAIN CLIPS OF YOUR PERFORMANCES AND PUT TOGETHER A PROFESSIONAL-LOOKING VIDEOTAPE THAT YOU CAN SUBMIT TO AGENTS AND CASTING DIRECTORS. HOMEMADE TAPES AND STAGED SCENES USUALLY DON'T IMPRESS AGENTS. NEVER SEND OUT YOUR ORIGINAL.

10. Join the appropriate guild(s):

Screen Actors Guild (SAG): feature films, filmed TV shows, filmed commercials, and industrial films.

American Federation of Television and Radio Artists (AFTRA): live and taped TV shows, taped commercials and industrials, radio and phonograph records.

Actor's Equity Association (Equity or AEA): performers and stage managers in play productions.

American Guild of Variety Artists (AGVA): live performers such as night club performers.

American Guild of Musical Artists (AGMA): opera singers, classical dancers, and choral singers.

Anyone can join AFTRA. The Union only requires an applicant to pay the initiation fee and dues.

Under the Taft-Hartley law[20] you can work up to 30 days on your first job on a union show before joining the union. In right-to-work states, unions cannot force you to join.

11. Get a reputable agent. Seek out those who are franchised by the guild that covers the area you want to work in. Franchised agents have to abide by guild rules. Agents get paid on a contingent basis (10% in California). Any agent asking for an upfront fee is probably in the business of exploiting actors, not finding work for them. Lists of franchised agents are available from national and local guilds.[21]

Agents often do not ask newcomers to sign a written contract until they secure work for them. Actors may prefer not to have a written agreement because, if the agent cannot find work for them, the actor may not want to be encumbered with a contract.

12. Personal Mangers: In California and other states, personal managers are not franchised or regulated. They often charge 15%, which is in addition to the fee you pay your agent. They are not legally allowed to solicit work for clients, although that is often what they do. Beginners generally do not need someone to tour with them or manage their careers, and mangers generally do not want to work for beginners.

Do not confuse business managers with personal managers. A business manager typically has an accounting background and helps you manage money and make investment decisions.

13. Do not wait for your agent to obtain work for you. Pursue whatever leads and opportunities you can on your own. Keep your agent informed of any auditions or interviews you have set up and any parts you get. Let the agent negotiate the deal even if you get the gig.

14. Get listed in the *Academy Player's Directory* (if you live in L.A.) or the *Player's Guide* (for those in New York) or the head sheet put out by agents in local communities. For the first two publications, a modest fee will enable you to have your name, photo, and agent's name listed in those directories. Many casting directors refer to these publications. For information on the *Player's Directory* contact The Academy of Motion Picture Arts and Sciences, 8949 Wilshire Blvd., Beverly Hills, CA 90211, (310) 247-3000. For information on the *Player's Guide* call (310) 247-3058 or visit www.playersdirectory.com.

15. Be careful about making commitments. Actress Kim Basinger was sued by producer Carl Mazzocone for breaching her promise to appear in the film *Boxing Helena*. The jury awarded Mazzocone $8.92 million in damages plus reimbursement of attorney's fees.

---

[20] 29 U.S.C. § 158(a)(3).
[21] Note that when this book went to press the franchise agreement with agents had expired.

DEALMAKING
IN THE
FILM AND
TELEVISION
INDUSTRY—
3RD EDITION

210

NOTABLE SAG RULES[22]

Once an actor joins SAG, she is subject to the Guild's rules and regulations. SAG members cannot work for non-signatory companies. In the past, actors could be represented only by agents who were franchised by SAG, which meant that the agents had signed an agreement with SAG that provided additional protections for SAG actors in their dealings with their agents. However, SAG does not currently have an agreement with The Association of Talent Agents or the National Association of Talent Representatives. So there are non-SAG franchised talent agents that represent actors. However, agents still must be licensed by the state if the state regulates agents. Actors cannot enroll in SAG under a name or professionally use a name that so closely resembles that of an existing member as to cause confusion. Members are required to carry their Guild card when working and not to turn possession of it over to any other person.

RIGHTS OF SAG MEMBERS[23]

Minimum Wages

SAG contracts cover film, television, and commercial producers. The current film and TV scale is more than $759 a day ($504 for low-budget pictures). Additional payment is required for location work, holidays, travel time, overtime, stunts, and wardrobe. Residual payments are required of producers who re-use film, television programs, and commercials. SAG also offers special terms with reduced compensation under its Short Film Agreement, Ultra-Low Budget Agreement, and Modified Low-Budget Agreement.

Working Conditions

For most productions, the SAG contract requires first-class air travel, flight insurance, private dressing rooms, meal breaks,

---

[22] When this 3rd edition of *Dealmaking* went to press, a new collective-bargaining agreement had not been reached.

[23] A more detailed description of SAG benefits is listed in the brochure *Basic Benefits, Acting in Your Interest*, available from SAG.

good meals, and rest time between calls. The contract also sets minimum safety and first-aid standards, provides for the education of minors, requires arbitration of disputes and grievances, and mandates affirmative action in auditions and hiring.

Pension and Health Plans

A major SAG benefit is participation in the Pension and Health Plans. Performers who meet the minimum earnings criteria are automatically enrolled for one year in the Health Plan, which may include coverage for spouses and dependent children. Dental benefits and life insurance are also available.[24]

These benefits are paid by employers when they contribute 14.8% of a performer's base salary to the Pension and Health fund.

Global Rule One

SAG has always required its members to perform in the United States under a guild contract; however, in recent years, more movies have been produced outside of the United States, causing members to lose access to benefits, residual payments, and in some cases, safety requirements. This movement of shooting American films overseas prompted SAG to expand its reach globally in 2002 by enacting Global Rule One. Since then SAG prohibits any member of

GUILDS

LOS ANGELES

SAG – 5757 WILSHIRE BLVD., 7TH FLOOR, LOS ANGELES, CA 90036, (323) 954-1600, WWW.SAG.ORG

AFTRA – 5757 WILSHIRE BLVD., 9TH FLOOR, LOS ANGELES, CA 90036, (323) 634-8100, WWW.AFTRA.ORG

AEA – 5757 WILSHIRE BLVD., SUITE 1, LOS ANGELES, CA 90036, (323) 964-1750, WWW.ACTORSEQUITY.ORG

AGVA – 4741 LAUREL CANYON BLVD., SUITE 208, NORTH HOLLYWOOD, CA 91607, (818) 508-9984

NEW YORK

SAG – 360 MADISON AVE., 12TH FLOOR, NEW YORK, NY 10017, (212) 944-1030, WWW.SAG.ORG

AFTRA – 260 MADISON AVE., NEW YORK, NY 10016, (212) 532-0800, WWW.AFTRA.ORG

AEA – 165 W. 46TH STREET, NEW YORK, NY 10036, (212) 869-8530, WWW.ACTORSEQUITY.ORG

AGVA – 363 7TH AVE., 17TH FLOOR, NEW YORK, NY 10001, (212) 675-1003

AGMA – 1430 BROADWAY, 14TH FLOOR, NEW YORK, NY 10018, (212) 265-3687, WWW.MUSICALARTISTS.ORG

---

[24] Information on pension and health plans are at www.sagph.org/html/bthw7.htm.

DEALMAKING
IN THE
FILM AND
TELEVISION
INDUSTRY—
3RD EDITION

212

SAG from performing anywhere without a SAG union contract in place.

This rule applies to all SAG theatrical, television, commercial, and industrial contracts. If a SAG member violates Global Rule One, he or she can be required to appear before a Trial Board (conducted by other SAG members), which has the power to discipline, impose fines, suspend, or expel union members from SAG.

AFTRA

AFTRA represents actors and other professional performers, as well as broadcasters, in television, radio, sound recordings, non-broadcast/industrial programming, and new technologies such as CD-ROMs. As with the other guilds, members generally are allowed to work only for employers who are signatories with AFTRA. Agents representing AFTRA members are required to be franchised by AFTRA (i.e., they have entered into a contract with AFTRA that protects the rights of AFTRA members). Unlike other guilds, AFTRA does not have stringent membership requirements. Any person who has performed or intends to perform in a medium covered by AFTRA is eligible for membership.

Membership

To become a member of AFTRA, one must complete an application and pay a one-time initiation fee of $1,300 plus dues for the current dues period. [25]

Minimum Wages

AFTRA contracts cover television, commercials, and radio productions, and the minimum scale varies depending on the production. Network primetime dramas and other types of productions are on par with SAG at $759 per day, but the numbers do vary depending on the project.

---

[25] Contact local office or National Membership Department at (866) 855-5191 or email membership@aftra.com.

Health and Retirement Benefits

ADVICE
FOR
WRITERS,
DIRECTORS &
ACTORS

213

AFTRA provides comprehensive medical and hospital benefits, a dental plan, prescription drug program, and mental health and substance-abuse programs. AFTRA also has a Retirement Fund, which allows employer contributions to be made on behalf of members. The fund is portable, allowing members working anywhere under an AFTRA contract to receive their contributions.

Questions and Answers

1. Does a director have the right to final cut on her picture?

Answer: The involvement and rights of director in post-production will depend on the terms of director's employment agreement, and the terms of the DGA Basic Agreement if it applies. The DGA Basic Agreement requires that a director be allowed to be present throughout the post-production period but does not give the director final cut. Most directors don't have final cut. If a producer or studio agrees to give you final cut, make sure the right is spelled out in your contract. A production company that is a DGA signatory does have to give the director the right to prepare his/her Director's Cut.[26]

2. Who owns the copyright to a writer's script?

Answer: If the writer creates a work on his own, he will own all rights to it. If the writer is an employee of a producer, usually the producer will own all rights to the writer's work product. Copyright to a script is property and can be assigned or transferred to others. It is advisable to register a script with the copyright office and record any assignment of rights.

---

[26] The creative rights of directors are explained at greater length in the DGA Creative Rights Handbook, available at www.dga.org/index2.php3?chg=

CHAPTER 8

MUSIC

This chapter does not cover many legal issues that concern composers and musicians as they pursue their careers.[1] The discussion is limited to the licensing of music for film and television soundtracks.[2]

SOUNDTRACKS

When it comes time to place music on a soundtrack, the producer has a choice: She can either obtain the right to use existing music (e.g., a popular song) or commission an original musical score (i.e., hire a composer to create something new for the movie). Of course, a producer could buy songs for part of the soundtrack and hire a composer for the remainder.

Buying Existing Music

Music is a work of authorship protected under copyright law. Determining ownership in music can be complex since several persons may share the copyright. For example, the composer

---

[1] A good reference source for those who seek this information is *The Musician's Business & Legal Guide*, edited and compiled by Mark Halloran, which can be obtained from the Beverly Hills Bar Association.

[2] Music rights can be exceedingly complex. The author recommends that an experienced music attorney be retained by persons not familiar with the issues presented.

DEALMAKING
IN THE
FILM AND
TELEVISION
INDUSTRY—
3RD EDITION

216

may own the copyright to the composition, the lyricist may own the copyright to the lyrics, the musicians may own the copyright to their performances, and the record label may own the copyright to the recording. So a film producer must determine which parties have ownership interests in each song and then license the appropriate rights.

Low-budget independent producers often run out of money by the time they reach post-production. One way to economize is by using songs by unknown songwriters that are available for little or no money. Fledgling songwriters often want to gain visibility and stature by having their music in a movie. The producer should keep in mind that a song performed in a movie that is broadcast can generate significant royalties for the songwriter (through ASCAP or BMI). Thus, songwriters have a financial incentive to have their music on a soundtrack, even if they receive no direct compensation from the producer. A Television Music Rights License is reprinted at the end of this chapter. This is a synchronization license for non-dramatic use only. It does not include any right to use a recording. For that right, the producer will need a Master Recording License.

Another way for a producer to reduce music acquisition costs is to use music that is in the public domain. One must make sure that all rights are in the public domain. Let's say a low-budget filmmaker decides to put Beethoven's Fifth Symphony on his soundtrack. He goes to the record store and buys the Boston Symphony Pops recording of Beethoven's Fifth. While the composition is in the public domain, this particular recording may not be. The filmmaker is free to use Beethoven's composition, but he will have to find a recording in the public domain or hire musicians and make his own recording.

To produce a new recording, a producer will have to strike a deal with a recording studio, musicians, and/or vocalists. AFofM, AFTRA, and SAG collective-bargaining agreements will apply to films made by Guild signatories. A star artist may receive $20,000 or more as a fee, as well as royalties based on the retail price of the soundtrack album. If the artist is exclusive to a record label, its permission will be needed.

If the producer wants to put recorded pre-existing music that is not in the public domain on the soundtrack, a MASTER USE LICENSE will be needed from the record company that owns the recording.[3] Fees range from several hundred dollars for use of a short excerpt to tens of thousands of dollars for the work of a superstar. The artist may have approval rights over licensing his/her music to another, in which case the artist's permission must also be obtained. Re-use payments to musicians and performers will be required if the recording was made by union members. A master use license is not necessary if the filmmaker creates his/her own original recording rather than incorporating another's recording.

Commissioning an Original Score

The producer must take care in hiring a composer/lyricist or songwriter. The agreement between the parties may determine whether the artist is an employee or an independent contractor, which may affect who the author is for copyright purposes. There can be joint ownership of a musical score (a participation agreement). Permission may also need to be obtained from a record company if you use an artist under contract.

The producer will usually want the work to be considered one that is "made-for-hire" so that he/she automatically owns the copyright. The composer will be entitled to a fee for his/her work and royalties from non-movie uses of his/her music.[4] A top songwriter may demand to share the copyright under a co-publishing agreement. The expenses of recording the soundtrack are borne by the producer.

For low-budget movies, a composer may wear several hats.[5] He/she may write, arrange, orchestrate, conduct, and perform the music. A composer may even agree to produce and deliver a

---

[3] A producer who has obtained synchronization and performance licenses from the artist's publisher could make its own sound-alike recording if the artist's record label refuses to grant a license to use its recording. That is, the producer could create his own recording that sounds exactly like the original as long as it was not copied from the original. See *Soundtrack Music* by Lionel S. Sobel, Chapter 184A, and *Entertainment Industry Contracts*, Volume 4, Mathew Bender.

[4] Composer's royalties from soundtrack albums are typically 50% of the mechanical license fees paid the studio by the record company that releases the album. Also, the composer will receive 50% of the public performance fees collected by the agencies ASCAP or BMI, which are paid directly to the composer by his agency. Additionally, the composer will receive a royalty from the sale of sheet music and in some circumstances may receive a royalty for conducting and/or producing the soundtrack album.

[5] Composers are not unionized. However, the American Federation of Musicians represents orchestrators and conductors, a role often performed by composers in delivering soundtracks.

DEALMAKING
IN THE
FILM AND
TELEVISION
INDUSTRY—
3RD EDITION

218

finished master recording at his/her own expense. Some produc-ers minimize costs by using non-union musicians or electronic synthesizers.

Sometimes artists anxious to break into movie composing will compose a soundtrack or song on speculation. Here the producer is not obligated to pay for the work unless he/she uses it.

A producer could also proceed under a step deal. The song-writer[6] is paid a modest upfront payment for composing the song, and then the producer decides if he/she wants to use it. If the producer uses the song, he/she will pay an additional fee. If he/she doesn't use the song, the writer will retain all rights to it. In that event, the producer may seek reimbursement of the upfront payment if the song ever generates income. A sample composer employment agreement is reprinted at the end of this chapter.

When a popular artist is commissioned to provide a song, the studio will pay him/her a creative fee for his/her services. The deal can be structured by providing the artist with a fund that includes payment for all writing and recording expenses. Thus the artist is paid a flat fee and is responsible for delivering the song and master and paying all recording expenses. Such a deal limits the studio's liability for recording costs and can provide greater compensation to the artist if expenses can be minimized.

Complications arise with popular songwriters because many have entered agreements granting a publisher the exclusive right to the songwriter's services. Both the publisher and the studio, which may have its own music publishing arm, may want copy-right ownership and management of a song written for a movie. The parties will need to reach an agreement, unless the artist has already fulfilled his/her songwriting contract.

Similarly, a soundtrack artist may be exclusive to a record label for recordings over a term of years or for several albums. The recording company may demand a royalty from the film studio in return for granting permission to use the artist on the soundtrack. Often the label and the artist share royalties.

There are other areas where the studio's interests and those of the record label may conflict. Studios want to release singles to promote movies and soundtrack albums. Record labels, on the other hand, want to use the single to promote their artists' albums.

---

[6] The songwriter creates a song for the soundtrack while the composer creates an entire score. The employment agreements are similar.

Ownership and control of a music video created to promote the movie is another issue. The studio will want to use the video as an integral part of the film's publicity campaign. The recording company will want to release the video in a manner that will best promote the artist.

Assuming all necessary permissions have been obtained from the artist's record label, a Soundtrack Recording Agreement will be used to employ an artist. The agreement will give the studio both the right to use the song on the soundtrack and the right to include it on a soundtrack album.

Since several artists may contribute material to a soundtrack, each will want to ensure that they receive a fair deal compared to the others. An artist will often ask for a MOST FAVORED NATIONS clause, which guarantees the artist as favorable terms as those given any other artist.

An artist may also seek to limit a studio's recoupment of recording costs and advances to those costs directly incurred by that artist. Thus, the artist's royalty will not be reduced by expenses attributable to others. If the studio agrees to such a provision, it must maintain a separate accounting for each artist.

NATURE OF MUSIC RIGHTS NEEDED

As discussed in Chapter 12, a copyright is a bundle of different rights, including the right to control the performance, copying, display, distribution (by sale, rental, or lease), and alteration of a work. The producer who wants to incorporate music on a soundtrack has to license several of these rights.

The PUBLIC PERFORMANCE RIGHT is the right to recite, play, sing, dance, or broadcast a musical composition in public. Music rights' owners virtually always use agencies such as ASCAP, BMI, or SESAC to license their performance rights. These agencies issue a blanket license to users.

First, the music rights' owner selects an agency (e.g., BMI) to represent her. Each agency represents thousands of songs. Television and radio broadcasters, nightclubs, theaters, amusement parks, discos, and other businesses that publicly perform music (except movie theaters in the United States) pay a yearly fee to the agencies. The agencies issue blanket licenses entitling the user to use any of the songs they represent without securing permission on an individual basis.

DEALMAKING
IN THE
FILM AND
TELEVISION
INDUSTRY—
3RD EDITION

220

The fees collected from users are pooled, and after the agency deducts its administrative costs, the money is divided among the songwriters and music publishers that the agency represents. The agency divides the money according to the popularity of the songs, which is determined through surveys and random samples. Thus, a famous songwriter will receive a larger check than some unknown songwriter whose song was played once on a local radio station.

The blanket license makes sense for everyone concerned. As a practical matter, the owner of rights to a piece of music can't monitor every public performance of his/her music and take action to enforce payment. Similarly, it would be cumbersome for a radio station to have to negotiate permission for every song it broadcasts.

Imagine a disc jockey having to share the broadcast booth with a dozen lawyers. After the DJ selects a record, he/she shouts "Get me permission from Bob Dylan for 'Blowin' in the Wind,'" as lawyers in pinstriped suits furiously dial phones and negotiate deals to obtain performance rights. Such a scheme would employ many lawyers but vex disc jockeys.

There are two important points to remember about the blanket license. First, it only covers non-dramatic or small performing rights. Performances such as a musical play or opera, where songs tell a story, are considered dramatic performances, and one cannot obtain a blanket license for this use. It may be difficult to distinguish a dramatic from a non-dramatic performance. A disc jockey who broadcasts a song would be making a non-dramatic use, whereas a small theater performance with props, costumes, and sets would be making a dramatic use. But there are many uses that fall in between.

Second, U.S. theater exhibitors cannot obtain a blanket license to perform music.[7] They are not covered by the license issued by ASCAP or BMI. Consequently, the rights to perform music in movie theaters (i.e., on the soundtrack of films) must be obtained from the music right's owner. Since it would be very cumbersome to require every theater owner to obtain these rights for each song in every movie they exhibit, the producer or distributor will secure these rights for all exhibitors who might show the film. However, if the music rights' owner refuses to license

---

[7] Movie theaters in Europe, however, do pay public performance fees.

the music, or the parties cannot agree on terms, the producer/ distributor can't use the music.

The SYNCHRONIZATION RIGHT is the right to reproduce the music[8] on the soundtrack of the movie in synchronization with video or filmed images. There is no blanket license available. Producers must negotiate with the music rights' owner. The fees are modest (e.g., a few thousand dollars) for television use since the music owners will receive fees from the blanket performance license. As a matter of convenience, the synchronization license is usually obtained simultaneously with the performance license for one fee and one license. Organizations like The Harry Fox Agency[9] license synchronization rights for many music owners.

ADAPTATION RIGHTS allow the producer to alter the musical composition by way of arrangement, parody, comedic use, and lyric change. If you want to use the title or story set forth in a song, you may need to obtain DRAMATIC RIGHTS. As mentioned above, dramatic use includes a film or television production of an opera or musical play. The composer or publisher may reserve certain rights, such as the right to make changes to the work.

Producers may also want to obtain the right to use the work in other markets such as home video, non-theatrical distribution, free television, cable television, subscription television, closed-circuit television, and airline exhibition.

Producers can negotiate for the necessary rights themselves, use an attorney, or retain an organization like the Copyright Clearance Center[10] to negotiate for them. Producers should always obtain all needed licenses before placing the music on the soundtrack. Otherwise, the producer risks having to remix the soundtrack if he/she cannot obtain the requisite rights.

Music Considerations

Soundtrack Album: Most indie films do not release a soundtrack album. Record companies are most interested in soundtrack albums for major studio films that are heavily promoted and advertised.

---

[8] For non-dramatic use of music. A non-dramatic use does not tell a story.
[9] The Harry Fox Agency is located at 405 Riverside Dr., Burbank, CA 91506, (818) 558-3480, www.harryfox.com.
[10] Copyright Clearance Center, 222 Rosewood Dr., Danvers, MA 01923, (978) 750-8500, www.copyright.com.

DEALMAKING
IN THE
FILM AND
TELEVISION
INDUSTRY—
3RD EDITION

222

Therefore, independent filmmakers may elect not to secure the right to release the music as a soundtrack album, or provide for royalties to the music owner if a soundtrack album is released.

Festival Rights: Securing the right to use the music for exhibiting your film only in film festivals may cause you problems down the road. If the movie is acquired for distribution, the music owner may demand a much greater license fee. The filmmaker must then either replace the music with something more affordable and re-edit the film with the new music, or pay a large fee for the music. Generally speaking, the inclusion of famous songs in a film does not significantly increase the revenue the filmmaker will receive.

Free or royalty-free music: There are numerous sources of free or royalty-free music, also referred to as Buyout Music. Royalty-free means you don't have to pay an ongoing royalty tied to how widely the motion picture is distributed. Further, the license is usually worldwide and in perpetuity. The license fee is typically an upfront flat fee. But it usually does not include any right to use the music separate from the motion picture or to release an album. You may need to supply a music cue sheet as well.

MUSIC RIGHTS NEEDED FOR A THEATRICAL FEATURE FILM

1) PUBLIC PERFORMANCE RIGHTS: No blanket license for movie theaters, so the producer must negotiate a license.

2) SYNCHRONIZATION RIGHTS: Obtained with above for one fee in one license.

3) MASTER USE LICENSE: To use existing recordings.

4) MECHANICAL RIGHTS: To use music on a soundtrack album.

Type into Google such words as "free film music," or "library music" and you can see some of the options such as productiontrax.com, mobygratis.com, stockmusic.net. You can also purchase a library of stock music on a CD or as a downloadable file (e.g., catovah.com).

Public Domain Music: Filmmakers can use public domain music without paying any fee. However, it is important to know that even if a composition is in the public domain, a particular recording may not be. So while Beethoven's compositions are in the public domain, a recent recording of his music by the Boston Symphony Orchestra may not be. In other words, the recording can have a separate copyright from the composition.

The motion picture studio will negotiate an agreement with a record label for the production and distribution of the soundtrack album. Record companies can earn significant revenue from such releases and will pay the studio a royalty and often an advance as well. Record companies prefer soundtracks with major artists and pop songs rather than orchestral performances.

The royalty will range from 10% to 19% of the retail price, although the studio will pay a portion to musical artists. The record company may ask the studio to put up matching funds for promotion. A studio will want the album's release to coincide with the film's release.

REVENUE FROM MUSIC USED IN FILM AND TELEVISION

SYNCHRONIZATION LICENSE FEE: For the right to use music in a motion picture. Generally $10,000 to $35,000 per song.

MASTER USE LICENSE: Record Companies may charge from $12,000 to $50,000 for the right to use their master recordings on a soundtrack.

PERFORMANCE ROYALTIES: For exhibition of the motion picture in theaters and television in foreign countries, and from exhibition in the U.S. on television. Publishers and songwriters receive performance rights payments from the performance rights societies such as ASCAP, BMI, and SESAC, as well as from affiliated performance rights organizations in foreign countries. The performing rights organizations also license music to radio stations, concert halls, and music services such as Muzak.

SOUNDTRACK ALBUM ROYALTIES: From the sale of records, tapes, and CDs.

HOME VIDEO: There are a number of approaches to licensing music for use on home videos. Some deals provide for a royalty (e.g., 6 cents to 12 cents per song) for each video sold. Many distributors, however, demand a one-time buy-out fee for all video rights regardless of sales.

PRINT PUBLICATIONS: Revenues derived from licensing songs or their lyrics for sheet music, folios, magazines, and books.

DEALMAKING
IN THE
FILM AND
TELEVISION
INDUSTRY—
3RD EDITION

224

MUSIC CHECKLIST

FOR EACH PIECE OF MUSIC ON THE SOUNDTRACK DETERMINE:

TITLE _____

COMPOSER(S)/SONGWRITER(S) _____

LYRICIST(S) _____

MUSICIAN (S) _____

SINGERS/PERFORMERS _____

PUBLISHER _____

RECORD COMPANY _____

USE OF MUSIC: ☐ BACKGROUND INSTRUMENTAL   ☐ BACKGROUND
VOCAL   ☐ VISUAL VOCAL   ☐ SOURCE MUSIC   ☐ THEME SONG
☐ OVER TITLES

FOR EACH PIECE OF MUSIC (SCORE OR SONG), DETERMINE WHETHER
THE MUSIC IS: ☐ PRE-EXISTING MUSIC OR   ☐ ORIGINAL MUSIC
CREATED FOR THE MOVIE.

PRE-EXISTING MUSIC

FOR PRE-EXISTING MUSIC, YOU MAY NEED TO OBTAIN TWO
LICENSES:

1) A MASTER USE LICENSE FROM THE RECORD COMPANY OR OWNER
IF AN EXISTING RECORDING IS BEING USED. (THIS LICENSE USUALLY
DOES NOT INCLUDE ANY RIGHT TO MAKE ANY CHANGE IN THE
FUNDAMENTAL CHARACTER OF THE MASTER, TO USE THE STORY
OR TITLE OF THE MASTER.) AND,

2) A SYNC LICENSE FROM THE MUSIC PUBLISHER THAT INCLUDES
THE RIGHT TO USE THE UNDERLYING COMPOSITION. THE SYNCHRO-
NIZATION LICENSE IS USUALLY OBTAINED SIMULTANEOUSLY WITH
THE PERFORMANCE LICENSE FOR ONE FEE AND ONE LICENSE. THE
PERFORMANCE LICENSE COVERS THE PUBLIC PERFORMANCE OF THE
MUSIC IN THEATERS SINCE THIS IS NOT COVERED BY THE MUSIC
PERFORMING AGENCIES.

IF A NEW RECORDING IS MADE, ONE WILL NEED AGREEMENTS
EMPLOYING MUSICIANS AND ARTISTS.

ORIGINAL SCORE OR SONG (MUSIC WRITTEN ESPECIALLY FOR A MOTION PICTURE)

FOR EACH PIECE OF MUSIC YOU NEED TO DETERMINE WHO IS OR
WILL BE THE COPYRIGHT OWNER. EITHER:

1) PRODUCER OWNS COPYRIGHT: USUALLY THE FILM PRODUCER HIRES THE COMPOSER UNDER A WORK-FOR-HIRE AGREEMENT, WHICH VESTS THE COPYRIGHT WITH THE PRODUCER (ALTHOUGH THE COMPOSER IS TYPICALLY ENTITLED TO RECEIVE MUSIC PUBLISHING ROYALTIES AND ALBUM ROYALTIES, AND WILL COLLECT PUBLIC PERFORMANCE FEES DIRECTLY FROM ASCAP OR ANOTHER PERFORMING RIGHTS SOCIETY); OR

2) COMPOSER OWNS THE COPYRIGHT: THE COMPOSER IS THE COPYRIGHT OWNER AND HE/SHE LICENSES THE MUSIC TO THE PRODUCER FOR THE INCLUSION ON THE SOUNDTRACK AND ON A SOUNDTRACK ALBUM. IN THIS CASE, THE PRODUCER NEEDS TO LICENSE THE SAME RIGHTS NEEDED TO LICENSE PRE-EXISTING MUSIC.

IN EITHER CASE, CHECK TO MAKE SURE THE COMPOSER HAS SIGNED AGREEMENTS WITH ANY OTHER CONTRIBUTORS (I.E., PERFORMERS, LYRICIST, MUSICIANS) TO THE MUSIC WHICH VESTS ALL NECESSARY RIGHTS IN THE COMPOSER (WHO WILL HAVE TO ASSIGN THESE RIGHTS TO THE FILM PRODUCER) OR VESTS THE RIGHTS DIRECTLY WITH THE PRODUCER.

RIGHTS NEEDED:

THE USE OF THE MUSIC IN ALL MEDIA NOW KNOWN OR HEREAFTER DEVISED (INCLUDING THEATRICAL, HOME VIDEO, TELEVISION, INTERNET DISTRIBUTION, AND IN ADVERTISING) THROUGHOUT THE UNIVERSE IN PERPETUITY. SHOULD INCLUDE RIGHT TO EDIT THE MATERIAL AND MAY INCLUDE THE RIGHT TO USE THE MUSIC ON A SOUNDTRACK ALBUM. THE RIGHTS ACQUIRED SHOULD INCLUDE:

1) SYNC RIGHTS WHICH IS THE RIGHT TO USE THE MUSIC IN SYNCHRONIZATION WITH MOTION PICTURE IMAGES;

2) PERFORMANCE RIGHTS, WHICH IS THE RIGHT TO THE PERFORMANCES (TO THE EXTENT THAT THE RIGHTS ARE NOT LICENSED THROUGH PERFORMING RIGHTS SOCIETIES);

3) MASTER USE RIGHTS IF AN EXISTING RECORDING IS BEING USED; AND

4) MECHANICAL RIGHTS FOR USE OF THE MUSIC ON A SOUNDTRACK ALBUM.

DEALMAKING
IN THE
FILM AND
TELEVISION
INDUSTRY—
3RD EDITION

226

TV MUSIC RIGHTS LICENSE

1. In consideration of the payment of $_____, and upon the payment of it to the undersigned, the undersigned does hereby grant to Licensee the non-exclusive, irrevocable right and license to record the following copyrighted musical composition(s) (the "Compositions") in synchronization or timed relation with a picture produced by Licensee (the "Picture") for television broadcast and exhibition only, and known as:

Title:

Composer:

Publisher:

Length of Composition & Manner of Use:

2. This is a license to record only, and the exercise of the recording rights herein granted is conditioned upon performance of the Composition(s) over television stations having valid licenses from the copyright owner (the "Owner"), or from the person, firm, corporation, or other entity having the legal right to issue performance rights licenses for the Owner in the respective territories in which the Composition(s) shall be performed. The Composition(s) shall not be used in any manner and media or be recorded for any other purpose, except those specifically set forth herein, without the express written consent of the Owner. No sound recordings produced pursuant to this license are to be manufactured, sold, and/or used separately from the Picture; and the Picture shall not be exhibited in or televised into theaters or other public places of amusement where motion pictures are customarily exhibited.

3. This license is granted for the following territory: The United States, its territories and possessions.

4. This license shall end on _____. Upon such date rights herein granted shall immediately cease and end, and the right derived from this license to make or authorize any further use or distribution of the Picture with the licensed music shall also cease and end upon such date.

5. This license cannot be assigned or transferred without the express consent of the undersigned in writing.

6. The undersigned warrants, on behalf of the principal for whom the undersigned is acting, that it is the owner of the recording rights herein licensed, and this license is given without other warranty or recourse, except to repay the consideration paid for this license if said warranty shall be

breached. The undersigned's warranty is limited to the amount of consideration paid for this license; and the undersigned further reserves all rights and uses in and to the Composition(s) not herein specifically granted.

_____

Publisher

AGREED AND ACCEPTED:

_____

Producer

COMPOSER AGREEMENT

FOR LOW-BUDGET FEATURE

_____, 20__

Mr. John Doe

Melody Lane

Los Angeles, CA

Dear Mr. Doe:

This letter, when signed by you (the "Composer"), will confirm our mutual agreement whereby Very Independent Productions, Inc. (the "Producer"), has engaged you as an employee for hire to render certain services and to furnish a complete and original musical score (the "Work") for the documentary feature "_____" (the "Picture").

Producer agrees to pay composer as full compensation, for all services required of him/her in connection with the Picture and for all the rights granted by the Composer, upon condition that the Composer shall fully and faithfully perform all the services required of him/her hereunder, the sum of $_____ and other valuable consideration, including one VHS copy of the Picture with musical score and a credit in the Picture.

Producer employs Composer to write, compose, orchestrate, perform, record, and submit to Producer music suitable for use as the complete background score for the Picture. Composer shall bear the full cost of any musicians, studio, or equipment rental, guild or union fees, or any other costs incurred in preparing the work except for tape-stock costs.

DEALMAKING
IN THE
FILM AND
TELEVISION
INDUSTRY—
3RD EDITION

228

The Composer grants the Producer the perpetual nonexclusive right to use and license others to use his name and likeness in any advertising or exploitation of the Picture.

The Composer agrees that Producer may perpetually use or authorize others to use any of the rights herein granted for commercial advertising or publicity in connection with any product, commodity, or service manufactured, distributed, or offered by the Producer or others, provided such advertising refers to the Picture, or to the Composer's employment by the Producer.

Composer warrants that all material written, composed, prepared, or submitted by him/her during the term hereof or any extension of it shall be wholly original with him/her and shall not be copied in whole or in part from any other work, except that submitted to the Composer by the Producer as a basis for such material. The Composer further warrants that said material will not infringe upon the copyright, literary, dramatic, or photoplay rights of any person. Composer warrants and agrees to indemnify and hold Producer and Producer's officers, shareholders, employees, successors, and assigns harmless from and against any claim, demand, damage, debt, liability, account, reckoning, obligation, cost, expense, lien, action, and cause of action (including the payment of attorneys' fees and costs incurred) arising out of any breach or failure of any of Composer's warranties, representations, or covenants herein contained.

The Composer further agrees that all the material which he/she may write, compose, prepare, or submit under this agreement shall be the sole property of the Producer. All of the material shall be written, composed, prepared, and submitted by him/her as the employee of the Producer, and not otherwise. The Producer shall be the author and first proprietor of the copyright and the Composer shall have no right, title, or interest in the material. Producer shall have the right to obtain copyrights, patents, and/or other protection therefore. The Composer further agrees to execute, verify, acknowledge, and deliver any documents which the Producer shall deem necessary or advisable to evidence, establish, maintain, protect, enforce, or defend its rights and/or title in or to the said material or any part of it. Producer shall have the right, but not the duty, to use, adapt, edit, add to, subtract from, arrange, rearrange, revise, and change said material or any part of it, and to vend, copy, publish, reproduce, record, transmit, broadcast by radio and/or television, perform, photograph with or without sound, including spoken works, dialogue, and/or music synchronously recorded, and to communicate the same by any means now known or from now on devised, either publicly and for profit, or otherwise.

Producer, its successors, and assigns shall, in addition to the Composer's services, be entitled to and own in perpetuity, solely and exclusively, all of the results and proceeds of said services and material, including all rights throughout the world of production, manufacture, recordation, and reproduction by any art or method, whether now known or from now on devised, and whether such results and proceeds consist of literary, dramatic, musical, motion picture, mechanical, or any other form of work, theme, idea, composition, creation, or product.

The Composer will at the request of the Producer execute such assignments or other instruments as the Producer may deem necessary or desirable to evidence, establish, or defend his/her right or title in the Work. The Composer hereby appoints the Producer the true and lawful attorney-in-fact of the Composer irrevocably to execute, verify, acknowledge, and deliver any such instruments or documents which the Composer shall fail or refuse to execute.

Producer shall have and is hereby granted the complete control of the publication of all or any of the musical material written by the Composer hereunder. Producer agrees, however, that in the event it publishes the musical material or causes the musical material to be published by a third party, Producer shall pay to the composer the following fees:

(a) Five cents (.05) per copy for each piano copy of the Composition and for each dance orchestration of the Composition printed, published, and sold in the United States and Canada by Publisher or its licensees, for which payments have been received by Publisher, after deduction of returns.

(b) Ten percent (10%) of the wholesale selling price upon each printed copy of each other arrangement and edition of the Composition printed, published, and sold in the United States and Canada by Publisher or its licensees, for which payment has been received, after deduction of returns, except that in the event the Composition shall be used or caused to be used, in whole or in part, with one or more other compositions in a folio, album, or other publication, Composer shall be entitled to receive that proportion of said royalty which the Composition shall bear to the total number of compositions contained in such folio, album, or other publication for which royalties are payable.

(c) Fifty percent (50%) of any and all net sums actually received (less any costs for collection) by Publisher in the United States from the exploitation in the United States and Canada by licensees of Publisher of mechanical rights, electrical

DEALMAKING
IN THE
FILM AND
TELEVISION
INDUSTRY—
3RD EDITION

230

transcription and reproducing rights, motion picture and television synchronization rights, and all other rights (except printing and public performance rights) in the Composition, whether such licensees are affiliated with, owned in whole or in part by, or controlled by, Publisher.

(d) Composer shall receive his/her public performance royalties throughout the world directly from his/her own affiliated performing rights society and shall have no claims at all against Publisher for any royalties received by Publisher from any performing rights society which makes payment directly (or indirectly other than through Publisher) to writers, authors, and composers.

(e) Fifty percent (50%) of any and all net sums, after deduction of foreign taxes, actually received (less any costs of collection) by Publisher in the United States from sales, licenses, and other uses of the Composition in countries outside of the United States and Canada (other than the public performance royalties as hereinabove mentioned in paragraph (d)) from collection agents, licensees, subpublishers, or others, whether same are affiliated with, owned in whole or in part by, or controlled by, Publisher.

(f) Publisher shall not be required to pay any royalties on professional or complimentary printed copies of the Composition which are distributed gratuitously to performing arts, orchestra leaders, and disc jockeys or for advertising, promotional, or exploitation purposes. Furthermore, no royalties shall be payable to Composer on consigned copies of the Composition unless paid for, and not until an accounting therefore can properly be made.

Notwithstanding anything to the contrary contained in this Agreement, Producer, its lessees, licensees, and all other persons permitted by Producer to distribute, exhibit, or exploit any picture in connection with which any material written, prepared, or composed by Composer hereunder is used, shall have the free and unrestricted right to use any such material and to make mechanical reproductions of it without the payment of any sums at all, and in no event shall Composer be permitted or entitled to participate in any rentals or other forms of royalty received by Producer, its licensees, or any other persons permitted by Producer to use any such material or mechanical reproductions of it in connection with the exhibition, distribution, exploitation, or advertising of any present or future kind of motion picture, nor shall Producer be obligated to account to Composer for any sums received by Producer from any other persons from the sale or licensing or other disposition of any material written, created, or composed by Composer hereunder in connection with the exhibition, distribution, exploitation, or advertising of any motion picture. Without limiting the foregoing, Composer shall not be entitled to any portion of any synchronization fee due to the use of the material or any portion of it in motion pictures produced by Producer or by any of its subsidiaries, affiliates, or related companies.

Provided Composer fully and satisfactorily renders his/her services pursuant to the terms and conditions of this Agreement, and that all of the original music contained in the Picture as released is the product of Composer's services, Producer shall accord Composer billing on a separate card by the phrase "MUSIC BY JOHN DOE" or a phrase substantially similar thereto on the positive prints of said Picture. Except as set forth in the preceding sentence, all other matters about billing shall be decided in Producer's sole discretion.

If Producer, its successors, or assigns shall exercise their right hereunder to make, distribute, and sell, or authorize others to make, distribute, and sell, commercial phonograph records (including, without limitation, discs of any speed or size, tape, and wire demos, and any and all other demos, whether now known or unknown, for the recording of sound) embodying the material for the Picture, and if said records contain Composer's performance as a conductor, they shall pay or cause to be paid to Composer in connection with it a reasonable royalty as is customarily paid in the industry.

Composer's sole remedy for any breach hereof shall be an action at law for damages, if any. In no event shall Composer have the right to rescind this Agreement or any of the rights granted hereunder nor to seek or obtain injunctions or other equitable relief restraining or enjoining the production, exhibition, or exploitation of any motion pictures based upon or using any portion of the Work.

Nothing contained in this Agreement shall be deemed to require Producer or its assigns to publish, record, reproduce, or otherwise use the Work or any part of it, whether in connection with the Picture or otherwise.

This instrument is the entire Agreement between the parties and cannot be modified except by a written instrument signed by the Composer and an authorized officer of the Producer.

This agreement shall be deemed to have been made in the State of California, and its validity, construction, and effect

DEALMAKING
IN THE
FILM AND
TELEVISION
INDUSTRY—
3RD EDITION

232

shall be governed by and construed under the laws and judicial decisions of the State of California applicable to agreements wholly performed therein.

Very truly yours,

By John Smith

President, Very Independent Prods.

ACCEPTED AND AGREED TO:

_____

John Doe

Composer

I hereby certify that I wrote the material hereto attached, as an employee of Very Independent Productions, Inc., pursuant to an agreement dated the ____ day of _____, 20___, in performance of my duties thereunder, and in the regular course of employment, and that said Very Independent Productions, Inc., is the author of it and entitled to the copyright therein and thereto, with the right to make such changes therein and such uses of it, as it may determine as such author.

IN WITNESS WHEREOF, I have hereto set my hands this _____ day of _____, 20__.

_____

John Doe

Questions and Answers

1. Do I need copyright clearance and permission to use an artist's music on my soundtrack if I am using it on an independent film for festivals only? If so, who/where do I contact?

Answer: Yes, you do need permission. There is no exemption in copyright law for film festivals or independent filmmakers. Many music rights holders may be willing to give a limited license for festival exhibition for free or for a nominal charge. It is best to negotiate a step deal where you pay according to the extent of your ultimate distribution. This might entail a payment of $500 for the right to use the music in the film for festivals, and larger sums paid if a distributor releases it theatrically, on television, or on home video.

Probably the easiest way to determine ownership rights in a particular song is to contact the music publisher for each song. If you have a copy of the song in the form of a record or CD, the label should list either the recording company, or the publisher, or both. You could also hire a clip clearance agency to help you clear these songs. Here are two: Copyright Clearance Center at www.copyright.com and Suzy Vaughan Associates, Inc., at www.suzyesq.com. You can locate the publisher of a particular song by contacting the performance right society such as ASCAP (www.ascap.com), BMI (www.bmi.com), or SESAC www.sesac.com).

2. I am currently trying to license two well-known songs for a very low-budget short film. What is the best way to obtain licenses for music under these circumstances?

Answer: Beg. If you know the musicians personally, that may help. Try to interest them in your project. Even if you can't pay them much of a fee up-front, they will receive fees from public-performing agencies when the film is televised and shown in theaters abroad. If the film is a hit, they may also benefit from the publicity. The owners of the song are under no obligation to let you use their music in your film.

3. Supposing that an agency wants to use a famous song in a commercial, yet the artist will not give up the rights. Can they use a "soundalike" to avoid copyright law violations and imply an endorsement by a well-known star?

Answer: You should proceed cautiously. You should review the Bette Midler case (*Midler v. Ford Motor Co.*, 849 F.2d 460 (9th Cir. 1988)) and the Tom Waits case (*Waits v. Frito-Lay*, 978 F.2d 1093 (9th Cir. 1992)) in this regard. The soundalike recording might violate the laws of unfair competition and rights of publicity—even if technically it's not copyright infringement.

CHAPTER 9

THE ACQUISITION/ DISTRIBUTION AGREEMENT

There are several ways to develop or produce a film. Beginning with an idea, or the movie rights to an existing literary property, a studio can hire a writer to create a script. The studio's development staff will work with the writer to develop the story. Most scripts developed by studios, however, never get produced.[1]

Other movies begin with a script developed outside the studio. Here a writer, working on his own or hired by an independent producer, writes a screenplay. After it is finished, it may be packaged (joined) with other elements (e.g., a star or director) and presented to the studio for financing and distribution. The big three talent agencies (CAA, ICM, and William Morris) are responsible for assembling many packages.

Other films are both developed and produced away from the studio that ultimately distributes them. These independently produced projects are often dependent on investors or pre-sale distribution deals (selling off various foreign-distribution rights) to finance production. The producer then enters an acquisition agreement with a distributor for release of the picture. This may be a so-called NEGATIVE PICK-UP DEAL, wherein the distributor doesn't have to provide any financing until the completed picture is delivered.

---

[1] Development, like research and development in scientific endeavors, doesn't always succeed. Many ideas sound promising at the concept stage, but the finished work may not be impressive enough to justify an investment of millions of dollars for production.

DEALMAKING
IN THE
FILM AND
TELEVISION
INDUSTRY—
3RD EDITION

236

While the terms of negative pick-up deals vary, the studio/ distributor typically pays for all distribution, advertising, and marketing costs. The studio and producer share profits. Because the producer has taken the risk of financing production, he/she probably can obtain a larger share of revenue than if the film was made the film with studio financing. Net revenue may be split 50/50 between the studio and producer. A so-called 50/50-net deal is illustrated on the opposite page. Alternatively, the distributor may take a distribution fee of gross revenues, recoup distribution expenses, and then remit the balance to the film-maker. Of course, the independent producer takes the risk that if the film turns out poorly, no distributor will want it. In that case, the producer can incur a substantial loss.

In a negative pick-up deal, the distributor will often agree to give the producer an advance of his share of revenue. The producer can use this money to repay investors. Producers will want to obtain as large an advance as possible because they know they may never see anything on the back end of the deal.

The distributor wants to pay as small an advance as possible, and usually resists giving an amount that is more than the cost of production. Its executives will propose, "We'll be partners. We will put up all the money for advertising and promotion. If the picture is successful, we will share in its success." Sound good?

Unfortunately, distributors have been known to engage in creative accounting, and profit participants rarely see any return on their share of "net profits" because of the way that term is defined. Consequently, the shrewd producer tries to get as large an advance as possible. He/she also tries to retain foreign rights and keep them from being cross-collateralized.[2]

Independent filmmakers often enter into agreements with multiple distributors for each film. A filmmaker will often license a film outside of North America by contracting with a foreign sales agent, who will in turn market the film to local territory distributors around the globe. For distribution within North America, the filmmaker will either enter into either an agreement with

---

[2] Cross-collateralized means the monies earned from several markets are pooled. For example, let's say your picture made $1 million dollars in England and lost $1 million dollars in France. If those territories were cross-collateralized, and you were entitled to a percentage of the net revenue, you would get nothing. On the other hand, if the territories were not cross-collateralized, you would get your percentage of the English revenues and the distributor would absorb the loss incurred in France. Different media may also be cross-collateralized so that loses from a theatrical release can be recovered from home video revenue.

one distributor for all rights, or if the film is not going to be exhibiting theatrically, enter into separate deals with a home video label and one or more television channels.

ORCHESTRATING THE DISTRIBUTION DEAL

The most important advice I can offer to filmmakers seeking distribution is DON'T BRAG ABOUT HOW LITTLE MONEY YOU SPENT TO MAKE THE PICTURE before you conclude your distribution deal. You may feel justly proud of making a great-looking picture for a mere $400,000. But if the distributor knows that is all you have spent, you will find it difficult to get an advance beyond that. It would be wiser not to reveal your investment, recognizing that production costs are not readily discernible from viewing a film. Remember, the distributor has no right to examine your books.[3]

Acquisition agreements can be negotiated before, during, or after production. Often distributors become interested in a film after viewing it at a film festival and observing audience reaction. All the studios and independent distributors have one or more staffers in charge of acquisitions. It is the job of these acquisition executives to find good films to acquire.

It is not difficult to get acquisition executives to view your film. Once production has been announced, don't be surprised if they begin calling you. They will track the progress of your film so that they can see it as soon as it is finished—before their competitors get a shot at it.

From the filmmaker's point of view, you will obtain a better deal if you have more than one distributor interested in acquiring your movie. That way you can play one off another to get the best terms. But what if one distributor makes a pre-emptive bid for the film, offering you a $500,000 advance, and you have only 24 hours to accept their offer? If you pass, you may not be able to secure a better deal later. It is possible you may fail to obtain any distribution deal at all. On the other hand, if you accept the offer, you may be foreclosing the possibility of a more lucrative deal that could be offered you later. Consequently, it is important to orchestrate the release of your film to potential distributors to maximize your leverage.

---

[3] Assuming the distributor has not provided any financing, what you have spent is between you, your investors, and the IRS.

DEALMAKING
IN THE
FILM AND
TELEVISION
INDUSTRY—
3RD EDITION

238

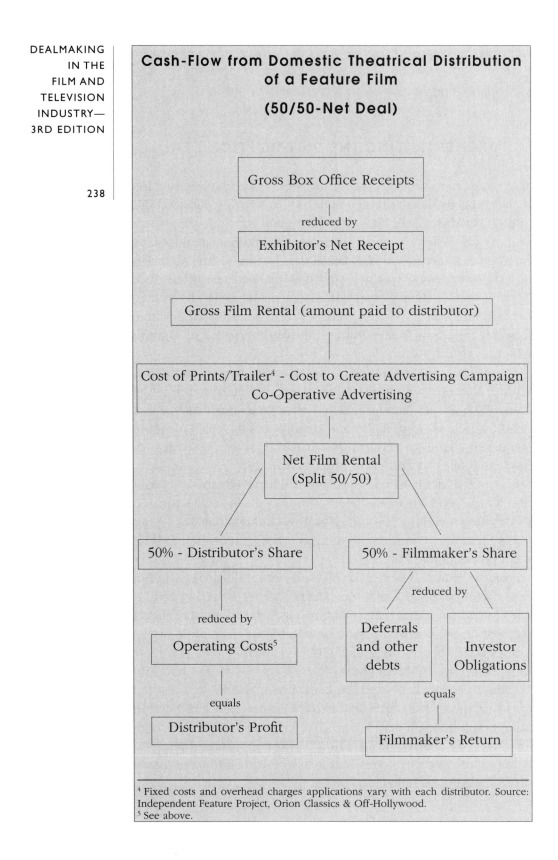

**Cash-Flow from Domestic Theatrical Distribution
of a Feature Film**

(50/50-Net Deal)

Gross Box Office Receipts

reduced by

Exhibitor's Net Receipt

Gross Film Rental (amount paid to distributor)

Cost of Prints/Trailer[4] - Cost to Create Advertising Campaign
Co-Operative Advertising

Net Film Rental
(Split 50/50)

50% - Distributor's Share   50% - Filmmaker's Share

reduced by

reduced by

Operating Costs[5]   Deferrals
and other
debts   Investor
Obligations

equals   equals

Distributor's Profit   Filmmaker's Return

[4] Fixed costs and overhead charges applications vary with each distributor. Source:
Independent Feature Project, Orion Classics & Off-Hollywood.
[5] See above.

ORCHESTRATING THE RELEASE

1) KEEP THE FILM UNDER WRAPS: Don't show your film until it is finished. Executives may ask to see a rough cut. They will say "Don't worry. We're professionals; we can extrapolate and envision what the film will look like with sound and titles." Don't believe them. Most people can't extrapolate. They will view your unfinished film and think it amateurish. First impressions last.

The only reason to show your film before completion is if you are desperate to raise funds to finish it. The terms you can obtain under these circumstances will usually be less than those given on completion. If you must show a work in progress, exhibit it on a Moviola or flatbed editing table. People have lower expectations viewing a film on an editing console than when it is projected in a theater.

2) ARRANGE A SCREENING: Invite executives to a screening; don't send them a DVD if you think you can get them to view the film in a theater. If you send a DVD to a busy executive, he/she will pop it into a DVD player and start to watch until the phone rings 10 minutes later and he/she pushes the pause button. Then, the executive watches another 10 minutes until he/she is interrupted again. After being distracted 10 times, he/she passes on your film because it is "too choppy." Well, of course it's choppy with all those interruptions. You want to get the executive in a dark room, away from diversions, to view your film with a live audience—hopefully one that will respond positively. So rent a screening room at MGM, invite all the acquisition executives you can, and pack the rest of the theater with your friends and relatives, especially Uncle Herb with his infectious laugh.

3) MAKE THE BUYERS COMPETE AGAINST EACH OTHER: Screen the film for all distributors simultaneously. Some executives will attempt to get an early look—that is their job. Your job is to keep them intrigued until it is complete. You can promise to let them see it "as soon as it is finished." They may be annoyed to arrive at the screening and see their competitors. But this will get their competitive juices flowing. They will know that they better make a decent offer quickly if they hope to get the film.

4) OBTAIN AN EXPERIENCED ADVISOR: Retain an experienced producer's rep or entertainment attorney to negotiate your deal. Filmmakers know about film, distributors know about distribution. Don't kid yourself and believe you can play in their arena and win. There are many pitfalls to avoid. Get yourself an experienced guide to protect your interests. Any decent negotiator can improve a distributor's offer enough to outweigh the cost of his services.

5) INVESTIGATE THE DISTRIBUTOR: Always check the track record and experience of potential distributors. As an entertainment attorney who represents many independent filmmakers, I often find myself in the position of trying to get unscrupulous distributors to live up to their contracts. I am amazed at how many distributors refuse to abide by the clear terms of their own distribution agreements.

I am not talking here about the major studios. While they engage in creative accounting by interpreting ambiguous clauses in their favor, they usually feel obliged to comply with the terms of their contracts. I am talking about the many small independent distributors who flagrantly breach contracts and take unconscionable advantage of inexperienced filmmakers. Their attitude seems to be: Promise anything to get the film. Then defraud, deceive, and fleece with abandon. If the victim has the audacity to complain, the distributor usually 1) lies, 2) claims the film wasn't any good and therefore its obligations are terminated, or 3) offers to settle for 10 cents on the dollar.

The savvy filmmaker will carefully investigate potential distributors by calling filmmakers who have contracted with them. I recently read a Standard & Poors report on a distributor and was shocked to learn that the company was $2.3 million in arrears on royalty payments. One can also check the Superior Court dockets in Los Angeles to see if a company has been sued.

DEALMAKING
IN THE
FILM AND
TELEVISION
INDUSTRY—
3RD EDITION

240

SELF-DEFENSE TIPS FOR FILMMAKERS

I represented a filmmaker who had signed an agreement with a small distributor. The filmmaker was entitled to an advance, payable in four installments. After the second installment was paid, the company changed hands and the new owners simply refused to make payments. There was no question that the company owed my client the money and that my client had lived up to all his obligations. The only excuse the distributor offered was that they were experiencing "financial problems." We offered to accept monthly payments to work off the debt. Payments were promised but never made. Only after I went to court and had the sheriff seize the distributor's film library did they cough up the dough.

Distributors of low-budget films know that the amounts at stake are often not enough for the filmmaker to hire an attorney. Consequently, filmmakers should include an arbitration clause in their contracts. This provision provides that, in case of a dispute, the matter will be settled through binding arbitration, not litigation. Arbitration clauses and procedures are discussed in Chapter 17.

My experience with distributors has taught me that filmmakers need to be very careful when entering distribution agreements. The experienced filmmaker will try to add incentives and/or penalties to the contract that will encourage the distributor to live up to its terms. In one contract,

CHECKLIST FOR SELECTING A DISTRIBUTOR

1. Amount of advance.

2. Extent of rights conveyed. Domestic and/or foreign. Ancillary rights? Are any markets cross-collateralized?

3. Is there a guaranteed marketing commitment?

4. Does the producer have any input or veto power over artwork and theater selection in the top markets?

5. Track record and financial health of distributor.

6. Are monthly or quarterly accounting statements required?

7. To what extent does the distributor plan to involve the filmmakers in promotion?

8. Marketing strategy: demographics of intended market, grassroots promotion efforts, film festivals, etc.

9. Split of revenues and accounting of profits: Is there a distribution fee? Overhead fees?

10. Distributor leverage with exhibitors. Can the distributor collect monies owed?

11. Any competing films handled by distributor? Conflicts of interest?

12. Does the producer have the right to regain distribution rights if the distributor pulls the plug early on distribution?

13. Personal chemistry between producer and distribution executives.

I inserted a special clause which said that if the distributor breached any promise, my client could recover all the money owed him AND regain all rights to his film. Nevertheless, the distributor breached the contract. My client recovered his money and film and promptly licensed the distribution rights to another distributor, from whom he received a second advance.

One of my cases involved a dispute with a home-video distributor. The filmmaker made an oral agreement with the distributor and delivered his film. The distributor began advertising and promoting the picture. Six weeks later, before the paperwork was signed, the company reneged on the deal and coerced the filmmaker into renegotiating the deal and granting better terms.

To protect yourself from such tactics, make sure all promises are in writing. Don't provide access to any materials until the deal is signed. Try to retain possession of your film negative; give the distributor a lab access letter. Have your lab directly report to you how many copies are duplicated for the distributor. Make sure your agreement guarantees a minimum amount to be spent on advertising.

An experienced negotiator can obtain many important provisions just for the asking. Don't sign the "sucker" contract the distributor sends out to unwary filmmakers. Remember, the terms of the proposed contract are negotiable.

The following agreement is for distribution of an independently made film through an international distributor (a.k.a Foreign Sales Agent).

DEALMAKING
IN THE
FILM AND
TELEVISION
INDUSTRY—
3RD EDITION

242

ACQUISITION/DISTRIBUTION AGREEMENT[6]

_____, 20__

PRODUCER FILMS, INC.
Sally Producer, Producer

_____

_____

Re: "Film title"

Agreement made and entered into as of _____, 20__, by
and between DISTRIBUTION, INC., a California Corporation
("Distributor") at ____ Sunset Blvd., West Hollywood, CA 90069,
and PRODUCER FILMS, INC., Inc., a California Corporation
("Producer") at _____. In consideration of their
respective covenants, warranties, and representations, together
with other good and valuable consideration, Distributor and
Producer hereby agree as follows:

1. PICTURE: Producer will deliver to Distributor the
documentation, advertising, and physical materials (the
"Materials") set forth in the attached Delivery Schedule, relating
to Motion Picture, currently entitled "_____" (the
"Picture").

2. RIGHTS GRANTED:

   a) Producer hereby grants to Distributor the irrevocable
right, title, and interest in and to the distribution of the Picture,
its sound, and music in the territory (as hereinafter defined),
including without limitation, the sole, exclusive, and irrevocable
right and privilege, under Producer's copyright and otherwise,
to distribute, license, and otherwise exploit the Picture, its
image sound and music, for the term (as hereinafter defined)
throughout the territory (as hereinafter defined) for Theatrical,
all forms of Home Video, all forms of Television media, and
limited Internet distribution rights..

Such rights do not include the rights to produce other Motion
Pictures, sequels, or other spin-offs, or remakes of the Picture or
any right to produce television series, mini-series, or programs
or other so-called ancillary programs or any rights reserved
(hereinafter called "Reserved Rights") to Producer. Without
limiting the generality of the foregoing, or any other rights
granted to Distributor elsewhere in this agreement, Producer
hereby grants to Distributor the following rights:

---

[6] For additional information about distribution agreements, see my book *Risky Business:
Financing and Distributing Independent Films* (Silman-James Press, 2nd Edition 2008).

i) Theatrical Rights: All rights in and to the manufacture, distribution, exhibition, marketing, and other exploitation of the Picture, its sound, and music, by and relating to the projection of visual images contained on positive film prints of any size or kind (including 35mm and 16mm), whether in movie theaters, drive-ins, or any other venues (herein the "Theatrical Rights"), throughout the territory for the term.

ii) Home Video Rights: All rights in and to the manu-facture, distribution, exploitation, and non-theatrical, non-admission free home use exhibition of the Picture, its sound, and music (whether by sale or by rental) by means of any and all forms of videocassette, videodisc, video cartridge, tape, DVD, or other similar device ("Videogram") now known or hereafter devised and designed to be used in conjunction with a reproduction apparatus which causes a visual image (whether or not synchronized with sound) to be seen on the screen of a television receiver or any comparable device now known or hereafter devised, including DVD (the "Home Video Rights" or "Video Rights").

iii) Free Television Rights: All rights in and to the distri-bution, exhibition, marketing, and other exploitation of the Picture, its sound, and music by free television utilizing means other than those provided for in Paragraph 2(a) above and including, without limitation, free television, by network, or by syndicated UHF or VHF broadcast (the "Free Television Rights").

iv) Pay Television/Pay-Per-View: All rights in and to the distribution, exhibition, marketing, and other exploitation of the Picture, its sound, and music by means of "Pay Television" as that expression is commonly understood in the motion picture industry, and including, without limitation, cable, wire, or fiber of any material, "over-the-air pay," all forms of regular or occasionally scrambled broadcast, master antenna, and multi-channel multi-point distribution, satellite transmission, and radio (for purposes of simulcast only), all on a subscription, pay-per-view, license, rental, sale, or any other basis ("the Pay Television Rights").

v) Internet: Distributor's rights include the right to distribute and exploit the Picture for Internet exhibition throughout the Territory; provided, that: (i) Distributor may only license the Internet rights to a licensee which is licensing some other right(s) (e.g., theatrical rights, television rights, and/or video rights) in connection with the Picture; and (ii) Distributor's licensees shall only have the right to exhibit the Picture on the Internet in a dubbed version of the foreign

DEALMAKING
IN THE
FILM AND
TELEVISION
INDUSTRY—
3RD EDITION

244

language rights granted to such licensee; and (iii) if English is the applicable licensee's native language, then Internet rights may not be granted to such licensee without the written approval of Producer unless such licensee can ensure that the Picture cannot be viewed in the United States via the Internet and unless such licensee agrees to indemnify Licensor against claims from the United States Distributor of the Internet rights to the Picture in the event that such an Internet exhibition crosses over into the United States.

b) Advertising: Distributor shall have the exclusive right throughout the territory during the Term to advertise and publicize (or have its sub-distributors advertise and publicize) the Picture by any and all means, media, and method whatsoever, including, by means of the distribution, exhibition, broadcasting, and telecasting of trailers of the Picture, or excerpts from the Picture prepared by Distributor or others, subject to any customary restrictions upon and obligations with respect to such rights as are provided for in the contracts in relation to the production of the Picture.

c) Title: Distributor shall have the right to use the present title of the Picture. Licensees may change and or translate the title for distribution in their territories. No other changes to the title shall be made without Producer's written approval.

d) Editing:

i) Distributor in its discretion will have the right to incorporate into the Picture preceding and/or following the main and end titles of the Picture and Trailers thereof, and in all advertising and publicity relating thereto, in such manner, position, form, and substance as Distributor may elect, Distributor's trademark, logo, and presentation announcement, and the designation of Distributor as the distributor of the Picture. Any re-edit of the credit sequence will be at Distributor's expense.

ii) Distributor's right to edit hereunder specifically excludes the right to make alterations whatsoever to the original negative and/or the Video Master of the Picture, to which Distributor shall have lab-access rights (irrevocable for the term of this Agreement) for duplication purposes only. Other than changes required to meet government censorship rules, or changes made allow for the insertion of television commercials and to meet broadcast standards and practices guidelines, Distributor shall not make any changes to the Picture without the prior written consent of Producer.

iii) Distributor hereby indemnifies Producer for any losses, including reasonable attorney fees, incurred as a result of any liability arising from Distributor's editing, adding, or changing material in the Picture.

e) Licensing: Distributor has the right to grant licenses and other authorizations to one or more third parties to exercise any or all of said rights and privileges provided herein, in countries throughout the territory. The maximum term for any license granted by Distributor shall be twelve (12) years except for licensees for exploitation in Germany, which can extend for up to fifteen (15) years. If Distributor appoints one or more sub-distributors in the Territory, each appointment shall be in writing with terms and conditions at least as restrictive as to the sub-distributor as this Agreement is with Distributor. Distributor shall be responsible for assuring that any sub-distributor does not act or fail to act in any manner which conflicts with any term or condition of this Agreement. The fees paid to sub-distributor shall be paid from the Distributor's compensation so as not to reduce the amount of revenue that Producer receives.

f) Territorial Minimums: Producer and Distributor have established mutually agreed minimum guarantee amounts per territory (hereinafter "Territorial Minimums"). Nothing contained herein or in the schedule of Territorial Minimums shall be deemed to require Distributor in fact to obtain any such Territorial Minimums, but rather, it is the intention of the parties hereto that Distributor may not enter into an agreement for an amount less than the applicable Territorial Minimum without first obtaining Producer's approval. The Territorial Minimums for the Picture are set forth in Schedule A, attached.

g) No Further Rights: This agreement confers no right on the part of the Producer to use, or authorize others to use the Picture or any of the rights granted Distributor, within the Territory, which is not authorized by the Distributor hereunder, except Producer shall have the right to exhibit the Picture in festivals, industry screenings, and screenings for non-profit and/or educational purposes.

3. RESERVED RIGHTS: All other rights not expressly granted herein, including, but not limited to, electronic publishing, print publication, music publishing, live-television, radio, and dramatic rights are reserved to the Producer.

4. TERRITORY: The territory (herein "Territory") for which rights are granted to Distributor consists of the World (in all languages and in all formats) with the exception of the United States, its territories, possessions, and military bases, and English-speaking Canada.

DEALMAKING
IN THE
FILM AND
TELEVISION
INDUSTRY—
3RD EDITION

246

5. TERM: The rights granted to Distributor under this Agreement will commence on the date of this Agreement and continue thereafter for two (2) years (the "Initial Term"). If Distributor pays Producer $800,000 or more in the Initial Term, Distributor shall automatically have the right to extend the term for another two (2) year term (the "First Extended Term"). During this First Extended Term (and additional terms if further extended), Distributor shall have the option of extending the term for additional two (2) year periods (up to a total term of no more than ten (10) years) if the following thresholds are met:

First Extended Term: If $1.4 million cumulatively has been paid to Producer during the Initial and First Extended Terms, then Distributor may extend the term another two (2) years (the Second Extended Term).

Second Extended Term: If $1.8 million cumulatively has been paid to Producer during the Initial, First and Second Extended Terms, then Distributor may extend the term for another two (2) years (the Third Extended Term).

Third Extended Term: If $2.2 million cumulatively has been paid to Producer during the Initial and First through Third Extended Terms, then Distributor may extend the term for another two (2) years (the Fourth Extended Term).

Fourth Extended Term: If $2.6 million cumulatively has been paid to Producer during the Initial and First through Fourth Extended Terms, then Distributor may extend the term for another two (2) years (the Fifth Extended Term).

In order to extend the term, Distributor shall notify Producer in writing of its intention at least thirty (30) days prior to expiration of the then current term.

6. ADVERTISING/PROMOTION: Distributor will consult in good faith with Producer on marketing plans before any artwork is commissioned and the marketing campaign has begun. Producer will supply to Distributor the advertising and marketing materials set forth on the attached delivery schedule Schedule A. Distributor will not disseminate any photos or bios of Producer unless they have been approved by Producer. If Distributor creates its own artwork and trailers for the Picture, Ownership of these materials shall vest in Producer, and Producer shall have the right to use said materials at any time for the release of the Picture outside the Territory, and anywhere in the Universe after the term of this Agreement expires. Any artwork or copyrightable material commissioned by Distributor shall be created pursuant to a written contract,

signed before the material is created, which states the work is a work-for-hire and that Producer is the owner of all rights.

7. COPYRIGHT:

a) Producer represents and warrants that the Picture is, and will be throughout the Term, protected by copyright. Each copy of the Picture will contain a copyright notice conforming to and complying with the requirements of the United States Copyright Act as amended from time to time.

8. PRODUCTION COSTS:

a) As between Producer and Distributor: Producer is and will be responsible for and has paid or will pay all production costs, taxes, fees, and charges with respect to the Picture and/or the Materials except as provided herein. As used herein, "production costs" will include all costs incurred in connection with the production of the Picture and the Materials, including payments to writers, producers, directors, artists, and all other persons rendering services in connection with the Picture and/or the materials, all costs and expenses incurred in acquiring rights to use music in connection with the Picture, including synchronization, performance, and mechanical reproduction fees and union residuals.

9. PRODUCER'S REPRESENTATIONS AND WARRANTIES: Producer warrants and represents to Distributor, to the best of Producer's knowledge and belief, as follows:

a) Producer has full right, power, and authority to enter into and perform this Agreement and to grant to Distributor all of the rights herein granted and agreed to be granted to Distributor.

b) Producer has acquired, or will have acquired prior to the delivery of the Picture hereunder, and will maintain during the term, all rights in and to the literary and musical material upon which the Picture is based or which are used therein, and any other rights necessary and required for the exploitation of the Picture, as permitted hereunder.

c) To the best of Producer's knowledge and belief, neither the Picture nor the Materials nor any part thereof, nor any literary, dramatic, or musical works, or any other materials contained therein or synchronized therewith, nor the exercise of any right, license, or privilege herein granted, violates or will violate, or infringes or will infringe, any trademark, trade name, contract, agreement, copyright (whether common law or statutory), patent, literary, artistic, dramatic, personal, private,

DEALMAKING
IN THE
FILM AND
TELEVISION
INDUSTRY—
3RD EDITION

248

civil, or property right or right of privacy or "moral right of authors," or any law or regulation or other right whatsoever of, or slanders or libels, any person, firm, corporation, or association.

d) Producer has not sold, assigned, transferred, or conveyed and will not sell, assign, transfer, or convey, to any party, any right, title, or interest in and to the Picture or any part thereof, or in and to the dramatic, musical, or literary material upon which it is based, adverse to or derogatory of, or which would interfere with the rights granted to Distributor, and has not and will not authorize any other party to exercise any right or take any action which will derogate from the rights herein granted or purported to be granted to Distributor.

e) Producer will obtain and maintain all necessary licenses for the production, exhibition, performance, distribution, marketing, and exploitation of the Picture and/or the Materials, including, without limitation, the synchronization and performance of all music contained therein, throughout the Territory during the term for any and all purposes contemplated hereunder. Producer further represents and warrants that as between the Producer and Distributor, the performing rights to all musical compositions contained in the Picture and/or the Materials will be controlled by Producer to the extent required for the purposes of the Agreement and that no payments will be required to be made by Distributor to any third party for the use of such music in the Materials or on television or in Videogram embodying the Picture other than Guild required residual payments (or, if any such music payments are required, Producer will be solely responsible therefore).

f) Producer represents and warrants all artists, actors, musicians, and persons rendering services in connection with the production of the Picture or the materials have been or will be paid by Producer the sums required to be paid to them under applicable agreements, and the sums required to be paid pursuant to any applicable pension or similar trusts required thereby will be made by Producer, in a due and timely manner.

g) It is understood that the Producer has not obtained Errors & Omissions insurance. However, if demand is made by a sub-licensee/distributor, a certificate of errors and omissions insurance as indicated above, Distributor will advance such cost and recoup the expense from Gross Receipts. Producer shall be added as an additional named insured on any E&O policy.

h) The Picture was shot on _____ film. The Picture and the television/airline version (when available) have a running time of __ minutes, and the Picture should receive an MPAA rating no more restrictive than "R." It is understood that the Picture has not received or applied for an MPAA rating. If and when it becomes necessary to receive an MPAA rating, Producer shall promptly perform any and all additional editing necessary in order to secure said MPAA rating. The expense of securing of such rating shall be advanced by Distributor and recouped from Gross Receipts.

i) At the time of delivery of the Picture to Distributor, the Picture will not have been exhibited anywhere in the Territory for commercial purposes, with the exception of festivals or industry screenings.

10. DISTRIBUTOR'S WARRANTIES:

Distributor warrants that:

a) Distributor has the authority to enter into this agreement and there are, and, to the best of Distributor's knowledge and belief, will be, no claims, actions, suits, arbitrations, or other proceedings or investigations pending or threatened against or affecting the Distributor's ability to fulfill its obligations under this agreement, at law or in equity, or before any federal, state, county, municipal, or other governmental instrumentality or authority, domestic or foreign.

b) Distributor is and will continue to be engaged during the Term as a distributor of motion pictures throughout the licensed territory. Distributor is not unable to pay its bills in the regular course of business, is not insolvent, or in danger of bankruptcy.

c) Distributor warrants that all payments from wholesalers, retailers, and other licensees will be by check, wire transfer, letter of credit, or money order payable in the name of Distributor. If cash is accepted, a copy of license agreement with the amount of the deposit will be sent to Producer. Distributor further warrants that Distributor will not accept any other consideration, whether cash, discounts on distribution for other Pictures, favors of any kind, or any other form of consideration, from any sub-distributor or Distributor in return for licensing the Picture, unless such consideration is approved by Producer. The amount paid by Licensees shall be divided into a license fee for distribution rights and reimbursement of any duplication and manufacturing costs needed to make delivery to the licensee. Duplication and manufacturing costs

DEALMAKING
IN THE
FILM AND
TELEVISION
INDUSTRY—
3RD EDITION

250

shall be limited to the direct out-of-pocket costs incurred by Distributor to create delivery materials for the licensees. These expenses shall not be marked up, and the reimbursement of these expenses shall not be included in Gross Receipts.

d) Distributor will obtain any necessary clearances needed for any advertising and marketing materials created to promote Producer's film, and will employ artists and designers on a work-for-hire basis with Producer designated as the Employer and copyright owner of such materials.

e) Distributor shall diligently promote and license the Film throughout the licensed territory.

f) The standard of quality of all Videograms, sub-masters, and other materials manufactured or duplicated by, or at the request of Distributor, shall be of a high quality.

g) Distributor shall not use the Film, or authorize the Film, to be used in any manner that is likely to bring Producer into disrepute or which is defamatory of any person.

h) Distributor shall not make any edits, cuts, alterations, or re-arrangements to the Film as released without the prior written approval of Producer.

11. INDEMNITY: Each party hereby agrees to defend, indemnify, and hold harmless the other (and its affiliates, and its and their respective successors, assigns, distributors, officers, directors, employees, and representatives) against and for any and all claims, liabilities, damages, costs, and expenses (including reasonable attorneys' fees and court costs) arising from or related to any breach by the indemnifying party of any of its undertakings, representations, or warranties under this Agreement, and/or arising from or related to any and all third-party claims which, if proven, would be such a breach. Each party agrees to notify the other in writing of any and all claims to which this indemnity will apply, and to afford the indemnifying party the opportunity to undertake the defense of such claim(s) with counsel approved by the indemnified party (which approval will not be unreasonably withheld), subject to the right of the indemnified party to participate in such defense at its cost. In no event shall any such claim be settled in such a way as which would adversely affect the rights of the indemnified party in the Picture without such party's prior written consent; provided, however, that Producer hereby consents to any settlement entered into under any of the following circumstances: (i) the applicable insurance carrier authorized the settlement; (ii) the settlement relates to a claim for injunctive relief which has remained unsettled

or pending for a period of thirty (30) days or longer which otherwise interferes with Distributor's distribution of the Picture hereunder; or (iii) the settlement is for not more than $10,000.00. All rights and remedies of the parties hereunder will be cumulative and will not interfere with or prevent the exercise of any other right or remedy which may be available to the respective party.

12. DELIVERY MATERIALS: The Picture will be delivered as follows:

a) On or before _____, 20__, Producer will deliver to Distributor the materials specified in Exhibit A hereto, accompanied by a fully executed lab-access letter (irrevocable for the term) for access to the Master materials. The lab-access letter shall provide that at Producer's request the Laboratory will disclose to Producer a complete listing of all orders fulfilled by Laboratory for Distributor, including a description of what materials were ordered, the prices charged for the work, and to whom each order was shipped.

b) Complete Delivery means acceptance by Distributor of all the items listed in Exhibit A annexed hereto. Distributor shall have three (3) weeks to review each delivery item from receipt thereof and either approve or disapprove of an item delivered to Distributor hereunder. If Distributor does not disapprove of an item in writing (which writing must specify any alleged defects) within said three (3) week period, then the item shall be deemed approved. If Distributor makes delivery to any third-party licenses (and said third-party licensee accepts such materials), Delivery shall be deemed accepted as to such Materials as was actually delivered to said third-party licensee. If Distributor disapproves a delivery item, Producer shall have three (3) weeks to correct any defect and resubmit the item, at which time Distributor shall have another three (3) weeks to review each delivery item. If Distributor does not approve the re-delivered items, then Distributor may elect to cure the deficiencies as set forth below in a prompt and timely manner (but no later than thirty [30] days) and then after making said cure pay the Advance or terminate the Term hereof and return all Materials to Producer. For purposes of clarification hereunder, acceptance by Distributor of less than all of the delivery items required by Distributor prior to or after the Delivery Date shall not be construed as a waiver by Distributor of Producer's obligations to delivery any item required by Distributor hereunder. Under no circumstances shall Producer be relieved of the obligation to deliver all of the materials and documents required in Exhibit A by the Delivery Date, nor shall Distributor be deemed to have waived any of

DEALMAKING
IN THE
FILM AND
TELEVISION
INDUSTRY—
3RD EDITION

252

said delivery requirements unless Distributor shall so notify Producer in writing designating the particular delivery item or items which need not be delivered by Producer to Distributor, or unless delivery is deemed accepted as set forth herein. In the event Producer does not supply to Distributor any of the required items set forth in Exhibit A by the Delivery Date or cure deficiencies in previously delivered items to Distributor in a timely fashion (no later than three [3] weeks after receipt of notification of a defect), then Distributor may (but shall not be obligated to) create such item, if possible, and recoup its direct-out-of pocket costs in doing so as set forth herein.

c) Producer will concurrently with the delivery of the materials deliver to Distributor a list of contractual requirements for advertising credits to persons who rendered services or furnished materials for such Picture and a list of any restrictions.

d) All materials delivered to Distributor shall be returned to Producer within thirty (30) days of the end of the term.

(e) If Distributor creates its own artwork and trailers for the Picture, Ownership of these materials shall vest in Producer, and Producer shall have the right to use said materials at any time outside the Territory, and anywhere in the Universe after the term of this Agreement expires. Any artwork or copyrightable material commissioned by Distributor shall be created pursuant to a written contract, signed before the material is created, which states the work is a work-for-hire and that Producer is owner of all rights.

13. ADVANCE/GUARANTEE:

a) Distributor shall advance the sum of $_____, which sum shall be non-refundable but recoupable from Gross Receipts. Time is of the essence in regard to the payment of this advance. If payment is not made by _____, then Distributor's rights under this agreement are void ab initio, and Distributor immediately loses its right to distribute this Picture. [7]

14. ALLOCATION OF GROSS RECEIPTS: As to proceeds derived

---

[7] If the distributor is not willing to pay an advance, an alternative approach is to have the Distributor agree to a minimum guaranteed (MG) amount to be paid to the producer within an agreed time frame, usually the first year or so of distribution. Another option is a 50/50 guarantee which provides that the Distributor agrees to delay recoupment of its expenses and receipt of its distribution fee so that at least fifty percent (50%) of Gross Receipts are paid to Producer each accounting period. In other words, regardless of the amount of money due Distributor for recoupable expenses and its distribution fee, at least fifty percent (50%) of all Gross Receipts are paid to Producer. Distributor may recoup any outstanding balance of fees owed it from future Gross Receipts. For example, if $100,000 in Gross Receipts is received by Distributor, and if Distributor is due a total of $60,000 for recoupment of expenses and its distribution fee, Distributor would receive only $50,000 out of the first $100,000 in Gross Receipts. The outstanding $10,000 balance due Distributor could be recouped from the next $20,000 of Gross Receipts, if any.

from Distributor's exploitation of all rights outlined in Paragraph 2, division of the Gross Receipts will be made as follows:

a) From the Distributor's exploitation of Theatrical, Television, Home Video, and any other Granted Rights, Distributor shall deduct and retain twenty percent (20%) of Gross Receipts. From the remaining revenues, Distributor may recoup all recoupable expenses related to the prints, marketing, advertising, and sale of the Picture. The net proceeds shall be paid to Producer.

b) Gross Receipts: As used herein, the term "Gross Receipts" shall mean all monies actually received by and credited to Distributor, less any refunds, returns, taxes, collection costs, and manufacturing or duplication costs. Distributor may be sent advances, guarantees, security deposits, and similar payments from persons or companies licensed by Distributor to sub-distributor or otherwise exploit the Picture (which monies shall be deposited in the collection account established for this Picture). Notwithstanding the receipt of such monies, if any, and notwithstanding anything to the contrary contained herein, no such monies will be deemed to be Gross Receipts hereunder unless and until such monies are earned or deemed forfeited, or become non-returnable.

c) Deductions from Gross Receipts shall be taken in the following order:

1) Distribution fee of twenty percent (20%).

2) Recoupment of any recoupable Delivery Expenses incurred by Distributor.

3) Recoupment of any advance and any recoupable Market and Promotional Expenses incurred by Distributor.

4) Net Proceeds shall be paid to Producer.

15. RECOUPABLE EXPENSES: As used herein, the term expenses and/or recoupable expenses shall mean all of Distributor's actual expenses on behalf of the Picture limited as follows:

a) Market Expenses: These expenses include all direct out-of-pocket costs to attend film markets such as AFM, Cannes, and Berlin. Such expenses include airfare, hotel, shipping, telephone, and staff expenses incurred to attend a film market. Such expenses shall be recoupable for the first year of distribution only, and only for those markets in which Distributor is actively participating (i.e., Distributor attends, rents a suite, and is actively selling the Picture). Distributor may recoup a total of $3,500 per market attended with an overall cap of no more than $10,000 overall market cap for the year.

DEALMAKING
IN THE
FILM AND
TELEVISION
INDUSTRY—
3RD EDITION

254

Distributor agrees to attend no less than three (3) markets during the first year of distribution. Should the distribution term extend beyond one (1) year, no market expenses shall be recoupable during the second and any subsequent years, unless the parties agree otherwise in writing.

b) Promotional Expenses: These expenses include the cost of preparing posters, one-sheets, trailers, and advertising. Distributor agrees to spend no less than $25,000 and no more than $40,000 on promotional expenses. These expenses are limited to direct out-of-pocket expenses actually spent on behalf of the Picture. At Producer's request, Distributor shall provide receipts for each and every expense or forego recoupment. Recoupable promotional expenses do not include any of Distributor's general office, overhead, legal, or staff expenses, or any of the aforementioned Market Expenses. Distributor agrees to spend the minimum necessary to adequately promote the Picture, including preparation of a trailer, poster, one-sheet, videocassette, and customary promotional material, if these items have not been supplied by Producer. Distributor will use its best efforts to promote the Picture, and will promote the Picture in a no less favorable manner than any of Distributor's other films.

c) Delivery Expenses: Delivery Expenses are the direct out-of-pocket costs incurred by Distributor to manufacture any of the film or video deliverables (as listed on Exhibit A) which Producer did not supply. Delivery Expenses also include the direct out-of-pocket costs incurred between markets for shipping, duplicating, delivery of marketing materials (i.e., screeners) to foreign buyers, and phone and fax calls. At Producer's request, Distributor shall provide receipts for each and every expense or forgo recoupment. Recoupable Delivery Expenses do not include any of Distributor's general office, overhead, legal, or staff expenses, or any of the aforementioned Promotional or Market Expenses.

d) "Gross Receipts" means the sum on a continuous basis of:

i) All monies or other consideration of any kind (including all amounts from advances, guarantees, security deposits, awards, subsidies, and other allowances) received by, used by, or credited to Distributor (including any sub-distributors, agents, or affiliated parties) from the lease, license, rental, exhibition, performance, or other exercise of the Rights Licensed in the Picture, all without any deductions; and

ii) All monies or other consideration of any kind received by, used by, or credited to Distributor and Affiliated Parties as recoveries for the infringement by third parties of any of the Licensed Rights in the Picture; and

iii) All monies and other consideration of any kind received by, used by, or credited to Distributor and Affiliated Parties from any authorized dealing in trailers, prints, posters, or advertising accessories supporting the release of the Picture.

iv) "Recoupable Expense" mean all direct, auditable, out-of-pocket, reasonable, and necessary costs, exclusive of salaries and overhead, and less any discounts, credits, rebates, or similar allowances, actually paid by Distributor for exploiting the Picture in arms-length transactions with third parties, all of which will be advanced by Distributor and recouped under this Agreement.

v) In no case may any item be deducted more than once. All costs not expressly covered by the above definition will be Distributor's sole responsibility.

vi) The "Wholesale Level" means the level of Videocassette distribution from which Videocassettes are shipped directly to retailers for ultimate sale or rental to the paying public. The "Wholesale Level" may include intermediate distribution levels between the manufacturer and the retailer, such as rack jobbers and the like if such distribution is performed by a parent, subsidiary, or affiliated company of Distributor, or unless Distributor participates in the profits from such intermediate distribution, but then only to the extent of such participation.

vii) Direct Consumer Level - Defined: The "Direct Consumer Level" means the level of Videocassette distribution at which Videocassettes are sold or rented directly to the paying public. The "Direct Consumer Level" includes the sale or rental of Videocassettes by means of retail outlets, mail order, video clubs, and similar methods. Where Commercial Video rights are licensed, the "Direct Consumer Level" also includes the authorized public performance, exhibition, or diffusion of Videocassettes in accordance with the Commercial Video Licensed Right. Distributor will not be deemed to be engaged in distribution at the Direct Consumer Level unless such distribution is performed by a parent, subsidiary, or affiliated company of Distributor or unless Distributor participates in the profits from such distribution, and then only to the extent of such participation.

viii) Free TV or Pay TV Gross Receipts means for each Picture the sum on a continuous basis of: All gross income or other consideration of any kind received by, used by or

DEALMAKING
IN THE
FILM AND
TELEVISION
INDUSTRY—
3RD EDITION

256

credited to Distributor or by Distributor's subsidiaries, parent or affiliated companies, or authorized sub-distributors or agents from the exercise of the Free TV or Pay TV Licensed Rights in the Picture, all without any deductions; and all gross income or other consideration of any kind received by, used by, or credited to Distributor and Affiliated Parties as recoveries for the infringement by third parties with any of the Free TV or Pay TV Licensed Rights in the Picture, less only the reasonable costs actually paid by Distributor in obtaining such recoveries.

e) Collection Account: All proceeds from the exploitation of the Picture shall be paid directly by each licensee in the Territory into a segregated account (the "Collection Account") held by the Collection Agent, and all receipts must be assigned directly to the Collection Account in accordance with the provisions of a collection account-management agreement ("Collection Account Agreement") entered into by Distributor, Producer, and Collection Agent, or as otherwise mutually agreed by Producer and Distributor. Distributor will include this requirement in all sub-license agreements regarding the Picture. In the event that Distributor receives any proceeds in connection with the Picture, Distributor will promptly forward such monies to the Collection Account. In the event of any conflict between the provisions of this Agreement with respect to Gross Receipts and the Collection Account Agreement, the provisions of the Collection Account Agreement shall prevail.

f) No Fees to Others: Distributor's subsidiaries, parent or affiliated company, and approved sub-distributors or agents may not deduct or charge any fee against Gross Receipts in calculating all amounts due Producer. It is the intent of this provision that, for the purpose of determining Producer's share of Gross Receipts, all Gross Receipts be calculated at "source." By way of clarification, Theatrical or Non-Theatrical Gross Receipts will be calculated at the level at which payments are remitted by local exhibitors of the Picture to the public. Home Video, or Commercial Video Gross Receipts will be calculated at the Wholesale Level or Direct Consumer Level, as appropriate, and Free TV or Pay TV Gross Receipts will be calculated at the level at which payments are remitted by local telecasters of the Picture.

16. CONTRACTS: Distributor will use exclusively IFTA deal memos and model contracts. Distributor will provide copies of all Deal Memos and contracts to Producer within fourteen (14) days of their execution.

17. PACKAGE SALES: The Picture may be included in any of Distributor's package of motion pictures provided that

Distributor shall make a fair and reasonable allocation of the package price to each of the pictures in the package, and provided that the price allocated to Producer's Picture shall be at least the minimum set forth in Schedule A, attached.

18. LATE PAYMENTS/LIEN: Producer shall hold a lien and security interest on the gross receipts and distribution contracts for the Picture. All monies due Producer shall be paid in accordance with this agreement. Distributor shall pay Producer interest on any amounts thirty (30) days past due at the lesser of 1) ten percent (10%) per annum, or 2) the maximum legal rate of interest. Time is of the essence hereof in regard to all payments due Producer.

19. SECURITY INTEREST: As security for payment of Producer's share of Gross Receipts, hereunder, Distributor hereby grants and assigns to Producer a lien and security interest in all of Distributor's right title and interest in and to (i) all rights granted to Distributor in the Picture and its underlying material, (ii) all film elements, videotapes, sound elements, and other physical materials of any kind to be used in the exploitation of the Picture by Distributor from exploitation of the Picture by Distributor, (iii) all proceeds realized by Distributor from exploitation of the Picture, to which Producer is entitled as Producer's share of Gross Receipts hereunder. With respect to said security interest, Producer shall have all the rights, power, and privileges of a secured party under the California Uniform Commercial Code as the same may be amended from time to time. Distributor agrees to sign and deliver to Producer all such financing statements and other instruments as may be legally necessary for Producer to file, register, and or record such security interests.

20. DEFAULT/TERMINATION:

a) Distributor Default: If it is found and proven that Distributor has defaulted on its obligations under this agreement, upon notification of that fact from Producer, Distributor will have thirty (30) days to cure said default. If the default is not cured within the allotted period, the Producer will have the right to initiate arbitration.

b) Producer Default: Distributor shall notify Producer in writing of any alleged default hereunder. Producer shall have thirty (30) days to correct alleged default before Distributor will have the right to initiate arbitration.

c) Termination Rights: No failure by either party hereto to perform any of its obligations under this Agreement shall be deemed to be a material breach of this Agreement until the

DEALMAKING
IN THE
FILM AND
TELEVISION
INDUSTRY—
3RD EDITION

258

non-breaching party has given the breaching party written notice of its failure to perform and such failure has not been corrected within thirty (30) business days from and after the giving of such notice. In the event of an uncured material breach, either party shall be entitled to terminate this Agreement (subject to arbitration) by written notice to the other party, obtain monetary damages and other appropriate relief, and, in the case of Producer, regain all of its rights in the Picture subject to existing executory contracts and licenses respecting Picture.

Producer shall have the right to terminate this Agreement and cause all rights herein conveyed to Distributor to revert to Producer subject, however, to third-party agreements conveying rights in the Picture (in respect to which Producer shall be deemed an assignee of all of Distributor's rights therein in respect to the Picture), by written notice to Distributor in the event that Distributor files a petition in bankruptcy or consents to an involuntary petition in bankruptcy or to any reorganization under Chapter 11 of the Bankruptcy Act. Notwithstanding anything to the contrary which may be contained in the preceding sentence, in the event that Distributor files a petition in bankruptcy or consents to an involuntary petition in bankruptcy or to any reorganization under Chapter 11 of the Bankruptcy Act, Producer shall not be entitled to terminate this Agreement if thereafter: (1) Distributor segregates Producer's share of the monies that Distributor receives in connection with the Picture and places the monies into a separate trust account, and that such monies are not commingled with Distributor's other funds, and Producer's share of such monies shall become Producer's property immediately upon the collection by Distributor, and (2) this procedure is approved by the Bankruptcy Court. In connection with the foregoing, Distributor hereby grants to Producer a security interest in the Picture and the right to receive monies from the exploitation of the Picture ("Security Interest"). Producer may by written notice to Distributor execute against the Security Interest if and only if Distributor files a petition in bankruptcy or consents to an involuntary bankruptcy or an organization under Chapter 11 and Producer is entitled to terminate this Agreement in accordance with the other provisions of this Paragraph.

21. ACCOUNTINGS:

a) Distributor will render, or cause to be rendered to Producer and his attorney, quarterly accounting statements ("Producer Reports") commencing forty-five (45) days after the first quarter in which any deposit or licensee fee has been paid for exploitation of the Picture in any portion of the territory, for the first year of this agreement. Thereafter, quarterly statements will be made within forty-five (45) days after the last day of Distributor's then-current fiscal accounting period. All monies due and payable to Producer pursuant to this Agreement shall be paid simultaneously with the rendering of such statements. Statements and payments shall be sent to: PRODUCER FILMS, INC., at _____ with a copy of statements to _____. Payments shall be made payable to "PRODUCER FILMS, INC."

b) Producer will be deemed to have consented to all accountings rendered by Distributor or its assignees, or successors and all such statements will be binding upon Producer unless specific objections in writing, stating the basis thereof, is given by Producer within thirty-six (36) months of Producer's receipt of each Producer Report.

c) Distributor shall keep and maintain at its office in Los Angeles County, California, until expiration of the Term and for a period of five (5) years thereafter, complete detailed, permanent, true, and accurate books of account and records relating to the distribution and exhibition of the Picture, including, but not limited to, detailed collections and sales by country and/or buyer, detailed billings thereon, detailed playdates thereof, detailed records of expenses that have been deducted from collections received from the exploitation of the Picture, and the whereabouts of prints, trailers, accessories, and other material in connection with the Picture. Records shall be kept in accordance with Generally Accepted Accounting Principles (GAAP). Producer shall be entitled to inspect such books and records of Distributor relating to the Picture during regular business hours and shall be entitled to audit such books and records of Distributor relating to the Picture upon ten (10) business days' written notice to Distributor and provided that not more than one audit is conducted every twelve (12) months during each calendar year and further provided that such audit shall last not more than ten (10) consecutive business days once begun and does not interfere with Distributor's normal operations. Within thirty (30) days of the completion of the audit, Producer will furnish Distributor with a copy of said audit. In the event that the audit discloses that Producer has been underpaid $5,000.00 or more, Distributor shall reimburse Producer for all audit costs. Otherwise, all audit expenses shall be borne by Producer.

d) Relationship Between Parties: Distributor will hold the Producer's portion of Gross receipts in trust for Producer. This agreement will not constitute a partnership or joint venture

DEALMAKING
IN THE
FILM AND
TELEVISION
INDUSTRY—
3RD EDITION

260

between Distributor and Producer, and neither of the parties will become bound or liable because of any representations, acts, or omissions of the other party hereto.

22. ASSUMPTION AGREEMENT: Distributor agrees to sign the customary assumption agreements required by any Union/ Guild agreements which are applicable to the Picture.[8]

23. NOTICES: All notices, correspondence, writings and statements shall be forwarded to the addresses and numbers as follows: PRODUCER FILMS, INC., at _____, fax number _____, with a copy to _____, at _____, fax number _____; DISTRIBUTION, INC., at _____, fax number _____, with a copy to _____, at _____, fax number _____. Fax receptions shall be deemed an acceptable mode of acceptance of all notices, writings, and statements unless otherwise agreed. In all instances hard copies will follow all telephonic or fax correspondence. Both parties reserve the right to change the address of service at any time with notice in writing to the receiving party.

24. ASSIGNMENT: This agreement will be binding upon and will inure to the benefit of the parties hereto and their respective successors and permitted assigns. Producer may assign its rights to payment of monies. Distributor may not assign its rights without the prior written consent of Producer, provided that nothing herein will prevent Distributor from assigning its rights to a successor company that may arise from Distributor merging, being acquired, or partnering with another company.

25. ARBITRATION AND JURISDICTION: This Agreement shall be interpreted in accordance with the laws of the State of California, applicable to agreements executed and to be wholly performed therein. Any dispute under this Agreement will be resolved by final and binding arbitration under the Independent Film & Television Alliance Rules for International Arbitration in effect as of the effective date of this Agreement ("IFTA Rules"). Each Party waives any right to adjudicate any dispute in any other court or forum, *except* that a Party may seek interim relief before the start of arbitration as allowed by the IFTA Rules. The arbitration will be held in the Forum designated in the Agreement, or, if none is designated, as determined by the IFTA Rules. The Parties will abide by any decision in the arbitration and any court having jurisdiction may enforce it. The Parties submit to the jurisdiction of the courts in the

---

[8] Note that many independent distributors will refuse to sign assumption agreements, not wanting to have to send residuals to any unions.

Forum to compel arbitration or to confirm an arbitration award. The Parties agree to accept service of process in accordance with the IFTA Rules. The prevailing party shall be entitled to reimbursement of attorney fees and costs.

26. ENTIRE AGREEMENT: This Agreement is intended by the parties hereto as a final expression of their Agreement and understanding with respect to the subject matter hereof and as a complete and exclusive statement of the terms thereof (unless amended in writing by both parties) and supersedes any and all prior and contemporaneous agreements and understanding thereto. This Agreement will be understood in all respects to lay under the jurisdiction of California law and the laws of the United States of America. All parties agree that because of the specialized interest of this Agreement pertaining to entertainment that it is in both parties' interests that confirmation of any arbitration award, and any other matters of law, be submitted to the jurisdiction of the U.S. District Court for the Central District of California, or the Superior Courts in Los Angeles County. The parties waive their rights to transfer such actions to any other jurisdictions and will be bound by the decisions of such courts.

In the event of any conflict or action between the parties, the prevailing party shall be entitled to recoup its reasonable attorney fees and court costs and expenses from the non-prevailing party.

Paragraph headings in this Agreement are used for convenience only and will not be used to interpret or construe the provisions of this Agreement.

IN WITNESS WHEREOF, the parties have executed this agreement as of the date hereof.

DISTRIBUTION, INC.

By: _____

Its: _____

ACCEPTED AND AGREED:

_____

Ms. Sally Producer on behalf of

PRODUCER FILMS, INC.

DEALMAKING
IN THE
FILM AND
TELEVISION
INDUSTRY—
3RD EDITION

262

EXHIBIT A

DELIVERY REQUIREMENTS[9]

Delivery of the Picture shall consist of Producer making delivery, at Producer's expense, to either DISTRIBUTOR or a laboratory designated by Producer (with a lab-access letter given to Distributor) for all the items set forth below.

IT IS UNDERSTOOD THAT ALL THEATRICAL ELEMENTS LISTED FOR THE FEATURE AND TRAILER ARE LISTED ON A "AS AVAILABLE BASIS" AND ARE NOT REQUIRED DELIVERY ITEMS.

All delivery Materials set forth below shall be of the highest technical quality, free from defects, and shall conform to the final edited version of the Picture and shall be in the same ratio of camera picture images in which the Picture was photographed. All Delivery Materials set forth below will be delivered either by Producer (a) making Physical Delivery of the following materials at Producer's sole expense, or (b) granting access to such materials by a fully executed irrevocable Laboratory Access Letter.

1. FEATURE FILM ELEMENTS – Each of the following must be new, fully color-corrected, and of the highest technical quality and condition. All picture and sound negatives must be free of physical damage.

a. Original Cut Picture Negative or Digital Intermediate Negative: Laboratory access to the original first-class completely edited color 35mm picture negative.

b. Original Textless Negative or Digital Intermediate Negative Backgrounds: Laboratory access to the original 35mm picture negative of the backgrounds used to create optical effects in the main, credit, insert, and end titles of the Picture, which shall be supplied as a separate reel of picture negative.

c. Textless Backgrounds & Overlays; Titles and Texted Scenes: As needed, Physical delivery of one (1) set of first-class, completely edited, color 35mm Interpositives made from the Original Picture Negative of the following: All main and end title textless backgrounds without lettering. Textless backgrounds without lettering of any forewords and/or other scenes carrying superimposed titles.

d. Answer Print: As needed, Physical delivery of one (1) first-

---

[9] This is a sample delivery list. Note that which delivery elements are required will depend how the motion picture was shot (i.e. HD, film stock) and the inclusion or deletion of some of these items is negotiable. Some distributors may agree to pay for some delivery items.

class, completely edited, 35mm composite answer print from the Original Picture Negative, fully timed and color-corrected, made from the items in paragraph A1 above.

e. Interpositive: As needed, Physical delivery of one (1) first-class 35mm fully timed Interpositive of the Picture made from the Original Picture Negative or from the Digital Intermediate Negative. The Interpositive shall be fully cut, main and end titled, edited and assembled, and conformed in all respects to the composite Answer Print and Original Picture Negative.

f. Internegative: As needed, Physical delivery of one (1) first-class 35mm Estar Internegatives of the Picture made from the first-generation Interpositive manufactured from the Original Picture Negative.

g. Check Print: As needed, Physical delivery of one (1) complete first-class composite 35mm check print of the Picture made from the Internegative, fully color corrected, fully cut, main and end titled, edited, scored, and assembled and conformed in all respects to the Answer Print.

h. Trims and Outtakes: Laboratory access to all unused takes and trims and all other film picture and soundtrack material produced for or used in the process of preparing the Picture, whether or not actually used in the Picture if the picture was completed using the Digital Intermediate Negative, access to all data files used to create the digital intermediate in LTO or DTF2 or an equivalent agreed upon format.

i. TV Cover Materials and ADR: Laboratory access to the negative and positive prints of all alternate takes, cover shots, looped dialogue lines (ADR), and other material ("Cover Material") used to create the television version if the picture was completed using the Digital Intermediate Negative, access to all data files used to create the digital intermediate in LTO or DTF2 or an equivalent agreed-upon format. The Cover Material shall be boxed separately and clearly marked for identification.

2. SOUND ELEMENTS

a. Soundtrack Negative: As needed, Physical delivery of one (1) first-class, fully mixed and recorded, 35mm optical soundtrack negative of the Picture, made from 2.d., capable of printing in perfect synchronization with the original Negative and conforming in all aspects to the answer print (including combined dialogue, sound effects, and music) on Estar base stock made from the DVD-R discs described below or from the 2-track Printmaster described below. The Soundtrack negative must contain the Dolby SR/Dolby SR-D (and/or SDDS and/

DEALMAKING
IN THE
FILM AND
TELEVISION
INDUSTRY—
3RD EDITION

264

or DTS, to be determined prior to delivery). The Soundtrack Negative must be ready in all respects for use in the manufacture of release prints.

b. 5.1 Printmaster + LT/RT: Physical Delivery of (2) DA88[10] 6+2-Track (5.1 mix) Printmasters of the Picture with the track configuration of left/center/right/left surround, right surround, sub woofer, LT/ RT. One (1) DA88 master in sync with Digibeta PAL 16/9 master and one (1) DA88 master in sync with Digibeta NTSC 16/9 master. Physical delivery of one (1) DVD-R.

c. 6+2 M&E Master: Physical Delivery of one (2) DA88 6-track (5.1 mix) fully filled and in perfect sync with the original soundtrack. M&E containing a stereo configuration of left/center/right/left surround, right surround, sub woofer, plus one track of extra or optional material containing any special sound elements peculiar to the Picture (e.g., grunts, groans, shouts, screams, breaths, echoes, foreign-language dialogue, dialogue from on-screen radios/computers/televisions, etc., and dialogue track. One (1) DA88 master in sync with Digibeta PAL 16/9 master and one (1) DA88 master in sync with Digibeta NTSC 16/9 master. Physical delivery of one (1) DVD-R.

d. DVD-R: Physical Delivery of one (1) DVD-R containing the Dolby SR and SR-D Printmasters, conformed to the final version of the Picture.

e. 6-track DME: Physical Delivery of one (1) DA88 stereo mix master with separate stereo dialogue tracks, separate stereo music track, and separate stereo effects

f. 5.1 Final Mix Stems: Physical Delivery of one (1) set of uncompressed DVD-R of the SR-D mix master stems, containing all separate stereo 6-track dialogue stems, all separate stereo 6-track music stems, all separate stereo 6-track effects stems, and one (1) set of DA88s of the Dolby SR-D mix master stems, containing all separate stereo 6-track dialogue stems, all separate stereo 6-track music stems, all separate stereo 6-track effects.

g. Musical Score and Source: Physical Delivery of One (1) CD-ROM w/AIFF files in original sample bit rate.

h. Closed Captions: The English-language closed-captioning disk containing pop-up style text for the NTSC version of the final feature.

---

[10] Instead of delivery by DA88, Pro Tools sessions can be accepted with the understanding that the files would need to be delivered with standard def EBU and DFTC time code and must conform to the PAL and NTSC down conversion feature masters along with a conformed set to the HD master (if the 5.1 Printmaster is not included on the HD master).

3. VIDEO ELEMENTS

a. High-Definition Video Masters: Physical Delivery of the following D-5 long-play 1080 24P high-definition versions, fully color-corrected and titled with stereo left and right mix of the original theatrical soundtrack on Channels 1&2 and the fully filled stereo M&E on Channels 3&4. The textless title backgrounds shall be properly slated and transferred at the end of the Picture end credit roll for each aspect ratio:

One (1) D5 long play 16/9 (1:33:1 side matted)

One (1) D5 long play 16x9 full height anamorphic 1:78

One (1) D5 long play 16/9 original aspect ratio anamorphic

b. Standard-Definition Video Masters: Physical Delivery of the following videotape masters, fully color-corrected and titled with audio Channels 1&2 containing a stereo left and right mix of the original sound and Channels 3&4 containing a stereo left and right mix of the fully filled music and effects tracks. The textless title backgrounds shall be properly slated and transferred at the end of the Picture end credit roll for each aspect ratio:

One (1) Digital Betacam NTSC 4x3/1.33:1 Full Frame

One (1) Digital Betacam NTSC 16x9 anamorphic 1.78:1 Full Frame

One (1) Digital Betacam NTSC 16x9 anamorphic original aspect ratio

One (1) Digital Betacam PAL 4x3/1.33:1 Full Frame

One (1) Digital Betacam PAL 16x9 anamorphic 1.78:1 Full Frame

One (1) Digital Betacam PAL 16x9 anamorphic original aspect ratio

c. Trailer Masters: If available, Physical Delivery of the following videotape masters with audio Channels 1&2 containing a stereo left and right mix of the original sound and Channels 3&4 containing a stereo left and right mix of the fully filled music and effects tracks. The textless title backgrounds shall be properly slated and transferred at the end of the Picture end credit roll for each aspect ratio:

One (1) Digital Betacam NTSC & PAL 4x3/1.33:1 Full Frame

4. TRAILER FILM ELEMENTS – If available (Flat & scope/ texted and textless versions), each of the following must be new, fully color-corrected, and of the highest technical quality and condition. All picture and sound negatives must be free of physical damage and all splices must be sound, secure, and transparent. The Trailer must be filmed in an aspect ratio

DEALMAKING
IN THE
FILM AND
TELEVISION
INDUSTRY—
3RD EDITION

266

(TBD) with a full frame at all times. Hard mattes are not acceptable.

a. Original Picture Negative or Digital Intermediate Negative: If available, laboratory access to the original first-class, completely edited, color 35mm Trailer negative, fully timed.

b. Original Textless Negative or Digital Intermediate Negative Backgrounds: If available, laboratory access to the original 35mm Trailer negative of the backgrounds used to create optical effects in the main, credit, insert, and end titles of the Picture, which shall be supplied as a separate reel of picture negative.

c. Textless Backgrounds & Overlays; Titles and Texted Scenes: If available, Physical delivery of one (1) set of first-class, completely edited, color 35mm Interpositives made from the Original Trailer Negative of the following:

All main and end title textless backgrounds without lettering.

Textless backgrounds without lettering of any forewords and/or other scenes carrying superimposed titles.

d. Answer Print: If available, Physical delivery of one (1) first-class, completely edited, 35mm composite answer print from the Original Trailer Negative, fully timed and color-corrected, made from the items in Paragraph A1 above.

e. Interpositive: If available, Physical delivery of one (1) first-class 35mm Interpositive of the Trailer made from the Original Trailer Negative. The Interpositive shall be fully cut, main and end titled, edited and assembled, and conformed in all respects to the composite Answer Print and Original Picture Negative.

f. Internegative: If available, Physical delivery of one (1) first-class 35mm Estar Internegative of the Trailer made from the first-generation Interpositive manufactured from the Original Trailer Negative.

g. Check Print: If available, Physical delivery of one (1) complete first-class composite 35mm check print of the Trailer made from the Internegative, fully color corrected, fully cut, main and end titled, edited, scored, and assembled, and conformed in all respects to the Answer Print.

5. TRAILER SOUND ELEMENTS

a. Soundtrack Negative: If available, Physical delivery of one (1) first-class, completely edited, 35mm synchronizing optical soundtrack negative (including combined dialogue, sound effects, and music) on Estar base stock made from the Modular Optical Discs described below or from the 2-track Printmaster described below. The Soundtrack negative must contain the Dolby SR/Dolby SR-D (and/or SDDS and/or DTS, to be determined prior to delivery.) The Soundtrack Negative must be ready in all respects for use in the manufacture of release prints.

b. 5.1 Printmaster + LT/RT: Physical Delivery of one (1) DA88 6-Track (5.1 mix) Printmasters of the Picture plus 2-track LT/RT Printmaster containing a stereo configuration of left/ center/right/surround, extra or containing any special sound elements peculiar to the Picture (e.g., grunts, groans, shouts, screams, breaths, echoes, foreign-language dialogue, dialogue from on-screen radios/computers/televisions). Physical delivery of one (1) DVD-R.

c. 4 + 2 M&E Master: Physical Delivery of one (1) DA88 6-track fully filled music and effects master of the Picture containing a stereo configuration of left/center/right/surround, extra or optional material containing any special sound elements peculiar to the Picture (e.g., grunts, groans, shouts, screams, breaths, echoes, foreign-language dialogue, dialogue from on-screen radios/computers/televisions, etc.) and dialogue guide track. Physical delivery of one (1) DVD-R.

d. 6-track DME: Physical Delivery of one (1) DA88 stereo mix master with separate stereo dialogue tracks, separate stereo music track, and separate stereo effects track, and one (1) Magneto Optical disc of the 6-track DME.

e. 5.1 Final Mix Stems: Physical Delivery of one (1) set of original uncompressed DVD-R mix master stems, containing all separate stereo 6-track dialogue stems, all separate stereo 6-track music stems, all separate stereo 6-track effects stems, and one (1) set of DA88s of the Dolby SR-D mix master stems, containing all separate stereo 6-track dialogue stems, all separate stereo 6-track music stems, all separate stereo 6-track.

6. PROTECTION ELEMENTS

a. Source and Feature Picture Elements: A fully executed and acceptable Laboratory Access Letter giving the Licensee irrevocable access to all picture materials in this schedule noted as Access items including, but not limited to, the original camera tapes and all pre-print and protection materials related to the Picture, and all of its trailers and TV spots that are being held by a laboratory or facility.

DEALMAKING
IN THE
FILM AND
TELEVISION
INDUSTRY—
3RD EDITION

268

b. Sound Elements: A fully executed and acceptable Laboratory Access Letter granting the Licensee irrevocable access to all audio materials in this schedule noted as Access items including, but not limited to, the original production recorded tapes, wild lines, looped lines, original music recorded masters, the individual dialogue, sound effects, music units, all resultant pre-dubs and dubbed masters of original language tracks of the Picture, and all of its trailers and TV spots, each as held by a storage or sound facility.

c. Audio Recordings, Tracks, and Masters: A fully executed and acceptable Access Letter giving the Licensee irrevocable access to the original music recorded tapes, the individual dialogue, sound effects, music units, all resultant pre-lay recordings and sweetened masters of original language tracks of the Picture, and all of its Trailers and TV spots, each as held by the storage or sound facility.

7. ADDED VALUE & PROMOTIONAL MATERIALS – Physical Delivery of all elements that are either produced by the Producers or domestic Theatrical/DVD distributor, fully cleared for international use and ready for inclusion in the DVD master:

a. EPK, featurette, deleted scenes, trims, outs, B-roll, alternate scenes, cover shots, audio commentary, alternate audio, and making-of footage.

8. RECORDS, DOCUMENTS, AND PUBLICITY MATERIALS

All items to be delivered below shall be in the English language and Physically Delivered.

a. Underlying Materials: One (1) typewritten copy of the final shooting script of the Film.

b. Combined Dialogue and Action Continuity: One (1) typewritten copy in the English language, including translations of all dialogue not in English, of the complete final dialogue and action continuity script conformed to the theatrical version of the Film containing all dialogue, narration, and song vocals, as well as a cut-by-cut description of the picture action (identified by footage) in a form suitable for use in connection with dubbing and subtitling the Film and conforming exactly to the photographic action and soundtrack of the Film.

c. Black & White Stills: Any and all available 35mm black and white stills, slides, or digital photos. All photographs shall be suitable for use in the preparation of advertising, exhibition, and publicity material for the Film. Negatives or transparencies, if negatives are not available, must be included with all still and slides. Producer shall deliver any and all releases from persons appearing in the photographs needed for Distributor's intended use thereof.

d. Color Stills: Any and all available 35mm color stills, slides, or digital photos. All photographs shall be suitable for use in the preparation of advertising, exhibition, and publicity material for the Film. Negatives or transparencies, if negatives are not available, must be included with all still and slides. Producer shall deliver any and all releases from persons appearing in the photographs needed for Distributor's intended use thereof

e. Publicity Materials: If and as available, one (1) typewritten copy of each of the following materials:

Approved biographies of each member of the principal cast and production staff

All available press clippings

Press kits

Epk

Synopses

Production notes

Flyers

Behind the scenes footage

Interviews and commentaries

Any other publicity material created

f. Final Main and End Credits: One (1) electronic file of the final main and end titles of the Film as they appear on the Original Negative.

g. Paid Ad Credits and Billing Block. One (1) electronic file of credit billings listing all cast and production credits for the theatrical, television, and video complete versions of the Film to be given in paid advertising (including posters, print, and outdoor ads) with the applicable contractual language relating to such advertising, together with a layout of the advertising copy in the form of a billing block.

h. Dubbing, Subtitling, and Editing Restrictions: One (1) electronic file specifying all of the following restrictions, if any:

All dubbing and subtitling restrictions relating to the replacement of any artist's voice,

Any other restrictions relating to dubbing or subtitling, including the dubbing of dialogue in a language other than that in which the Film was originally recorded.

DEALMAKING
IN THE
FILM AND
TELEVISION
INDUSTRY—
3RD EDITION

270

All contractual rights granted to any party to supervise or otherwise participate in the foreign dubbing and translations of the Film, the video formatting, editing for television or other post-production or editing processes.

i. Residual Materials: One (1) copy of each of the following materials:

Final cast list as prepared by Producer's payroll company from which all residuals are to be calculated.

IATSE pro-rata sheet, if applicable.

Written statement setting forth any and all guilds which may be applicable to the Film (i.e., SAG, WGA, DGA, IATSE, AFofM, AFTRA, ACTRA, DGC [Directors Guild of Canada], etc.)

j. Guild Approvals:

Directors Guild Credit Approval: If the Film is produced under the jurisdiction of the Directors Guild of America ("DGA"), a letter from the DGA approving the list of screen credits for the Film submitted to the DGA pursuant to Article 8-201 of the DGA Basic Agreement.

Writers Guild Credit Verification: If the Film is produced under the jurisdiction of the Writers Guild of America ("WGA"), a copy of the Notice of Tentative Writing Credits submitted to the WGA and, if the writing credits were submitted to a WGA credit arbitration, a copy of a letter from the WGA setting forth the final writing credits as determined by the WGA Credits Committee.

Production Designer Credit Waiver: If the Film is produced under the jurisdiction of the Society of Motion Picture and Television Art Directors Local 876 ("Art Directors Guild") and Producer desires to accord credit to the art director in the form "Production Designer," a copy of a written waiver from the Art Directors Guild approving the use of such "Production Designer" credit.

k. Music Cue Sheet: One (1) electronic file of the music cue sheet detailing the particulars of all music contained in the final version of the Film, including the title of each composition; the usages and the number of such uses; the place of each composition showing the film footage and running time of each cue; the performing rights society involved for each composer and publisher; the percentage of ownership for each composer and publisher; and any other information customarily set forth in music cue sheets.

l. Music License Materials: One (1) fully executed copy of each music synchronization, master use, and performance license covering each musical composition embodied in each version of the Film. Where any music performance license is claimed to be available by blanket license from a performing rights society, Producer may, in lieu of an individual license, provide copies certified by Producer to be complete and accurate in all material respects, of the composer, lyricist, and publisher affiliation agreements with the applicable performing rights society and the inclusion of the subject musical composition in the performing rights society's catalogue.

m. Final Cast and Crew List: One (1) electronic file of a list indicating: (i) the names, addresses, and telephone numbers of each cast member (including the character they portrayed); and, (ii) the names, addresses, and telephone numbers of all technical personnel (including their title or assignment) involved in the production of the Film.

n. Service Agreements: One (1) fully executed copy of all agreements or other documents related to the engagement of all personnel and facilities in connection with the Film, including those for individual producer(s), the director, editor, casting director, director of photography, unit production manager, 1st and 2nd assistant directors; one (1) typewritten statement setting forth any and all nudity restrictions with respect to any actor's services with the applicable contractual language relating to any such nudity restrictions.

o. Rating Certificate: A fully paid certificate by the Code and Rating Administration of the MPAA granting the Film the rating required under the Agreement.

p. Dolby, SDDS, and DTS Licenses: One (1) fully executed copy of the applicable license agreement in full force and effect between Producer and the sound laboratory(ies) in connection with the Film.

q. TV Version Records and Documentation: One (1) typewritten copy of a statement setting forth in specific detail all cover shots taken for the TV version of the Film, including all dialogue changes and film cuts.

r. Inventory Listing: One (1) typewritten copy setting forth in specific detail the complete contents of all production boxes of film and sound elements which are Physically Delivered to Distributor or to which Distributor has been granted Laboratory Access, including, but not limited to:

DEALMAKING
IN THE
FILM AND
TELEVISION
INDUSTRY—
3RD EDITION

272

Conductor's score of all music recorded for the Film

Music scoring logs

s. Chain of Title Documents: Producer shall deliver the following documents to Distributor:

Contracts: One (1) fully executed copy of any and all documents, instruments and contracts pertaining to the acquisition of all underlying materials, including all literary and/or screenplay material, upon which the Film is based, including, but not limited to, assignments, licenses, consents, and releases pertaining to all works of authorship and rights under copyright, trademark, and other property or third-party rights purchased and/or licensed by Producer which evidences Producer's chain of ownership in and to the rights granted to Distributor in connection with the Film. With respect to any non-English documents, a certified copy of the English translation thereof will be concurrently delivered to Distributor.

Short-Form Assignment: One (1) fully executed original copy of a Short-Form Assignment executed by duly authorized principals or officers of Producer in the presence of a Notary Public.

Copyright Certificates: One (1) fully executed copy of a Form PA copyright registration certificate(s) and any renewal certificate(s) for the Film and the Underlying Material plus evidence of filing with the U.S. Copyright Office for recordation (i.e., a copy of the cover letter and payment of the filing fee or a copy of the recorded Form PA as registered with the U.S. Copyright Office).

Copyright and Title Opinions and Reports: One (1) copy of a Copyright Opinion and Report and one (1) copy of a Title Opinion and Report issued within the last six (6) months by Thomson & Thomson or a similar institution known within the entertainment industry to provide such services.

Other Documentation: Need Physical Delivery of fully executed original copies of each of the following documents:

Copyright Mortgage and Assignment: Two (2) fully executed original copies executed by a duly authorized principal or officer of Producer in the presence of a Notary Public.

Final Certified Cost Statement: One (1) fully executed original copy certified by Producer's Chief Financial Officer as being a true, correct, and complete accounting of the final negative cost of the Film.

Form UCC-1: Two (2) fully executed original copies executed by a duly authorized principal or officer of Producer.

t. Insurance Certificates and Endorsements: Physical Delivery of separate original Certificates of Insurance and Endorsements thereto evidencing Producer's Errors & Omissions coverage reflecting no material exclusions and in a form and substance satisfactory to Distributor reflecting inclusion of all of the following language:

Certificates: Each of the following will be named as additional insured on separate original Certificates of Insurance:

Distributor, and any direct or indirect parent, subsidiary, and affiliate, and the successors, licensees, assigns, and customers of each of them, and the officers, directors, agents, attorneys, and employees of each of them, at 3907 W. Alameda Ave., Burbank CA, 91505.

Producer's limits of coverage not less than US$1,000,000 for each claim and US$3,000,000 aggregate for all claims.

A policy deductible no greater than US$25,000.

A policy term expiring not earlier than three (3) years following either (i) the start of principal photography of the Film provided the production of the Film has not been completed as of the date of the Agreement; or (ii) Delivery of the Film to Distributor.

Inclusion of all media, title, and music coverage.

Endorsements: Each of the above-referenced separate original Certificates of Insurance must be accompanied by separate original Endorsements thereto evidencing the named additional insureds interest in the Film and reflecting inclusion of all of the following language:

During the term of Producer's coverage, Producer's coverage will be primary and any insurance coverage provided by the named additional insured will apply solely to the benefit of the named additional insured as excess insurance over and above Producer's coverage.

Producer's insurance may not be modified, revised, or canceled without separate thirty (30) days prior notice to each named additional insured at their addresses indicated above.

With respect only to Distributor's Endorsement, the following additional language must be reflected thereon: The insurance carrier will, at no additional cost, name any other person(s) as additional insured and issue to such person(s) a separate original Certificate of Insurance and separate original Endorsement thereto evidencing Producer's Errors

DEALMAKING
IN THE
FILM AND
TELEVISION
INDUSTRY—
3RD EDITION

274

& Omissions coverage upon the request and designation of Distributor at any time during the policy term.

Each separate original Certificate of Insurance and separate original Endorsement thereto will be delivered to Distributor on the date Producer obtains the policy, but, with respect to any Film which has not commenced production as of the date of the Agreement, in no event later than commencement of principal photography or the date any such policy or binder of coverage or endorsement is provided to the production lender. Distributor will be responsible to deliver such original documents to each named additional insured.

SCHEDULE A

TERRITORIAL MINIMUMS

TERRITORY	ASKING PRICES	MINIMUMS THEATRICAL	MINIMUMS VIDEO	MINIMUMS TELEVISION	MINIMUMS ALL RIGHTS
ARGENTINA/CHILE/URUGUAY/PARAGUAY	$40,000	$20,000			$20,000
ASIA (PAY TELEVISION)	25,000			10,000	12,500
AUSTRALIA/NZ	75,000	30,000	5,000	15,000	50,000
BANGLADESH	12,000	4,000	1,000	1,000	6,000
BENELUX	60,000	25,000	2,000	5,000	32,000
BRAZIL	50,000	20,000	5,000		25,000
BULGARIA	10,000	3,000	1,000	1,000	5,000
CANADA (ENGLISH)	80,000	25,000	5,000	10,000	40,000
CANADA (FRENCH)	30,000	10,000	2,000	2,000	14,000
CHINA	30,000	10,000	2,000	2,000	14,000
COLOMBIA	15,000	5,000			5,000
CROATIA/SLOVENIA	7,500	2,000	1,000	1,000	4,000
CZECH/SLOVAK REPUBLICS	7,500	2,000	1,000	1,000	4,000
DOMINICAN REPUBLIC	5,000	1,500			1,500
EAST & WEST AFRICA	25,000	10,000	5,000		15,000
ECUADOR/PERU/BOLIVIA	15,000	5,000			5,000
FRENCH-SPEAKING EUROPE	100,000	40,000	STRAIGHT DIST	10,000	50,000
GERMAN-SPEAKING EUROPE	200,000	70,000	20,000	35,000	125,000
GREECE/CYPRUS	20,000	7,500	2,000	2,000	11,500
HONG KONG	20,000	7,500	2,000	3,000	12,500
HUNGARY	10,000	2,000	1,000	2,000	5,000
INDIA	20,000	5,000	2,000	2,000	9,000
INDONESIA	25,000	7,500	2,000	2,000	11,500
ISRAEL	15,000	5,000	1,500	1,500	8,000
ITALIAN-SPEAKING EUROPE	100,000	30,000	5,000	15,000	50,000
JAPAN	200,000	50,000	20,000	50,000	120,000
KOREA	75,000	20,000	5,000	10,000	35,000
SPANISH-SPEAKING LAT-AM VIDEO	25,000		5,000		
LATIN AMERICAN TV	40,000			15,000	15,000
MALAYSIA	7,500	2,000	1,000	1,000	4,000
MEXICO/CENTRAL AMERICA	35,000	17,500			17,500
MIDDLE EAST	12,500	5,000	1,000	1,000	7,000
PAKISTAN	20,000	7,500	1,000	1,000	9,500
PHILIPPINES	30,000	10,000	1,000	3,000	14,000
POLAND	25,000	5,000	2,000	4,000	11,000
PORTUGAL	20,000	5,000	1,000	2,000	8,000
ROMANIA	15,000	3,000	1,000	2,000	6,000
RUSSIA/CIS	125,000	35,000	10,000	20,000	65,000
SCANDINAVIA	STRAIGHT DISTRIBUTION DEAL				
SINGAPORE	10,000	2,000	2,000	1,000	5,000
SOUTH AFRICA	STRAIGHT DISTRIBUTION DEAL				
SPAIN	100,000	25,000	5,000	15,000	45,000
SRI LANKA	8,000	2,000	1,000	1,000	4,000
TAIWAN	25,000	10,000	1,000	2,000	13,000
THAILAND	10,000	2,000	1,000	2,000	5,000
TURKEY	20,000	5,000	1,000	3,000	9,000
UNITED KINGDOM	100,000	30,000	10,000	20,000	60,000
VENEZUELA	10,000	5,000			5,000
TOTAL (excluding USA)	$1,910,000	$588,000	$134,500	$273,500	$996,000

Where Pay TV and Free TV are sold separately in any territory, the minimum price for each of Pay TV and Free TV shall be deemed to be 50% of the applicable price set forth in the "MINIMUMS TELEVISION" column.

DEALMAKING
IN THE
FILM AND
TELEVISION
INDUSTRY—
3RD EDITION

276

Questions and Answers

1. If I obtain $4 million in financing for a picture with name actors, can I get a U.S. distributor to provide my entire budget for the rights and some guaranteed advances so my investors will see their cash back, regardless of whether there are profits?

Answer: While possible, it is not likely that you will get your money back and then some from a domestic distributor. But, of course, everything depends on the quality of the film that is to be produced and the track record of those associated with it. However, if you look at what most indie films earn domestically, it is not likely. The U.S. market may be considerably less than half of worldwide revenue generated for a film. You should try to reduce your budget, put as much as possible up on the screen, and check beforehand with experienced distributors to determine the appeal of the cast in both the domestic and international market.

2. I am raising money for my production through both investors and friends. Can I take small amounts of money from friends and local businesses ($100-$500 at a time) as gifts, without having to comply with securities laws?

Answer: There is no problem with people giving you gifts, and there is no problem with giving credits or acknowledging people for gifts in your screen credits. Gifts and loans are not an investment, and those are not a "security." Consequently, the security laws do not apply. As far as taking money from investors, however, if these investors are passive investors, that is, they are not actively involved in making the movie; you should make sure that you comply with state and federal securities laws. You should not take money from investors until you have given them a written limited offering memorandum or PPM. This should be prepared by a lawyer who is knowledgeable in entertainment and securities laws. It is more than a business plan.

3. I am in negotiations with a studio to obtain payment for home video domestic distribution rights to a film made some years ago. The studio earns about $25,000-$30,000 per year from these rights. What is an average range for distribution royalties for such a title?

Answer: Producers of films often receive a royalty of 20%-25% of the wholesale price of home videos sold, but the amount of revenue that one film generates has no relation to what another film may generate. Keep in mind that many studios license their films to their own home video subsidiaries. Those subsidiaries may pay a royalty to the parent company, which, in turn, shares revenue with the producer. So I would first make sure whether the amount you mention is what the parent company or the subsidiary receives. Ascertain exactly which rights they are using and reserve all other rights. Then try to obtain at least 20% of the wholesale price as a royalty. There are other formulas for sharing revenue with producers, such as a 50/50 Net Deal, in which expenses come off the top and the balance is shared equally.

CHAPTER 10

NEGOTIATING TACTICS & STRATEGIES[1]

The top Hollywood dealmakers are sometimes referred to as "players." These agents, attorneys, studio executives, and producers regularly conduct business with one another and observe an unwritten code of behavior. While players are admired for being tough and shrewd, dishonesty is not respected.

For an industry with a reputation for chicanery, outsiders may be surprised to find that many players take great pride in keeping their word. They make oral agreements with one another that are relied upon by their clients. An agent may commit his/her client to a project, and the written contract may not be signed until the project has been completed.

The honor code among players does permit a certain amount of hype and exaggeration. Agents talking about a client will stress the positive and ignore the negative. Other shenanigans are allowed, although these tactics may only work against the uninitiated.

HIGH-BALLING is asking for an excessive amount of money or staking out an extreme position in order to position oneself favorably for compromise. If a fair fee for an actor would be

---

[1] Portions of this chapter are derived from the author's prior work *Reel Power*.

DEALMAKING
IN THE
FILM AND
TELEVISION
INDUSTRY—
3RD EDITION

280

$80,000, a request for $180,000 leaves plenty of room to compromise and still walk away with a good deal. If the other side counters with an unreasonably low bid, the stage is set for a protracted struggle.

LOW-BALLING is suggesting an unduly low amount. In attempting to persuade a studio to produce a picture, producers may give a low estimate of its budget. The producer may reason that once the studio is committed to a picture, and has invested a significant amount of money, it will be loathe to shut down a production if it goes over budget. However, if the producer has agreed to an EAT-IN CLAUSE, the studio may have the last laugh. An eat-in clause provides that a producer's profits and/or fees are eaten into if the film goes over budget.

High-balling and low-balling tactics don't work against experienced negotiators since they understand how salaries are set. The unwritten rule is that everyone is entitled to a modest raise over what they earned on their last deal. Salary information is hard to keep secret, so the parameters within which to negotiate are fairly narrow. Unless the artist has recently won an Academy Award or starred in a blockbuster film, he/she ordinarily cannot obtain a substantial increase in his/her fee.

Creating confusion is a technique some dealmakers use. If one party does not understand what is being discussed—and is too embarrassed to ask for clarification—it is difficult for that party to protect its interests. Some people create confusion by being long-winded or going off on tangents. Some deals are so complex that no additional confusion need be added. Parties should always carefully read each draft to make sure the agreed changes have been made. As a courtesy, the drafting attorney will often send a "redlined copy" showing changes from the previous draft.

Intimidation can be another ploy. Strong-arm tactics work only when one's opponent needs a deal so badly that he/she will submit to such abuse. This tactic is usually avoided among players because they deal with each other regularly. "If I use leverage and kill somebody, tomorrow he is going to kill me," says attorney Eric Weissmann. "In the old days, negotiating was filled with much more histrionics. There was much more ranting and raving and screaming, barring people from the lot, and fistfights. Today people try to reason with each other."

Even insanity can be useful, it being difficult to negotiate with the insane. "If one person is nuts, then he cannot be reached logically and the other person who is desperately trying to reach him is already at a disadvantage," says Weissmann, who adds that the approach works best when the party is truly insane, since it's a hard thing to fake.

Bursts of irrational behavior can be useful. "There's nothing more unsettling when you are negotiating with someone and they do something completely unexpected," says Weissmann. "When I was a young lawyer, I was negotiating with the head of the legal department at a studio, who buzzed the secretary and told her to call the studio police and have me escorted from the place and to bar me from the lot forever. Well I decided right then that I didn't feel that strongly about the point."

A variation of these last two approaches could be called "my boss is insane." A negotiator will concede an opponent's position is reasonable but profess that he/she cannot agree to it because his/her employer is crazy. It is tough to argue with someone who agrees with you and denounces the person he represents.

Even silence can be a negotiating ploy. If it makes the other party uncomfortable, that party may talk itself into compromising its position. A similar passive technique is for a negotiator never to propose solutions but to maneuver the conversation so that the other party suggests them.

The best negotiators are versatile, employing tactics appropriate to the situation and the personality of their counterpart. Often first encounters are a time of testing. Parties who regularly deal with each other, however, don't engage in a lot of gamesmanship.

The preeminent dealmakers are not necessarily those who make the toughest demands. An attorney may build a reputation for being tough, but it is often at the expense of clients who suffer the consequences of blown deals. An attorney who has the client's best interests at heart will try to obtain the optimum deal available under the circumstances and will not blow a deal unless that is what the client wants.

DEALMAKING
IN THE
FILM AND
TELEVISION
INDUSTRY—
3RD EDITION

282

TECHNIQUES TO INDUCE A STUDIO TO MAKE A DEAL

Here are some gambits that can be used to lure a studio into a development or production deal. Considering that these techniques have been around a long time, it is surprising that they still work. One would think that at some point everyone would wise up to them.

When a studio executive knows that OTHER BUYERS ARE INTERESTED in a project, his/her interest often grows exponentially. I suppose a Sony executive who learns that a counterpart at Fox is actively pursuing you figures that you must be worth pursuing. Pretty soon you have several suitors fighting over you, and that can produce a lucrative deal.

Of course, one cannot directly inform a Sony executive of Fox's interest in your project. The Sony executive might ask, "If Fox is so interested in the project, how come you are here talking with us instead of making the movie at Fox?"

So the masters of this technique use the trade papers and the grapevine to spread the word that they have a hot project. With smoke and mirrors and gossip and innuendo, they try to generate the illusion that they have something desirable. Their goal is to get several buyers into a feeding frenzy and auction the project off to the highest bidder.

Another gambit capitalizes on studio executives' desire to SEE A PROJECT FIRST. Everyone wants a first look or at least an early look at a project. So if your screenplay has been making the rounds for a couple of years and is looking kind of ragged, you would be well advised to make a fresh photocopy. If your script looks like it has been rejected everywhere, buyers may assume that it can't be any good.

Remember that evaluating a screenplay is subjective, and some people don't trust their own instincts. A common phenomenon is for a new writer to labor many years submitting scripts in an attempt to break into the industry. Then the writer sells his/her sixth screenplay to Steven Spielberg or another reputable buyer. Suddenly the writer's old screenplays sell like hotcakes. Did those old screenplays on the shelf get better with age, like fine wine? Of course not. The sale to Spielberg gave this writer the imprimatur of success. Buyers now view his/her work in a different light. The unspoken assumption is, "If Spielberg bought a script from this guy, he must be good." The same screenplay that was rejected six months ago is now enthusiastically received.

Everyone loves a BARGAIN, including studio executives. Stars will sometimes agree to do a favorite project for scale wages. Such movies are often prestige films that cost little and have the potential of winning an Oscar. Status-hungry executives also like these projects.

Executives are often attracted to a HOT TOPIC. A story off the front page of the newspaper or a subject that "everybody is talking about" can be easier to market because the public is already aware of it. Studios will avoid topical stories, however, if they think television will tackle the subject first. Television movies can be produced in less than a year, while features generally take several years to develop and produce. No studio will want to invest a lot of money developing a story that is likely to appear on television first.

How then does one distinguish those stories appropriate for television from those meant to be features? Sexy or violent subject matter may prevent the networks from tackling certain stories. The most important difference, however, is budget. The typical network movie costs several million dollars, while feature films often cost more than $50 million. Any story that involves numerous locations, expensive sets, special effects, herds of wild animals, costly costumes, or crowds of extras is probably too expensive to be made for television.

BUILDING RELATIONSHIPS: Savvy dealmakers know that the motives of studios differ from their executives. Studios want to make hit movies for as little money as possible. To some extent, studio executives want the same. However, realizing that their tenure is limited, executives want to prepare for their next job. That job is often as an independent producer, sometimes affiliated with the same studio they used to work for. What is important to these executives? They want to build relationships with important stars, directors, and writers. As one executive told me, "Working as a studio executive is like going to producer school."

Thus, a smart dealmaker knows that one way to make a project appealing to a studio executive is to present it as an opportunity for the executive to develop a relationship with an up-and-coming star. The executive may want to develop the project, because it presents an opportunity to have several meetings with the talent and forge a strong relationship.

DEALMAKING
IN THE
FILM AND
TELEVISION
INDUSTRY—
3RD EDITION

284

Similarly, studios may develop or produce a project just to placate a star with whom the studio has an important relationship. What are a few hundred thousand dollars in development expenses if it keeps a major star happy and earning the studio millions of dollars?

Finally, keep in mind that experienced dealmakers always want to appear passionate about their project, but they never want to appear desperate to make a deal. The best attitude is one of great determination. You would love to work with the studio, but if they pass on your project, you intend to pursue it elsewhere. Sometimes playing hard-to-get can be useful. When an executive asks to read a screenplay and the producer tries to keep it under wraps, the executive's appetite may be whetted.

Questions and Answers

1. I will soon be pitching a TV series to production companies and networks, but I do not have an agent. Would it be wise to have an entertainment lawyer already on retainer? And how important is it in picking one? Can some actually help steer you toward agents and production companies?

Answer: You do not need a lawyer to accompany you when you go in to pitch your TV series. This is a meeting about creative matters. Only at the point where the other side says they want to make a deal is it important that you retain someone to advise you on the business aspects of a deal. If you are not familiar with such deals, it is best not to negotiate an agreement on your own. When a studio or network says they want to do a deal, they will have their business affairs person contact your attorney or agent. In answer to your second question, yes, entertainment attorneys can help steer you toward agents and production companies, although many of them may be reluctant to take you on as a client if that is the sole purpose for retaining them.

2. If I write a script, it is made into a movie, and then five years later I decide to write another script, or maybe a book, which deals with one of the supporting characters from that first script. Would I have to have contracted at the time of sale to keep the rights to the characters?

Answer: If you reserved author written sequel rights, you may be able to use the characters in a subsequent work. You need to carefully review the language in your agreement to determine what rights you may have retained.

If you sold the entire copyright to your script, then the new owner now has all rights to it, until such time as it goes into the public domain. Those rights include the use of the characters in the work to the extent that characters are copyrightable. Finely drawn characters, especially those with a visual component such as a comic book character, can be protected under copyright law. Likewise, characters with a name, such as "James Bond" might be protectable under the laws of unfair competition. But general character and personality traits, such as a "hard-boiled private eye," are not copyrightable, and freely available for all writers to use. There are dozens of hard-boiled private-eye characters created by different authors. So even if your character is now owned by someone else, you could create a new and different character that might share some of the same personality characteristics of some of your prior characters.

When writers create an original script on their own (i.e., not as a work-for-hire for another), they often are able to reserve certain rights to their scripts when they option or sell the motion picture rights. These reserved rights may include dramatic, radio, live television, print publication, and author-written sequel rights. Moreover, if the writer has a reversion clause in the purchase agreement, it might provide that if the buyer does not produce a movie based on the script within a certain time (i.e., five years), all rights revert back to the writer. Finally, if a writer is a member of the Writers Guild, he/she may be entitled to certain "separated rights" by virtue of the collective-bargaining agreement between the guild and its signatory companies.

CHAPTER 11

CREATIVE ACCOUNTING

ART BUCHWALD V. PARAMOUNT

Art Buchwald was angry. The Pulitzer Prize-winning columnist had just seen the movie *Coming to America* while vacationing in Martha's Vineyard. The Paramount picture was about an African prince, played by Eddie Murphy, who came to America to find a bride. It seemed similar to a story Buchwald had optioned to Paramount several years earlier, a project the studio had developed for Eddie Murphy.

Buchwald's story, *King for a Day*, as written in his three-page treatment, was about an extremely wealthy, handsome, and spoiled young emperor from an oil-rich African country who comes to Washington and is stranded after losing his throne and wealth in a coup d'état staged in his absence. The King must cope with life in the ghetto, where he works a menial job and falls in love with a former CIA call girl. Eventually he is able to reclaim his throne, return home, and make the former call girl his queen.

Under Buchwald's agreement with Paramount, he was entitled to receive a fixed fee of $65,000 plus 1½% of the net profits if a film based on his story was made. Alain Bernheim signed a

287

DEALMAKING
IN THE
FILM AND
TELEVISION
INDUSTRY—
3RD EDITION

288

similar deal with the studio to produce the project; he was set to receive a fee of $200,000 and 17½% of the net profits. Buchwald and Bernheim received $42,500 during the two years the story was in development at Paramount.

The film grossed more than $128 million the year it was released, making it the third-highest-grossing film of 1988. But neither Buchwald nor Bernheim received any further compensation, and Buchwald didn't receive a screen credit because Eddie Murphy claimed he had conceived the story.

Murphy earned $8 million for his starring role in the movie as well as 15% of Paramount's gross revenues from the film—an astronomical sum in light of the combined salaries of the rest of the cast: $906,000. After the film's release, Murphy's salary rose to $9 million per picture. Nevertheless, he was reportedly dissatisfied with his five-picture deal at Paramount.

In 1987, Bernheim lunched with Paramount production chief Ned Tanen in the studio commissary and accused Paramount of stealing Buchwald's story. The conversation quickly degenerated into a heated disagreement, and the two have not spoken since. Buchwald and Bernheim discussed the matter and decided they might have to sue.

First, however, Buchwald told his friend, Paramount Communications, Inc., Chairman Martin Davis, what had happened and of his intention to sue the studio. Davis responded by sending the writer a bottle of champagne and a record of a song titled "Sue Me." Buchwald did, and then promptly went on the Larry King radio show to denounce the film.

The trial gave outsiders a rare glimpse into the highest echelons of studio decision-making. Buchwald and Bernheim asked the court for $5 million in damages for breach of contract as well as unspecified punitive damages. Paramount responded that *Coming to America* was not based on Buchwald's story. Furthermore, the studio said that even if the movie were based on the story, Buchwald wasn't due any "net profits" from the film according to the studio's contract with him. The film had generated an estimated $350 million dollars in revenue and was one of the top 20 highest-grossing movies of the decade.

Hollywood writers and other net-profit participants have long complained that studios engaged in creative accounting, cheating them out of participating in "profits." But most writers just grumble because they don't have the financial means to finance a protracted legal struggle, and attorneys often don't want to take such cases on a contingency fee basis. Besides, many writers fear that instigating such a suit might make them unemployable.

Buchwald, however, was a nationally syndicated columnist and a wealthy man who didn't need the movie industry for his livelihood. Over the years he had written 20 movie treatments, none of which was produced, but it didn't much matter because movie-writing was merely a diversion for him. He could afford to challenge the studios on behalf of all writers.

Executives at other studios quietly griped that Paramount's refusal to settle the lawsuit could result in a legal precedent that would have disastrous repercussions for the industry. Insiders speculated that Paramount, on its own, would have preferred to quietly settle the case. Fear of alienating Eddie Murphy apparently drove the studio to trial.

Although Murphy was not a named party in the suit, his testimony was relevant. The star swore that he and his talk-show-host friend Arsenio Hall had conceived the story for *Coming to America*. But correspondence written by Murphy's manager, Bob Wachs, revealed that he knew Buchwald's story was being developed by Paramount for Murphy.

Other documents obtained through discovery revealed that within a few months of taking an option on Buchwald's story, Paramount began developing the story for Murphy. In a letter stamped "confidential," then-Paramount production head Jeffrey Katzenberg sent John Landis a list of 13 projects in development for him to consider directing. On that list was *King for a Day*, which was described as a political satire for Eddie Murphy inspired by Art Buchwald.

Paramount spent approximately $500,000 to have screenwriters Tab Murphy and Francis Veber develop Buchwald's story into a screenplay. But when Paramount's management changed in 1985, the new regime let the option on Buchwald's story lapse. Bernheim then sold the story to Warner Bros. under the title *Me and the King*. Warner's spent more than $200,000 developing the concept. When they learned that Paramount had a similarly themed movie in production, they dropped the project.

The trial was presided over by Judge Harvey Schneider, an admitted film buff, who decided all factual issues himself after both sides waived a jury trial. After reviewing the evidence, Schneider ruled that *Coming to America* was based upon Buchwald's story.

DEALMAKING
IN THE
FILM AND
TELEVISION
INDUSTRY—
3RD EDITION

290

TERMS

EACH STUDIO CAN DEFINE THE TERMS USED IN ITS AGREEMENTS AS IT LIKES. THERE ARE NO INDUSTRY-WIDE DEFINITIONS FOR "GROSS," "ADJUSTED GROSS," OR "NET" DEALS. WHAT ONE STUDIO CALLS AN ADJUSTED GROSS DEAL, ANOTHER CALLS A NET DEAL. BEFORE YOU CELEBRATE THE "GROSS" DEAL YOU OBTAINED, CHECK THE FINE PRINT AND SEE HOW THE TERM IS DEFINED.

GENERALLY, INDUSTRY TERMS ARE DEFINED AS FOLLOWS:

BOX OFFICE RECEIPTS: WHAT THE THEATER OWNER TAKES IN FROM TICKET SALES TO CUSTOMERS AT THE BOX OFFICE.

FILM RENTAL: WHAT THE THEATER OWNER PAYS THE DISTRIBUTOR FOR THE RIGHT TO SHOW THE MOVIE.

GROSS RECEIPTS: ALL REVENUES DERIVED FROM ALL MEDIA, INCLUDING FILM RENTALS, TELEVISION SALES, MERCHANDISING, AND ANCILLARY SALES. THE AMOUNT OF REVENUES CONTRIBUTED BY HOME VIDEO SALES, HOWEVER, IS TYPICALLY ONLY 20% OF WHOLESALE SALES.

GROSS PARTICIPATION: A PIECE OF GROSS RECEIPTS WITHOUT ANY DEDUCTIONS FOR DISTRIBUTION FEES OR EXPENSES OR PRODUCTION COSTS. HOWEVER, DEDUCTIONS FOR CHECKING AND COLLECTION COSTS, RESIDUALS, AND TAXES ARE USUALLY TAKEN.

ADJUSTED GROSS PARTICIPATION: GROSS PARTICIPATION MINUS CERTAIN COSTS, SUCH AS COST OF ADVERTISING AND DUPLICATION OF FILM PRINTS.

ADVANCES: UP-FRONT PAYMENT THAT COUNTS AGAINST MONIES THAT MAY BE PAYABLE AT SOME TIME IN THE FUTURE. NON-RECOUPABLE ADVANCES ARE PAYMENTS THAT ARE NOT REFUNDABLE, EVEN IF FUTURE MONIES ARE NEVER GENERATED.

NET PROFIT: WHAT IS LEFT, IF ANYTHING, AFTER ALL ALLOWABLE DEDUCTIONS ARE TAKEN. THIS USUALLY AMOUNTS TO ZERO. TYPICALLY EXPRESSED IN TERMS OF 100% OF NET PROFITS, ALTHOUGH PAYABLE OUT OF THE PRODUCER'S SHARE (E.G., OUT OF HIS 50%).

THEATRICAL DISTRIBUTION FEES: GENERALLY BETWEEN 30% AND 40% OF GROSS RECEIPTS.

DOUBLE DISTRIBUTION FEES: WHERE DISTRIBUTOR USES A SUB-DISTRIBUTOR TO SELL TO A TERRITORY. IF BOTH DISTRIBUTORS ARE ALLOWED TO DEDUCT THEIR STANDARD FEES, THE FILMMAKER IS UNLIKELY TO SEE ANY MONEY.

TELEVISION DISTRIBUTION FEE: TYPICALLY 10% FOR NETWORK BROADCAST, 35%-40% FOR DOMESTIC SYNDICATION, AND 45%-50% FOR FOREIGN DISTRIBUTION. MANY FILMMAKERS CONSIDER THESE FEES EXCESSIVE SINCE THE STUDIO DOESN'T INCUR A LOT OF EXPENSE TO DISTRIBUTE TO TELEVISION. THERE ARE MINIMAL DUPLICATION EXPENSES (I.E., THE STUDIO SENDS ONE VIDEO COPY TO THE BUYER).

DISTRIBUTION EXPENSES: INCLUDES TAXES, GUILD PAYMENTS, TRADE ASSOCIATION DUES, CONVERSION/TRANSMISSION COSTS, COLLECTION COSTS, CHECKING COSTS, ADVERTISING AND PUBLICITY COSTS, RE-EDITING COSTS, PRINTS, FOREIGN VERSION COSTS, TRANSPORTATION AND SHIPPING COSTS, COPYRIGHT COSTS, COPYRIGHT INFRINGEMENT COSTS, INSURANCE, ROYALTIES, AND CLAIMS AND LAWSUITS.

In a partial victory for Paramount, however, the judge ruled that the plaintiffs were not entitled to punitive damages. The studio had not acted in bad faith or with fraudulent intent, according to Schneider, when it failed to honor its contract with Buchwald and Bernheim. The ruling didn't settle all outstanding issues because now the court had to decide what the plaintiffs' share of net profits was worth. If, as Paramount contended, there were no net profits, Buchwald and his attorney would have won a Pyrrhic victory, having incurred more in legal fees than any recovery from Paramount.[1]

For the second part of the trial, Buchwald's attorney, Pierce O'Donnell, asked the court to invalidate Paramount's definition of net profits on the ground that it was unconscionable. According to O'Donnell, Paramount and other major studios exploit ambiguities in their contracts to the detriment of profit participants. They abuse their "awesome power," he said, by imposing terms on talent which allow the studios to make "hidden profits" and charge "exorbitant interest."

Defenders of the major studios point out that the studios bear all the financial risks of making movies and, therefore, deserve the lion's share of revenues. Paramount charged that Buchwald was trying to rewrite his agreement after the fact. The studio protested that it had hardly taken advantage of a vulnerable and unsophisticated writer, noting that Buchwald was represented in his negotiations by one of the top executives at the William Morris Agency.

According to Paramount's calculations, the movie cost more than $58 million. Buchwald claimed the studio spent $22.9 million on the film. He claims that certain payments such as $1 million for Murphy's entourage, $900,000 for excessive fringe benefits, and a uniform 15% overhead charge shouldn't be allocated to the production budget. According to Buchwald, $1.65 million of the $8 million in overhead charges was "merely for writing gross-participation checks to Eddie Murphy and [director] John Landis."

Buchwald won his case at the trial level but was awarded damages of only $900,000—not nearly enough to cover the $4 million in legal fees that his attorney's firm had amassed. Paramount appealed and later settled the case before the appellate court issued a decision.

---

[1] Since Buchwald's attorney took the case on a contingency-fee basis, the law firm would be the big loser.

DEALMAKING
IN THE
FILM AND
TELEVISION
INDUSTRY—
3RD EDITION

292

COMING TO AMERICA[2]

PROFIT PARTICIPATION STATEMENT, JUNE 23, 1990

GROSS RECEIPTS:	$140,566,278
LESS UNCOLLECTED BILLINGS:	300,300
LESS STUDIO DISTRIBUTION FEES:	47,137,610
LESS DISTRIBUTION EXPENSES:	38,233,946
BALANCE:	54,894,422
LESS NEGATIVE COST:	62,717,606
INTEREST ON NEGATIVE COST:	7,165,859
BALANCE (NET LOSS):	(14,989,043)

[2] Financial information on *Coming to America* and *Three Men and a Baby*, from "Net Profits" by David Robb, *The Hollywood Reporter*, reprint of series appearing from August 17 to September 4, 1992.

CREATIVE ACCOUNTING— TRICKS OF THE TRADE

Creative accounting problems are widespread in the industry. Most films are not profitable by any standard, so the profit participants don't bother with an audit. For those films that do generate significant revenue, audits invariably pay for themselves. Audits usually cost a minimum of $20,000 to $30,000.

There are two types of errors revealed by an audit. The first are clerical errors. For example, a studio accountant added up a row of numbers incorrectly, or expenses were deducted twice. For some mysterious reason, these errors usually favor the studio. Studios often correct such errors without a fuss when the profit participant points them out.

The other type of error arises out of contract interpretation. The philosophy of most studios is, "When in doubt, resolve it in our favor and we will fight it out later if it is contested." Despite the great care taken by lawyers to draft contracts, new areas of ambiguity always arise.

Creative-accounting disputes frequently arise when a net-profit participant feels cheated. Gross-profit participants—people who receive a piece of the gross—usually don't experience problems because determining gross revenues is fairly straightforward since few deductions are permitted.

To understand the difference between a "net" and a "gross" deal, let us review the cash flow from ticket sales to the profit participant. BOX OFFICE RECEIPTS is the sum that the theater owner (exhibitor) takes in from ticket sales at the box office. A theater owner is entitled to retain some of these revenues to cover costs and hopefully earn a profit.

The exhibitor/distributor agreement states the terms on which the film is licensed to the exhibitor. For example, the exhibitor may agree to play the film for a minimum of eight weeks and make a guaranteed payment in advance. The agreement also sets the exhibitor's share of box office revenue. If a distributor is releasing a highly desirable picture, the revenues may be split on a 90:10 ratio[3] for the first few weeks: The distributor receives 90% of the revenue, the exhibitor 10%. In subsequent weeks, the split may shift to 70/30, 60/40, or 50/50.[4]

A sliding scale gives the exhibitor an incentive to show the picture as long as possible. From the distributor's point of view, as long as the picture is in a theater, there is the possibility that someone may buy a ticket to see it. Once the film is no longer in the theaters, no revenue can be earned from this market.

Before revenues are split, the exhibitor may be allowed to deduct certain expenses or his House NUT. The nut is an amount that is supposed to represent the exhibitor's overhead expenses. This figure is arrived at through negotiation with the distributor, and often it is greater than the actual overhead expenses. In such a case, the figure has some AIR in it. The exhibitor retains 100% of all revenue from the concession stand. This is a major profit center for exhibitors.

After the exhibitor deducts his house nut and splits revenue according to the distribution/exhibition contract, he/she remits the distributor's share. This payment is called the Film RENTAL. Generally, exhibitors retain about half of the box office receipts and pay the other half as rental payments.

The DISTRIBUTOR'S GROSS receipts comprise rentals from all exhibitors and revenue derived from other markets such as television, foreign sales, cable, home video, and merchandising.

---

[3] The exhibitor typically gets to deduct his "house nut," or overhead expenses, before the split.
[4] These splits may be without any deduction for the house nut.

DEALMAKING
IN THE
FILM AND
TELEVISION
INDUSTRY—
3RD EDITION

294

Profit participants with a PIECE OF THE GROSS share in gross revenue, although a few deductions like taxes are allowed. Only the top stars and directors have the clout to obtain a piece of the gross. Studios dislike gross deals because gross-profit participants share in revenue from a picture even if the studio has not earned its investment back.

Suppose a studio has given Paul Newman 10% of the gross from a film. If the film's gross revenues from all sources are $50 million, and if the film's production, marketing, and distribution costs total $50 million, the distributor has broken even. However, Newman is due $5 million beyond his up-front fee. So the studio is losing money while Newman is making a bundle. To avoid this situation, studios prefer to pay participants after the studio recoups at least some expenses such as advertising and duplication costs. This arrangement is an ADJUSTED GROSS or MODIFIED GROSS deal.

Filmmakers and studios have devised all kinds of variations on these deals. For instance, a participant's piece of the gross might not be payable until the movie grosses two or three times its negative cost. The parties could also agree to split some markets (e.g., home video) off into separate profit pools and pay part of the gross in these markets to participants.

The least desirable deal from the profit participant's point of view is a NET PROFIT[5] deal. Here, so many deductions are allowed that what is left is often zero or less. Although the net-profit participant may not see any money from his POINTS, or percentage of profits, the studio may make a "profit" because it receives 30% to 40% of the gross as a distribution fee. This fee is usually far more than the actual costs the studio incurs to distribute a film. Thus the release of a picture may be very profitable to the studio although, technically, there are no "profits" for the participants.

Net profits, if there are any, are often shared 50/50 between the studio and the producer. Net profit participants typically receive their pieces of the profit pie from the producer's half. Nevertheless, net profits are customarily defined in terms of the whole (100%). We say the writer is entitled to 5% of 100% of the net profits. This means the writer is entitled to 5% of all the net profits, although his percentage comes from the producer's

---

[5] A "net profit" deal does not represent anyone's economic net profit but is simply an amount determined by a contract formula.

half. We define net profits this way to avoid ambiguity. If the contract simply said the writer was entitled to 5% of the net profits, the question might arise, is he/she due 5% of the producer's half (which would amount to 5% of 50%) or is he/she entitled to 5% of the whole?

There is more room for dispute when a participant is entitled to a piece of the net because the studio can deduct various expenses as well as interest, distribution, and overhead fees. Any payments made to gross-profit participants are also deductible before payment is due a net-profit participant. Thus, even if there is no creative accounting, a net-profit participant is unlikely to see any profits if the studio is obligated to pay gross-profit participants.

Other problems arise when improper deductions are made. For example, a studio may try to deduct the cost of an ad used to promote a different movie. Other deductions may seem unfair but are technically proper according to the terms of the distribution agreement.

THREE MEN AND A BABY[6]

PROFIT PARTICIPATION STATEMENT, SEPTEMBER 30, 1991

FILM REVENUES

DOMESTIC THEATRICAL	$80,990,413
FOREIGN THEATRICAL	32,559,620
FREE TELEVISION	8,779,571
PAY TELEVISION	14,615,518
HOME VIDEO	13,242,932
NON-THEATRICAL	2,451,131
OTHER SOURCES	12,445
TOTAL REVENUE:	$152,651,630
LESS ACCTS. RECEIVABLE	41,421
GROSS RECEIPTS:	152,610,209
DISTRIBUTION FEES:	49,798,213
ADVERTISING & PUBLICITY	35,125,096
CHECKING & COLLECTION	428,316
OTHER VERSIONS	621,920
RESIDUALS	2,990,426
TRADE DUES	50,000
TAXES, LICENSES, INSURANCE	2,289,052
PRINTS	4,617,978
TRANSPORTATION	696,350
MISCELLANEOUS	172,405
NET RECEIPTS AFTER DIST. COSTS & FEES	55,820,453

NEGATIVE COSTS

DIRECT COST	$13,241,723
OVERHEAD @ 15%	1,986,258
INTEREST	1,291,866
GROSS PARTICIPANTS	1,983,750
TOTAL NEGATIVE COST	18,503,597
BALANCE	37,316,856
LESS OTHER PARTICIPATIONS & DEFERMENTS	10,284,593
NET PROFITS	27,032,263

[6] Financial information on *Coming to America* and *Three Men and a Baby*, from "Net Profits" by David Robb, *The Hollywood Reporter*, reprint of series appearing from August 17 to September 4, 1992.

DEALMAKING
IN THE
FILM AND
TELEVISION
INDUSTRY—
3RD EDITION

296

Here are some problem areas to watch out for when reviewing a studio's accounting:

1) EXCESSIVE BILLS: If the studio used a film lab that is a subsidiary, has the film processing been charged at the prevailing rate? If the studio has used its own vehicles in a shoot, is it fair for them to charge the production the highest daily rate that Hertz might charge?

2) REBATES: If a studio receives year-end rebates, have all the films been credited with their fair share?

3) OVERHEAD CHARGES: Studio overhead charges may apply even if a film is not shot on a studio lot. This fee is meant to compensate a studio for the fixed costs of running the production and for the corporate functions performed by the studio. Distributors also may charge a 10% advertising overhead charge, which is meant to reimburse the studio for the fixed costs of operating the marketing division. But what if all the advertising work is contracted out? Is it proper to take an overhead fee? What does the contract say?

4) INTEREST: Studios charge the production interest on money used to make each film. They often mark up the rate. For example, they may borrow the money at prime and charge you prime plus two. Does the contract allow this? Also, advances from exhibitors are often not credited against interest charged. Thus, the studio collects interest on advances while refusing to credit this interest against the interest charged the producer.

5) MISALLOCATION OF EXPENSES: It is in the studio's interest to tack on expenses to successful pictures to avoid having to pay profit participants. Unsuccessful pictures will never earn enough revenue to pay participants under any circumstances. Thus the cost of limos, lunches, executive travel, and other expenses that were incurred on flops may find their way onto the books of hits.

6) MISALLOCATION OF REVENUES: If the studio sells a package of its films to television, how have the revenues been allocated? If one film is a hit and the others are flops, is it fair to apportion the revenue equally among the pictures? The studios prefer to allocate revenue to flops that have no chance of earning a profit to avoid paying profit participants.

7) HOME VIDEO: Many studios have home-video subsidiaries. These subsidiaries will typically pay the studio 20% of the wholesale price as a royalty for the right to distribute the movie in the home-video market. The royalty payments are then added to the studio's gross receipts, and a distribution fee is deducted. Is it fair for the studio to license the product to its own subsidiary for only 20%? Is it fair for both the subsidiary and the parent company to each make a profit from home-video distribution?

8) ADVERTISING & MERCHANDISING REVENUE: The studio may earn a fee from putting a Coca-Cola commercial on its videocassettes, or a manufacturer may pay to have a product shown in a picture. Has the studio accounted for this revenue? A studio may license a manufacturer to produce spin-off toys and merchandise. Has the studio accounted for this revenue?

9) FOREIGN DUBS: Has the film been dubbed into a foreign language? Are the charges appropriate? What is the local practice? Pictures released in Japan, for example, are subtitled, not dubbed.

10) TAXES: Some governments impose a remittance tax on money taken out of the country. The U.S. government allows a credit on these taxes on the distributor's U.S. tax return. If the tax doesn't really cost the studio anything, should it be deductible?

11) CALCULATION OF INTEREST: Studios may charge interest on items that are not out-of-pocket expenses. Did the studio charge simple interest or compound interest? What is the period for which interest is charged? Is the studio assessing interest based on a 360-day year? If interest is tied to the prime rate, was it properly calculated? What does the contract say?

12) PAYMENTS TO GROSS PARTICIPANTS: Are these payments considered part of the negative cost? Will an overhead fee be assessed on it? Suppose the gross-profit participants earn $5 million. The studio could deduct an overhead fee of $750,000 for the task of writing and mailing a few checks.

13) OVER-BUDGET PENALTY: This penalty may be added to negative cost, even if the studio was responsible for the film going over budget. Perhaps the budget never was realistic in the first place.

DEALMAKING
IN THE
FILM AND
TELEVISION
INDUSTRY—
3RD EDITION

298

Because of all the creative-accounting disputes that have arisen in the industry, top talent demands large up-front payments or a piece of the gross. They know that it is unlikely that they will ever see anything from net points. Thus budgets escalate to accommodate large up-front fees, and talent has little incentive to keep production expenses down since it doesn't affect their earnings.

Remember that not all complaints about creative accounting are legitimate. Sometimes studios account according to the terms of their contracts. The contract may be unfair and the talent never bothered to read it. Now the film is a big hit, and the talent can't understand why they are not sharing in the riches. This is not creative accounting. This is an example of a studio using its clout to bargain hard and extort favorable terms.

CHAPTER 12

COPYRIGHT

You are writing the Great American Screenplay. After completing 119 pages of your 120-page script, you put your work aside for the evening and leave your writer's garret for dinner.

Late that night, through a window you carelessly left open, a burglar enters. He/she is a literary thief who doesn't take your money or stereo but steals your almost-finished manuscript. The script has not been registered with the copyright office and you didn't place a copyright notice on it.

The thief takes the script to the nearest film studio, which immediately recognizes its value. Before one can say "Oprah Winfrey," the movie is produced, it becomes a blockbuster hit, and the thief is interviewed on talk shows about "his" new work.

Question: Can you sue the thief for copyright infringement? Answer: Yes. You obtained the copyright to your work when you created it. It doesn't matter that you didn't put a notice on the manuscript, nor does it matter that you didn't register it with the Copyright Office. Incidentally, the thief may be liable for burglary, trespass, and conversion, too.

There is a common misunderstanding that copyright registration is required for copyright protection.

Now, you may wonder in this situation how you could prove you wrote the script. That is a question of evidence. Both parties to the dispute will present their evidence and the jury will decide whom to believe. Your attorney will have an opportunity to cross-examine the thief to discredit that person's claim of authorship.

DEALMAKING
IN THE
FILM AND
TELEVISION
INDUSTRY—
3RD EDITION

300

You could have your spouse testify that he/she read an early draft of the work. Of course, spouses may not have as much credibility as an impartial third party. That is why it is a good idea to register your manuscript with the Copyright Office or the Writers Guild.[1]

PROTECTING YOUR COPYRIGHT AND TITLE

Writers and filmmakers will want to take steps to fully protect their works. Although copyright law protects unregistered works, registration with the Copyright Office confers additional benefits and protections. As will be explained, a filmmaker may protect work under other legal doctrines, such as using contract law as a remedy for theft of one's work.

Titles can be protected under state and federal unfair competition and trademark laws. Titles can also be protected under contract law, typically by registration with the Motion Picture Association of American (MPAA), as explained at the end of this Chapter.

COPYRIGHT BASICS

What Is a Copyright?

A copyright is a form of intellectual property. It is a bundle of rights the owner has in certain products of the mind. Copyright law protects works of authorship such as literary works, musical works, paintings, and photographs. A copyright owner can prevent others from copying, distributing, performing, and displaying works, and from preparing derivative works.

Other forms of intellectual property include trademarks and patents. Trademarks are words, symbols, and logos that identify and distinguish products or services. Patents protect inventions. All of these creations are considered a form of property, albeit an unusual form of property because they do not come from wood, steel, or other tangible material, but are derived from the human mind. Like other forms of property, however, intellectual property can be sold and rights transferred. Thus, intellectual property is a "thing," created by people, but is not a person. Products of the mind should not be confused with personality rights people may possess to protect the use of their name and

---

[1] See Chapter 7 for information on how to register.

likeness (the right of publicity), their privacy (the right of privacy), or their reputation (protection from defamation).

A copyright is essentially intangible in nature. Compare a copyright, for example, to a tangible product, such as a car (personal property) or a piece of land (real property). People are often confused as to the nature of a copyright because, while a copyright is intangible, it may be expressed in a tangible form (e.g., a story fixed in a book, or a painting on canvas). Indeed, a copyright will only be protected under the law when it is fixed in a tangible medium of expression. But the medium in which the copyright is expressed must be distinguished from the copyright itself. The medium can be sold without transferring the copyright.

In other words, there are different levels of rights a person may have in a piece of work. There is ownership of the actual physical work, such as a painting. The owner of a painting can display it in his/her home and sell it to another. The owner cannot duplicate the painting, however, unless the owner also owns the copyright to it. The copyright permits its owner to duplicate, distribute, and prepare derivative works such as a T-shirt with the image of the painting on it. Ownership of the actual painting is not the same as ownership of the underlying copyright. Thus, the copyright owner of a painting could authorize the printing of a thousand reproductions in the form of posters. Each purchaser owns his/her own poster, but none of them owns the underlying copyright. Likewise, if you buy a videocassette copy of the motion picture *Titanic*, you would own your copy but would gain no rights in the underlying work. If you tried to duplicate your copy, or create a derivative work from it, you would violate the rights of the copyright owner.

Then there are the moral rights an author may have in his/her work. These rights are separate and distinct from the ownership of a painting and the copyright to it. If a painter has moral rights in his/her work, then he/she can sell the work, transfer the copyright, and still assert his/her moral right to prevent others from taking his/her name off the work or changing it. In the United States moral rights are generally limited to fine art.

The Source of Copyright Law

The United States Constitution gives Congress the power to enact copyright statutes to secure the property rights of authors.

DEALMAKING
IN THE
FILM AND
TELEVISION
INDUSTRY—
3RD EDITION

302

"Author" is broadly defined to encompass creators of all works eligible for copyright protection. This includes photographers, painters, musicians, and sculptors as well as computer animators and programmers.

Pursuant to the Constitution, Congress has enacted various copyright laws. These federal laws apply to residents of all states. At one time both the states and the federal government had laws affecting copyrights. This dual system of copyright protection protected unpublished works under state law (often referred to as common-law copyright), while published works were protected under federal law. The 1976 Copyright Act abolished this bifurcated system of copyright protection by providing that federal law "preempts" state law. Thus, the states no longer enact their own copyright laws. The only area left for state regulation is that of works not falling within the purview of federal law. Thus the states could enact laws concerning works that are not copyrightable under federal law (e.g., protection of ideas, or protection of works not in a tangible form).

International Application of Copyright Laws

The United States has joined several international copyright conventions to protect American works from infringement in foreign countries. These accords essentially provide for reciprocity of treatment of foreign nationals. For example, France agrees to protect the works of American authors in France. In return, we agree to protect the work of French authors in the United States.

This means that the United States will protect a French author in the United States in the same manner and extent as the United States protects American authors. It does not mean that French authors will have the same rights in the United States that they have in France under French law. Thus it is often said that copyright laws are territorial in their application. French law applies in France; American law applies in the United States. This application can produce unexpected results because American copyright law and French copyright law are significantly different.

American law, for example, recognizes the work-for-hire doctrine under which the "author" of a work can be the employer of an artist, not the artist himself/herself. This doctrine is not recognized in many countries. On the other hand, some countries have doctrines that do not exist under American law. France expressly recognizes the moral rights ("droit moral") authors have in their work. American copyright law only recognizes moral rights in the realm of fine art. Moral rights prevent others from changing the author's work (the right of integrity), or taking the author's name off of it (the right of paternity), even if the author has sold the physical work and the copyright to it.[2]

Under French law, the rights of integrity and paternity are perpetual, inheritable, inalienable, and imprescriptible.[3] Thus, the heirs of an artist can object to the use of their ancestor's work, even if that work's copyright has expired. In Huston v. Turner Entertainment,[4] the late American director John Huston was determined by a French court to be the author of the American film *The Asphalt Jungle*. Under American law, Huston's employer was deemed the author.

CRITERIA FOR COPYRIGHT PROTECTION

Not every work is copyrightable. To be eligible for copyright protection a work must meet four criteria. These criteria are:

1) It must be original.
2) It must be an "expression of an author."
3) It must be of a non-utilitarian nature.
4) It must be in a fixed, tangible medium of expression.

A work has to meet all four criteria; three out of four is not good enough.

If a work meets all four criteria, the creator automatically has a copyright in her work. The copyright comes into existence when the work has been created. The creator does not need to send any forms into the Copyright Office, say any magic words or perform any rituals in order to be protected under copyright law. No copyright notice is required to gain a copyright.[5]

---

[2] French law provides authors with a limited right to decide when to release their works to the public (the right of divulgation) and the right to remove the works from the public arena (the right of retraction).

[3] André R. Bertrand, *Multimedia: Stretching the Limits of Author's Rights in Europe,* 7. Propriety Rights, November 1995, p. 4.

[4] *Huston v. Turner Entertainment*, French Court of Cassation, 1991, cited in article "International Copyright Litigation in U.S. Courts: Jurisdiction, Damages, and Choice of Law," by Lionel S. Sobel, *Emerging Issues in Intellectual Property Practice*, CEB Program Handbook, p. 83, April 1994, California Continuing Education of the Bar.

[5] Although, before March 1, 1989, failure to put a copyright notice on your work, if you published it, could result in the loss of the copyright.

TYPES OF WORKS THAT <u>CAN</u> BE COPYRIGHTED

LITERARY WORKS

MUSICAL WORKS

DRAMATIC WORKS

PANTOMIMES

PHOTOGRAPHS

GRAPHIC DESIGN

SCULPTURE

MOTION PICTURES

SOUND RECORDINGS

CHOREOGRAPHY

COMPUTER PROGRAMS

WHAT <u>CAN'T</u> BE COPYRIGHTED?

INVENTIONS

IDEAS

THEMES

INDUSTRIAL DESIGN

TYPEFACE DESIGN

TITLES

HISTORICAL EVENTS

ANYTHING IN THE PUBLIC DOMAIN

NOTE THAT THE CATEGORIES ARE BROAD AND THEY OVERLAP. LYRICS FOR A SONG CAN FIT INTO EITHER THE LITERARY-WORK CATEGORY OR THE MUSICAL-WORK CATEGORY. PANTOMIMES AND CHOREOGRAPHY CAN SOMETIMES DOUBLE AS DRAMATIC WORKS.

Perhaps the simplest way of understanding copyright law is to view it as a three-tiered scheme. First, the author gets a copyright in a work when he/she creates it (assuming it meets the four criteria). Second, before 1989 authors were obliged to put a copyright notice (the word copyright, or the abbreviation or the symbol ©, the name of the copyright holder, and the year of publication) if they choose to publish the work. And third, if the author registers the work, he/she will be eligible for some extra, super-duper benefits, like reimbursement of attorneys' fees and recovery of statutory damages in a copyright-infringement suit. But if the author does not publish or register the work, he/she is nevertheless protected under copyright law.

Note that since the United States joined the Berne international copyright convention in 1989,[6] notice is no longer required to protect a copyright. Nowadays an American author who publishes his/her work and fails to attach a copyright notice is protected anyway. However, it remains a good practice to routinely put a copyright notice on your work so that nobody can claim they didn't know it was copyrighted material. You don't need the Copyright Office's permission to put a copyright notice on your work.

[6] The Berne Convention Implementation Act of 1988 enabled the United States to establish copyright relations with 25 more countries. Notice requirements were dropped for works published after March 1, 1989. Recordation of an interest in a copyrighted work is no longer required as a prerequisite to bringing an infringement suit.

1) THE WORK MUST BE ORIGINAL

In order for a work to meet the originality requirement it must be created through the independent effort of the author. The creator cannot copy it from another's work.

The work need not have any merit. No one at the copyright office reviews applications for copyright registration to determine artistic or literary value. You can register a badly written novel or a child's finger-painted picture. You can register a brilliant scientific article or the *National Enquirer*. In other words, there are no aesthetic or scholarly standards for copyright protection. The work has to be original, not good. Besides, artistic worth is subjective. What one person considers great art another may think is junk.

How much originality is required? Could you, for instance, take a picture of an ordinary white wall with a Brownie Instamatic camera and receive copyright protection for your work? Yes, because not much originality is required. Here, the creator chose how to frame the picture and how to light it. You may not think this picture is interesting or worth much, but it is original enough for copyright protection.

CLASSIFICATION OF WORKS

THE CLASSIFICATION OF A WORK AFFECTS WHAT RIGHTS CAN BE CONFERRED UPON THE AUTHOR. FOR EXAMPLE, THE OWNER OF A COPYRIGHT IN A SOUND RECORDING DOES NOT ENJOY A PERFORMANCE RIGHT. ONLY NON-DRAMATIC MUSICAL WORKS ARE SUBJECT TO A COMPULSORY LICENSE FOR REPRODUCTION. A LIBRARY'S REPRODUCTION RIGHT IS MUCH WIDER FOR LITERARY AND DRAMATIC WORKS THAN FOR OTHER CATEGORIES. IT IS IMPORTANT TO FILE THE CORRECT FORM TO OBTAIN THE PROPER COPYRIGHT.

THE COPYRIGHT CLASSIFICATION SYSTEM HAS FOUR BROAD CATEGORIES OF REGISTRATION:

CLASS TX: NON-DRAMATIC LITERARY WORKS
CLASS PA: PERFORMING ARTS
CLASS VA: VISUAL ARTS
CLASS SR: SOUND RECORDINGS

2) THE WORK MUST BE AN EXPRESSION OF AN AUTHOR

Ideas, themes, and titles are never copyrightable. On the other hand, books, plays, and movies are copyrightable. The former are not considered expressions of an author, while the latter are.

Copyright law protects the craftsmanship of the writer, the writer's approach, and his/her skill in fashioning the material. But the writer can never copyright an idea—whether it is

DEALMAKING
IN THE
FILM AND
TELEVISION
INDUSTRY—
3RD EDITION

306

incorporated in a sentence or a 400-page book—and prevent others from creating works based on the same idea.

In other words, ideas are as free as the air. Nobody can possess them. If you want to write a book about George Washington, you may do so and be protected under copyright law. But you cannot preclude subsequent authors from writing their own books on George Washington as long as they don't copy your work.[7]

It is sometimes difficult to distinguish an idea from the expression of an author. I'm sure everyone would agree that a 500-page book is an expression of an author. But what about a 250-page book? A 100-page book? A ten-page book? A one-page book? What about a one-page book with just one letter on each page? We'll call it the Alphabet Book Series. The first book contains just the letter "A."

If this book deserves copyright protection, then could I prevent anyone else from using the letter "A" in his/her writings? Of course not. You can't copyright a letter or a word. But when you string together words, at a certain point you will be protected if somebody copies your expression. At what point does that occur? It's not clear because it is difficult to determine precisely when an idea becomes sufficiently embellished to become an expression of an author. And even when a work is an expression of an author, the underlying idea is not protected.

To understand why Congress protects only expressions of authors, you have to understand the competing policy considerations underlying the Copyright Act. On one hand, Congress wants to protect the work of authors to encourage them to create new works. If anyone who owned a printing press could freely copy, sell, and compete against authors, authors would not reap the full fruits of their labor. Authors would have little incentive to invest time and energy to create new works. Because Congress wants to encourage authors to create new works for the good of society, Congress gives the author certain exclusive rights over the use of their work—the so-called copyright.

---

[7] Except they may be able to borrow small portions of your book under the Fair Use Doctrine, discussed on page 312, and they could borrow historical facts because these are in the public domain.

But Congress also believes that, in an open and democratic society, people should be able to freely exchange ideas and create new works based on the ideas of others. So the copyright is not absolute. The right is limited in several ways.

First, it is restricted in time. The creator (or the employer of the creator if it is a work-for-hire) has a copyright to his/her work for a limited term. Before 1978, the author of a work had a copyright in his/her work for 28 years and could renew it for an additional 28 years, for a total of 56 years of copyright protection.[8] Under current law, a copyright for a work created on or after January 1, 1978, lasts for the lifetime of the author plus 70 years. However, if the work is a "work-made-for-hire," the employer owns the copyright, and the duration of copyright is 95 years from publication or 120 years from creation, whichever is shorter.[9] Once a copyright expires, the work goes into the public domain and anyone can use it. Second, Congress restricts the copyright by limiting it to expressions of authors. Mere ideas, titles, and themes are not protected.[10]

3) THE WORK MUST BE OF A NON-UTILITARIAN NATURE

Works of a utilitarian nature are not eligible for copyright protection. An ordinary lighting fixture, for example, cannot be copyrighted. A bookkeeping ledger or the contest rules on the side of a cereal box are utilitarian forms of writing. If there is no other way, or few other ways, to express something, the writing will be considered utilitarian.

Note that works of an ingenious design, although utilitarian, may be eligible for patent protection.[11] There is some overlap between patent and copyright law, and some works can be protected by both.

Since a lighting fixture cannot be copyrighted, and a statue is an aesthetic work that can be copyrighted, what

---

[8] Works in the second term when the law changed received an extra 19-year extension for a total of 75 years.

[9] Since the employer could be a corporation, which doesn't die or have to ever dissolve, a different term is required. Otherwise, corporations would have an unfair advantage in being able to keep their work copyrighted indefinitely.

[10] Protection could be obtained in some situations, however, under contract, trademark, or unfair competition laws.

[11] Patents protect technological information and they arise from government grant. Copyrights protect expressive information and they arise automatically upon creation assuming all the criteria for copyright eligibility have been meet. Trademarks protect symbolic information (e.g., product marks and logos), and they arise from use.

DEALMAKING
IN THE
FILM AND
TELEVISION
INDUSTRY—
3RD EDITION

308

happens if you mount a lighting fixture on top of a piece of sculpture? In other words, you make the sculpture the base of a lamp. Can you obtain copyright protection for the hybrid work? Well, you retain copyright to the base, but you don't gain a copyright in the fixture.

On the other hand, what if an avant-garde artist welds 200 old lighting fixtures into an intricate design? Although lighting fixtures are not ordinarily copyrightable, here they are being used in a non-utilitarian way, so the work should be copyrightable.

4) THE WORK MUST BE IN A FIXED, TANGIBLE MEDIUM OF EXPRESSION

The work must be expressed in a fixed, tangible form that is relatively stable and permanent. Such mediums as paper, videotape, audio-tape, paint, clay, film, and metal meet the requirement. A work that is comprised solely of an impromptu speech or an unrecorded live performance, or a work embodied in an ice sculpture or a sand castle, will not be protected under copyright law.

The author or someone under his/her authorization must reduce the work to a tangible form. Recordation by an audience member listening to an improvised jazz performance would not constitute fixation for purpose of copyright protection.

Fixation before a public performance is preferred. But what about simultaneous fixation as a work is performed? The Copyright Act protects live broadcasts that are simultaneously recorded.

There is a practical reason for the requirement that copyrighted material be put in tangible form. How else could a judge determine the extent of a copyright in an ethereal work?

Can one copyright choreography? Yes, if it is put in a fixed form. Either written stage directions or a videotaped performance will suffice. Of course, choreography must meet the other criteria for copyright protection. You could not copyright a single dance step because that would not be considered an expression of an author.

COPYRIGHT NOTICE

Proper copyright notice contains three elements:

1) either the word "copyright," the abbreviation for the word copyright, or the symbol ©,
2) the name of the copyright owner, and
3) the date of first publication.

The order of the elements does not matter. Authors may also add the phrase "All Rights Reserved," which can provide additional protection in foreign jurisdictions.

The date may be omitted where a pictorial, graphic, or sculptural work with accompanying text matter, if any, is reproduced in or on greeting cards, postcards, stationery, jewelry, dolls, toys, or any useful articles. The full name of the copyright owner is not required.

The notice should be located in such a manner as to give reasonable notice. A copyright is not affected if notice is taken off a work without authorization of the copyright owner.

The 1976 Copyright Act reduces the importance of publication because federal copyright now begins when a work is created. For works created between 1978 and March 1, 1989, the 1976 Act retains the notice requirement, although omission of notice can be cured by taking certain steps. Until the 1988 Amendments the United

CONTINUING IMPORTANCE OF PUBLICATION:

1) DEPOSIT REQUIREMENTS: For works published since the Berne Amendments deposit requirements remain. You have three months to deposit a copy with the Library of Congress. Criminal fines can be assessed.

2) NEED TO REGISTER AFTER PUBLICATION AS PREREQUISITE TO BRINGING ABOUT SUIT AND TO SECURE CERTAIN ADVANTAGES:

In addition, registering a work provides the following advantages:

a) Registration within five years of publication confers prima facie evidence of the validity of a copyright. In other words, it will create evidence sufficient to prove copyright ownership if not rebutted or contradicted by the other party.

b) One can obtain statutory damages and attorney fees for published works only if registration preceded an infringement or if the work was registered three months after publication.

3) INTERNATIONAL COPYRIGHT IMPLICATIONS: Under both Berne and Universal Conventions the act of publication is important. Works first published in a member state or by a national of a member state must be given the same protection in every other country as works first published in its own territory.

4) DURATIONAL CONSEQUENCES: The date of publication determines length of copyright for certain categories of works. Under the 1976 Act and its amendments, the term for anonymous and pseudonymous works and works-for-hire is measured either by 95 years from the year of first publication or by 120 years from creation, whichever is shorter.

DEALMAKING
IN THE
FILM AND
TELEVISION
INDUSTRY—
3RD EDITION

310

States was alone in the world in requiring compliance with notice formalities. After March 1, 1989, notice is permissive.

The provisions of the 1988 Amendments are not retroactive, so works that went into the public domain for failure to comply with notice provisions remain in the public domain.

Copyright notice remains important because section 405(b) limits remedies against innocent infringers misled by lack of notice. An innocent infringer is shielded from actual damages and statutory damages. This limitation lasts until the infringer is put on notice of the claim of copyright.

Summary of Notice Requirements

For works published before 1978, the harsh notice provisions of the 1909 Act apply.

For works published between 1978 and March 1, 1989, the less-strict notice provisions of the 1976 Act apply.

For works published after March 1, 1989, the permissive notice requirements apply.

THE RIGHTS OF THE COPYRIGHT HOLDER

When you own a copyright, you possess a bundle of rights: the right to control the reproduction of your work, the right to control preparation of derivative works, the right to distribute copies of the work to the public by sale, rental, or lease, the right to perform the works publicly,[12] and the right to display the works publicly.[13] Graphic, pictorial, sculptural works, and sound recordings, however, don't enjoy the same full range of exclusive rights as do literary, musical, and dramatic works. The copyright owner of a sound recording, for example, cannot control the right of performance and display of the work. Also, graphic, pictorial or sculptural works do not enjoy a performance right.[14]

---

[12] A performance is public at any place where a substantial number of persons outside of the normal circle of family and friends is gathered. Thus, singing in the bathtub is not a public performance. Renting a movie and showing it in one's house to friends is not a public performance.

[13] These rights are subject to limitations in sections 107-118 of the Copyright Act.

[14] Moreover, Section 106 limits the exclusive rights of performance and display to public performance and display.

Moreover, a copyright is limited by various compulsory licenses—licenses required to be given to all persons who comply with the statutory requirements (i.e., payment of royalties).[15]

There are other limitations as well. The distribution right is limited by the First Sale Doctrine, which permits the owner of a copy to sell or rent it. This doctrine allows a video retailer to buy a tape from a movie studio and rent it out repeatedly to customers. An owner of a copy can dispose of it physically, can resell it, rent it, give it away, and rebind it. He/she cannot, however, reproduce it or perform it publicly. Record stores cannot do the same, however, because they fall within an exception to the First Sale Doctrine that prevents the renting of sound recordings.[16]

LIMITS ON COPYRIGHT

Sometimes people can utilize copyrightable works by obtaining a license that covers many works (a blanket license), or they may be entitled under the law to be granted a license for a set fee (a compulsory license), or they may be allowed to borrow a small amount of material without permission because such a use is in the public interest (the Fair Use doctrine).

Blanket License

Under a blanket license a user can secure permission to use many different works for one fee. For instance, a radio station can obtain a blanket license from ASCAP to obtain the right to publicly perform music in ASCAP's catalog, which includes music from thousands of artists. ASCAP and BMI, as well as other groups such as SESAC, are performing rights societies that act as agents in licensing their members' work.

---

[15] There are currently six compulsory licenses: 1) Cable television license; 2) Mechanical recording license and digital audio-transmission license; 3) Digital audio transmission of a sound recordings license; 4) Public broadcasting license; 5) Satellite retransmission license; and 6) Digital audio-tape device license. Licenses are administered by the Copyright Royalty Tribunal, an administrative agency.

[16] See § 109(b) of the Copyright Act. The Record Rental Amendment of 1984 prohibits an owner of a phonorecord which embodies a sound recording of a musical work from renting it to the public for direct or indirect commercial advantage. It does not apply to resale or other transfers, and it is limited to commercial establishments (i.e., does not apply to libraries and educational institutions).

DEALMAKING
IN THE
FILM AND
TELEVISION
INDUSTRY—
3RD EDITION

312

It makes sense for artists to let these societies license their music. This arrangement is administratively convenient for both the artist and the licensee. Can you imagine the burden it would place on a radio disc jockey to individually license every song he/she wants to broadcast? The payment for each use would be minuscule, and the administrative burden great.

Compulsory License

The compulsory license allows anyone to make his/her own recording of a non-dramatic musical work once a phonorecord of that work has been distributed to the public. This means anyone can hire a group of musicians to independently record a song, which can then be distributed to the public. This licensee obtains the so-called Mechanical Rights. This right is limited in several ways. The license applies only to non-dramatic musical works; one cannot obtain a license for opera, Broadway musicals, ballets, or motion picture soundtracks. In making the recording, the compulsory licensee cannot change the basic melody or the fundamental character of the work beyond that which is necessary to conform the musical work to the range and style of the licensee's performers.

To obtain a compulsory license, the party making the independent sound recording of the song must notify the copyright owner by filing a notice of intention. This notice must be filed before distribution of the phonorecords, or within 30 days of making the new recording. The compulsory licensee must pay a monthly statutory royalty known as mechanical royalties. This requirement is burdensome, which is why most licensees prefer to license these rights from the music rights' owner. Typically, the license is obtained through an agent, the Harry Fox Agency, which specializes in licensing mechanical rights. The fee is usually less than the statutory rate.

Fair Use

In some situations no license is needed to borrow from a copyrighted work. The law protects the right of the public to draw

upon copyrighted works to produce separate works of authorship under the fair use doctrine. Such uses include fair comment
and criticism, parody, news reporting, teaching, scholarship, and
research. Thus, a movie or literary critic does not need permission to include a small quote from a work being reviewed. It is
sometimes said of writers that if you borrow extensively from
another's work, you are a literary thief; but if you borrow bits
from thousands, you are considered a scholar. Of course, the
scholar adds value by synthesizing information from prior works
and creating something new.

In determining whether the use of a copyrighted work is fair
use, courts weigh four factors:

1) The purpose and character of the work: A non-profit
   educational use is more likely to be considered a fair
   use than a commercial use. A commercial use is one that
   earns a profit.
2) The nature of the copyrighted work: There is greater public
   interest in allowing borrowing for scientific, biographical,
   and historical works than for entertainment works.
3) The amount and substantiality of the portion borrowed
   in relation to the copyrighted work as a whole: Taking
   one sentence from a 500-page book is more likely to be
   considered a fair use than taking a sentence from a 10-
   line poem.
4) The potential adverse effect on the market for, and value of,
   the copyrighted work: If borrowing from the copyrighted
   work harms the market for it, the use is less likely to be
   considered a fair use. Borrowing a sentence from a novel
   and incorporating it in another, completely different, kind
   of work, such as a scholarly work, is unlikely to have any
   effect on sales of the novel. Likewise, borrowing from a
   book that is out of print is not likely to have an adverse
   impact on its sales.

In applying these factors to a specific factual situation, it can
often be difficult to predict whether a use will fall within the
doctrine. Generally speaking, a greater amount of material may
be borrowed from non-fiction works than from fictional works.
Clearly, a writer can borrow historical facts from a previous work
without infringing upon the first author's copyright. Moreover,
since factual works, unlike works of fiction, may be capable of

DEALMAKING
IN THE
FILM AND
TELEVISION
INDUSTRY—
3RD EDITION

314

being expressed in relatively few ways, only verbatim reproduction or close paraphrasing will be an infringement.[17]

Writers should be cautious in borrowing from novels and other fictional works. In one case, the author of the book *Welcome to Twin Peaks: A Complete Guide to Who's Who and What's What* was found to have infringed the television series *Twin Peaks*. The book contained detailed plot summaries and extensive direct quotations of at least 89 lines of dialogue.[18]

One encounters a lot of gray areas in applying the fair use doctrine. It is safe to say that a schoolteacher will be protected if she photocopies a *Newsweek* article and distributes it to her class on one occasion. If the schoolteacher, however, photocopies an entire textbook and distributes it to her students in order to save them the expense of purchasing their own texts, this would not be a fair use. But there are many factual situations that lie between these two extremes; and in those cases it can be difficult to predict whether the fair use doctrine will be a good defense.

Many writers and filmmakers are confused about the fair use doctrine and whether they need permission to borrow from copyrighted works. Documentary filmmakers are often uncertain whether they can borrow and how much they can borrow to incorporate in their film without a license. Obviously, a filmmaker preparing an exposé or even taking a critical look at a subject cannot expect the subject to grant him/her a license. Robert Greenwald is not going to get, nor did he even bother to ask, for permission from the Fox Network for inclusion of their television footage in his film *Outfoxed: Rupert Murdoch's War on Journalism*.

If the fair use doctrine applies, no license is needed to borrow from a copyrighted work. It gives the public a limited right to draw upon copyrighted works to produce separate works of authorship. Such uses include fair comment and criticism, parody, news reporting, teaching, scholarship, and research. Thus, a movie or literary critic does not need permission to include a small quote from a work being reviewed. An excellent reference for documentary filmmakers is *Documentary Filmmakers' Statement of Best Practices in Fair Use*, which is

---

[17] *Apple Computer, Inc. v. Microsoft Corp.*, 821 F. Supp. 616 (N.D. Cal. 1993)(citing *Landsberg v. Scrabble Crossword Game Players, Inc.*, 736 F.2d 485 (9th Cir. 1984)).

[18] *Twin Peaks Prod. v. Publications Int'l.*, 996 F.2d 1366 (2d Cir. 1993).

published by and can be downloaded for free from the Center for Social Media, American University (www.centerforsocialmedia .org/resources/fair_use/).

The *Statement* addresses common situations faced by filmmakers, such as when can they quote works of popular culture without permission, and when will an incidental use of background music or visuals on a television set be considered a fair use.

OWNERSHIP OF COPYRIGHT

Works created pursuant to one's employment are works made for hire. Works created by the collaborative effort of several authors are joint works. Like other property, copyrights can be sold and transferred.[19]

Work for Hire

The employer is considered the copyright owner of works made for hire. The employee has no ownership rights at all.

How does one determine if a work is made for hire? First, all works prepared by employees within the scope of their employment are presumed to be works for hire unless the parties have expressly agreed otherwise in a written instrument signed by them.

Second, certain works[20] that are specially made or commissioned from independent contractors are considered works for hire if the parties expressly agree so in writing. The agreement must be signed by both parties and must consist of explicit wording that the work is a work for hire.[21]

---

[19] Grants made after 1978 can be terminated under certain circumstances by serving written notice and filing a notice with the copyright office 35 years from date of grant or if grant covers right of publication, then 35 years from date of publication or 40 years from date of grant, whichever is earlier. Works for hire and dispositions by will cannot be terminated. See § 203 of the Copyright Act.

[20] Works that are contributions to a collective work, part of a motion picture or other audiovisual work, a translation, supplementary work, a compilation, an instructional text, a test, answer material for a test or an atlas. See 17 USC § 101.

[21] The presumption differed under the 1909 Act which provided that the commissioning party was the author unless the parties intended the contrary. The 1976 Act reversed that presumption.

DEALMAKING
IN THE
FILM AND
TELEVISION
INDUSTRY—
3RD EDITION

316

Joint Works

A joint work is one prepared by two or more authors with the intention that their contributions be merged into inseparable or interdependent parts of a unitary whole.

Critical to determining whether a joint work exists is whether the authors intended when they created their contributions that they be integrated into one work. A joint work can be created if the contributions of the authors are unequal, so long as the author makes more than a de minimus (trifling) contribution and intends his/her work to be part of a joint work.

A joint work can also be created when a copyright owner transfers a copyright to more than one person, or when a copyright passes by will or intestacy to two or more persons, or when a work is subject to state community property laws. Thus, a joint work can be broadly defined as one in which copyright is owned in undivided shares by two or more persons.

Derivative Works

A derivative work is any work based on one or more preexisting works. Examples include a translation, musical arrangement, dramatization, fictionalization, motion picture version, sound recording, abridgement, or condensation. Also, works consisting of editorial revisions, annotations, elaborations, or other modifications that, as a whole, represent an original work of authorship are derivative works.

A derivative work infringes on the copyright of the original. To avoid infringement it must be based on public domain material or made with permission of the copyright owner of the original.

DURATION OF COPYRIGHT

All works are either copyrighted or in the public domain. There is no twilight zone in between. Until the 1909 Copyright Act was revised in 1976 (effective 1978), copyright lasted for 28 years and could be renewed for one additional 28-year term. For works published before 1978, the 1909 Act's two 28-year-term scheme continues to apply.[22] The first term is measured from the date of publication.

The copyright for works created since 1978 will last for the lifetime of the author plus 70 years.[23] For anonymous works and works made for hire, copyright generally lasts 95 years from first publication or 120 years from creation, whichever expires first.

Termination of Copyright Transfers

Prior to passage of the current copyright law, a copyright reverted to the author or his/her beneficiaries if a renewal claim was filed in the 28th year of the original term. Now, however, instead of requiring a renewal, an author can terminate a grant of rights after 35 years if he/she provides written notice to the transferee within certain time limits.

DIFFERENCE BETWEEN 1909 AND 1976 COPYRIGHT ACTS

Under the 1909 Copyright Act, a work enjoyed perpetual protection (under state common-law copyright law) until it was published. Then the work became subject to federal protection, which limited the copyright to two 28-year terms. Notice was required to be affixed to each copy; failure to do so could place the work in the public domain. Thus, publication divested common-law rights. The '76 Act reduces the importance of publication because federal copyright now begins when the work is created.

---

[22] The renewal term reverted to the author automatically, upon filing for renewal between the 27th and 28th year. Failure to comply resulted in forfeiture of copyright. The 1976 Act retains this system for works copyrighted before 1978, and the second term has been lengthened from 28 to 47 years. Moreover, works in their renewal term between December 31, 1976, and December 31, 1977, receive an extra 19 years added to the second term, for a total copyright of 75 years.

[23] For works created but not copyrighted or published before 1978, copyright will not expire before December 31, 2002. If published before this expiration date, copyright protection will last until December 31, 2027. These works are often letters, diaries, and other manuscripts that were never sold or publicly distributed.

DEALMAKING
IN THE
FILM AND
TELEVISION
INDUSTRY—
3RD EDITION

318

COPYRIGHT REGISTRATION AND DEPOSIT

No other country has anything like the United States' elaborate system of copyright registration. The advantage of our system is that it protects owners by establishing priority of authorship and provides evidence of the validity of a copyright. It also facilitates transfers, assignments, and licenses of copyrighted works because prospective transferees have more confidence in the validity of a registered copyright than an unregistered one.

The registration system has several shortcomings, however. A search of copyright records may be unrewarding or misleading because the absence of any mention of a work in the records does not mean it is unprotected. Registration is voluntary, and many copyright owners choose not to register.[24]

Furthermore, information in records may be inaccurate or incomplete. The copyright office assumes all information submitted is accurate. No independent investigation is conducted. Consequently, searches of copyright records are rarely conclusive.

ADVANTAGES OF REGISTRATION

There are a number benefits conferred on those who register their copyrights. These benefits are:

1) PUBLIC RECORD: Registration establishes a public record of a copyright claim.

2) RIGHT TO SUE: Registration secures the right to file an infringement suit for works whose country of origin is the United States.

    The 1976 Copyright Act originally required registration as a prerequisite for bringing a suit. Effective March 1, 1989, registration is only necessary for works whose country of origin is the United States.[25] If registration has taken place, suit can be brought for all infringing acts occurring before or after registration.

    Registration is not required for a work whose country

---

[24] The only exceptions to voluntarily registration were for works copyrighted before 1978 (published with notice) when the copyright owner had to file a renewal registration to claim a second term. For unpublished works, copyright protection was perpetual. Also under the 1976 Act registration is required to preserve copyright when proper notice has been omitted on a significant number of published copies.

[25] 17 U.S.C. § 411(A), *as amended* by Berne Convention Implementation Act of 1988.

of origin is a Berne Convention signatory. The location of publication determines whether a work is published in a Berne country, not the nationality of the author.

3) PRESUMPTIONS: Registration establishes prima facie validity of the copyright (if registration takes place within five years of publication). Thus the copyright will be presumed to be true unless disproved by evidence to the contrary.

4) BROADER RANGE OF REMEDIES: Registration makes available a broader range of remedies in an infringement suit, allowing statutory damages and attorneys' fees if 1) registration occurs before the infringement for an unpublished work; or 2) if registration occurs within three months of first publication. Statutory damages are often the only viable remedy for a copyright owner.

As provided by the Copyright Act, courts may award statutory damages of no less than $750 nor more than $30,000.[26] However, under some circumstances courts have the discretion to award more or less than the amounts specified by the Copyright Act. For example, if the copyright owner has proven a knowing and willful infringement, the court has the discretion to award up to $150,000.[27] Alternatively, if the infringer proves that he or she was unaware of the infringement, or had no reason to know the acts were infringing, the recovery may be reduced to as low as $200.[28]

5) RECORDATION OF TRANSFERS: Only if registration is made will recordation of a document in the Copyright Office give notice of a transfer. The 1976 Copyright Act permits recording in the copyright office of all documents of copyright ownership, whether assignments, exclusive licenses, or non-exclusive licenses.[29]

Recordation is important because it puts the world on legal notice as to the existence of your copyright.[30] Recordation also establishes priority of ownership between conflicting transfers of copyright.

---

[26] *Id.* § 504(c)(1), *as amended* by Berne Convention Implementation Act of 1988.
[27] *Id.* § 504(c)(2), as amended by Berne Convention Implementation Act of 1988.
[28] *Id.*
[29] For causes of action arising before March 1, 1989, recordation is a prerequisite to bringing a suit for copyright infringement.
[30] Constructive notice is notice implied by law as compared with actual notice. In other words, recordation of a copyright gives everyone legal notice, even if they are not actually aware of the copyright.

DEALMAKING
IN THE
FILM AND
TELEVISION
INDUSTRY—
3RD EDITION

320

Form PA should be completed to register published or unpublished works of the performing arts. This class includes works prepared for the purpose of being performed directly before an audience or indirectly by means of any device or process. Works of performing arts include musical works, dramatic works, including any accompanying music, pantomimes, and choreographic works, and motion pictures and other audiovisual works.

COPYRIGHT REGISTRATION

IF YOUR MOTION PICTURE IS FINISHED, YOU SHOULD REGISTER IT BY SENDING IN FORM PA WITH A COPY OF THE FINISHED FILM AND AN ATTACHED SYNOPSIS DESCRIBING THE FILM. IF YOU ARE STILL AT THE SCRIPT STAGE, YOU CAN REGISTER THE SCRIPT NOW AND REGISTER THE FILM WHEN IT IS COMPLETED. IN EITHER CASE, CLOSELY FOLLOW THE INSTRUCTIONS ON FORM PA. THE FOLLOWING GUIDE ADDRESSES THOSE SECTIONS THAT APPLICANTS OFTEN FIND CONFUSING WHEN REGISTERING SCRIPTS OR MOTION PICTURES. REMEMBER TO COMPLETE ALL APPLICABLE SECTIONS OF THE FORM, NOT JUST THOSE DISCUSSED BELOW.

REGISTERING A SCRIPT

UNDER #1, NATURE OF THIS WORK, YOU COULD WRITE "SCREENPLAY FOR MOTION PICTURE."

UNDER #2, "NAME OF AUTHOR": NOTE THAT IF A SCREENPLAY HAS BEEN WRITTEN FOR YOU OR YOUR COMPANY—IN OTHER WORDS, IF YOU HIRED SOMEONE TO WRITE THE SCREENPLAY—THEN IT MAY BE A WORK-MADE-FOR-HIRE. IN THIS CASE, YOU OR YOUR COMPANY IS THE COPYRIGHT HOLDER AND SHOULD BE LISTED UNDER "NAME OF AUTHOR." ON THE OTHER HAND, IF A WRITER HAS CREATED THE SCREENPLAY ON HIS/HER OWN, AND HE/SHE IS THEN SELLING IT TO YOU, THE WRITER WOULD BE THE AUTHOR. IF THIS WRITER HAS ALREADY REGISTERED THE SCRIPT WITH THE COPYRIGHT OFFICE, YOU SHOULD NOT REGISTER IT AGAIN, BUT MERELY RECORD THE TRANSFER (ASSIGNMENT) OF THE COPYRIGHT TO YOU. THE COPYRIGHT SHOULD BE ASSIGNED TO YOU OR YOUR COMPANY WITH A WRITTEN CONTRACT, AND A SHORT-FORM COPYRIGHT ASSIGNMENT RECORDED WITH THE COPYRIGHT OFFICE.

UNDER "NATURE OF AUTHORSHIP," YOU SHOULD GIVE A BRIEF GENERAL DESCRIPTION OF THE AUTHOR'S CONTRIBUTION TO THE WORK. IF THE AUTHOR WROTE THE ENTIRE SCRIPT YOU MIGHT WRITE: "ENTIRE TEXT." IF YOU ARE CLAIMING COPYRIGHT TO SOMETHING LESS THAN THE ENTIRE SCRIPT, DESCRIBE YOUR CONTRIBUTION: FOR EXAMPLE, "EDITORIAL REVISIONS."

THEN ENTER THE YEAR IN WHICH THE CREATION OF THE WORK WAS COMPLETED AND THE COPYRIGHT CLAIMANT (THE AUTHOR OR WHOMEVER HAS LEGALLY ACQUIRED THE COPYRIGHT).

UNDER #5, IF THE SCREENPLAY CONTAINS A SUBSTANTIAL AMOUNT OF PREVIOUSLY REGISTERED MATERIAL, ANSWER YES TO THE FIRST QUESTION AND CHECK THE BOX INDICATING THE REASON FOR THIS REGISTRATION. ADD THE REGISTRATION NUMBER AND YEAR OF THE PREVIOUSLY REGISTERED MATERIAL. IF NO PORTION OF THE WORK WAS PREVIOUSLY REGISTERED, ANSWER NO TO THE FIRST QUESTION AND LEAVE THE REST OF THE SPACE BLANK. FILL OUT #6A & B ONLY IF THE WORK HAS A SIGNIFICANT AMOUNT OF PREVIOUSLY REGISTERED, PREVIOUSLY PUBLISHED, OR PUBLIC DOMAIN MATERIAL.

UNDER #6A, "DERIVATIVE WORK OR COMPILATION," YOU MIGHT WRITE "PREVIOUSLY REGISTERED SCREENPLAY."

UNDER #6B, "MATERIAL ADDED TO THIS WORK," YOU MIGHT WRITE "ADDITIONAL DIALOGUE AND TEXT."

REGISTERING A COMPLETED FILM

UNDER #1, "NATURE OF THIS WORK," WRITE: "MOTION PICTURE."

UNDER #2, "NAME OF AUTHOR": USUALLY THIS WILL BE THE NAME OF THE PRODUCTION COMPANY OR ENTITY THAT HIRED EVERYBODY WHO MADE THE MOTION PICTURE. IF THIS IS PROJECT WAS ENTIRELY A WORK-MADE-FOR-HIRE, CHECK YES UNDER "WAS THIS CONTRIBUTION TO THE WORK A 'WORK MADE FOR HIRE.'" UNDER "NATURE OF AUTHORSHIP," WRITE IN "SCREENPLAY AND ADAPTATION AS MOTION PICTURE."

IF THIS MOTION PICTURE WAS NOT AT ALL A WORK-FOR-HIRE, FILL IN THE NAME OF THE PERSON(S) WHO MADE THE MOTION PICTURE, AND CHECK "NO" UNDER "WAS THIS CONTRIBUTION TO THE WORK A 'WORK MADE FOR HIRE.'" UNDER "NATURE OF AUTHORSHIP," WRITE IN "SCREENPLAY AND ADAPTATION AS MOTION PICTURE."

IF THIS MOTION PICTURE WAS PARTLY A WORK-FOR-HIRE, AND PARTLY NOT, YOU'LL NEED TO FILL IN A SPACE FOR EACH PART. FOR EXAMPLE, IF YOUR PRODUCTION COMPANY MADE THE MOTION PICTURE AS A WORK-FOR-HIRE BUT BOUGHT A COMPLETED SCREENPLAY FROM A WRITER WHO WAS ITS AUTHOR, THEN YOU WOULD FILL OUT TWO SPACES:

IN ONE SPACE, YOU COULD FILL IN THE WRITER'S NAME AS AUTHOR, CHECK NO TO THE QUESTION OF WHETHER IT WAS A "WORK MADE FOR HIRE," AND FILL IN "SCREENPLAY" OR "SCRIPT" IN "NATURE OF AUTHORSHIP."

IN ANOTHER SPACE, YOU COULD FILL IN THE PRODUCTION COMPANY'S NAME, CHECK YES INDICATING IT IS A "WORK MADE FOR HIRE," AND FILL IN "ALL OTHER CINEMATOGRAPHIC MATERIAL" UNDER NATURE OF AUTHORSHIP."

UNDER SECTION 5, IF THE MOTION PICTURE CONTAINS A SUBSTANTIAL AMOUNT OF PREVIOUSLY REGISTERED MATERIAL, ANSWER YES TO THE FIRST QUESTION AND CHECK THE BOX INDICATING THE REASON FOR THIS REGISTRATION. INCLUDE THE REGISTRATION NUMBER AND YEAR OF THE PREVIOUSLY REGISTERED MATERIAL.

FILL OUT #6A & B ONLY IF THE WORK HAS A SIGNIFICANT AMOUNT OF PREVIOUSLY REGISTERED, PREVIOUSLY PUBLISHED, OR PUBLIC DOMAIN MATERIAL.

UNDER #6A, "DERIVATIVE WORK OR COMPILATION," YOU COULD WRITE IN "PREVIOUSLY REGISTERED SCREENPLAY."

UNDER #6B, "MATERIAL ADDED TO THIS WORK," WRITE "MOTION PICTURE."

YOU ARE REQUIRED TO DEPOSIT A COPY OF YOUR FILM WITHIN THREE MONTHS OF PUBLICATION. IF YOU DO NOT, YOU MAY BE SUBJECT TO FINES AND PENALTIES.

IN GENERAL

COMPLETE #4, "COPYRIGHT CLAIMANTS," EVEN IF THE CLAIMANT IS THE SAME AS THE AUTHOR. THE CLAIMANT IS THE PERSON OR COMPANY THAT HAS LEGALLY ACQUIRED THE COPYRIGHT. IT WILL BE EITHER THE AUTHOR OR THE ENTITY TO WHICH THE COPYRIGHT HAS BEEN TRANSFERRED. WHEN THE CLAIMANT IS NOT THE AUTHOR, YOU NEED TO DESCRIBE UNDER "TRANSFER" HOW THE COPYRIGHT WAS OBTAINED BY THE CLAIMANT. YOU COULD STATE, FOR EXAMPLE, "BY WRITTEN ASSIGNMENT."

DON'T FORGET TO INCLUDE A COPY OF YOUR SCRIPT OR FILM WHEN YOU SEND IN YOUR REGISTRATION FORM.

YOU NEED TO SIGN FORM PA AND SEND IT IN WITH A CHECK FOR $45 PAYABLE TO "REGISTER OF COPYRIGHTS." RETAIN A PHOTOCOPY OF EVERYTHING YOU SEND THE COPYRIGHT OFFICE INCLUDING THE COMPLETED FORM PA AND YOUR COVER LETTER. IT IS A GOOD IDEA TO SEND YOUR PACKAGE BY CERTIFIED MAIL.

IF YOU WOULD LIKE TO PUT YOUR ATTORNEY'S NAME UNDER "CORRESPONDENCE" SO THAT HE/SHE CAN ANSWER ANY QUESTIONS THE COPYRIGHT OFFICE MAY HAVE, YOU MAY DO SO. IN THIS EVENT, YOU SHOULD SEND YOUR ATTORNEY A PHOTOCOPY OF THE FORM AND YOUR COVER LETTER SO HE/SHE WILL HAVE A RECORD OF WHAT YOU HAVE SUBMITTED.

MAIL TO:

LIBRARY OF CONGRESS
COPYRIGHT OFFICE
101 INDEPENDENCE AVE., S.E.
WASHINGTON, D.C. 20559-6000

COPYRIGHT CIRCULARS AND FORMS ARE AVAILABLE FROM THE FORMS AND PUBLICATIONS HOTLINE, (202) 707-9100 (LEAVE A RECORDED MESSAGE REQUESTING THE DOCUMENTS YOU WANT MAILED TO YOU), OR ON THE COPYRIGHT OFFICE WEBSITE, WWW.COPYRIGHT.GOV. THE WEBSITE ALSO OFFERS EXTENSIVE COPYRIGHT INFORMATION. CIRCULAR 45 FOUND AT WWW.COPYRIGHT.GOV/CIRCS/CIRC45.HTML SPECIFICALLY ADDRESSES COPYRIGHT REGISTRATION FOR MOTION PICTURES. TO SPEAK TO AN INFORMATION SPECIALIST, CALL (202) 707-3000.

DEALMAKING
IN THE
FILM AND
TELEVISION
INDUSTRY—
3RD EDITION

322

Online Registration

Online registration through the electronic Copyright Office (eCO) is usually the best method to register your copyright. Advantages of online filing include a lower filing fee, faster processing, online status tracking, and the ability to pay by credit or debit card, electronic check, or a Copyright Office deposit account. Some types of deposits can be uploaded directly as electronic files.

You can still register online and save on fees even if you deposit by sending in a hard copy. The system will prompt you to specify whether you intend to submit an electronic or a hard-copy deposit, and it will provide instructions. To access eCO, go to the Copyright Office website at www.copyright.gov and click on electronic Copyright Office.

REGISTRATION AFTER BERNE

For causes of action arising after March 1, 1989, the Berne Convention Implementation Act has ended the requirement of registering as a prerequisite to bringing a suit for infringement for non-U.S. works. Registration remains important because it gives constructive notice to the world of one's copyright. This notice may be critical if there arises a conflict between two transfers of an interest in one copyright.

REQUIREMENT OF REGISTRATION UPON PUBLICATION

You are not required to publish your work. If you do publish it, however, you are required to deposit two copies of the work within three months of publication.[31] If you do not deposit the copies, you may be fined but you do not forfeit your copyright.[32]

---

[31] §407. This requirement does not apply to published works not having notice, and works published in foreign countries.

[32] Under the 1909 Act, failure to comply with the deposit and registration requirements after a Demand by the Register of Copyrights would subject the claimant to a fine and void his copyright.

The deposit requirement serves two purposes. It adds a copy of the work to the collection of the Library of Congress, and it identifies the work with the copyright registration.

TRANSFERS OF COPYRIGHT INTERESTS

Copyright is comprised of a bundle of rights, and the 1976 Copyright Act expressly recognizes the divisibility of copyright: any subdivision of the rights may be transferred and owned separately.

Each transferee enjoys all the rights of a copyright owner, and each has standing to sue. By contrast, under the 1909 Act the licensee was not considered an owner of copyright and was forced to join the copyright holder in a suit.

To be effective, transfers of copyright must be in writing and signed by the copyright owner. The requirement does not apply to a nonexclusive license.

CASES

Estate of Hemingway v. Random House, Inc. (1966)[33]

FACTS: Hotchner wrote a book, *Papa Hemingway*. It incorporated long conversations between the author and Hemingway. They had been close friends for 13 years and went on drinking escapades and travels together. Hotchner took notes and published several articles incorporating their conversations. Hemingway liked the articles. Hemingway's estate sues Hotchner, seeking an injunction against the book and damages for infringement of common-law copyright.

ISSUE: Were Hemingway's conversations protected under common-law copyright?

HOLDING: No.

RATIONALE: It is presumed that, in ordinary conversations the parties are not reserving any rights. Here Hemingway's conduct demonstrates no intention to reserve rights; indeed, it appears he approved of Hotchner quoting him.

---

[33] 49 Misc. 2d 726, 268 N.Y.S.2d 531 (1966).

DEALMAKING
IN THE
FILM AND
TELEVISION
INDUSTRY—
3RD EDITION

324

One cannot copyright an extemporaneous conversation unless it is put in a tangible form. Absent an express or implied agreement between the parties, the plaintiff has no remedy.

Common-law copyright refers to the rights authors have in unpublished works protected by state court decisions. Since the Copyright Act of 1976, federal copyright law extends to unpublished as well as published works. Thus, the field has now largely been preempted by federal statutory law.

Sheldon v. Metro-Goldwyn Pictures Corp. (1936)[34]

FACTS: MGM attempted to secure the movie rights to Edward Sheldon's copyrighted play *Dishonored Lady*. The play was based, in part, on a true story. When MGM couldn't secure the movie rights from Sheldon, the studio produced a movie of its own, *Letty Lynton*, based on the same historical incident. Although much of the movie was original, certain details and sequences of events were identical to those expressed in Sheldon's play. The lower court held for MGM on the grounds that the use of Sheldon's play only involved general themes or ideas. Sheldon appealed.

ISSUE: Did MGM infringe upon Sheldon's copyright?

HOLDING: Yes.

RATIONALE: MGM'S work was identical in details and sequence of events to Sheldon's work in matters unrelated to the underlying true story. This is more than merely appropriating an idea or a theme. It doesn't matter that the plagiarized material only comprises a small portion of the entire film. It is not okay to steal a little bit.

Sheldon wrote a play based on a historical event. Historical events are in the public domain, and anyone, including MGM, is free to use them.

MGM wanted to make a movie of Sheldon's play. The parties were unable to agree on terms. So MGM decided to make its own movie based on the historical events underlying Sheldon's play. MGM hired a writer to write a screenplay and the movie was made. Some incidents and sequences of events in the movie were similar to Sheldon's play, and these similarities were not matters of historical record. In other words, Sheldon wrote a play based on a historical event and other events he created

---

[34] 81 F.2d 49 (1936).

from his imagination. Some of the imaginary material appeared in MGM's movie.

While MGM had every right to make a movie about the historical events in Sheldon's play, it had no right to borrow material created by Sheldon if that material was copyrightable—in other words, if the material was more than an idea. Here the court felt the MGM writer borrowed more than an idea.

MGM should have been more careful in hiring a writer. The studio should have declined to hire writers who had read Sheldon's play. Once hired, the studio should have told the writer not to read Sheldon's play to ensure against any inadvertent copying.

Musto v. Meyer (1977)[35]

FACTS: Plaintiff wrote an article in a medical journal titled "A Study in Cocaine: Sherlock Holmes and Sigmund Freud." It concerned the history of cocaine use in Europe in the 1800s and speculated that Holmes was a heavy cocaine user, which led him to believe that Professor Moriarty was after him. The author also speculated that Holmes' famous disappearance was due to his going to see Freud for treatment of his cocaine addiction.

Nicholas Myer subsequently wrote a book titled *The Seven Percent Solution*. It had Watson tricking Holmes into seeing Freud for treatment of cocaine addiction, Freud curing Holmes, and both of them embarking on a Holmesian adventure. Universal Pictures made a movie from the book. Plaintiff sued, claiming the book and movie infringed his copyrighted article.

ISSUE: Was Plaintiff's copyright infringed?

HOLDING: No.

RATIONALE: The book is not similar to the article except for the idea that Holmes was addicted to cocaine and this addiction was cured by Freud. They are not similar as far as reader appeal, fashioning of plot, delineation of characters, or literary skill.

Nicholas Meyer didn't deny that he read the plaintiff's article. Indeed, he gave the plaintiff a credit in his book.

Meyer's book resembles the plaintiff's article because both are based on the premise of Sherlock Holmes seeing Freud

---

[35] 434 F. Supp. 32 (1977).

DEALMAKING
IN THE
FILM AND
TELEVISION
INDUSTRY—
3RD EDITION

326

for cocaine addiction. Sherlock Holmes is a fictional character, a creation of Sir Arthur Conan Doyle, whose copyright in the work has long since expired. Therefore, Sherlock Holmes is in the public domain and is available to everybody. Freud was a real person, so clearly this meeting between Holmes and Freud never took place but is a product of the plaintiff's imagination. Articles, whether fiction or non-fiction, are copyrightable.

Nicholas Meyer prevailed because the court found that he only borrowed an idea, and it's permissible to borrow ideas. The facts of this case are not much different from the Sheldon case. But in Sheldon the court found infringement because the borrower took "certain details and sequence of events," while what Meyer took was characterized merely as an idea. Because it's not always easy to know when one has borrowed more than an idea, attorneys are often conservative when counseling their clients.

Warner Bros. v. ABC (1983)[36]

FACTS: Plaintiff, Warner Bros., owns the copyright in various works embodying the character Superman and have exploited its rights in various media, including *Superman, The Movie* and two sequels. In these works, Superman is a brave, fearless hero, endowed with superhuman powers. The commercial success of the Superman movie led defendant ABC to seek a license for a production called *Superboy*, based on the early adventures of Superman. Warner Bros., which was planning to make their own sequels and derivative works, refused ABC permission to proceed with the proposed project.

ABC then asked Stephen J. Cannell to create a pilot program for a TV series involving a super hero. The program, *The Greatest American Hero*, was described as what happens when an average person becomes Superman. Its protagonist, Ralph Hinkley, was an ordinary guy. He was a young high-school teacher attempting to cope with a recent divorce, a dispute over custody of his son, and his relationship with his girlfriend.

While attractive, Hinkley was not physically imposing. He derived his superhuman powers from a magical caped costume—a red leotard with a tunic top, no boots, and a black cape—which was a gift from an intergalactic visitor.

---

[36] 720 F.2d 231 (1983).

However, he lost the instruction book and uses his powers awkwardly and fearfully, often making crash landings.

The *Hero* series contained several visual effects and lines that inevitably called Superman to mind, sometimes by mention of Superman or another character from Superman works, and by humorous parodying or ironic twisting of well-known Superman phrases. For example, when Hinkley first viewed himself in a mirror, he says, "It's a bird . . . It's a plane . . . It's Ralph Hinkley."

ISSUE: Did ABC infringe the copyright of Warner Bros.' character Superman?

HOLDING: No.

RATIONALE: The total perception of the Hinkley character is not substantially similar to that of Superman. Superman is portrayed as a brave, proud hero. Hinkley is a timid, reluctant hero who accepts his mission grudgingly and exercises his powers in a bumbling, comical fashion. In the genre of super heroes, Hinkley follows Superman as Inspector Clouseau follows Sherlock Holmes.

As for Superman phrases and references in the series, this is not an infringement. The lines are used to highlight the differences with Superman, often to laughable effect. The defendant is poking fun at, rather than copying, a copyrighted work.

While Warner Bros. has a copyright to the Superman character, they don't have a copyright on the idea of a superhuman hero and cannot prevent others from inventing their own super-human characters.

Characters may be copyrightable, especially those with pictorial or visual elements such as comic book characters. With literary characters that are not represented visually, protection may depend on how finely drawn the character is. One could not, for example, gain any rights over a character defined simply as "a hard-boiled private eye." Other authors would be free to borrow these personality traits. Note that names of characters might be protectable under unfair competition and trademark laws.

DEALMAKING
IN THE
FILM AND
TELEVISION
INDUSTRY—
3RD EDITION

328

Estate of Martin Luther King, Jr., Inc. v. CBS, Inc.[37]

FACTS: Dr. Martin Luther King (P) delivered his "I Have a Dream" speech before thousands during a civil rights march in Washington, D.C. The speech was widely reported by the news media, and they received an advance copy of the text. In 1994, Defendant CBS (D) produced a historical documentary called *The 20th Century with Mike Wallace*, which included approximately 60% of Dr. King's speech without P's permission. P sued for copyright infringement while D argued that the delivery of the speech was a general publication which divested it of common-law copyright.

ISSUE: Does the general publication of a speech occur when it is orally delivered to a vast audience or its text is distributed to the press?

HOLDING: Yes.

RATIONALE: While, oral delivery does not constitute a dedication of the speech to the public, Dr. King's speech was made widely available to members of the public at large without regard to who they were or what they proposed to do with it, thus constituting a general publication and thrusting it into the public domain.

At common law there was a property right in unpublished works (the "common-law copyright"). After publication, the common law copyright did not exist, and a work would only be protected if it met the criteria for statutory copyright (federal copyright).

Ordinarily, the public performance of a work is not considered a publication. Note that the copyright law has been changed since this case was decided. First, copyright law was amended to provide ways to cure the effects of a general publication without proper notice, so the act of publication has lost some of its importance. Later, notice became optional.

Gross v. Seligman (1914)[38]

FACTS: Rochlitz, an artist, posed a model in the nude and produced a photograph that he named Race of Youth. He sold his copyrighted photo to Gross (P). Two years later, Rochlitz placed the same model in an identical pose, but the woman wore a smile and held a cherry stem between her teeth. This photograph, called Cherry Ripe, was pub-

---

[37] 13 F.Supp.2d 1347 (N.D. Ga. 1998).
[38] 212 F. 930 (2nd Cir. 1914).

lished by Seligman (D). P contends that the new photo infringes his copyright of the first photo.

ISSUE: When an artist sells all rights in a work to another and then produces a similar work that is only marginally different, is the subsequent work an infringement?

HOLDING: Yes.

RATIONALE: If an author grants all his rights to another and then attempts to reproduce the identical work with minor differences, the latter work is an infringement of the owner's copyright. This is not true if the subsequent work, although substantially similar, was independently created without reference to the prior work.

The test of infringement is twofold. Copying exists where the infringer has had access to the original work and where the subsequent work is substantially similar to the first. The access does not have to be deliberate or in bad faith, and access may be inferred from circumstantial evidence.

COPYRIGHT REQUIREMENTS

1) An original work
2) An expression of an author
3) Non-utilitarian nature
4) Fixed in a tangible medium of expression

COPYRIGHT NOTICE

1) Either the word "copyright," abbreviation, or the symbol ©
2) Name of the copyright owner
3) Date of first publication
Optional: the phrase "All Rights Reserved" may provide additional protection in foreign jurisdictions.

WHAT RIGHTS DOES THE COPYRIGHT HOLDER HAVE?

1) Right to reproduce (copy)
2) Right to prepare derivative work (e.g., screenplays)
3) Right to distribute copies to the public by sale, rental, or lease
4) Right to perform works publicly
5) Right to display works publicly

DEALMAKING
IN THE
FILM AND
TELEVISION
INDUSTRY—
3RD EDITION

330

ARTIST'S MORAL RIGHTS

Certain foreign countries recognize what is known as moral rights (droit moral), which are personal to authors. They are separate and apart from the author's copyright.

These rights include:

1) The right to be known as the author of a work;
2) The right to prevent others from falsely attributing to the writer authorship of work he/she has not written;
3) The right to prevent others from making deforming changes to the work;
4) The right to withdraw a published work from distribution if it no longer represents the views of the author;
5) The right to prevent others from using the work or the author's name in such a way as to reflect adversely on one's professional standing.

United States copyright law has not expressly incorporated moral rights, and several federal and state decisions have noted that moral rights are not recognized in the United States. However, the Visual Artists Rights Act of 1990 conferred limited moral rights on artists who create certain works of fine art. In addition, American law accords protection to some moral rights under other legal doctrines such as unfair competition, defamation, invasion of privacy, and breach of contract.

The Berne Convention, to which the United States is now a signatory, expressly recognizes moral rights. However, the treaty is not self-executing, which means that the terms of the convention are not binding without implementing American legislation. The American implementation act, however, prohibits the use of Berne as the basis for recognizing more moral rights while reaffirming the protection given under existing American law.

Gilliam v. ABC (1976)[39]

FACTS: "Monty Python" (the plaintiffs) retained the copyright in its scripts that the BBC produced as television programs. While the BBC retained final authority to make revisions, plaintiffs exercised primary control over the scripts, and only minor changes were permitted without consultation. Nothing in the agreement allowed the BBC

---

[39] 538 F.2d 14 (2nd Cir., 1976).

to alter the scripts once they were recorded. The BBC owned the copyright to the recorded programs.

The BBC sold the U.S. distribution rights to Time-Life Films and gave Time-Life the right to edit the programs and add commercials. ABC obtained from Time-Life the right to broadcast two 90-minute specials, each comprised of three 30-minute programs. After editing for commercials, the original 90 minutes were reduced by 24 minutes. ABC deleted some material on the grounds that it was obscene or offensive.

Plaintiffs claimed that showing a truncated and distorted version of their work was an impairment of the integrity of their copyright and caused the program to lose its iconoclastic verve. Plaintiffs sought an injunction to prevent any further showing.

ISSUE: Should the court grant the injunction?

HOLDING: Yes.

RATIONALE: The authors retained the copyright to their work. The license given the BBC does not give it the right to broadcast a truncated version. The BBC can give ABC no greater rights than the BBC possesses.

Moreover, broadcasting the deformed version as the work of the plaintiffs misrepresents the work's origins, an instance of unfair competition.

While the United States does not expressly recognize the doctrine of moral rights (except for fine art), legal remedies can often be found under other legal doctrines such as unfair competition.

In this case, ABC was representing to the public that their program was the work of the plaintiffs but in a form that substantially departs from the original work. The Lanham Act was invoked to prevent misrepresentation that may injure one's business or personal reputation by creation of a false impression of the product's origin. Thus there is a statutory basis for the type of protection other countries recognize under the principle of author's moral rights.

DEALMAKING
IN THE
FILM AND
TELEVISION
INDUSTRY—
3RD EDITION

332

WRITERS GUILD REGISTRATION

Registering a work with the Writers Guild does not have the same effect as registering your work with the Copyright Office. Guild registration, however, is simpler than Copyright Registration and confers an important benefit.

Guild registration creates evidence that can be used in the event of a plagiarism dispute. The outcome of such a lawsuit may turn on which party can persuade the jury that he/she created the story first. The first writer will be presumed to be the originator, while the second will be presumed to be a copier.[40]

How do you prove that you came up with the story first? You could bring a friend into court to testify as a witness that she read an early version of the manuscript. Or you could mail a copy of the manuscript to yourself, registered mail, in a post-marked and sealed envelope. But friends are not impartial witnesses, and envelopes can be steamed open and their contents changed. The best evidence is a signed declaration by a neutral third-party custodian who swears that he/she received your manuscript on a certain date and has kept it in seclusion ever since. This is what registration with the Writers Guild accomplishes.

As soon as you write your story, register it with the Copyright Office or with the Writers Guild. You need not be a member to register a script with either their East or West Coast office. Copyright registration also confers evidence that you created a work at a certain time. Thus, if you register your work with the Copyright Office, there is little need to register it with the Writers Guild. Moreover, copyright registration confers some additional benefits, such as entitling the author to reimbursement of attorney's fees and making statutory damages available.

---

[40] If the second writer can prove that he independently created the same story, without copying the first writer, he will be entitled to the copyright to the second story just as the first writer will have the copyright to the first story. Thus, both writers will own the copyright to their work, notwithstanding their similarities. Of course, if the two sources are very similar, it is highly unlikely that one writer didn't copy from the other.

1. If I write a screenplay, do I need to register each draft with the copyright office?

Answer: There is only one copyright for each work. You can make a supplemental filing to your original filing to protect any additions to the draft already registered. If subsequent drafts do not differ materially from earlier drafts, you may not want to bother with a supplemental filing. You might choose not to register early drafts if you plan extensive revisions and you're not going to show the work to anyone. In such a case there is little danger of copyright infringement.

2. During a bus ride I overheard two people engaged in an interesting conversation. Can I incorporate snatches of their talk in my screenplay?

Answer: Yes. Typically, speakers don't have any rights in ordinary conversation because the conversation has not been put in tangible form. Assuming you don't identify the person and violate any right of privacy or defame them, and assuming you are not party to an agreement not to quote them, you should be free to incorporate their conversation in your screenplay.

However, if you subsequently discover that the speakers were not engaged in an ordinary conversation but were actors rehearsing a play, you would not be privileged to borrow any of the conversation (assuming the play was copyrighted material).

CHAPTER 13

THE FIRST AMENDMENT AND THE RIGHT OF PUBLICITY

The Right of Publicity is the right that individuals have to control the use of their name and likeness[1] in a commercial setting. You cannot put a picture of another person on your spaghetti sauce without their permission. The right of publicity is typically exploited by celebrities, who earn large fees from endorsing products.

The Right of Publicity is similar to the appropriation form of invasion of privacy. The principal difference is that the right of publicity seeks to ensure that a person is compensated for the commercial value of his/her name or likeness while the right of privacy seeks to remedy any hurt feelings or embarrassment that a person may suffer from such publicity.

Celebrities might have difficulty proving invasion of privacy because frequently they do not make a habit of seeking solitude and privacy. How can James Garner claim that the unauthorized use of his likeness on a product embarrassed and humiliated him at the same time that he appears in commercials encouraging

---

[1] Voice and signature are also protected.

DEALMAKING
IN THE
FILM AND
TELEVISION
INDUSTRY—
3RD EDITION

336

consumers to eat beef or drive Mazda cars or use Polaroid film? By thrusting themselves into the public eye, celebrities waive much of their right of privacy. On the other hand, celebrities have an especially valuable property right in their name and likeness, for which they are often paid handsomely.

Under either a publicity or privacy theory, subjects can recover for some unconsented uses of their names and likenesses. A problem arises, however, when one person's publicity/privacy rights come in conflict with another person's rights under the First Amendment. Suppose a newspaper publisher wants to place a picture of Cher on the front page of its paper. Is her permission required? What if *60 Minutes* wants to broadcast an exposé of a corrupt politician? What if Kitty Kelly wants to write a critical biography of Frank Sinatra?

In each of these instances, a person's name and likeness is being used on a "product" that is sold to consumers. Products such as books, movies, and plays, however, are also forms of expression protected by the First Amendment. The First Amendment allows journalists and writers to freely write about others without their consent. Otherwise, subjects could prevent any critical reporting of their activities. When one person's right of publicity conflicts with another person's rights under the First Amendment, the rights under the First Amendment are often paramount.

When a person's name or likeness is used on a coffee cup or T-shirt or poster, however, there is no expression deserving protection. The seller of these products is not making a statement or expressing an opinion. He/she is simply trying to make money by exploiting the name and likeness of another. Since there are no competing First Amendment concerns, the right of publicity will prevent the unauthorized use of a subject's name or likeness. Thus the law draws a distinction between products that contain protected expression and those that don't.

Courts have struggled with the issue of whether the right of publicity descends to a person's heirs. In other words, when a celebrity dies, does his/her estate inherit his/her right of publicity? Can the estate continue to control the use of the celebrity's name or likeness, or can anyone use it without permission?

Some courts have held that the right of publicity is a personal right that does not descend. These courts consider the right similar to the right of privacy and the right to protect one's reputation (defamation). When a person dies, heirs don't inherit these rights. Suppose you were a descendent of George Washington. An unscrupulous writer publishes a defamatory biography claiming that George was a kleptomaniac and reveals the contents of his diary. You couldn't sue for defamation or invasion of privacy. Perhaps this is why many scandalous biographies are not published until the subject dies.

In California, the courts have held that the right of publicity is personal and doesn't descend.[2] In 1984, however, the California legislature changed the law. California Civil Code Section 3344.1 provides that the right of publicity descends for products, merchandise, and goods, but does not descend for books, plays, television, and movies. Protection extends for 70 years after death. California Civil Code Section 3344 prohibits the unauthorized use of the name and likeness of living persons on products. News and public affairs uses are excepted. Both statutes attempt to balance First Amendment rights against rights of publicity and privacy.

In other states, the right to publicity may descend. The rights of the heirs, however, may be outweighed by other people's First Amendment rights when protected expression is at stake.

CASES

Hicks v. Casablanca Records (1978)[3]

FACTS: Casablanca Records begins to film a movie called *Agatha* about the well-known mystery writer Agatha Christie. The story is a fictionalized account of an 11-day disappearance of Christie in 1926. The film portrays Christie as an emotionally unstable woman who is engaged in a sinister plot to murder her husband's mistress. An heir to Christie's estate brings suit to enjoin Casablanca from distributing the movie, alleging infringement of Agatha Christie's right of publicity.

ISSUE: Can Casablanca use Agatha Christie's name and likeness without the estate's permission?

HOLDING: Yes. Although the right of publicity descends, Casablanca's rights under the First Amendment are paramount to the estate's rights.

---

[2] See *Lugosi v. Universal Pictures*, 25 Cal. 3d at 819 (1979).
[3] 464 F. Supp 426 (S.D.N.Y. 1978)

DEALMAKING
IN THE
FILM AND
TELEVISION
INDUSTRY—
3RD EDITION

338

RATIONALE: The First Amendment outweighs the right of publicity because the subject was a public figure, and the events portrayed were obviously fictitious.

Here is a movie based on a real-life individual set in a fictional plot. In other words, Agatha Christie was a famous mystery writer, but the story presented in this movie is fictional.

Note that Christie's estate couldn't win a defamation action although the movie portrayed Christie as a criminal. A defamation action isn't possible because the right to protect one's reputation is a personal right that doesn't descend to the estate.

While the right of publicity in this jurisdiction descended, the Christie estate lost. The court felt Casablanca's First Amendment rights outweighed the estate's right to control the name and likeness of Christie.

Zacchini v. Scripps-Howard Broadcasting Co.[4]

FACTS: Zacchini, the "human cannonball," is shot from a cannon into a net 200 feet away at a county fair. A news reporter videotapes the entire 15-second act without Zacchini's consent. The film clip is shown on the eleven o'clock news program that night. Zacchini brings an action for damages, alleging that the reporter unlawfully infringed upon his right of publicity. The reporter claims that the news broadcast is protected under the First Amendment.

ISSUE: Does the news reporter have the right to broadcast Zacchini's act without his consent?

HOLDING: No. Zacchini prevails.

RATIONALE: The First Amendment does not immunize the press from infringing on the right of publicity. By broadcasting the whole segment, the press threatened the economic value of Zacchini's performance.

Here Zacchini's right of publicity is considered more important than the First Amendment rights of the news reporter. So the First Amendment is not always the paramount right.

The court cited three factors in support of its position:

1) the news reporter knew that Zacchini objected to having his entire act televised,

---

[4] 433 U.S. 562, 97 S. Ct. 2849 (1977)

2) the entire act was broadcast,[5] and

3) Zacchini did not seek to enjoin the press; he just wanted to be paid for his performance.[6]

THE FIRST
AMENDMENT
AND THE
RIGHT OF
PUBLICITY

339

Motschenbacher v. R.J. Reynolds Tobacco Co.[7]

FACTS: Motschenbacher (P), an internationally known racing-car driver, is paid by manufacturers of commercial products for his endorsement. Since 1966 his cars have been painted red with distinctive narrow-white pinstriping and the number 11 on an oval white background.

In 1970 Reynolds Tobacco (D) produced and televised a cigarette commercial. It depicted several cars on a race-track, one of which appeared to belong to P. The car's number had been changed to 71 and a spoiler device attached to the car. The car had the same white pinstriping, oval medallion, and red color as P's car. Several persons who saw the commercial immediately recognized P's car and believed that Winston was sponsoring the car.

ISSUE: Is P's interest in his identity afforded legal protection?

HOLDING: Yes. These markings were peculiar to P's cars and they caused some person to think the car in question was his and to infer that the person driving the car was P.

In another case, Bette Midler successfully sued the Ford Motor Co. and its ad agency.[8] They had hired a singer to imitate Midler's distinctive voice. The Midler case is discussed on pages 34-35.

Questions and Answers

1. If I shoot a documentary film and interview a subject without obtaining a written release, can I be held liable?

Answer: The First Amendment would likely protect this use within a documentary. Moreover, a subject who sits still for an interview may have implicitly consented to the use of his/her

---

[5] If the news reporter had stood outside the performance arena and merely informed viewers of the nature of Zacchini's act, the result would be different. Likewise, if only a portion of Zacchini's act were broadcast, the holding might differ.

[6] Courts are reluctant to issue injunctions when they prevent people from expressing themselves. They often prefer to allow the defendant to express himself/herself, and compensate the plaintiff with monetary damages for any wrong.

[7] 498 F.2d 821 (9th Cir., 1974)

[8] *Bette Midler v. Ford Motor Company*, 849 F.2d 460 (1988).

DEALMAKING
IN THE
FILM AND
TELEVISION
INDUSTRY—
3RD EDITION

340

name and likeness. However, it never hurts to obtain a signed release. You should make it a practice to secure one whenever possible. And you definitely should secure a release if you plan to use the footage for some other purpose, such as in a commercial or advertisement.

2. How does the right of publicity differ from a copyright?

Answer: You can copyright a work of authorship, such as a book, play, or other literary or artistic work. You cannot copyright your personality, name, or likeness per se. Simply put, copyright law protects things that people make, while the Right of Publicity protects the commercial value of one's persona. Copyright is a form of property, and often referred to as "intellectual property." Like other property, it can be assigned or inherited by another (until such time as the copyright expires and the material goes into the public domain).

CHAPTER 14

DEFAMATION OF PERSONS DEPICTED IN LITERARY WORKS

Defamation is a communication that harms the reputation of another so as to lower that individual in the opinion of the community or to deter third persons from associating or dealing with him/her. For example, those communications that expose another to hatred, ridicule, or contempt, or reflect unfavorably upon their personal morality or integrity, are defamatory. One who is defamed may suffer embarrassment and humiliation, as well as economic losses such as loss of a job or the ability to earn a living.

CONSTITUTIONAL LIMITATIONS

The law of defamation can be very confusing. That is because the common law[1] rules that have developed over the centuries are subject to constitutional limitations. To determine the terms of the law, one must read a state's defamation laws in light of various constitutional principles. For example, recent U.S.

---

[1] The common law is the law of precedent that arises from cases decided by courts. Another type of law is statutory, or law that has been enacted by a legislative body, like Congress.

DEALMAKING
IN THE
FILM AND
TELEVISION
INDUSTRY—
3RD EDITION

342

Supreme Court decisions have imposed significant limitations on the ability of public officials and public figures to win defamation actions. If a state's law is inconsistent with a constitutional principle, the law is invalid.

TYPES OF DEFAMATION

There are two types of defamation. Libel is defamation by written or printed words, or defamation embodied in some physical form. Slander is spoken defamation.

There are historical reasons for the distinction. Libel has been considered the more damaging form of defamation. Printed defamation generally has greater permanency and reaches more people than oral defamation. At least that was the rationale several hundred years ago, in the days before microphones, amplifiers, and broadcasting. Today, however, an oral remark can be heard by millions. Surely a slanderous remark uttered on a popular national talk-show would reach far more people than a libelous one printed in an obscure journal.

To take account of the damage that can be done by slanderous broadcasts, California treats all broadcasts as libel.[2] Why is the difference between libel and slander important? The criteria for liability are different. Plaintiffs have to prove more to win a slander action. They must prove special damages. Special damages are specific identifiable economic losses, such as lost wages. General harm to one's reputation is not enough.

There is, however, a form of slander that is actionable without special damages. This is called slander per se, and it occurs when the defamatory remark carries an imputation in one of the following areas:

1) a criminal offense,
2) a loathsome disease,
3) a matter incompatible with the proper exercise of the plaintiff's business, trade, profession, or office, or
4) sexual misconduct.

---

[2] Cal. Civ. Code § 46.

PUBLICATION

DEFAMATION
OF PERSONS
DEPICTED
IN LITERARY
WORKS

343

In order for a plaintiff to prevail in a defamation action, she must prove that the matter was "published." Publication is a legal term of art. A statement is published when it has been communicated to at least one person other than the plaintiff. The statement need not be in writing or printed.

For example, suppose I was in a room with you alone, and I said, "You dirty low-down rotten bicycle thief." I could not defame you unless there was someone else in the room. That is because, unless a third party heard the remark, there was no publication.

The reason for this limitation makes sense when you understand that the gist of a defamation action is harm to one's reputation. People do not possess their own reputations. Your reputation is held by the community, and if the community is not exposed to a defamatory remark, your reputation can't possibly suffer.

DEFENSES AND PRIVILEGES

There are a number of defenses and privileges to defamation. In other words, sometimes a person can publish a defamatory remark with impunity. Why? Because protecting people's reputations is not the only value we cherish in a democratic society. When the right to protect one's reputation conflicts with a more important right, the defamed person may not recover for harm to his/her reputation.

The most important privilege, from a filmmaker's point of view, is truth. If your remarks hurt someone's reputation, but your statement is true, you are absolutely privileged. An absolute privilege cannot be lost through bad faith or abuse. So even if you maliciously defame another person, you will be privileged if the statement is true.[3] Truth is an absolute privilege because society values truth more than it values protection of people's reputations.

Keep in mind that while truth is an absolute defense, the burden of proving truth will sometimes fall on the defendant. So if you make a defamatory statement, you should be prepared to prove its truth. And that may not be easy to do.

---

[3] Truth is not a privilege, however, against invasion of privacy.

DEALMAKING
IN THE
FILM AND
TELEVISION
INDUSTRY—
3RD EDITION

344

Another absolute privilege covers communications that occur during judicial, legislative, and executive proceedings. Statements made in a court of law are absolutely privileged.[4] Why? Again, as a matter of public policy, the courts have found that it is more important that witnesses speak freely and candidly without fear of being sued than that we protect the reputation of others. Similarly, statements made in a Congressional hearing or in executive proceedings will be privileged.

Conversations between husbands and wives are also privileged. In other words, all pillow talk is protected. If you come home from a hard day at work and make disparaging remarks about your boss to your spouse, you cannot be sued for defamation. This policy encourages candid conversations between spouses. But the privilege does not extend beyond the marriage. So if your spouse the next day communicates the disparaging remark to a friend, that statement would not be privileged.

There is also a conditional common-law privilege of fair comment and criticism. This privilege applies to communications about a newsworthy person or event. Conditional privileges may be lost through bad faith or abuse. This privilege has been largely superseded, however, by a constitutional privilege for statements about public officials or public figures.

HOW DOES THE LAW OF DEFAMATION AFFECT WRITERS, DIRECTORS, AND PRODUCERS?

HERE ARE SOME GUIDELINES TO AVOID LIABILITY:

1) BE ESPECIALLY CAREFUL ABOUT PORTRAYING LIVING INDIVIDUALS WHO ARE NOT PUBLIC OFFICIALS OR FIGURES.

2) MAKE SURE YOU CAN PROVE THAT ANY DEFAMATORY STATEMENTS ARE TRUE. ANNOTATE YOUR SCRIPT WITH THE SOURCES OF YOUR INFORMATION SO THAT YOU CAN DOCUMENT ITS TRUTH AND SHOW THAT YOU ACTED WITHOUT "ACTUAL MALICE."

3) OBTAIN RELEASES WHENEVER POSSIBLE. IT NEVER HURTS TO HAVE A RELEASE, EVEN IF IT IS NOT LEGALLY REQUIRED.

4) HAVE YOUR ATTORNEY CLOSELY REVIEW YOUR SCRIPT FOR POTENTIAL LIABILITY BEFORE PRODUCTION. IF YOU CAN CHANGE THE NAMES OF SUBJECTS AND THE SETTING WITHOUT DETRACTING FROM THE DRAMATIC VALUE OF THE STORY, DO SO.

5) MAKE SURE THE PRODUCTION OBTAINS ERRORS & OMISSIONS (E&O) INSURANCE POLICY INCLUDING YOU AS A NAMED INSURED.

[4] Provided the remarks are relevant to the proceedings.

PUBLIC FIGURES AND PUBLIC OFFICIALS

Public figures,[5] such as celebrities or public officials (a Senator), have a much higher burden to bear to prevail in a defamation action. They must prove that the defendant acted with "actual malice." Actual malice is a legal term that means that the defendant intentionally defamed another or acted with reckless disregard of the truth.

Plaintiffs find it difficult to prove that a defendant acted with actual malice. That is why so few celebrities bother suing the *National Enquirer*. To successfully defend itself, the *Enquirer* need only show that it did not act with malice. In other words, the newspaper can come into court and concede that its report was false, defamatory, and the result of sloppy and careless research. But unless the celebrity can prove that the *Enquirer* acted with actual malice, the court is obliged to dismiss the case. Mere negligence is not enough for liability.

There is also a constitutional privilege for the mass media. The Supreme Court has said that liability without fault can never be imposed upon the mass media. Even private individuals need to show that the mass media was at least negligent to recover in a defamation action. The court reasoned that the mass media must be allowed a certain amount of breathing room to exercise its First Amendment rights. If *The New York Times* were strictly liable for any mistakes it made, the paper would be inhibited from the robust debate essential to a vital democracy.

---

[5] There are two types of public figures: 1) persons of pervasive fame or notoriety, such as a celebrity sports figure; and 2) persons who voluntarily inject themselves into a particular public controversy and become public figures for that limited range of issues.

DEALMAKING
IN THE
FILM AND
TELEVISION
INDUSTRY—
3RD EDITION

CASES

Youssoupoff v. MGM (1934)[7]

FACTS: MGM produced a movie in which a character named Princess Natasha resembled real-life Russian Princess Irina Youssoupoff. In the movie, the princess is ravaged or seduced by Rasputin, a despicable character. Rasputin is murdered by several men, including the prince whom the princess intended to marry.

Princess Irina brought suit for libel, claiming that the public had come to identify her as a female of questionable repute because of the movie. Before the release of the movie, Irina's husband had published a book discussing his participation in the murder of Rasputin. As a result, viewers were likely to perceive that the prince character in the film, Prince Chegodieff, was Prince Youssoupoff and, consequently, that Natasha was Irina.

MGM described the film as factual, although it was a fictionalized account, and the studio said that some principal characters were alive. The jury concluded that reasonable people would perceive the Princess Natasha character to be Princess Irina.

ISSUE: Can one be defamed unintentionally and without being named?

HOLDING: Yes.

RATIONALE: You don't need to name the defamed person if

DEFAMATION

DEFINITION: A COMMUNICATION THAT HARMS THE REPUTATION OF ANOTHER AS TO LOWER THAT PERSON IN THE ESTIMATION OF THE COMMUNITY OR TO DETER THIRD PERSONS FROM ASSOCIATING OR DEALING WITH HIM/HER.

Types Of Defamation

LIBEL: PUBLICATION BY WRITTEN OR PRINTED WORDS.

SLANDER: SPOKEN WORDS, TRANSITORY GESTURES.

Slander Per Se

NO RECOVERY ALLOWED IN A SLANDER ACTION ABSENT SHOWING OF SPECIAL DAMAGES UNLESS THE SLANDER CARRIES AN IMPUTATION IN ONE OF THE FOLLOWING AREAS:

1) CRIMINAL OFFENSE
2) A LOATHSOME DISEASE
3) A MATTER INCOMPATIBLE WITH THE PROPER EXERCISE OF THE PLAINTIFF'S BUSINESS, TRADE, PROFESSION, OR OFFICE.
4) SEXUAL MISCONDUCT

DEFENSES & PRIVILEGES[6]

1) TRUTH
2) JUDICIAL, LEGISLATIVE, AND EXECUTIVE PROCEEDINGS
3) CONVERSATIONS BETWEEN HUSBANDS AND WIVES.
4) CONDITIONAL COMMON-LAW PRIVILEGE OF FAIR COMMENT AND CRITICISM.
5) CONSTITUTIONAL PRIVILEGE: PUBLIC OFFICIALS AND PUBLIC FIGURES MUST PROVE ACTUAL MALICE.

---

[6] This list is not exclusive. There are other privileges.

---

[7] Eng. C.A., 50 Times L.R. S81, 99 A.L.R. 864 (1934).

reasonable people could identify the person from the facts and circumstances.

DEFAMATION
OF PERSONS
DEPICTED
IN LITERARY
WORKS

347

Princess Irina contended that, although she wasn't mentioned by name in the movie, she was defamed. She asserted that viewers thought she was portrayed by the Princess Natasha character and that she had slept with Rasputin. The inference was possible because her husband had published a book recounting his role in Rasputin's death.

The court found that although the MGM movie never mentioned Princess Irina by name, viewers would reasonably conclude that the movie was about incidents in her life. This deduction was likely since MGM billed the movie as a true story and said some people involved were still alive.

Thus, a filmmaker cannot insulate himself/herself from defamation merely by changing the names of people depicted in a movie. If the person depicted is identifiable from the circumstances, liability may result. Similarly, a disclaimer in the credits such as "Any resemblance to people, living or dead is purely coincidental . . ." will not protect the filmmaker if viewers nevertheless believe the movie is depicting a real person.

Suppose a writer published a novel about the widow of an American president who was assassinated in office during a visit to Dallas, and the widow later marries a Greek shipping tycoon. The book is clearly labeled a novel, and there is a prominent disclaimer on the first page saying that everything in it is fiction. Nevertheless, readers believe the book reveals true incidents in the life of Jackie Kennedy and dismiss the disclaimer as a device to protect the author from a lawsuit. Under such circumstances, the disclaimer will not be sufficient to shield the author from a defamation action.[8]

Filmmakers can protect themselves from liability by:

1) changing the names and circumstances so that the people depicted are not identifiable,
2) obtaining a depiction release from those persons portrayed, or
3) excising any potentially defamatory material.

---

[8] However, the defendant has another defense because reputation is a personal right that does not descend to heirs, and Jackie Kennedy is now deceased.

DEALMAKING
IN THE
FILM AND
TELEVISION
INDUSTRY—
3RD EDITION

348

Of course, a filmmaker could defend a defamation action by raising one or more defenses or privileges, such as truth. But the burden may be on the filmmaker to prove the truth of his/her statements.

CASES

New York Times Co. v. Sullivan (1964)[9]

FACTS: Sullivan was one of three elected commissioners of the city of Montgomery, Alabama. His duties included supervision of the police department.

In 1960, a group of black clergymen took out a full-page ad in *The New York Times* discussing the plight of black students involved in the civil-rights movement. The ad claimed that the students were terrorized by the Montgomery police. It described various abuses, some of which never occurred.

Sullivan felt that Montgomery residents would believe these statements reflected poorly on himself as Commissioner of the police department. He sued for libel.

ISSUE: Are the clergymen who took out the ad liable for defamation? Is *The New York Times* liable for defamation?

HOLDING: Judgment for *The Times*.

RATIONALE: You can't defame a public official for statements about his official conduct unless the statements were made with actual malice (i.e., knowledge of falsity or reckless disregard of the truth). Here *The Times* was at most negligent in failing to discover the misstatements. Also, the evidence was insufficient to establish that the statements were made "of and concerning" Sullivan.

This is the landmark decision that established the actual malice standard required of public officials in defamation suits. Subsequent cases have extended the New York Times Co. v. Sullivan rule to public figures.

The court also ruled against Sullivan because the defamatory statements were not "of and concerning" Sullivan. In other words, Sullivan himself was not defamed, only the police officers he supervised. This was not considered direct enough to be

---

[9] 376 U.S. 254 (1964).

actionable. Similarly, if someone said, "The New York Yankees stink," a die-hard New Yorker could not sue because such a statement reflected poorly on him.

Gertz v. Robert Welch, Inc. (1974)[10]

FACTS: In 1968, a Chicago policeman shot and killed a youth. The policeman was later convicted of murder in the second degree. The family of the slain boy retained attorney Gertz (P) to represent them in a civil action against the policeman.

A John Birch Society publication published by Welch (D) portrayed Gertz as having framed the policeman and said Gertz was a Communist. Because these statements constituted libel per se under Illinois law, Gertz received a jury award of $50,000. The District Court, however, overturned the jury verdict and entered judgment for D because P should have been required to meet the N.Y. Times Co. v. Sullivan standard that requires a showing of actual malice.

ISSUE: Does the New York Times Co. standard apply?

HOLDING: No. A newspaper or broadcaster that publishes defamatory falsehoods about an individual, who is neither a public official nor public figure, may not claim a constitutional privilege against liability for the injury inflicted by those statements.

RATIONALE: Public figures, by virtue of their public status, have more of an opportunity to counteract false statements.

This case is instructive for three reasons. First, it establishes that an attorney involved in a prominent case is not necessarily a public figure. The status of an individual can often be difficult to determine. Another Supreme Court case[11] held that a socially prominent person involved in a celebrated divorce trial was not a public figure.

Second, the Gertz case says that a plaintiff must show actual malice to recover more than actual damages. Thus, if liability is predicated on negligence, a plaintiff ordinarily cannot recover presumed or punitive damages.[12]

---

[10] 418 U.S. 323, 94 S. Ct. 2997 (1974).
[11] *Time, Inc. v. Firestone*, 424 U.S. 448, 96 S. Ct. 958 (1976).
[12] An exception occurs when no public issues are involved. See *Dun & Bradstreet, Inc. v. Greenmoss Builders, Inc.*, 472 U.S. 749, 105 S. Ct. 2939 (1985).

DEALMAKING
IN THE
FILM AND
TELEVISION
INDUSTRY—
3RD EDITION

350

Third, the Gertz court held that the mass media can never be held strictly liable for defamation. If a newspaper could be held strictly liable for any misstatement, the paper's exercise of its First Amendment Right of free expression would be greatly inhibited.

Street v. NBC (1981)[13]

FACTS: In 1931, nine black youths were accused of raping two young white women while riding a freight train. The youths were promptly tried in Scottsboro, Alabama, found guilty, and sentenced to death. The case was the subject of widespread media coverage.

In reversing the convictions, the United States Supreme Court said that the defendants were denied the right to counsel. The defendants were retried separately after a change in venue. In a trial before Judge Horton, the jury found defendant Patterson guilty and sentenced him to death. Judge Horton then set the verdict aside. Upon retrial Patterson and several other defendants were convicted and sent to prison.

The case against the Scottsboro defendants was based on the testimony of Victoria Price. She gave some press interviews at the time but then disappeared from sight.

Forty years after the case, NBC televised a historical drama entitled *Judge Horton and the Scottsboro Boys*. The movie was based on a book by a historian who portrayed Price in a derogatory light. She was shown to be a perjurer, a woman of bad character, and a person who falsely accused the Scottsboro boys of rape knowing that the verdict would likely condemn them to the electric chair. Witnesses who corroborated Price's version of the facts were omitted from the movie. Portions of the trial that showed her to be a perjurer and a promiscuous woman were emphasized. NBC incorrectly stated in the movie that she was no longer living. After the first showing, Price informed NBC that she was living and sued. NBC rebroadcast the dramatization omitting the statement that she was no longer living.

ISSUE: Is Price a public figure?

HOLDING: Yes.

RATIONALE: Price remains a public figure notwithstanding the passage of time.

---

[13] 645 F.2d 1227 (6th Cir. 1981).

The defendant NBC prevailed because *The New York Times* standard applies, and the plaintiff could not prove that NBC acted with actual malice. There is no evidence that NBC had knowledge that its portrayal of Price was false or that NBC recklessly disregarded the truth. The author of the history and the producer of the movie may have had their facts wrong, but the law will not punish them unless they acted with actual malice.

Questions and Answers

1. If a person is writing a screenplay about a historical event, does the filmmaker need a release from every living person in order to use his or her name in a story?

Answer: Not necessarily. Unauthorized biographies and films are produced and protected under the First Amendment guarantee of free speech. If the subject is a public figure or public official, you won't be liable for defamation unless you recklessly publish defamatory matter. You will also need to make sure not to reveal any intimate details of subjects' lives that would be considered an invasion of privacy, or borrow more material than allowed as a fair use of any copyrighted material. If you are writing about a private individual, rather than a public official or public figure, you should proceed more cautiously because private individuals may only need to show you acted negligently to recover damages. Prior to production you should submit your screenplay for review by an experienced entertainment attorney to identify any legal problems. Often potential liability can be avoided by simply changing character names, locations, and adding disclaimers.

2. Why do I need to obtain someone's life-story rights?

Answer: Essentially, the purchaser of life-story rights is obtaining a release protecting the buyer of the rights from a suit predicated on defamation, invasion of privacy, or right of publicity and may be obtaining cooperation and access to information that the purchaser might not otherwise have access to. When the subject is deceased, there's much less reason to option life-story rights because the rights of defamation and invasion of privacy are personal and do not descend to one's heirs.

CHAPTER 15

THE RIGHT OF PRIVACY

The United States Constitution does not mention a right of privacy. According to the United States Supreme Court, however, such a right is implicit in the Constitution and the Bill of Rights.

The right of privacy has been defined as the right to live one's life in seclusion, without being subjected to unwarranted and undesired publicity. In other words, it is the right to be left alone.

Like defamation, the right of privacy is subject to constitutional restrictions. The news media, for example, is not liable for defamatory statements that are newsworthy unless they are made with knowing or reckless disregard of the truth (i.e., actual malice). Unlike defamation, a cause of action for invasion of privacy does not require any injury to one's reputation.

Suppose you were in your backyard sunbathing in the nude. Your backyard is surrounded by a solid wood fence preventing passersby from seeing you. Suddenly a photographer for the *National Enquirer* hops over the fence and snaps your picture. Soon the photograph is displayed in newspaper tabloids near supermarket check-out stands across the nation. Can you sue for defamation?

No, because you were sunbathing in the nude and truth is an absolute defense to defamation. Could you sue for invasion of privacy? Yes. You have a reasonable expectation of privacy in your enclosed backyard.

DEALMAKING
IN THE
FILM AND
TELEVISION
INDUSTRY—
3RD EDITION

354

Suppose you were sunbathing in the nude on your front porch, in open public view. Could you bring a successful action for invasion of privacy? No, because you do not have a reasonable expectation of privacy under these circumstances. Thus, whether an intrusion into your privacy will be actionable depends on whether you have a reasonable expectation of privacy.

Many defenses to defamation apply to invasion of privacy. But truth is not a defense. Revealing matters of public record cannot be the basis for an invasion of privacy action. Express and implied consent are valid defenses. If you voluntarily reveal private facts to others, you cannot recover for invasion of your privacy.

Privacy actions typically fall into four factual patterns.[1]

INTRUSION INTO ONE'S PRIVATE AFFAIRS

This category includes such activities as wiretapping and unreasonable surveillance. The intrusion must be highly offensive. Whether an intrusion is highly offensive depends on the circumstances. Most people would find it offensive to discover a voyeur peering through their bedroom window. On the other hand, a salesman knocking on your front door at dinner time may be obnoxious but will not be sufficiently offensive to state a cause of action.

PUBLIC DISCLOSURE OF EMBARRASSING PRIVATE FACTS

One who gives publicity to a matter concerning the private life of another is subject to liability for invasion of privacy, if the matter publicized is of a kind that:

a) would be highly offensive to a reasonable person, and
b) is not of legitimate concern to the public. In other words, it is not newsworthy.

An example of this type of invasion of privacy would occur if someone digs up some dirt on another person, publicizes it, and the information is not of legitimate interest to the public.

---

[1] Privacy actions need not fall within one of these four categories to be actionable.

THE WRITER/FILMMAKER AS INVESTIGATOR

Entering Private Premises

WRITERS AND FILMMAKERS WISHING TO ENTER PRIVATE PROPERTY NEED PERMISSION. THERE IS NO FIRST AMENDMENT RIGHT TO TRESPASS ON PRIVATE PROPERTY. CONSENT MAY NOT BE EFFECTIVE IF YOU EXCEED THE SCOPE OF THE CONSENT GIVEN. JUST BECAUSE SOMEONE LETS YOU INTO THEIR LIVING ROOM DOES NOT MEAN YOU CAN RIFLE THROUGH THEIR DESK DRAWERS.

Receiving Private Documents from Inside Sources

GENERALLY, A PERSON WILL NOT BE LIABLE FOR INVASION OF PRIVACY IF HE/SHE DID NOT PARTICIPATE IN, ENCOURAGE, OR SUGGEST ANY UNLAWFUL ACTS TO OBTAIN THE PROPERTY BUT IS MERELY A PASSIVE RECIPIENT OF THEM. THIS HOLDS TRUE EVEN IF THE PERSON KNOWS PAPERS ARE STOLEN.

Taping Telephone Calls

FEDERAL

WIRETAPPING IS PROHIBITED BY FEDERAL CRIMINAL STATUTE 18 U.S.C. § 2511. THE LAW DOES NOT PROHIBIT, HOWEVER, TAPING OF PHONE CALLS BY A PARTY TO A CONVERSATION IF THE RECORDING IS NOT DONE FOR AN ILLEGAL PURPOSE.[2]

FEDERAL LAW GOVERNS ONLY INTERSTATE PHONE CALLS.

STATE

LAWS VARY BY STATE. MANY STATES REQUIRE CONSENT OF ALL PARTIES TO A CONVERSATION.

CALIFORNIA PENAL CODE § 632 PROHIBITS RECORDING TELEPHONE CALLS WITHOUT THE CONSENT OF ALL PARTIES TO THE CONVERSATION. AN EXCEPTION IS PROVIDED FOR CONVERSATIONS WHICH ARE NOT CONFIDENTIAL.

CONSENT SHOULD BE OBTAINED IN WRITING OR RECORDED ON TAPE.

Obtaining Government Information

CITIZENS ARE GENERALLY PERMITTED ACCESS TO GOVERNMENT RECORDS UNDER STATE OR FEDERAL FREEDOM OF INFORMATION ACTS (FOIA).

FEDERAL FOIA[3]

EXEMPT AREAS:

1) NATIONAL SECURITY - FOREIGN AFFAIRS
2) INTERNAL PRACTICES OF AN AGENCY
3) INTERAGENCY MEMORANDA
4) INVESTIGATORY FILES
5) TRADE OR COMMERCIAL SECRETS
6) PERSONNEL AND MEDICAL FILES
7) REPORTS ON REGULATION OF FINANCIAL INSTITUTIONS
8) GEOLOGICAL DATA
9) DATA SPECIFICALLY EXEMPT FROM DISCLOSURE UNDER OTHER LAWS

EXEMPTIONS UNDER CALIFORNIA'S FREEDOM OF INFORMATION ACT ARE SET FORTH IN CALIFORNIA GOVERNMENT CODE § 6254.

---

[2] *U.S. v. Wright,* 573 F.2d 681 (1978).
[3] 5 U.S.C. § 552

DEALMAKING
IN THE
FILM AND
TELEVISION
INDUSTRY—
3RD EDITION

356

APPROPRIATION

An action for appropriation of another's name or likeness is similar to action for invasion of one's right of publicity. The former action seeks to compensate the plaintiff for the emotional distress, embarrassment, and hurt feelings that may arise from the use of one's name or likeness on a product. The latter action seeks to compensate the plaintiff for the commercial value arising from the exploitation of one's name and likeness.

As with the right of publicity, a person cannot always control the use of his or her name and likeness by another. While you can prevent someone from putting your face on their pancake mix, you cannot stop *Time* magazine from putting your face on its cover. Thus the use of someone's name or likeness as part of a newsworthy incident would not be actionable.

FALSE LIGHT

Publicity placing a plaintiff in a false light will be actionable if the portrayal is highly offensive. This type of invasion of privacy is similar to defamation but harm to reputation is not required. An example of false-light invasion of privacy could entail a political dirty trick such as placing the name of a prominent Republican on a list of Democratic contributors. Although this person's reputation may not be harmed, he/she has been shown in a false light.

CASES

Melvin v. Reid (1931)[4]

FACTS: In 1925, Reid (D) released a motion picture entitled *The Red Kimono*. The movie told the true story of the unsavory incidents in the life of Melvin (P). The film portrayed Melvin as a prostitute who was tried and acquitted of murder in 1918. The film used the real maiden name of Melvin, who had since reformed, married, assumed a place in respectable society, and made many friends who

---

[4] 112 Cal. App. 285, 297 P. 91 (1931)

were unaware of her previous activities. She sued Reid
for invasion of privacy.

ISSUE: Did Reid invade Melvin's privacy?

HOLDING: Yes. Plaintiff wins.

RATIONALE: Publication of past unsavory incidents after
she has reformed, coupled with use of her real name,
is an invasion of privacy. This incident was no longer
newsworthy.

While the public has a legitimate interest in Melvin's illegal
activities, these incidents happened some time ago, and there
was no good reason for revealing her identity now. The story
could have been told just as well without using her real name.
Had the producer changed the character's name, the court's decision would likely be different. Thus, changing the identity of a
character can sometimes insulate a filmmaker from liability.

Note that material taken from court records is privileged. However, the filmmaker here went beyond the public record. Writers
usually find it difficult to tell a true story without going beyond
the public record since it is rare for subjects' lives to be so fully
documented. Of course, if one presented a courtroom drama
limited to the trial transcripts, the material would be completely
privileged.

Why didn't the plaintiff file a defamation action? Because
the events were true, and truth is an absolute defense to
defamation.

Bernstein v. NBC (1955)[5]

FACTS: In 1919, Bernstein (P) was convicted of bank
robbery and sentenced to prison for 40 years. After serving nine years, he was paroled and pardoned. In 1933,
Bernstein, under another name, was tried and convicted
of first degree murder and sentenced to death. Later the
sentence was commuted to life imprisonment. In 1940,
Bernstein received a conditional release and in 1945 a
presidential pardon. After that, Bernstein lived an exem-
plary, quiet, and private life, shunning publicity.

In 1952, NBC (D) telecast a fictionalized dramatization
of Bernstein's conviction and pardon. The movie did not
mention Bernstein's real name. He alleges, however, that
the actor who portrayed him resembled him physically,

---

[5] 129 F. Supp. 817 (D.D.C. 1955).

DEALMAKING
IN THE
FILM AND
TELEVISION
INDUSTRY—
3RD EDITION

358

and that his words and actions were reproduced, creating a portrayal recognizable to his friends and identifying him in the public mind. Bernstein alleged that the program was a willful and malicious invasion of his right of privacy.

ISSUE: Did NBC invade Bernstein's right of privacy?

HOLDING: No.

RATIONALE: The events in question were already known by the public from the prior publicity. The passage of time was not enough to make them private facts. Also, the program did not identify Bernstein. Bernstein conceded that only those people who already knew about the story would recognize him.

The facts of this case are not much different from Melvin v. Reid. However, here defendant NBC fictionalized Bernstein's name and moved the events from Minneapolis to Washington, D.C.

Why didn't Bernstein sue for defamation? First, because the story was true. Second, it appears his reputation was not damaged. He was portrayed sympathetically, as a man unjustly convicted of a crime. Note that this movie focused most of its attention on the crusading news journalist who proved Bernstein's innocence. The journalist found an eyewitness who revealed that Bernstein wasn't the killer. The journalist also deduced that a witness against Bernstein couldn't possibly have seen the murder because leaves on a tree at that time of year blocked her view.

Gill v. Hearst Publishing (1953)[6]

FACTS: As part of an article in *Ladies' Home Journal* entitled "Love," Hearst (D) published a photo of Mr. and Mrs. Gill (P) taken without their permission. The photo captured the Gills in an affectionate pose, at their place of business, a confectionery and ice cream store in the Farmer's Market in Los Angeles.

ISSUE: Is publication of a photo without the consent of the subjects an invasion of their privacy?

HOLDING: No.

RATIONALE: Persons do not have an absolute legal right to prevent publication of any photo taken of them without their permission. If every person had such a right, no

---

[6] 40 Cal. 2d 224 (1953).

photo could be published of a street scene or a parade. Liability exists only if publication of a photo would be offensive to people of ordinary sensibilities. Here the Gills voluntarily assumed this pose in a public place. The photo merely permitted others to see them as they publicly exhibited themselves.

The Gills were not a subject of the *Ladies' Home Journal* article. The magazine did not interview them or mention them by name. The magazine merely bought a stock photo of them taken by a photographer who happened to snap their picture one day. This photograph was taken inside the Gill's store in open public view.

This case stands for the principle that people do not have an absolute right to control the use of their name and likeness. A television news reporter could broadcast footage of an individual without his permission. It is always a good idea, however, to get a release, to preclude any possibility of a lawsuit.

The decision would be different if the Gills were photographed in a place where they had a reasonable expectation of privacy, such as their bedroom, or if the Gill's picture was used on a commercial product.

Spahn v. Julian Messner, Inc. (1967)[7]

FACTS: Spahn, a well-known baseball player, sued over the publication of an unauthorized biography, alleging that his rights under New York's misappropriation (privacy) statute had been invaded. In the purported biography, the author took great literary license, dramatizing incidents, inventing conversations, manipulating chronologies, attributing thoughts and feelings to Spahn, and fictionalizing events. The invented material depicted the plaintiff's childhood, his relationship with his father, the courtship of his wife, important events in their marriage, and his military experience.

The defendant argues that the literary techniques he used are customary for juvenile books. The defendant never interviewed Spahn, any members of his family, or any baseball player who knew him. The author's research was comprised of newspaper and magazine clippings, the veracity of which he rarely confirmed.

ISSUE: Did the defendant invade P's privacy?

---

[7] 21 N.Y. 2d 124, 233 N.E. 2d 840 (1967).

DEALMAKING
IN THE
FILM AND
TELEVISION
INDUSTRY—
3RD EDITION

360

HOLDING: Yes.

RATIONALE: The New York privacy statute protects a public person from fictionalized publication only if the work was published with knowledge of the falsification or with reckless disregard for the truth (actual malice). D acted with at least reckless disregard of the truth in incorporating so much fictional and false material.

Factual reporting of newsworthy persons and events is in the public interest and is protected. The fictitious is not. The Plaintiff does not seek an injunction and damages for the unauthorized publication of his biography. He seeks only to restrain the publication of that which purports to be his biography.

New York has enacted a statute protecting the privacy of its citizens.[8] The court found the law to be constitutional provided actual malice was shown because Spahn is a public figure. Since the defendant writer invented large portions of the book, he obviously knew his statements were not true. Spahn could not prevent publication of an unflattering biography simply because he didn't like its contents.

Leopold v. Levin (1970)[9]

FACTS: In 1924, Nathan Leopold (P) and a partner pleaded guilty to kidnapping and murdering a young boy. Because of the luridness of the crime, the case attracted international notoriety, which did not wane over time. In 1958, a paroled Leopold published a publicized autobiography.

In 1956, Levin (D) wrote a novel, *Compulsion*, whose basic framework was the Leopold case, although Leopold's name did not appear in it. The book was described as a fictionalized account of the Leopold murder case. A motion picture based on the book was released with fictitious characters that resembled actual persons in the case. The promotional materials referred to the crime but made it clear that the story was a work of fiction suggested by the case. Leopold sues for invasion of privacy.

ISSUE: Does a person who fosters continued public attention, after having engaged in an activity placing him in the public eye, have a right of privacy in fictitious accounts of that activity or in the use of his name in promoting such account?

---

[8] New York Civil Rights Law §§ 50, 51.
[9] 45 Ill. 2d 434, 259 N.E. 2d 250 (1970).

HOLDING: No.

RATIONALE: Books, magazines, newspapers, and motion pictures are forms of public expression protected by the First Amendment, even if they are sold for profit. While the book and movie were "suggested" by Leopold's crime, they were evidently fictional and dramatized works. The core of the novel and film were a part of Leopold's life that he had caused to be placed in public view. The fictionalized aspects, minor in offensiveness, were reasonably conceivable from the facts of record from which they were drawn. Similarly, reference to Plaintiff in advertising materials concerned his notorious crime. His participation was a matter of public and historical record so that his conduct was without benefit of privacy.

The court noted that a documentary account of the Leopold case would be constitutionally protected. Also, a completely fictional work inspired by the case would be protected if matters such as locale were changed and there was no promotional identification with the plaintiff.

Questions and Answers

1. I recently completed a documentary which contains close-ups of people who may or may not want to be included in my film, and some of them are engaged in rather unflattering behavior. Everything was taped outside, in open public view. Should I be concerned about any invasion of privacy issues?

Answer: Generally speaking, any conduct in public is fair game in regards to other people photographing or observing it. You waive your right of privacy when you publicly exhibit yourself to others. The documentary will probably be protected under the First Amendment, even if some of the subjects are not happy with their portrayal. When Mike Wallace does a *60 Minutes* investigation, he does not obtain a release from the perpetrators of a scam. However, if you want to use the names or likenesses of people on products or merchandise, or in an entertainment program, you should secure releases. And you should not misrepresent the nature of what you are showing. So while you might be able to include footage of a person walking down a

DEALMAKING
IN THE
FILM AND
TELEVISION
INDUSTRY—
3RD EDITION

362

street, that does not mean you can have a narrator comment that this person is committing a crime when they are not.

2. I've written a biographical script about a famous person who recently died. Do I need permission from his or her estate to proceed? What about other people in the script who are still living?

Answer: Some rights, such as the right of privacy and the right to protect one's reputation (defamation), are considered personal rights and they expire when the person dies. In regard to the other people in your script who are alive, they might be able to sue for invasion of privacy or defamation should you violate their rights. Some subsidiary characters you might be able to fictionalize, and if they are not identifiable, they might have difficulty proving they had been damaged. A disclaimer that the story is fictional may also give you some protection. Some rights, such as the right of publicity, which may be needed if any merchandising spin-offs are planned, do not expire on death. State law varies on this issue.

CHAPTER 16

TRADEMARKS AND UNFAIR COMPETITION

TRADEMARKS

A trademark or service mark[1] is a brand name that can be a word, a symbol, or a device used by a business to distinguish its goods or services from those of others. "Coca-Cola" written in its distinctive script is a trademark, as are "IBM," "Disney," and thousands of other marks used to identify the source of goods or services. In the entertainment industry, titles of television series and some movies may be trademarked.[2]

Trademarks can theoretically last forever as long as they are used to distinguish goods. They can be abandoned by non-use or can fall into the public domain if they become the generic term of a product. For example, former trademarks "zipper," "thermos," "aspirin," and "brassiere" are now considered generic names for all such products, regardless of their manufacturer.

Unlike patents and copyrights,[3] protection of trademarks is not based exclusively on federal law. State law may provide important remedies. Note also that federal trademarks can be

---

[1] A trademark is used on a product; a service mark designates a service. Unless otherwise noted, all references to the rights of trademark holders apply to service mark holders.
[2] Marks may be portrayed in a motion picture. See Chapter 2 for a discussion of merchandising and product-placement deals and the legality of showing trademarked products in films without permission.
[3] Before 1978, unpublished works were protected under state law. Since then, federal copyright law has largely preempted the field.

DEALMAKING
IN THE
FILM AND
TELEVISION
INDUSTRY—
3RD EDITION

364

obtained only for products or services used in interstate commerce (i.e., sold in more than one state).

Federal trademark law provides for a registration system administered by the U.S. Trademark Office. You are not required to register a trademark to establish your right to use it. Simply using a particular mark to distinguish your goods from those manufactured by others may prevent third parties from using the mark. Registration of a mark confers several advantages, such as allowing the trademark owner to obtain triple damages and reimbursement of attorneys' fees.

To federally register a mark, one must submit an application. An examiner in the Trademark Office reviews the application to verify:

1) that the mark is not deceptive;
2) that the mark is not confusingly similar to another mark; and
3) that the mark is not merely descriptive of goods or mis-descriptive, geographically descriptive or misdescriptive, or is primarily a surname.

Whether one mark infringes another is determined by whether use of the two marks would cause consumers to be mistaken or confused about the origin of manufacture. Registration forms and information are available on websites: www.uspto.gov (federal); www.ss.ca.gov/business/ts (California); www.dos.state.ny.us/corp/miscfae.html (New York). One can conduct an Internet search of federal trademarks by using the Trademark Electronic Search System (TESS).[4] Forms can be downloaded through the Trademark Electronic Application System (TEAS).[5] TEAS can be used to file an application for registration of a mark, respond to examining attorney's office action, provide notice of change of address, amendment to allege use, statement of use, or request an extension of time to file a statement of use. Forms are also available through the Trademark Assistance Center at (800) 786-9199 or (571) 272-9250.

---

[4] http://tess2.uspto.gov/bin/gate.exe?f=tess&state=j18118.1.1
[5] http://www.uspto.gov/teas/index.html

CREATION OF TRADEMARK RIGHTS

Federal trademark rights arise from 1) use of the mark, or 2) a bona fide intention to use a mark, along with the filing of an application to federally register that mark.

Therefore, before a trademark owner may file an application for federal registration, the owner must 1) use the mark on goods which are shipping or sold, or services which are rendered in interstate commerce (or commerce between the U.S. and a foreign country), or 2) have a bona fide intention to use the mark in such commerce in relation to specific goods or services.

THE FEDERAL REGISTRATION PROCESS

When an application has been filed, an Examining Attorney in the Patent and Trademark Office will review the application and decide whether the mark may be registered. The Office will make an initial determination about three months after the application has been filed. The applicant must respond to any objections within six months or the application will be deemed abandoned.

Once the Examining attorney approves a mark, the mark is published in the *Trademark Official Gazette*. Thirty days are allowed for anyone to object to the registration. If no opposition is filed, the registration will issue about 12 weeks later for marks in use in commerce. For applications based on intent to use, a notice of allowance will issue about 12 weeks after publication. The applicant then has six months to either use the mark in commerce or request a six-month extension of time to file a statement of use.

BENEFITS OF REGISTRATION

The benefits of federal registration include the following:

1) The right to sue in federal court for trademark infringement;
2) The right to recover profits, damages, and costs from an infringer, and up to triple damages and attorney fees;

DEALMAKING
IN THE
FILM AND
TELEVISION
INDUSTRY—
3RD EDITION

366

3) Gives others constructive notice of your mark;

4) Allows the use of the federal registration symbol, R in a circle, with the mark;

5) Allows one to deposit copies of the registration with the Customs Service to stop importation of goods bearing an infringing mark;

6) Permits one to sue for counterfeiting the mark, providing civil and criminal penalties;

7) Enables one to file a corresponding application in many foreign countries.

State registration gives one important additional benefit—it prevents another from registering the same mark with the state.

GROUNDS FOR REFUSING FEDERAL REGISTRATION

1) It is scandalous or disparaging.

2) It is an insignia of a governmental entity.

3) Without consent it identifies a living individual or a deceased President during the life of his widow.

4) It is confusingly similar to a previously registered mark, or to a mark previously used in the United States by another and not abandoned.

5) It is merely descriptive or deceptively misdescriptive of goods or services. Or it is primarily a surname, and is not distinctive of such goods or services.

MAINTENANCE OF THE MARK

Continued use of the mark is necessary to avoid abandonment of the mark. Federal registrations must be renewed every 10 years. Moreover, between the fifth and sixth year after the date of the registration, you must file an affidavit stating that the mark is currently in use in commerce. If no affidavit is filed, the registration will be canceled. California registrations must be renewed every 10 years.

MADRID PROTOCOL

The Madrid Protocol is a system for international registration of trademarks. It permits one to file a single trademark application with his or her national trademark office, which will then enable it to be protected in various countries designated by the applicant if those countries are signatories to the Madrid agreement. The single filing has the same effect as if the trademark was filed in each designated country separately. This process makes protecting one's trademark much more efficient. Furthermore, management of trademarks such as recording subsequent changes and renewals can be done with one filing. [6]

UNFAIR COMPETITION

Section 43 of the federal Lanham Act, 15 U.S.C. § 1125, provides:

> (a) Civil action (1) Any person who, on or in connection with any goods or services, or any container for goods, uses in commerce any word, term, name, symbol, or device, or any combination thereof, or any false designation of origin, false or misleading description of fact, or false or misleading representation of fact, which (A) is likely to cause confusion, or to cause mistake, or to deceive as to the affiliation, connection, or association of such person with another person, or as to the origin, sponsorship, or approval of his or her goods, services, or commercial activities by another person, or (B) in commercial advertising or promotion, misrepresents the nature, characteristics, qualities, or geographic origin of his or her or another person's goods, services, or commercial activities, shall be liable in a civil action by any person who believes that he or she is or is likely to be damaged by such act.

Under the law of unfair competition, a person cannot open a hamburger stand and name it "McDonald's" if they are not affiliated with the well-known chain. A competitor would also be barred from displaying golden arches or using any device that would mislead and confuse consumers and make them think its burgers are genuine McDonald's burgers when they are not.

---

[6] Additional information can be found at the World Intellectual Property Organization at www.wipo.int/madrid/en/.

DEALMAKING
IN THE
FILM AND
TELEVISION
INDUSTRY—
3RD EDITION

368

Placing a misleading title on a movie could be actionable as unfair competition. Suppose a sleazy movie producer decides to release a low-budget movie with the title *Raiders of the Last Ark* soon after George Lucas has released his *Raiders of the Lost Ark*. Since the public has come to identify the title with the work of George Lucas, the words have acquired a secondary meaning. Thus consumers would likely be confused about the origin of *Raiders of the Last Ark*.

CASE

Allen v. National Video, Inc. (1985)[7]

FACTS: National Video, a video-rental chain, placed a series of ads in which a Woody Allen look-alike is portrayed in a picture as one of its customers. The look-alike appears at a counter checking out the videotapes of *Annie Hall*, *Bananas*, *Casablanca*, and *The Maltese Falcon*. He is holding a National Video V.I.P. card, and the woman behind the counter is smiling and gasping in exaggerated excitement at the presence of a celebrity.

The copy reads, "Become a V.I.P. at National Video. We'll make you look like a star," and, "You don't need a famous face to be treated to some pretty famous service." A small disclaimer stating that a celebrity double was being used appeared in one ad. Allen sued, claiming that his portrait was used without permission and that the ads were misleading and likely to confuse consumers and lead them to believe he had endorsed National Video.

ISSUE: Does Allen have a cause of action?

HOLDING: Yes.

RATIONALE: Consumers are likely to be confused. There is a likelihood of confusion, even with the ad containing the disclaimer. The disclaimer is small and says only that a celebrity double is being used, which doesn't by itself dispel the inference that Allen may be involved with National's products or services. The disclaimer must be bold and make clear that Allen in no way endorses the service.

---

[7] 610 F.Supp. 612 (S.D.N.Y., 1985).

Allen also sued on Invasion of Privacy and infringement of his Right of Publicity. The court said that since the defendant didn't use Allen's name or likeness, there was no privacy cause of action. Whether Allen stated a cause of action for invasion of his Right of Publicity was a question for the jury to decide. They would need to decide whether the look-alike created the illusion of Woody Allen's actual presence.

Questions and Answers

1. What are the legalities of using actual business names (e.g., McDonald's, Nike, or Staples) in a screenplay?

Answer: The legalities depend on the circumstances. In many instances you may be able to refer to actual names of people, hospitals, or restaurants without their permission. However, if you defame these entities by portraying them in a derogatory light, you may be liable for defamation. Likewise, if you invade the privacy of actual living people by revealing intimate details of their lives, you could be liable. Moreover, if you use names or trademarks to indicate an affiliation that does not exist, you could potentially be liable for unfair competition and/or trademark infringement. Under the First Amendment, you are permitted to mention other people in books and films without their permission. Before you go into production, it would be a good idea to have your script reviewed by an experienced entertainment attorney to point out any potential pitfalls. Of course, it never hurts to obtain a release. And to play it safe, you may want to have your prop person come up with a pseudo product so there is no chance of liability. Distributors and insurance companies are often very conservative as to the amount of risk they will accept, so it is best to steer clear of any questionable uses.

2. Prior to a movie being announced, marketed, promoted, and released, can a movie title be registered as a trademark?

Answer: Trademarks protect product and service names, and company names. When a certain name becomes associated with a certain product or service, trademark rights arise. Some of these rights arise simply from use of the mark. Additional protections arise if the mark is registered. Examples of famous trademarks

DEALMAKING
IN THE
FILM AND
TELEVISION
INDUSTRY—
3RD EDITION

370

are Xerox, Google, and Mercedes. If you are in the computer business, you cannot market your computers as Apple computers unless you have the permission of the company known by that name. Likewise, you cannot set up a hamburger stand across the street from McDonald's and call yourself McDonald's, put up golden arches, or in any way try to pass off your hamburgers as legitimate McDonald's hamburgers, if they are not.

However, titles of individual products like a book or a movie are generally not eligible for trademark protection. Only a series of products from a single source, such as sequels or a television series such as *Bonanza* can be protected under trademark law. So a one-shot product like a movie or its title would not be protected, although a studio that produced a series of films, such as Paramount Pictures, could serve as a trademark.

In some circumstances a title could be protected under the laws of unfair competition once the title had acquired a secondary meaning. A movie title cannot have a secondary meaning with the public before it is released. Thus, after George Lucas had produced and distributed *Star Wars*, another filmmaker could not distribute a movie called *Star Wars II*, and try to trade on the goodwill and name recognition of the original. This would be unfair competition, and would violate various federal and state laws.

Trademark rights are often restricted to a geographical area or type of product. For example, if you operate the Acme Hardware Store in Los Angeles, it would not be necessarily to prevent someone else from opening an Acme Hardware Store in Brooklyn, a location where you do not do business. Likewise, the fact that you operate a Hardware Store under the mark "Acme" would not prevent someone from setting up the Acme Supermarket because people do not associate hardware and food together. In other words, there is little likelihood of confusion.

Another way to protect titles is registration with the MPAA. This is protection by contract law, through an arrangement between the MPAA companies and any independent producers who choose to sign the agreement. It is a contract wherein all parties agree not to infringe each other's titles. There are some limitations because the agreement is only binding on those people who choose to sign it. You can contact the MPAA Title Registration Bureau at (818) 995-6600. While signing this agreement may offer you a measure of protection, it can also subject you to legal action from one of the other signers to the agreement if you have selected a title that might be confused with a previously registered title.

3. How can I protect the name and look of my main character before my animated short is released? Are characters trademarkable, or will a copyright of an image of the character protect it?

Answer: After you complete your script, and after you complete your film, you should register each with the Copyright Office, using a Form PA. Copyright law can, to some extent, protect characters that are sufficiently well defined. However, copyright law does not prevent others from creating characters with similar personality traits. Just because you wrote a detective story featuring Detective Sam Spade does not mean that you can thereafter preclude others from writing their own stories that feature other hard-boiled private eyes. A character, which is represented visually, such as a cartoon character, may receive greater protection under Copyright law because of its visual representation.

A character might also be protected under trademark law, if for example, it was used as a mark to identify the source of a product or service. Mickey Mouse is a trademark used on a variety of toys and other products.

CHAPTER 17

REMEDIES

If you carefully investigate potential partners before going into business with them, you may never need to refer to this chapter. Contrary to conventional wisdom, there are honorable people in the movie business. There are also sleazy operators. If you do some checking, you can usually figure out who you are dealing with.

In the event you find yourself in business with a shark, or a well-meaning incompetent, you will first need to review your contract to determine your rights and remedies. You may want to get out of the deal, force the other party to abide by the terms of the agreement, and/or obtain a monetary award to compensate you for damages you have suffered.

For union/guild members, the first step may be to ask your union/guild for assistance. While the guilds do not have the resources to file a lawsuit every time a member's rights have been infringed, they can bring a great deal of pressure to bear on a recalcitrant party. The guilds can place a production company or a producer on a strike list, which prevents other guild members from working for the wrongdoer. Moreover, some issues, such as allocation of writing credits, are determined by guild rules, with the guild resolving disputes through its own arbitration process.

DEALMAKING
IN THE
FILM AND
TELEVISION
INDUSTRY—
3RD EDITION

374

GUILD REMEDIES

Collective-bargaining agreements of the Screen Actors Guild (SAG), the American Federation of Television and Radio Artists (AFTRA), the Directors Guild of America (DGA), and the Writers Guild of America (WGA) all require that certain disputes involving their members be arbitrated. In general, disputes involving alleged violations of guild rules go to a grievance hearing and/ or arbitration.

Arbitration rules and procedures are set forth in the collective-bargaining agreement for each guild. Guild rules provide for a hearing before single or multiple arbitrators. In the case of the DGA, WGA, and SAG, the arbitrators are chosen from a panel designated during the collective-bargaining process.

Each guild has its own rules as to which types of disputes can be litigated and which must be arbitrated. The WGA and SAG exclude from arbitration those disputes where an injunction or a large amount of money damages is sought. On the other hand, DGA arbitrators have broader power, including the right to order a member company to correct advertising and film titles. In some instances the guilds require the parties to engage in a grievance procedure prior to filing a demand for arbitration. Contact the appropriate guild to determine if a grievance procedure is mandated.

As with most collective-bargaining agreements, entertainment-guild arbitration decisions are final and binding. However, guild rules do not prohibit petitioning a court to confirm, set aside, or modify an arbitration award. For example, if an arbitrator rules that a production company owes money to a writer, and the company does not pay promptly, the WGA may go to court to secure an enforcement order. Contact information for industry guilds and unions is in the Appendix.

For those persons not in a guild, and for disputes not subject to guild arbitration, one should consider providing for arbitration by including an arbitration clause in one's contract. Such a provision requires that disputes be resolved through arbitration, not litigation. Arbitration usually offers a speedier, more informal, and less expensive method of settling disputes. Conflicts are often settled in a matter of months. Instead of going to court, the parties meet in a conference room. The usual rules of evidence and court procedure don't apply. The arbitrator is typically an attorney or retired judge with knowledge of the entertainment industry.

Arbitration and mediation are forms of Alternative Dispute Resolution (ADR), the generic term for settling disputes in a manner other than traditional civil litigation. In the past decade there has been tremendous growth in ADR. In mediation, the parties submit their dispute to an impartial third party, who assists them in reaching a mutually acceptable resolution. The mediator tries to negotiate a settlement between the parties. If the parties are unable to agree, however, the mediator (unlike an arbitrator) cannot impose a settlement or make a binding decision.

It is particularly important to provide for ADR if the party you are contracting with is wealthier

ARBITRATION ORGANIZATIONS

AMERICAN ARBITRATION ASSOCIATION (AAA):
WWW.ADR.ORG; CORPORATE HEADQUARTERS ñ 1633 BROADWAY, 10TH FLOOR, NEW YORK, NY 10019, (212) 716-5800, FAX (212) 716-5905; LOS ANGELES- MICHAEL R. POWELL, VICE PRESIDENT, 725 S. FIGUEROA ST., SUITE 2400, LOS ANGELES, CA 90017, (213) 362-1900.

IFTA:
WWW.IFTA-ONLINE.ORG; ARBITRAL AGENT AND ASSOCIATE COUNSEL, 10850 WILSHIRE BLVD., 9TH FLOOR, LOS ANGELES, CA 90024-4321, (310) 446-1000, FAX (310) 446-1600, RSTARKEY@IFTA-ONLINE.ORG.

CALIFORNIA LAWYERS FOR THE ARTS:
WWW.CALAWYERSFORTHEARTS.ORG; SOUTHERN CALIFORNIA- 1641 18TH ST., SANTA MONICA, CA 90404, (310) 998-5590, FAX (310) 998-5594, USERCLA@AOL.COM, (ARBITRATION IN SOUTHERN CALIFORNIA).

INTERNATIONAL COURT OF ARBITRATION (INTERNATIONAL COURT OF ARBITRATION (INTERNATIONAL CHAMBER OF COMMERCE) :
WWW.ICCWBO.ORG; INTERNATIONAL SECRETARIAT, ICC INTERNATIONAL COURT OF ARBITRATION, 38, COURS ALBERT, 1ER, 75008 PARIS, FRANCE, 011-33-1-49-53-29-05, FAX 011-33-1-49-53-29-29, ARB@ICCWBO.ORG.

JAMS:
WWW.JAMSADR.COM; LOS ANGELES- 707 WILSHIRE BLVD., 46TH FLOOR, LOS ANGELES, CA 90071, (213) 620-1133, FAX (213) 620-0100; NEW YORK- 620 8TH AVE., 34TH FLOOR, NEW YORK, NY 10018, (212) 751-2700, FAX (212) 751-4099.

DEALMAKING
IN THE
FILM AND
TELEVISION
INDUSTRY—
3RD EDITION

376

SAMPLE ADR CLAUSES

ARBITRATION: This Agreement shall be interpreted in accordance with the laws of the State of California applicable to agreements executed and to be wholly performed therein. Any dispute under this Agreement will be resolved by final and binding arbitration under the Independent Film & Television Alliance Rules for International Arbitration in effect as of the effective date of this Agreement ("IFTA Rules"). Each Party waives any right to adjudicate any dispute in any other court or forum, *except* that a Party may seek interim relief before the start of arbitration as allowed by the IFTA Rules. The arbitration will be held in the Forum designated in the Agreement, or, if none is designated, as determined by the IFTA Rules. The Parties will abide by any decision in the arbitration and any court having jurisdiction may enforce it. The Parties submit to the jurisdiction of the courts in the Forum to compel arbitration or to confirm an arbitration award. The Parties agree to accept service of process in accordance with the IFTA Rules. The prevailing party shall be entitled to reimbursement of attorney fees and costs.

Any dispute, claim, or controversy arising out of or relating to this Agreement or the breach, termination, enforcement, interpretation, or validity thereof, including the determination of the scope or applicability of this agreement to arbitrate, shall be determined by arbitration in (insert the desired place of arbitration), before (one) (three) arbitrator(s). The arbitration shall be administered by JAMS pursuant to its (Comprehensive Arbitration Rules and Procedures) (Streamlined Arbitration Rules and Procedures). Judgment on the Award may be entered in any court having jurisdiction. This clause shall not preclude parties from seeking provisional remedies in aid of arbitration from a court of appropriate jurisdiction. The arbitrator may, in the Award, allocate all or part of the costs of the arbitration, including the fees of the arbitrator and the reasonable attorneys' fees of the prevailing party.[1]

ARBITRATION: This agreement shall be interpreted and construed according to the laws of the State of New York, applicable to contracts made and entirely performed therein. The parties select the American Arbitration Association expedited arbitration using one arbitrator, to be a disinterested attorney specializing in entertainment law, as the sole forum for the resolution of any dispute between them. The venue for arbitration shall be either New York City or Los Angeles, California, to be determined by the party who first files a demand for arbitration. The determination of the arbitrator in such proceeding shall be final, binding, and non-appealable.

ARBITRATION: Any controversy or claim arising out of or relating to this Agreement or any breach thereof shall be settled by arbitration in accordance with the Rules of the American Arbitration Association. The parties select expedited arbitration using one arbitrator, to be a

---

[1] JAMS can be reached at (800) 352-5267 or www.jamsadr.com.

DISINTERESTED ATTORNEY SPECIALIZING IN ENTERTAINMENT LAW, AS THE SOLE FORUM FOR THE RESOLUTION OF ANY DISPUTE BETWEEN THEM. THE VENUE FOR ARBITRATION SHALL BE LOS ANGELES, CALIFORNIA. THE ARBITRATOR MAY MAKE ANY INTERIM ORDER, DECISION, DETERMINATION, OR AWARD HE/SHE DEEMS NECESSARY TO PRESERVE THE STATUS QUO UNTIL HE/SHE IS ABLE TO RENDER A FINAL ORDER, DECISION, DETERMINATION, OR AWARD. THE DETERMINATION OF THE ARBITRATOR IN SUCH PROCEEDING SHALL BE FINAL, BINDING, AND NON-APPEALABLE. JUDGMENT UPON THE AWARD RENDERED BY THE ARBITRATOR MAY BE ENTERED IN ANY COURT HAVING JURISDICTION THEREOF. THE PREVAILING PARTY SHALL BE ENTITLED TO REIMBURSEMENT FOR COSTS AND REASONABLE ATTORNEYS' FEES.

ARBITRATION AND JURISDICTION: THIS AGREEMENT SHALL BE INTERPRETED IN ACCORDANCE WITH THE LAWS OF THE STATE OF CALIFORNIA, APPLICABLE TO THE AGREEMENTS EXECUTED AND TO BE WHOLLY PERFORMED THEREIN. ANY CONTROVERSY OR CLAIM ARISING OUT OF OR IN RELATION TO THIS AGREEMENT, OR TO THE VALIDITY, CONSTRUCTION, OR PERFORMANCE OF THIS AGREEMENT, OR THE BREACH THEREOF, SHALL BE RESOLVED BY ARBITRATION IN ACCORDANCE WITH THE RULES AND PROCEDURES OF THE INTERNATIONAL FILM AND TELEVISION ALLIANCE, AS SAID RULES MAY BE AMENDED FROM TIME TO TIME. SUCH RULES AND PROCEDURES ARE INCORPORATED AND MADE A PART OF THIS AGREEMENT BY REFERENCE. IF THE INTERNATIONAL FILM AND TELEVISION ALLIANCE SHALL REFUSE TO ACCEPT JURISDICTION OF SUCH DISPUTE, THEN THE PARTIES AGREE TO ARBITRATE SUCH MATTER BEFORE AND IN ACCORDANCE WITH THE RULES OF THE AMERICAN ARBITRATION ASSOCIATION UNDER ITS JURISDICTION IN LOS ANGELES BEFORE A SINGLE ARBITRATOR FAMILIAR WITH ENTERTAINMENT LAW.

THE PARTIES SHALL HAVE THE RIGHT TO ENGAGE IN PRE-HEARING DISCOVERY IN CONNECTION WITH SUCH ARBITRATION PROCEEDINGS. THE PARTIES AGREE HERETO THAT THEY WILL ABIDE BY AND PERFORM ANY AWARD RENDERED IN ANY ARBITRATION CONDUCTED PURSUANT HERETO, THAT ANY COURT HAVING JURISDICTION THEREOF MAY ISSUE A JUDGMENT BASED UPON SUCH AWARD AND THAT THE PREVAILING PARTY IN SUCH ARBITRATION AND/OR CONFIRMATION PROCEEDING SHALL BE ENTITLED TO RECOVER ITS REASONABLE ATTORNEYS' FEES AND EXPENSES. THE ARBITRATION WILL BE HELD IN LOS ANGELES, AND ANY AWARD SHALL BE FINAL, BINDING, AND NON-APPEALABLE. THE PARTIES AGREE TO ACCEPT SERVICE OF PROCESS IN ACCORDANCE WITH THE IFTA OR AAA RULES. THE PARTIES FURTHER AGREE THAT IF AN ARBITRATION AWARD IS AWARDED AGAINST DISTRIBUTOR, AND DISTRIBUTOR FAILS TO PAY THE AWARD AFTER IT IS CONFIRMED BY A COURT, THE IFTA MARKET BARRING RULE WILL APPLY AGAINST _____, THE PRESIDENT OF DISTRIBUTOR. _____ AGREES TO SIGN THE IFTA RIDER ATTACHED TO THIS AGREEMENT (ATTACHED AS EXHIBIT _____).

MEDIATION: IF A DISPUTE ARISES OUT OF OR RELATES TO THIS CONTRACT, OR THE BREACH THEREOF, AND IF THE DISPUTE CANNOT BE SETTLED THROUGH NEGOTIATION, THE PARTIES AGREE TO FIRST TRY IN GOOD FAITH TO SETTLE THE DISPUTE BY MEDIATION ADMINISTERED BY THE AMERICAN ARBITRATION ASSOCIATION UNDER ITS COMMERCIAL MEDIATION RULES BEFORE RESORTING TO ARBITRATION, LITIGATION, OR SOME OTHER DISPUTE RESOLUTION PROCEDURE.

DEALMAKING
IN THE
FILM AND
TELEVISION
INDUSTRY—
3RD EDITION

378

than you; in such a case the other party may prevail in litigation simply because he/she has more staying power (i.e., the other party is better able to finance a protracted court battle). With an ADR clause, the playing field is more level.

An ADR clause may provide that the prevailing party is entitled to reimbursement for costs and attorneys' fees. Otherwise, the prevailing party may not be able to recoup these expenses.

ADR can be conducted by the American Arbitration Association (AAA), California Lawyers for the Arts, IFTA[2] or any other impartial organization or person. The AAA is a national non-profit organization with 37 regional offices. AAA handles well over 100,000 cases a year and has settled rules of procedure. Unless otherwise noted, the following descriptions are of AAA arbitration procedures and practices.

State and Federal law govern arbitration.[3] As explained later, arbitration awards can be enforced by the courts, and the local sheriff's office can help the prevailing party collect an outstanding judgment.

Parties are not required to be represented by an attorney in arbitration proceedings, although parties often feel it is helpful to have an attorney. The attorney can draft the Demand for Arbitration, submit a written brief, help select the arbitrator, and prepare witnesses and exhibits. At the hearing, the attorney can make an opening statement, examine and cross-examine witnesses, introduce evidence, and make a closing argument.

COMMENCING AAA ARBITRATION

Arbitration commences with the filing of a document called a Demand for Arbitration. The party who initiates arbitration is the "claimant." The other party is the "respondent."

---

[2] In the event a party is unable to collect an IFTA arbitration award, the International Film and Television Alliance Market Barring Rule can be invoked to bar a company from participating in the American Film Market. However, this rule will not be invoked against executives of such a company. To bar a company's executives, you need the executive to sign either a guarantee or the IFTA Rider agreement. For additional information about IFTA arbitration, contact IFTA, 10850 Wilshire Blvd., 9th Floor, Los Angeles, CA 90024, (310) 446-1051.

[3] See, *e.g.*, Cal. Code Civ. Proc. § 1280 *et seq.* (California arbitration); 9 U.S.C. §§ 1-15 (Federal Arbitration Act).

Demand forms are available from AAA at no cost, and can be downloaded from the AAA website (www.adr.org). The use of the form is not mandatory, but a demand must contain a statement setting forth the nature of the dispute, the names and addresses of all other parties, the amount involved, if any, the remedy sought, and the hearing locale requested.

Under AAA rules, the claimant must file two copies of the demand at an AAA office, with a copy of the contract arbitration clause attached to each copy, and the filing fee. The original demand is sent to the respondent. Some states require that it be sent by certified mail.

The amount of the filing fee depends on the size of the claim, and ranges from $950 for a claim between $0 and $10,000 to $14,000 for a claim of $5 to $10 million. In addition, the AAA requires a case service fee (also determined by the amount of the claim) to be paid for all cases that proceed to a first hearing. The arbitrator's fees are in addition to these administrative fees, and each arbitrator sets his/her own fee.

Parties may voluntarily submit a dispute to arbitration even though their contract doesn't provide for arbitration. In this case both parties must agree to submit the dispute to arbitration by signing a submission agreement.

SELECTING AN ARBITRATOR

Parties to an arbitration select their own arbitrator. The arbitrator is often an expert in the field with specialized knowledge of the customs and practices of the industry. The AAA entertainment panel in Los Angeles is comprised of arbitrators/mediators, most of whom are entertainment attorneys.

Arbitrators must disqualify themselves if they have a relationship with either of the parties that would prevent them from being completely impartial. Any relationship between the arbitrator and the parties or their attorneys must be disclosed.

DEALMAKING
IN THE
FILM AND
TELEVISION
INDUSTRY—
3RD EDITION

380

THE ARBITRATION HEARING

The arbitration hearing is conducted in an informal setting. Usually the parties, their attorneys, and the arbitrator sit around a conference table. The parties may request that the hearing be recorded or that a stenographer be present to create a written record.

The claimant and the respondent will have an opportunity to introduce evidence in the form of exhibits and witnesses to prove their contentions. Attorneys can use subpoenas to require testimony from people who would prefer not to testify. With a subpoena duces tecum, a witness can be compelled to bring books and documents to the hearing.

The rules of evidence and court procedure do not apply. That does not mean, however, that the parties can be rude and obnoxious or interrupt each other while testifying. The hearing should be conducted in a dignified manner with each party given ample opportunity to prove its case and cross-examine the other party's witnesses.

The hearings are closed—that is, they are not open to the public, and disinterested third parties cannot sit in or review any record of the proceedings.

Under California law an arbitrator is required to include in his/her award a determination of all the questions submitted to the arbitrator.[4] AAA rules allow the arbitrator to grant any remedy that the arbitrator deems just, as long as it is within the scope of the powers given the arbitrator under the arbitration clause. An arbitrator can award monetary damages as well as equitable relief (i.e., the arbitrator can order a party to do something). In California, arbitrators can award punitive damages, the costs of arbitration and reimbursement of attorneys' fees (if the arbitration clause so provides) to the prevailing party.

AFTER THE AWARD

Binding arbitration awards are difficult to overturn. Grounds for appeal are limited. If the losing party does not voluntarily comply with the arbitration award, the prevailing party can confirm the

---

[4] Cal. Code Civ. Proc. § 1283.4.

award in court. Once confirmed, the award is no different from a court judgment, and the judgment creditor can have the sheriff seize the judgment debtor's assets to satisfy the award.

For more information on AAA rules and procedures, call the AAA Customer Service department at (800) 778-7879 or visit their website at www.adr.org.

IFTA ARBITRATION

IFTA (formerly known as the American Film Marketing Association or AFMA) arbitration was established in 1984 to serve the needs of the entertainment industry. IFTA arbitrators are all entertainment attorneys. IFTA screens arbitrators for conflicts before they are assigned to a particular case. Like AAA arbitration, the rules of evidence don't apply. In fact, either of the parties may request that the dispute be resolved solely or in part on the basis of documents filed instead of through a hearing. Arbitration is available to both IFTA members and non-members for disputes arising from production, financing, licensing, and domestic and international exhibition of motion pictures, television and multimedia works.

An IFTA arbitration claim may be filed if the parties expressly opt for IFTA arbitration either in their contract or in a subsequent agreement at the time the claim is filed. There is a $500 surcharge for claims not involving IFTA members. The basic filing fee for a monetary claim is 1% of the amount claimed, with a minimum of $200 and maximum of $3,500 ($4,500 for nonmember claims).[5] If the claim does not seek monetary damages, the filing fee is $200. For more detailed information, visit the IFTA website at www.ifta-online.org.

COMMENCING IFTA ARBITRATION

Notice of Arbitration: The first step is to make a demand by sending a Notice of Arbitration to the other party. There is no standard form, but the IFTA website (www.ifta-online.org/

---

[5] These rates are effective as of July 2007. Rates subject to change.

DEALMAKING
IN THE
FILM AND
TELEVISION
INDUSTRY—
3RD EDITION

382

IndustryServices/Publications/samplenotice.aspx) does provide a sample notice. A letter that states the following information will suffice under IFTA Rules:

- A demand that the dispute be referred to IFTA Arbitration;
- The names, addresses, phone, and fax numbers of the parties and of the filing party's counsel;
- A description of the nature of the dispute and the amount involved;
- A statement of the relief or remedy sought;
- A copy of the contractual clause or agreement providing for IFTA arbitration; and
- A complete copy of the contract relating to the dispute.

Filing the Demand: All documents and the filing fee should be sent to: Arbitral Tribunal, c/o The Arbitral Agent, IFTA, 10850 Wilshire Blvd., 9th Floor, Los Angeles, CA 90024.

The claimant can choose to use the optional pre-arbitration settlement period (see discussion below) or begin the arbitration. IFTA will notify both parties that arbitration is formally initiated. Once notified, the respondent will have 21 days to respond to the demand for arbitration.

IFTA PRE-ARBITRATION SETTLEMENT PROCEDURE

One of the advantages of IFTA Arbitration is the optional, pre-arbitration settlement procedure that the parties may choose to undergo. For $50 (with a $100 surcharge for cases that don't involve at least one IFTA member), IFTA will send a letter to the other party offering a 10-day period of time for the parties to settle the dispute before arbitration is formally commenced. Many disputes have been resolved this way. If the case does go forward, IFTA will apply this fee toward the full filing fee.

ARBITRATOR FEES

Participating IFTA arbitrators have agreed, as a service to the entertainment industry, to work at rates less than their customary fees. A $1,500 deposit from each party is usually required once an arbitrator is designated. If one party fails to send in their deposit, the arbitrator has the discretion to have the other party provide the deposit for both sides. The arbitrator then can draw from the deposit amount, deducting his/her hourly fee in direct proportion to the amount of work done on the arbitration.

An IFTA arbitrator's fee for members is $300 per hour; for non-members, $350 per hour. If the deposit does not cover the fees incurred, the arbitrator may require additional deposits. When an arbitration award is made, the fees to the arbitrators can be included and recovered from the losing party. Any unused portion of the deposit is returned to the parties.

IFTA RIDER TO
INTERNATIONAL DISTRIBUTION AGREEMENT

LICENSOR: _____

DISTRIBUTOR: _____

PICTURE: _____

TERRITORY: _____

CONTRACT REFERENCE CODE: _____

DATE: _____

THE UNDERSIGNED, IN ORDER TO INDUCE THE LICENSOR TO ENTER INTO THE "AGREEMENT" WITH THE DISTRIBUTOR FOR THE PICTURE IN THE TERRITORY WITH THE DATE AND CONTRACT REFERENCE CODE LISTED ABOVE, EXECUTES THIS RIDER TO THE DISTRIBUTION AGREEMENT (HEREINAFTER THE "AGREEMENT") AND AGREES AND CONFIRMS AS FOLLOWS:

1. ARBITRATION

THE UNDERSIGNED AGREES THAT THE UNDERSIGNED SHALL BE A PARTY RESPONDENT IN ANY ARBITRATION AND RELATED COURT PROCEEDING(S) WHICH MAY BE ORIGINALLY BROUGHT OR BROUGHT IN RESPONSE BY THE LICENSOR AGAINST THE DISTRIBUTOR UNDER THE AGREEMENT. THE UNDERSIGNED SHALL HAVE THE RIGHT TO RAISE IN SUCH PROCEEDINGS ONLY THOSE DEFENSES AVAILABLE TO THE DISTRIBUTOR. NO FAILURE OF LICENSOR TO RESORT TO ANY RIGHT, REMEDY, OR SECURITY WILL REDUCE OR DISCHARGE OBLIGATIONS OF THE UNDERSIGNED. NO AMENDMENT, RENEWAL, EXTENSION, WAIVER, OR MODIFICATION OF THE AGREEMENT WILL REDUCE OR DISCHARGE THE OBLIGATION OF THE UNDERSIGNED. THE UNDERSIGNED WAIVES ALL DEFENSES IN THE NATURE OF SURETYSHIP, INCLUDING, WITHOUT LIMITATION, NOTICE OF ACCEPTANCE, PROTEST, NOTICE OF PROTEST, DISHONOR, NOTICE OF DISHONOR, AND EXONERATION. SUBJECT TO PARAGRAPH 2 BELOW, ANY AWARD OR JUDGMENT RENDERED AS A RESULT OF SUCH ARBITRATION AGAINST THE DISTRIBUTOR SHALL BE DEEMED TO BE RENDERED AGAINST THE UNDERSIGNED. IN THE EVENT THAT LICENSOR SHALL OBTAIN AN AWARD FOR DAMAGES AGAINST DISTRIBUTOR, LICENSOR SHALL RECEIVE A SIMILAR AWARD AGAINST THE UNDERSIGNED.

CONTINUED

DEALMAKING
IN THE
FILM AND
TELEVISION
INDUSTRY—
3RD EDITION

384

LITIGATION

Litigation may not provide a viable remedy for an actor, writer, or filmmaker who has been victimized. Lawsuits cost money, and the amount of money at stake may not be enough to justify the expenditure of large legal fees. Moreover, unless there is a contract that provides for reimbursement of attorneys' fees and costs, the prevailing party may not be entitled to recover these expenses. So a filmmaker defrauded by a distributor might be

AFMA RIDER TO
INTERNATIONAL DISTRIBUTION AGREEMENT
(CONTINUED)

2. REMEDIES

NOTWITHSTANDING ANYTHING IN THIS RIDER, IN THE EVENT OF AN AWARD AGAINST THE DISTRIBUTOR, LICENSOR SHALL HAVE NO REMEDY AGAINST THE UNDERSIGNED OTHER THAN THE REMEDY PROVIDED UNDER THE MARKET BARRING RULE OF THE INTERNATIONAL FILM AND TELEVISION ALLIANCE. IN THAT REGARD, THE UNDERSIGNED HEREBY AGREES TO BE BOUND BY THE PROVISIONS OF THE MARKET BARRING RULE WITH RESPECT TO THE AGREEMENT, AS THOUGH THE UNDERSIGNED WERE THE DISTRIBUTOR. LICENSOR CONFIRMS THAT ITS ONLY REMEDY AGAINST THE UNDERSIGNED IN THE EVENT OF A BREACH OF THE AGREEMENT BY, AND BY AN ARBITRATION AWARD FOR DAMAGES AGAINST, THE DISTRIBUTOR SHALL BE APPLICATION OF THE MARKET BARRING RULE, TO THE SAME EXTENT THAT THE MARKET BARRING RULE MAY BE APPLIED AGAINST THE DISTRIBUTOR. LICENSOR WAIVES ANY AND ALL OTHER REMEDIES OF EVERY KIND AND NATURE WHICH IT MAY HAVE WITH RESPECT TO THE UNDERSIGNED'S INDUCEMENTS AND AGREEMENTS HEREIN.

3. ASSIGNMENT

THIS RIDER WILL INURE TO THE BENEFIT OF AND BE FULLY ENFORCEABLE BY LICENSOR AND ITS SUCCESSORS AND ASSIGNS.

4. GOVERNING LAW

THIS RIDER WILL BE GOVERNED BY AND INTERPRETED IN ACCORDANCE WITH THE AGREEMENT, INCLUDING, WITHOUT LIMITATION, THE ARBITRATION PROVISIONS, GOVERNING LAW, AND FORUM PROVISIONS THEREIN STATED.

THE UNDERSIGNED CONFIRMS THAT SERVICE OF ARBITRATION NOTICE, PROCESS, AND OTHER PAPERS SHALL BE MADE TO THE UNDERSIGNED AT THE ADDRESS FIRST SET FORTH IN THE AGREEMENT PERTAINING TO DISTRIBUTOR, UNLESS OTHERWISE SET FORTH BELOW.

WHEREFORE, THE UNDERSIGNED AND THE LICENSOR HEREBY EXECUTE THIS RIDER AS OF THE DATE FIRST SET FORTH ABOVE,

THE "UNDERSIGNED"

NAME: _____

faced with the prospect of spending $50,000 on legal fees to recover $30,000 in damages.[6]

Sometimes an attorney will take cases on a contingency-fee basis. Here the attorney doesn't charge an hourly fee for her time, but if she wins the case, she gets a percentage of the damages (e.g., 30%). Depending on the particular contingency arrangement, the client may be expected to pay for filing fees and other court costs, which can amount to thousands of dollars. Attorneys generally won't take cases on a contingency-fee basis unless the case is likely to be a winner and the potential recovery is large (e.g., $100,000 or more).

Of course, a filmmaker could bring suit himself or herself in Small Claims Court, but the potential recovery is limited to a maximum of $5,000 in California. A filmmaker could bring suit in Municipal or Superior Court without an attorney, but he/she will have to invest a lot of time and energy learning how to prepare and present his/her case. Moreover, unless the filmmaker has had a legal education or is being coached by an attorney, he/she may make fatal mistakes and be denied a recovery altogether.

COURT INFORMATION

FOR MORE INFORMATION ON BOTH STATE (INCLUDING SMALL CLAIMS) AND FEDERAL COURTS, GO TO THESE WEBSITES:

WWW.USCOURTS.GOV (FEDERAL JUDICIARY HOMEPAGE)

WWW.FINDLAW.COM/11STATEGOV (INFORMATION ON COURTS, LAWS AND GOVERNMENT OF ALL 50 STATES)

WWW.COURTS.NET (LINKS TO STATE AND FEDERAL COURTS' WEBSITES)

WWW.NCSCONLINE.ORG/D_KIS/INFO_COURT_WEB_SITES.HTML (NATIONAL CENTER FOR STATE COURTS SITE, FEATURING LINKS TO STATE COURT WEBSITES)

CALIFORNIA COURTS:
GENERAL STATE COURT INFORMATION:

WWW.COURTINFO.CA.GOV

CALIFORNIA SMALL CLAIMS COURT INFORMATION:

WWW.COURTINFO.CA.GOV/SELFHELP/SMALLCLAIMS

NEW YORK COURTS:
GENERAL STATE COURT INFORMATION:

WWW.COURTS.STATE.NY.US/

NEW YORK SMALL CLAIMS COURT INFORMATION:

WWW.NYCOURTS.GOV/COURTS/NYC/SMALLCLAIMS/INDEX.SHTML, AND

WWW.TENANT.NET/COURT/HOWCOURT/SCLAIM.HTML

---

[6] This is why it is important to include an arbitration clause in all your contracts, as well as a provision that the prevailing party is entitled to reimbursement of attorneys' fees and costs.

DEALMAKING
IN THE
FILM AND
TELEVISION
INDUSTRY—
3RD EDITION

386

JURISDICTION

The party who claims they have been injured and files a lawsuit is the plaintiff. The party who is being sued is the defendant.

A plaintiff can only sue a defendant in the proper court. The court must have both personal and subject-matter jurisdiction. Personal jurisdiction requires that the state wherein the suit is filed have some contact with the defendant. If the defendant resides in that state or does business in that state, its courts will have personal jurisdiction over the defendant. Thus a filmmaker could sue a producer who has an office in California, or who conducts business in California, but could not sue a Montana producer in California if the producer had no contact with California.[7]

Subject-matter jurisdiction concerns the competence of a court to adjudicate (judge) the kind of action brought. The type of lawsuit filed and the amount or kind of relief sought will generally determine whether a court has jurisdiction.

Each state is free to label its courts as it chooses. In New York, the highest court is called the Court of Appeal, and the trial-level courts are called the Supreme Court. In California, the highest court is called the Supreme Court, and the trial-level court is called the Superior Court. The following discussion is based on California nomenclature; other states arrange their courts in a similar fashion, although the names of their courts may differ.

Suits can be filed in California Small Claims courts for damages up to $5,000. One cannot use an attorney in Small Claims Court. However, the procedures are fairly simple and information is readily available on how to serve your papers and prepare your case. The hearing is informal; the parties may sit in an ordinary room and present their case to a lawyer who has volunteered to serve as a temporary judge.

The California Superior Courts are courts of general jurisdiction, which means they have jurisdiction over all matters except for those given by statute to other courts.

California courts sometimes share jurisdiction with federal courts unless a federal statute provides that federal jurisdiction is exclusive. Under the U.S. Constitution, in order to bring a case in federal court, one's case must either 1) involve a "federal question";

---

[7] Personal jurisdiction in California is governed by the Code of Civil Procedure Section 410.10, which provides for the broadest possible jurisdiction permitted under the Constitution.

or 2) involve parties that have "diversity of citizenship," which is when the parties reside in different states, or where one party is a citizen of the U.S. and one is a citizen of another country. A case that raises a "federal question" is one that a) involves the U.S. government, the Constitution, or federal laws; or b) involves a controversy between states or between the U.S. and another country. Federal courts have exclusive jurisdiction over federal question cases, as well as over all bankruptcy matters.

To bring a federal case based on diversity, the plaintiff must have a claim involving more than $75,000 in potential damages. Diversity cases are not the exclusive jurisdiction of federal courts; any such case may also be brought in an appropriate state court.

CHAPTER 18

RETAINING ATTORNEYS, AGENTS, AND MANAGERS

ATTORNEYS

California requires lawyers to have written fee agreements with their clients whenever the client's total expense, including fees, will likely exceed $1,000 (Business and Professions Code § 6148).[1] A written fee agreement protects the client by explaining how the lawyer charges for services.

The agreement must disclose the lawyer's hourly rate and other charges, the general nature of legal services to be provided, and the responsibilities of the lawyer and client under the agreement.

If the lawyer fails to comply with the above requirements, the fee agreement becomes voidable at the client's option. In that case the lawyer would be entitled to collect a "reasonable" fee.

Lawyers are regulated and subject to discipline by the bar association of the state or states in which they are licensed. There is an elaborate set of ethical rules governing lawyers' con-

---

[1] The attorney is also required to provide a duplicate copy of the contract signed by both the attorney and the client, or the client's guardian or representative, to the client or to the client's guardian or representative.

DEALMAKING
IN THE
FILM AND
TELEVISION
INDUSTRY—
3RD EDITION

390

duct.[2] For example, an attorney is prohibited from simultaneously representing clients with conflicting interests unless the clients are aware of the conflict and give their written consent.

Attorneys also have a fiduciary duty to their clients. This means the attorney should be putting the client's interests first, ahead of what is convenient or profitable for the attorney.

Before retaining an attorney, you should carefully review the retainer agreement. The rate an attorney charges is often negotiable, and some attorneys may charge a reduced rate to fledgling filmmakers. Some large firms may not consider it worth their while to take on a small client.

An attorney's hourly rate is not always a good measure of how much the client will ultimately spend on legal fees. That is because an experienced $400-per-hour attorney who can draft a contract in an hour may prove less expensive than a $150-an-hour novice who spends four hours to complete the same task, and then may not even get it right.

When hiring an entertainment attorney, it is advisable to retain someone who specializes in the field. A real estate attorney may think it exciting to dabble in entertainment law, but he or she probably does not have the specialized knowledge that an expert in the field possesses. Only someone who is immersed in the industry will know the going rates for services and how to overcome common obstacles. A good entertainment attorney can do more than draft contracts. He/she can open doors for you, recommend distributors and potential partners, and provide strategic advice which may be based more on knowledge of the industry than knowledge of court decisions.

Within the entertainment law field, there is considerable specialization. Some attorneys handle litigation while others may restrict their practice to transactional work (dealmaking). Some attorneys specialize in music, others may focus on television, film, book publishing, or multimedia.

---

[2] A copy of the Business and Professions Code, which outlines the ethical rules for California lawyers, can be found at www.netlawlibraries.com.

SAMPLE ATTORNEY-CLIENT FEE AGREEMENT

Larry Lawyer ("Attorney") and Carole Client ("Client") hereby agree that Attorney will provide legal services to Client on the terms set forth below.

1. CONDITIONS. This Agreement will not take effect, and Attorney will have no obligation to provide legal services, until Client returns a signed copy of this Agreement and pays the initial deposit called for under Paragraph 4.

2. SCOPE OF SERVICES. Client hires Attorney to provide legal services in the following matter: _____ _____ [describe matter]. Attorney will provide those legal services reasonably required to represent Client. Attorney will take reasonable steps to keep Client informed of progress and to respond to Client's inquiries. If a court action is filed, Attorney will represent Client through trial and post-trial motions. This Agreement does not cover representation on appeal or in execution proceedings after judgment. Separate arrangements must be agreed to for those services. Services in any matter not described above will require a separate written agreement.

3. CLIENT'S DUTIES. Client agrees to be truthful with Attorney, to cooperate, to keep Attorney informed of any information or developments which may come to Client's attention, to abide by this Agreement, to pay Attorney's bills on time, and to keep Attorney advised of Client's address, telephone number, and whereabouts. Client will assist Attorney in providing necessary information and documents and will appear when necessary at legal proceedings.

4. DEPOSIT. Client agrees to pay Attorney an initial deposit of $_____ by _____. The hourly charges will be charged against the deposit. The initial deposit, as well as any future deposit, will be held in a trust account. Client authorizes Attorney to use that fund to pay the fees and other charges as they are incurred. Payments from the fund will be made upon remittance to client of a billing statement. Client acknowledges that the deposit is not an estimate of total fees and costs, but merely an advance for security.

Whenever the deposit is exhausted, Attorney reserves the right to demand further deposits, each up to a maximum of $_____ before a trial or arbitration date is set. Once a trial or arbitration date is set, Client shall pay all sums then owing and deposit the attorneys' fees estimated to be incurred in preparing for and completing the trial or arbitration, as well

DEALMAKING
IN THE
FILM AND
TELEVISION
INDUSTRY—
3RD EDITION

392

as the jury fees or arbitration fees, expert witness fees, and other costs likely to be assessed. Those sums may exceed the maximum deposit.

Client agrees to pay all deposits after the initial deposit within _____ days of Attorney's demand. Unless otherwise agreed in writing, any unused deposit at the conclusion of Attorney's services will be refunded.

5. LEGAL FEES AND BILLING PRACTICES. Client agrees to pay by the hour at Attorney's prevailing rates for all time spent on Client's matter by Attorney's legal personnel. Current hourly rates for legal personnel are as follows:

Senior partners	/hour
Partners	/hour
Associates	/hour
Paralegals	/hour
Law clerks	/hour

The rates on this schedule are subject to change on 30 days' written notice to Client. If Client declines to pay increased rates, Attorney will have the right to withdraw as attorney for Client.

The time charged will include the time Attorney spends on telephone calls relating to Client's matter, including calls with Client, witnesses, opposing counsel, or court personnel. The legal personnel assigned to Client's matter may confer among themselves about the matter, as required and appropriate. When they do confer, each person will charge for the time expended, as long as the work done is reasonably necessary and not duplicative. Likewise, if more than one of the legal personnel attends a meeting, court hearing, or other proceeding, each will charge for the time spent. Attorney will charge for waiting time in court and elsewhere and for travel time, both local and out of town.

Time is charged in minimum units of one-tenth (.1) of an hour. The following have higher minimum charges:

Telephone calls:
Letters:
Other:

6. COSTS AND OTHER CHARGES.

(a)   Attorney will incur various costs and expenses in performing legal services under this Agreement. Client agrees to pay for all costs, disbursements, and expenses in addition to the hourly fees. The costs and expenses commonly include: service of process charges, filing fees, court and deposition reporters' fees, jury fees, notary fees, deposition costs, long-distance telephone charges, messenger and other delivery fees, postage, photocopying and other reproduction costs, travel costs including parking, mileage, transportation, meals and hotel costs, investigation expenses, consultants' fees, expert witness, professional, mediator, arbitrator, and/or special master fees, and other similar items. Except for the items listed below, all costs and expenses will be charged at Attorney's cost.

In-office photocopying:	/page
Facsimile charges:	/page
Mileage:	/mile
Other:	

(b)   Out-of-town travel. Client agrees to pay transportation, meals, lodging and all other costs of any necessary out-of-town travel by Attorney's personnel. Client will also be charged the hourly rates for the time legal personnel spend traveling.

(c)   Experts, Consultants, and Investigators. To aid in the preparation or presentation of Client's case, it may become necessary to hire expert witnesses, consultants, or investigators. Client agrees to pay such fees and charges. Attorney will select any expert witnesses, consultants, or investigators to be hired, and Client will be informed of persons chosen and their charges.

Additionally, Client understands that if the matter proceeds to court action or arbitration, Client may be required to pay fees and/or costs to other parties in the action. Any such payment will be entirely the responsibility of Client.

7. BILLING STATEMENTS. Attorney will send Client periodic statements for fees and costs incurred. Each statement will be payable within _____ days of its mailing date. Client may request a statement at intervals of no less than 30 days. If Client so requests, Attorney will provide one within 10 days. The statements shall include the amount, rate, basis of calculation, or other method of determination of the fees and costs, which costs will be clearly identified by item and amount.

8. LIEN. Client hereby grants Attorney a lien on any and all claims or causes of action that are the subject of the

DEALMAKING
IN THE
FILM AND
TELEVISION
INDUSTRY—
3RD EDITION

394

representation under this Agreement. The lien will be for any sums owing to Attorney at the conclusion of services performed. The lien will attach to any recovery Client may obtain, whether by arbitration award, judgment, settlement, or otherwise. The effect of such a lien is that Attorney may be able to compel payment of fees and costs from any such funds recovered on behalf of Client, even if Attorney has been discharged before the end of the case. Because a lien may affect Client's property rights, Client may seek the advice of an independent lawyer of Client's choice before agreeing to such a lien. By initialing this paragraph, Client represents and agrees that Client has had a reasonable opportunity to consult such an independent lawyer and—whether or not Client has chosen to consult such an independent lawyer—Client agrees that Attorney will have a lien as specified above.

_____ (Client Initial Here) _____ (Attorney Initial Here)

9. DISCHARGE AND WITHDRAWAL. Client may discharge Attorney at any time. Attorney may withdraw with Client's consent or for good cause. Good cause includes Client's breach of this Agreement, refusal to cooperate or to follow Attorney's advice on a material matter or any fact or circumstance that would render Attorney's continuing representation unlawful or unethical. When Attorney's services conclude, all unpaid charges will immediately become due and payable. After services conclude, Attorney will, upon Client's request, deliver Client's file, and property in Attorney's possession, unless subject to the lien provided in Paragraph 8 above, whether or not Client has paid for all services.

10. DISCLAIMER OF GUARANTEE AND ESTIMATES. Nothing in this Agreement and nothing in Attorney's statements to Client will be construed as a promise or guarantee about the outcome of the matter. Attorney makes no such promises or guarantees. Attorney's comments about the outcome of the matter are expressions of opinion only. Any estimate of fees given by Attorney shall not be a guarantee. Actual fees may vary from estimates given.

11. ENTIRE AGREEMENT. This Agreement contains the entire agreement of the parties. No other agreement, statement, or promise made on or before the effective date of this Agreement will be binding on the parties.

12. SEVERABILITY IN EVENT OF PARTIAL INVALIDITY. If any provision of this Agreement is held in whole or in part to be unenforceable for any reason, the remainder of that provision and of the entire Agreement will be severable and remain in effect.

13. MODIFICATION BY SUBSEQUENT AGREEMENT. This Agreement may be modified by subsequent agreement of the parties only by an instrument in writing signed by both of them, or an oral agreement only to the extent that the parties carry it out.

14. EFFECTIVE DATE. This Agreement will govern all legal services performed by Attorney on behalf of Client commencing with the date Attorney first performed services. The date at the beginning of this Agreement is for reference only. Even if this Agreement does not take effect, Client will be obligated to pay Attorney the reasonable value of any services Attorney may have performed for Client.

THE PARTIES HAVE READ AND UNDERSTOOD THE FOREGOING TERMS AND AGREE TO THEM AS OF THE DATE ATTORNEY FIRST PROVIDED SERVICES. IF MORE THAN ONE CLIENT SIGNS BELOW, EACH AGREES TO BE LIABLE, JOINTLY AND SEVERALLY, FOR ALL OBLIGATIONS UNDER THIS AGREEMENT. CLIENT SHALL RECEIVE A FULLY EXECUTED DUPLICATE OF THIS AGREEMENT.

DATED: _____   _____

                                      Carole Client
                                        Address:_____

                                        _____

                                        Telephone:_____

DATED: _____   Larry Lawyer & Associates

                                        By:_____

                                        Larry Lawyer

AGENTS

An agent differs from an attorney in several important respects. First, the agent is a salesperson whose primary role is to find employment for his or her clients. An agent spends a great deal of time covering the town to learn what kinds of projects and talent potential buyers (i.e., studios, producers) are seeking and then tries to fill those needs from his/her client list. While a lawyer may incidentally help a client find work, the lawyer's primary role is to negotiate deals and protect the legal rights

DEALMAKING
IN THE
FILM AND
TELEVISION
INDUSTRY—
3RD EDITION

396

of the client. Lawyers don't systematically cover the town the way agents do.

Second, agents work on a contingency-fee basis. In California, agents charge a 10% commission. For instance, if an agent sells a client's screenplay for $50,000, the agent would receive a fee of $5,000. Lawyers, on the other hand, usually work on an hourly basis, often charging $300 or more for each hour of their time. Some law firms charge clients a percentage of earnings, often 5%, for their services. This type of deal, however, is typically offered only to clients who are established and who are employed on a regular basis.

From the client's point of view, the advantage of a contingency fee is that the client doesn't incur any expense unless and until a deal is closed. Thus, the agent or attorney has a strong incentive to reach an agreement. But if the representative only spends a few hours on a deal, a contingency fee may produce an excessive fee compared to one computed on an hourly basis.

Agents sometimes negotiate routine deals for clients without the assistance of a lawyer. For complex matters, though, talent should consult an attorney. Clients may want both an agent and an attorney to review their deals. In my experience, lawyers tend to be more aggressive than agents on many deal points. As salespeople, agents may be reluctant to push too hard because they need to return to the buyer next week to sell another client or script.

Artists need to understand the difference between agents and managers. Agents try to find work for their clients; managers advise clients on career matters and help manage their careers.

Under some states' laws, including California, managers are prohibited from soliciting work for their clients, but they often do so anyway. In such a case, the personal manager is in a vulnerable position because, under the law, the client may be able to rescind the representation agreement and not pay the manager.

California and several other states license talent agents. California Labor Code § 1700.5 requires that talent agents must first procure a license from the Labor Commissioner.[3] An agent who engages in wrongdoing may lose his/her license.[4] A con-

---

[3] The website www.netlawlibraries.com also includes the California Labor Codes, which govern talent agents.
[4] The Labor Commissioner cannot grant a license to a person whose license has been revoked within three years prior to the date of application.

tract between an unlicensed agent and artist is void.[5] Personal managers, on the other hand, are not licensed.[6]

Agents may enter into franchise agreements with one or more talent guilds. These franchise agreements take precedence over any agreement between the agent and a guild member. The franchise agreements provide artists with certain protections in addition to what the states require of agents. For example, talent may have the right to terminate the agency agreement if the agent is unable to secure any offers of employment within a certain time.

Since 1937, SAG and the Association of Talent Agents (ATA) and its East Coast counterpart, the National Association of Talent Representatives (NATR), had a franchise agreement that provided benefits to both actors and agents. The agreement ended in 2002 when SAG members voted down a referendum that would have made broad-based changes to the franchise agreement.

The relationship fell apart when agents wanted to renegotiate the deal so that they could have some of the flexibility that managers, who are unregulated, retain. Managers can serve as producers on projects their actor clients are employed on, which could potentially pose a conflict of interest in representing clients. Agencies also wanted to be able to sell parts of their companies to ad agencies or independent production companies.

No replacement agreement has been made to date, although sister union AFTRA did enter into a franchise agreement with the agents. The SAG National Board has temporarily suspended application of Rule 16(a) of the Rules and Regulations section of the SAG Constitution, which requires SAG members to be represented only by a franchised agent. Therefore, SAG members may continue to be represented by talent agents who are not franchised. Consequently, actors now sign agreements with their agents that are approved by the state but allow agents to share in more residual income than they were entitled to under the prior franchise agreement.

Agents don't always enter into written representation agreements with their clients. They may work on a handshake. This may be acceptable to the client since the agent's conduct is regulated by the state and one or more guilds. Moreover, a written

---

[5] *Waisbren v. Peppercorn Productions, Inc.*, 48 Cal. Rptr. 2d 437, 41 Cal. App. 4th 246, (Cal. Dist. Ct. App. 1995)(interpreting California Labor Code § 1700.5).
[6] *Id.*

DEALMAKING
IN THE
FILM AND
TELEVISION
INDUSTRY—
3RD EDITION

398

agreement doesn't guarantee that an agent will find the client work. From a practical point of view, if an agent is unable to secure work, there may be no sense in continuing the relationship for either party.

The agency agreement defines the fields in which the agent will represent the client. A client involved in multi-disciplinary activities may need several agents. For example, the client may sign a New York literary agent to represent her for publishing, a Hollywood talent agent for screenwriting, and a personal-appearance agent for live performances. Some agencies cover several fields while others focus on one. For example, an agency may specialize in dancers, another may only deal in television commercials. While a person may have several agents, agents will usually insist on exclusivity within their field of practice.

SAG MOTION PICTURE/TELEVISION AGENCY CONTRACT

THIS AGREEMENT, made and entered into at _____ (Location of Agreement), by and between _____ (Talent Agent), a talent agent, hereinafter called the "Agent", and _____ (Actor Name), _____ (Social Security Number), hereinafter called the "Actor."

WITNESSETH:

1. The Actor engages the Agent as his/her agent for the following fields as defined in Screen Actors Guild Codified Agency Regulations Rule 16(g) (hereinafter "Rule 16(g)"), and the Agent accepts such engagement:

[Mark appropriate space(s)]
Theatrical Motion Pictures
Television Motion Pictures

If television motion pictures are included herein for purposes of representation and if during the term of this agency contract the Actor enters into a series or term employment contract for services in television motion pictures, under which he/she agrees also to render services in program commercials or spots, this agency contract shall include representation of the Actor in connection with his/her employment in said commercials, and representation of the Actor in said commercials shall not be deemed included in any separate agency contract which the Actor may have entered into covering commercials.

This contract is limited to motion pictures in the above-designated field(s) and to contracts of the Actor as an actor in such motion pictures, and any reference herein to contracts or employment whereby Actor renders his/her services refers to contracts or employment in such motion pictures unless otherwise specifically stated.

2. The term of this contract shall be for a period of _____ (Contract Term) commencing _____ (Term Commencement).

3. (a) The Actor agrees to pay to the Agent a commission equal to _____ percent (Commission to Agent) of all monies or other consideration received by the Actor, directly or indirectly, under contracts of employment (or in connection with his/her employment under said employment contracts) entered into during the term specified in Paragraph 2 or in existence when this Agency Contract is entered into except to such extent as the Actor may be obligated to pay commissions on such existing employment contracts to another agent. Commissions shall be payable when and as such monies or other consideration are received by the Actor, or by anyone else for or on the Actor's behalf. Commission payments are subject to the limitations of Rule 16(g).

(b) Commissions on compensation paid to Actor for domestic reruns, theatrical exhibition, foreign exhibition, or supplementary market exhibition of television motion pictures are subject to the provisions of Rule 16(g).

(c) Commissions on commercials included herein under Paragraph 1 above shall be subject to the rules governing commercials provided by Rule 16(g).

(d) No commissions shall be payable on any of the following:

(i) Separate amounts paid to Actor not as compensation but for travel or living expenses incurred by Actor;

(ii) Separate amounts paid to Actor not as compensation but as reimbursement for necessary expenditures actually incurred by Actor in connection with Actor's employment, such as for damage to or loss of wardrobe, special hairdresser, etc.;

(iii) Amounts paid to Actor as penalties for violations by Producer of any of the provisions of the SAG collective-bargaining contracts, such as meal period violations, rest period violations, penalties or interest on delinquent payments;

(iv) Sums payable to Actor for the release on free television or for supplemental market exhibition of theatrical motion pictures produced after January 31, 1960, under the provisions

DEALMAKING
IN THE
FILM AND
TELEVISION
INDUSTRY—
3RD EDITION

400

of the applicable collective-bargaining agreement providing for such payment. However, if the Actor's individual theatrical motion picture employment contract provides for compensation in the event the motion picture made for theatrical exhibition is exhibited over free television or in supplemental market exhibition, in excess of the minimum compensation payable under the applicable collective-bargaining agreement in effect at the time the employment contract was executed, commissions shall be payable on such compensation.

(v) Sums payable to Actor for foreign telecasting on free television of television motion pictures and commercials under the provisions of the applicable collective-bargaining agreements. However, if the Actor's contract provides for compensation in excess of minimum under the applicable collective-bargaining agreements in effect at the time of employment, commissions shall be payable on such sums.

(vi) On any employment contract which is in violation of SAG collective bargaining agreements. For example, employment contracts providing for "free days," "free rehearsal," "free looping," "a break in consecutive employment," etc., shall not be commissionable. This paragraph is not subject to SAG waiver.

(vii) On any employment contract for television motion pictures which provides for any prepayment or buyout of domestic or foreign residuals or theatrical release, or supplemental market fees, other than those permitted by the appropriate SAG collective-bargaining agreement, unless such provisions of individual employment contracts are expressly approved by SAG.

(e) Any monies or other consideration received by the Actor, or by anyone for or on his/her behalf, in connection with any termination of any contract of the Actor by virtue of which the Agent would otherwise be entitled to receive commission, or in connection with the settlement of any such contract, or any litigation arising out of any such contract, shall also be monies in connection with which the Agent is entitled to the aforesaid percentage. However, in such event the Actor shall be entitled to deduct attorneys' fees, expenses, and court costs before computing the amount upon which the Agent is entitled to his/her percentage. The Actor shall also be entitled to deduct reasonable legal expenses in connection with the collection of monies or other consideration due the Actor arising out of an employment contract in motion pictures before computing the amount upon which the Agent is entitled to his/her percentage.

(f) The aforesaid percentage shall be payable by the Actor to the Agent during the term of this contract and thereafter only where specifically provided herein and in the Regulations.

(g) The Agent shall be entitled to the aforesaid percentage after the expiration of the term specified in Paragraph 2 for so long a period thereafter as the Actor continues to receive monies or other consideration under or upon employment contracts entered into by the Actor during the term specified in Paragraph 2 hereof, including monies or other consideration received by the Actor under the extended term of any such employment contract, resulting from the exercise of an option or options under such an employment contract, extending the term of such employment contract, whether such options be exercised prior to or after the expiration of the term specified in Paragraph 2, subject, however, to the applicable limitations set forth in the Regulations.

(h) If, during the period in which the Agent is entitled to commissions, a contract of employment of the Actor is terminated before the expiration of the term thereof, as said term has been extended by the exercise of options therein contained, by joint action of the Actor and employer, or by the action of either of them, other than on account of Act of God, illness, or the like, and the Actor enters into a new contract of employment with said employer within a period of sixty (60) days, such new contract shall be deemed to be in substitution of the contract terminated as aforesaid, subject, however, to the applicable limitations set forth in the Regulations. No contract entered into after said sixty (60) day period shall be deemed to be in substitution of the contract terminated as aforesaid. Contracts of substitution have the same effect as contracts for which they were substituted. However, any increase or additional salary, bonus, or other compensation payable to the Actor thereunder over and above the amounts payable under the contract of employment which was terminated shall be deemed an adjustment, and, unless the Agent shall have a valid agency contract in effect at the time of such adjustment, the Agent shall not be entitled to any commissions on any such additional or increased amounts. In no event may a contract of substitution with an employer extend the period of time during which the Agent is entitled to commission beyond the period that the Agent would have been entitled to commission had no substitution taken place. A change in form of an employer for the purpose of evading this provision or a change in the corporate form of an employer resulting from reorganization or the like shall not preclude the application of these provisions.

DEALMAKING
IN THE
FILM AND
TELEVISION
INDUSTRY—
3RD EDITION

402

(i) So long as the Agent receives commissions from the Actor, the Agent shall be obliged to service the Actor and perform the obligations of this Agency Contract with respect to the services of the Actor on which such commissions are based, unless the Agent is relieved therefrom under express provisions of the Regulations.

(j) The Agent has no right to receive money unless the Actor receives the same, or unless the same is received for or on his/her behalf, and then only in the above percentage when and as received. Money paid pursuant to legal process to the Actor's creditors, or by virtue of assignment or direction of the Actor, and deductions from the Actor's compensation made pursuant to law in the nature of a collection or tax at the source, such as Social Security, Old Age Pension taxes, State Disability taxes, or income taxes, shall be treated as compensation received for or on the Actor's behalf.

4. Should the Agent, during the term specified in Paragraph 2, negotiate a contract of employment for the Actor and secure for the Actor a bona fide offer of employment, which offer is communicated by the Agent to the Actor in reasonable detail and in writing or by other corroborative action, and the Actor declines such offer, and if, within sixty (60) days after the date upon which the Agent gives such information to the Actor, the Actor accepts said offer of employment on substantially the same terms, then the Actor shall be required to pay commissions to the Agent upon such contract of employment. If an agent engaged under a prior agency contract is entitled to collect commissions under the foregoing circumstances, the Agent with whom this contract is executed waives his/her commission to the extent that the prior agent is entitled to collect the same.

5. (a) The Agent may represent other persons who render services in motion pictures, or in other branches of the entertainment industry.

(b) Unless and until prohibited by the Actor, the Agent may make known the fact that he/she is the sole and exclusive representative of the Actor in the motion picture fields covered hereby. However, it is expressly understood that even though the Agent has not breached the contract, the Actor may at any time, with or without discharging the Agent, and regardless of whether he/she has legal grounds for discharge of the Agent, by written notice to the Agent prohibit him/her from rendering further services for the Actor or from holding himself/herself out as the Actor's Agent, and such action shall not give Agent any rights or remedies against Actor. The Agent's rights under this paragraph continue only as long as Actor consents thereto, provided, however, that this does not apply to the Agent's right to commissions. In the event of any such written notice to the Agent, the ninety-one (91) day period set forth in Paragraph 6 of this Agency Contract is suspended and extended by the period of time that the Agent is prohibited from rendering services for the Actor.

6. (a) If this is an initial agency contract and if Actor fails to be employed and receive, or be entitled to receive compensation for ten (10) days' employment in the initial one hundred fifty-one (151) days of the contract, provided further that if no bona fide offer of employment is received by the Actor within any consecutive period of one hundred twenty (120) days during the initial one hundred fifty-one (151) day period, or if during any other period of ninety-one (91) days immediately preceding the giving of the notice of termination hereinafter mentioned in this Paragraph, the Actor fails to be employed and receive, or be entitled to receive compensation for ten (10) days' employment, whether such employment is from fields under SAG's jurisdiction or any other branch of the entertainment industry in which the Agent may be authorized by written contract to represent the Actor, then either the Actor or Agent may terminate the engagement of the Agent hereunder by written notice to the other party, subject to the qualifications hereinafter in this Paragraph set forth. Each day the Actor renders services or may be required to render services in motion pictures shall count as one (1) day's employment. For the purpose of determining what constitutes a day's employment in other fields of the entertainment industry, the following rules shall govern:

(i) Each separate original radio broadcast (including rehearsal time), whether live or recorded, and each transcribed program shall be considered a day's employment.

(ii) Each separate live television broadcast shall be considered a minimum of two (2) days' employment. However, each day spent in rehearsal over the minimum of two (2) days inclusive of the day of telecast, shall be considered an additional one-half (½) day's employment.

(iii) A rebroadcast, whether recorded or live, or by an off-the-line recording, or by a prior recording, or time spent in rehearsal for any employment in the radio broadcasting or radio transcription industry, shall not be considered such employment. A re-telecast of a live television program and a rerun of television motion picture entertainment film or commercial shall likewise not be considered such employment.

DEALMAKING
IN THE
FILM AND
TELEVISION
INDUSTRY—
3RD EDITION

404

(iv) Each master phonograph record recorded by the Actor shall be one (1) day's employment.

(v) In all other branches of the entertainment industry, except as set forth above, each day the Actor renders services or may be required to render services for compensation shall count as one (1) day's employment.

(b) The ninety-one (91) day period which is the basis of termination shall be extended by the amount of employment the Actor would have received from calls for his/her services in any other branch of the entertainment industry in which the Actor is a recognized performer and at or near the Actor's usual places of employment at a salary and from an employer commensurate with the Actor's prestige, which calls are actually received by the Agent and reported to the Actor in writing or by other corroborative action, when the Actor is in such a locality (away from his/her usual places of employment) that he/she cannot return in response to such a call, or when the Actor is unable to respond to such a call by reason of physical or mental incapacity or any other reason beyond his/her control, or by reason of another engagement in a field in which the Actor is not represented by the Agent, provided, however, that if the Actor is rendering services in another engagement in a field in which the Agent is authorized to represent the Actor, then the time spent in such engagement shall not be added to the ninety-one (91) day period. Regardless of whether or not the Agent is authorized to represent the Actor on the legitimate stage, if the Actor accepts an engagement on the legitimate stage under a run of the play contract, the ninety-one (91) day period which is the basis of termination shall be extended by the length of such run of the play contract, including rehearsals. The ninety-one (91) day period which is the basis of termination shall also be extended for any period of time during which the Actor has declared himself/herself to be unavailable and has so notified the Agent in writing or by other corroborative action or has confirmed in writing or by other corroborative action a communication from the Agent to such effect.

(c) In the event that the Agent has given the Actor notice in writing, or by other corroborative action, of a bona fide offer of employment as an actor in any branch of the entertainment industry in which the Actor is a recognized performer at or near his/her usual place of employment at a salary and from an employer commensurate with the Actor's prestige (and there is in fact such an offer), which notice sets forth in detail the terms of the proposed employment and the Actor refuses or fails within a reasonable time after receipt of such notice to accept such proffered employment, then the period of guaranteed employment in said offer shall be deemed as time worked by the Actor in computing time worked with reference to the right of the Actor to terminate under the provisions of this Paragraph.

(d) The Actor may not exercise the right of termination if at the time he/she attempts to do so the Actor is under a contract or contracts for the rendition of his/her services in the entertainment industry, in any or all fields in which the Agent is authorized by written contract to represent the Actor, which contract or contracts in the aggregate guarantee the Actor:

(i) Compensation for such services of seventy thousand dollars ($70,000) or more; or

(ii) Fifty (50) or more days' employment, during the ninety-one (91) days in question plus the succeeding two hundred seventy-three (273) days after said ninety-one (91) day period.

(e) Saturdays, Sundays, and holidays are included in counting days elapsed during the ninety-one (91) and two hundred seventy-three (273) day periods provided.

(f) No termination hereunder shall deprive the Agent of the right to receive commission or compensation on monies earned or received by the Actor prior to the date of termination, or earned or received by the Actor after the date of termination of the Agent's engagement, on contracts for the Actor's services entered into by the Actor prior to the effective date of any such termination.

(g) Periods of lay-off, leave of absence, or any periods during which the Actor is not performing and is prohibited from rendering services for others in the motion picture field under and during the term of any motion picture employment contract shall not be deemed periods of unemployment hereunder. The "term of any motion picture employment contract" as used in this subparagraph shall not include any unexercised options.

(h) Where the Actor does not actually render his/her services for which he/she has been employed but nevertheless is compensated therefore, the same shall be considered as employment hereunder. This shall not apply to employment on live television shows, which employment is computed according to the formula set forth in Subparagraph (a) (ii) of this Paragraph.

(i) If, at any time during the term of the agency contract,

DEALMAKING
IN THE
FILM AND
TELEVISION
INDUSTRY—
3RD EDITION

406

the production of motion pictures in general (as distinguished from production at one or more studios) should be suspended, thereupon the ninety-one (91) day period herein mentioned shall be extended by the period of such suspension.

(j) If the Actor is under an employment contract which provides that any part of the Actor's guaranteed compensation shall be deferred or if said compensation is spread over a period prior or subsequent to the time of the actual performance of Actor's services under said employment contract, then for the purpose of determining the Actor's right to terminate under the provisions of Subparagraph (d) of this Paragraph, the guaranteed compensation shall be deemed to have been paid to the Actor during the period of the actual performance of Actor's services under said employment contract.

(k) Anything herein to the contrary notwithstanding, if the Agent submits to the Actor a bona fide offer of employment in writing or by other corroborative action, as defined in Paragraph 6(c), after the right of termination has accrued under Paragraph 6 but the Actor has not yet terminated the agency contract, and if the Actor thereafter terminates the agency contract pursuant to Paragraph 6 and thereafter accepts the offer within sixty (60) days of the date of submission of the offer to the Actor by the agent, the Actor shall pay the Agent commission on the compensation received by the Actor pursuant to such offer.

(l) Other than in cases of initial agency contracts subject to the one hundred fifty-one (151) day clause provided by Paragraph 6(a), the right of termination provided by the ninety-one (91) day termination provisions of this Paragraph 6, the Actor shall also have the right of termination beginning with the eighty-second day of the ninety-one (91) day period whenever it becomes apparent that the Agent will be unable to procure the required employment pursuant to this Paragraph 6 during such ninety-one (91) day period. In considering whether it has become so apparent, the possibility that after the Actor exercises the right of termination the Agent might preclude exercise of the right by compliance with Subparagraphs (b), (c) or (d) hereof shall be disregarded. To illustrate: If the Actor has had no employment for eighty-two (82) days, Actor may terminate on the eighty-second day, since only nine (9) days remain, and Agent cannot obtain ten (10) days' employment for the Actor in such period. If Actor received one day's employment in eighty-three (83) days, Actor may terminate on the eighty-third day, since only eight (8) days remain, and Agent cannot obtain ten (10) days' employment for Actor in such period.

(m) Employment at SAG minimum shall be deemed "employment" and/or "work" for purposes of this Paragraph 6.

7. Rule 16(g) of the Screen Actors Guild Codified Agency Regulations, which contains regulations governing the relations of its members to talent agents, is hereby referred to and by this reference hereby incorporated herein and made a part of this Contract. The provisions of said Rule are herein sometimes referred to as the "Regulations," and the Screen Actors Guild, Inc., is herein sometimes referred to as "SAG."

8. The Agent agrees that during the term of this Contract the following persons only shall have the responsibility of personally supervising the Actor's business and of servicing and being available to the Actor. The name of one of the persons shall be inserted in the Actor's own handwriting.

(This provision is a note from SAG to the Actor and not a part of the contract. If the Actor is executing this contract in reliance on the fact that a particular person is connected with the Agent, then the Actor should insert only such person's name in the space. If the Actor is not executing this contract in reliance on such fact, then the Agent shall insert not more than one name, and the Actor shall insert one name.)

The Agent, upon request of the Actor, shall assign either one of such persons who may be available (and at least one of them always shall be available upon reasonable notice from the Actor) and whom the Actor may designate to conduct negotiations for the Actor at such city or its environs and such person shall do so; it being understood that subagents employed by the Agent who are not named herein may handle agency matters for the Actor or may aid either of the named persons in handling agency matters for the Actor. In the event both of the persons above named shall cease to be active in the affairs of the Agent by reason of death, disability, retirement, or any other reason, the Actor shall have the right to terminate this contract upon written notice to the Agent. The rights of the parties in such case are governed by Sections XI and XII of the Regulations.

9. The Agent agrees to maintain telephone service and an office open during all reasonable business hours (emergencies such as sudden illness or death excepted) within the city of _____ (Agent City), or its environs, throughout the term of this agreement, and agrees that some representative of the Agent will be present at such office during such business hours. This Contract is void unless the blank in this paragraph is filled in with the name of a city at which the Agent does maintain an office to render services to actors.

DEALMAKING
IN THE
FILM AND
TELEVISION
INDUSTRY—
3RD EDITION

408

10. If the Actor is employed under a series or term contract, the Actor shall have the right to terminate this Contract during the thirty (30) day period immediately following any annual anniversary date of the series or term contract then in effect by giving the Agent thirty (30) days' written notice of his/her intention to so terminate this contract. Exercise of this termination right shall not affect the Actor's commissions obligation hereunder.

11. Any controversy under this Contract, or under any contract executed in renewal or extension hereof or in substitution hereof or alleged to have been so executed, or as to the existence, execution, or validity hereof or thereof, or the right of either party to avoid this or any such contract or alleged contract on any grounds, or the construction, performance, nonperformance, operation, breach, continuance, or termination of this or any such contract, shall be submitted to arbitration in accordance with the arbitration provisions in the Regulations, regardless of whether either party has terminated or purported to terminate this or any such contract or alleged contract. Under this Contract, the Agent undertakes to endeavor to secure employment for the Actor. This provision is inserted in this Contract pursuant to a rule of the SAG, a bona fide labor union, which Rule regulates the relations of its members to talent agents. Reasonable written notice shall be given to the Labor Commissioner of the State of California of the time and place of any arbitration hearing hereunder. The Labor Commissioner of the State of California, or his/her authorized representative, has the right to attend all arbitration hearings. The clauses relating to the Labor Commissioner of the State of California shall not be applicable to cases not falling under the provisions of Section 1700.45 of the Labor Code of the State of California.

12. Both parties hereto state and agree that they are bound by the Regulations and by all of the modifications heretofore or hereafter made thereto pursuant to the SAG Basic Contract and by all waivers granted by SAG pursuant to said Basic Contract or to the Regulations.

13. (a) Anything herein to the contrary notwithstanding, if the Regulations should be held invalid, all references thereto in this Contract shall be eliminated; all limitations of the Regulations on any of the provisions of this Contract shall be released, and the portions of this contract which depend upon reference to the Regulations shall be deleted, and the provisions of this Contract otherwise shall remain valid and enforceable.

(b) Likewise, if any portion of the Regulations should be held invalid, such holding shall not affect the validity of remaining portions of the Regulations or of this Contract; and if the portion of the Regulations so held invalid should be a portion specifically referred to in this Contract, then such reference shall be eliminated herefrom in the same manner and with like force and effect as herein provided in the event the Regulations are held invalid; and the provisions of this Contract otherwise shall remain valid and enforceable.

Whether or not the Agent is the Actor's agent at the time this contract is executed, it is understood that in executing this Contract each party has independent access to the Regulations and has relied exclusively upon his/her own knowledge thereof.

IN WITNESS WHEREOF, the parties hereto have executed this agreement the _____ day of _____, 20__.

_____
Actor

_____
Agent

By: _____

This talent agent is licensed by the Labor Commissioner of the State of California.

This talent agent is franchised by the Screen Actors Guild, Inc.

The form of this contract has been approved by the State Labor Commissioner of the State of California on January 11, 1991.

This form of contract has been approved by the Screen Actors Guild, Inc.

The foregoing references to California may be deleted or appropriate substitutions made in other states.

PERSONAL MANAGERS

As previously noted, personal managers are not licensed by the state or federal government.

In the entertainment industry, recording and performing artists often retain managers. Personal managers can give more personal attention than a talent agent. The manager will often tour with the client, handle the details of pursuing a career and act as an advisor.

DEALMAKING
IN THE
FILM AND
TELEVISION
INDUSTRY—
3RD EDITION

410

Personal managers should be distinguished from business managers. The latter manage one's investment portfolio and assets. Personal managers should also be distinguished from publicists. Publicists either help a client obtain publicity, or in the case of a celebrity, try to manage the publicity by deciding which interview requests to grant and how to minimize negative publicity.

Here is an agreement between a personal manager and a novice actor. A star would be able to negotiate a more favorable agreement.

MANAGEMENT AGREEMENT

(DATE)

Via U.S. Mail And Facsimile:

_____

_____

_____

_____

Re: Management Agreement

Dear _____:

This letter is to confirm upon signature of both parties the terms between you ("Artist") and _____ ("Representative") as your managerial representation in the entertainment industry. The terms are as follows:

1. Term: The Term of this Agreement shall commence on the date hereof and continue for a period of two (2) years from the date upon which Representative receives from you a new set of acting "Head Shots" and a professional videotape of you in acting situations. The Term shall automatically be extended for successive one (1) year terms unless either party notifies the other party in writing not later than sixty (60) days prior to the end of the applicable term that it wishes to terminate this Agreement.

2. Exclusivity: During the Term stated above, Representative shall have the sole and exclusive right to perform said Managerial services in all forms of entertainment and media except modeling unless Representative secures a modeling agent for Artist, in which event this Agreement shall apply to modeling as well. Artist understands and acknowledges that Representative may represent other artists who may compete with Artist in the entertainment and media business.

3. Services: Representative agrees to use its reasonable efforts to perform one or more of the following services for you:

a) To represent you and act as your advisor in all business negotiations and matters of policy relating to your career and the media and entertainment businesses;

b) To cooperate with and supervise your relations with any theatrical, television, or literary agents employed on your behalf; to advise and counsel you in the selecting of third parties, to assist, accompany, or improve your artistic presentation and to make himself/herself or staff members reasonably available at reasonable times to confer with you in all matters concerning your career;

c) To perform other reasonable services customarily rendered by personal managers in the entertainment business.

4. Compensation: In consideration of Representative's services, Artist agrees that Representative shall be entitled to receive a fee equal to fifteen percent (15%) of all gross compensation received by or credited to Artist in connection with services rendered or rights granted by Artist in the entertainment and media business payable as and when Artist receives such compensation. Said compensation shall continue in perpetuity with respect to services rendered and/or rights granted during the Term hereof notwithstanding any prior termination of this Agreement for any reason. Artist also agrees to pay Representative said commission following the Term hereof upon and with respect to all of Artist's gross compensation received after the expiration of the Term hereof but derived from any and all employments, engagements, contracts, agreements, and activities negotiated, entered into, commenced, or performed during the Term hereof relating to any of the foregoing, and upon any and all extensions, renewals, and substitutions thereof and therefor, and upon any resumptions of such employments, engagements, contracts, agreements, and activities which may have been discontinued during the Term hereof and resumed within one (1) year thereafter. The term "gross compensation" shall include, but not be limited to, salaries, earnings, fees, royalties, gifts, bonuses, shares of profit, shares of stock, partnership interests, percentages and the total amount paid for a television or radio program (live or recorded), motion picture, or other entertainment products or services, earned or received directly or indirectly by Artist or by Artist's heirs, executors, administrators, or assigns, or by any person, firm, or corporation on Artist's behalf.

5. Receipt of Compensation: Representative is hereby authorized to receive, on Artist's behalf, all "gross compensation and other

DEALMAKING
IN THE
FILM AND
TELEVISION
INDUSTRY—
3RD EDITION

412

considerations" and to deposit all such funds into a separate trust account in a bank or savings and loan association. Representative shall have the right to withdraw from such account all expenses and commissions to which Representative is entitled hereunder and shall remit the balance to Artist or as Artist shall direct. Notwithstanding the foregoing, Artist may, at any time, require all "gross compensation or other considerations" to be paid to a third party, provided that such party shall irrevocably be directed in writing to pay Representative all expenses and commissions due hereunder.

6. Authority of Manager: Representative is hereby appointed Artist's exclusive, true, and lawful attorney-in-fact, to do any or all of the following, for or on behalf of Artist, during the Term of this Agreement:

(a) approve and authorize any and all publicity and advertising, subject to Artist's previous approval;

(b) approve and authorize the use of Artist's name, photograph, likeness, voice, sound effects, caricatures, and literary, artistic, and musical materials for the purpose of advertising any and all products and services, subject to Artist's previous approval;

(c) execute in Artist's name contracts for the granting of rights and rendering of services by Artist, subject to Artist's previous consent to the material terms thereof; and

(d) execute Artist's name on checks or other negotiable instruments for the purpose of depositing same into Representative's Client's Trust Account for disbursal to Artist and Representative in accordance with the terms hereof;

(e) without in any way limiting the foregoing, generally do, execute, and perform any other act, deed, matter, or thing whatsoever, that ought to be done on behalf of the Artist by a personal manager.

7. Producing: In the event Representative elects to become "attached" as, and is actually engaged, as a Producer of a project created by Artist and/or for which Artist is also rendering services and/or granting rights, Artist and Representative shall either negotiate in good faith directly Representative's producing compensation or Representative shall negotiate said compensation directly with the financier, and in either such event Representative shall not commission Artist's services or rights granted in connection with such project.

8. Assignment: Representative may assign this agreement to any corporation or entity which acquires Representative or

with which Representative becomes affiliated with at any time during the term of this agreement.

9. Disclaimer; Waiver: Nothing in this Agreement and nothing in Representative's statements to Artist will be construed as a promise or guarantee about the outcome or the results of Representative's services hereunder. Artist understands and acknowledges that the entertainment picture business is risky, unpredictable, and subject to cultural trends and the whims and personal tastes of buyers of entertainment products and services. Artist acknowledges that Representative makes no such promises or guarantees as to the results of the services hereunder. Artist also understands, acknowledges, and agrees that the nature of the entertainment business and the personal relationships that develop from the production, financing, and distribution of entertainment products and services may result in conflicts of interest or perceived conflicts of interest. Artist nevertheless hereby waives any claims against Representative concerning conflicts of interest.

10. Advertising: During the Term hereof, Representative shall have the exclusive right to advertise and publicize Representative as Artist's personal manager and representative with respect to the entertainment industry.

11. Advances: Artist shall pay directly for all photographs, videos, and other materials reasonably necessary to promote Artist's career. Representative shall not be obligated to, but may make loans or advances to Artist or for Artist's account and incur some expenses on Artist's behalf for the furtherance of Artist's career in amounts to be determined solely by Representative in Representative's best business judgment. Artist hereby authorizes Representative to recoup and retain the amount of any such loans, advances, and/or expenses, including, without limitation, transportation and living expenses while traveling, promotion and publicity expenses, and all other reasonable and necessary expenses, from any sums Representative may receive on behalf of Artist. Artist shall reimburse Representative for any reasonable expenses incurred by Representative on behalf of Artist, including, without limitation, long-distance calls, faxes, courier expenses, and travel expenses, but no single item of expense in excess of one hundred dollars ($100) shall be incurred by Representative without the prior approval of Artist. Representative shall provide Artist with monthly statements of all expenses incurred hereunder, and Representative shall be reimbursed by Artist within fourteen (14) days of receipt by Artist of any such statement. Interest shall be charged on the unpaid monthly balance at the rate of one and one-half percent (1½%) per month.

DEALMAKING
IN THE
FILM AND
TELEVISION
INDUSTRY—
3RD EDITION

414

12. California Law: Any dispute under this Agreement will be resolved by final and binding arbitration under the Independent Film & Television Alliance Rules for International Arbitration in effect as of the effective date of this Agreement ("IFTA Rules"). Each Party waives any right to adjudicate any dispute in any other court or forum, *except* that a Party may seek interim relief before the start of arbitration as allowed by the IFTA Rules. The arbitration will be held in the Forum designated in the Agreement, or, if none is designated, as determined by the IFTA Rules. The Parties will abide by any decision in the arbitration and any court having jurisdiction may enforce it. The Parties submit to the jurisdiction of the courts in the Forum to compel arbitration or to confirm an arbitration award. The Parties agree to accept service of process in accordance with the IFTA Rules. The prevailing party shall be entitled to reimbursement of its reasonable attorney fees and costs.

13. Entire Agreement: This agreement constitutes the entire agreement between parties hereto. This Agreement shall not be revised or modified or terminated except by an agreement in writing, executed by the party against whom enforcement of the change or modification or termination is sought.

Please feel free to have an independent representative or attorney of your choosing review the terms and conditions of this Agreement with you. If the foregoing accurately reflects your agreement, please so indicate by signing a copy of this Agreement in the space provided below.

Very truly yours,

_____ ("Representative")

By: _____

AGREED TO AND ACCEPTED:

_____ ("Artist")

Questions and Answers

1. I do not have relationships with any agents or other industry insiders. What might be the best route to pitching my series concept? Do some agencies consider concepts, and then package them with talent and pitch those packages to networks?

Answer: Unfortunately, writers are not judged solely on their writing ability. Many times, agencies will not even consider looking at a concept or script by a newcomer unless it is recommended by an existing client, an industry insider, or someone the agency respects. Assuming you are able to get in the door, and meet with an agency, you may find that the agents are not particularly interested in pitches from newcomers without a track record. They may be more open to reviewing completed scripts, especially if there is a respected director, producer, or actor who has expressed interest in it. These are easier to sell for a novice screenwriter. Networks and studios generally don't hire beginning writers to write a screenplay until they have demonstrated their writing ability.

2. I have written a few freelance scripts, but I discovered that production companies only accept scripts that are submitted through agents or entertainment attorneys. How can I find representation?

Answer: You can write to entertainment attorneys and see if they are willing to represent you. Many attorneys do not like to be retained by clients simply to act as a script-submission service. This is not really legal work. Selling a script is more the role of an agent. The companies that require that scripts be submitted through an agent or attorney may be using the lack of representation to screen out novices. They figure if a person is able to obtain an attorney or an agent, he/she is probably not an amateur.

CHAPTER 19

GLOSSARY OF TERMS

Above-The-Line Costs   Portion of the budget that covers major creative participants (writer, director, actors, and producer), including script and story development costs.

Access   To make available a motion picture copy on the Internet or Wireless system in a manner that allows a user to copy, view, stream, download, or use, or to obtain data or information about, or related to, the motion picture copy or its embodied Motion Picture.

Adaptations   Derivative works. When a motion picture is based on a book, the movie has been adapted from the book.

Adjusted Gross Participation   Gross participation minus certain costs, such as cost of advertising and duplication. Also called "Rolling Gross." If many deductions are allowed, the participant is essentially getting a "net profit" deal.

Administrator   Person appointed by a court to manage the assets of a deceased person.

Advance   Up-front payment that counts against monies that may be payable at some time in the future. Non-recoupable advances are payments that are not refundable, even if future monies are never due.

Advertiser-Supported   Web software that makes a motion picture copy available on the Internet or Wireless system for accessing, downloading, or streaming, by either: (i)

DEALMAKING
IN THE
FILM AND
TELEVISION
INDUSTRY—
3RD EDITION

418

including trailers, commercials, or other advertising before, after, or within the continuity of the motion picture copy; or (ii) including banners, logos, icons, text, hypertext, meta tags, symbols, or other identifying information of a product or service or a supplier of such product or service provider on the same webpage or viewing screen as the motion picture copy or any of its elements or identifying information. This is also known as *adware*.

Aforesaid Previously said.

Airline Rights: A type of exploitation of a motion picture for direct exhibition in airplanes that are operated by an airline flying the flag of any country in the licensed territory for which Airline exploitation is granted, but excluding airlines that are customarily licensed from a location outside the licensed territory or that are only serviced in but do not fly the flag of a country in the licensed territory.

Ancillary Rights: Airline, ship, and hotel exploitation of a motion picture.

Answer Print The first composite (sound and picture) motion picture print from the laboratory with editing, score, and mixing completed. Usually color values will need to be corrected before a release print is made.

Art House Theater A movie venue that shows specialized art films, generally in exclusive engagements, rather than mass-market studio films.

Aspect Ratio (A.R.) The proportion of picture width to height.

Assign Transfer.

Assignee Person or business entity receiving property by assignment.

Assignor Person or business entity giving or transferring property to another.

Assigns Those to whom property has or may be assigned.

Attorney-In-Fact A person named in a written power-of-attorney document to act on behalf of the person who signs the document, called the principal. The attorney-in-fact's power and responsibilities depend on the specific powers granted in the power of attorney document. An attorney-in-fact is an agent of the principal.

Auteur   [See *Auteur Theory*]

Auteur Theory   A French-born theory that holds that the director is the true creator, or author ("auteur" simply means "author" in French), of a film, bringing together script, actors, cinematographer, and editor and molding everything into a work of cinematic art with a cohesive vision. Anyone who has worked on a movie knows what nonsense this is. Filmmaking is a collaborative endeavor, and the director is only one of the contributors.

Author   Creator, originator. Under U.S. copyright law, the author may be the employer of the person who actually creates the work. [See *Work-For-Hire*]

Back End   Profit participation in a film after distribution and/or production costs have been recouped.

Below-The-Line Costs   A film's technical and labor expenses, which include set construction, crew, camera equipment, film stock, developing, and printing.

Blind Bidding   When theater owners bid on a movie without seeing it. Several states and localities require open trade screenings for each new release. Guarantees and advances may also be banned.

Blow-Up   A film print that has been optically enlarged, usually from 16mm to 35mm.

Box Office Receipts   What the theater owner takes in from ticket sales to customers at the box office. A portion of this revenue is remitted to the studio/distributor in the form of rental payments.

Box-Office Gross   [See *Gross Box Office*]

Break   Simultaneously open a film in a few or many theaters.

Breakout   To expand bookings after an initial period of exclusive or limited engagement.

DEALMAKING
IN THE
FILM AND
TELEVISION
INDUSTRY—
3RD EDITION

420

Broadcast The communication to the public of a motion picture by means of wire, cable, wireless diffusion, or radio waves, terrestrially or by satellite, which allows the motion picture to be viewed on a television screen. Broadcast means the same as telecast or diffusion.

Cable Free TV The originating transmission by coaxial or fiberoptic cable of a motion picture for television reception in private living places without a charge to the viewer for the privilege of viewing the motion picture, provided that for this purpose neither government television assessments or taxes nor the regular periodic service charges (but not a charge for Pay-Per-View or Pay TV) paid by a subscriber to a cable television system will be deemed a charge to the viewer.

Cable Pay TV An originating transmission of a motion picture by means of an encoded signal over cable for television reception where a charge is made: (i) to viewers in private living places for use of a decoding device to view a channel that transmits the motion picture along with other programming; or (ii) to the operator of a hotel or similar temporary living place located distant from where the broadcast signal originated for use of a decoding device to receive a channel that broadcasts the motion picture and other programming and retransmit it throughout the temporary living place for viewing in private rooms.

CD-i [See *Compact Disc Interactive* below]

Cel A transparent sheet of cellulose acetate used as an overlay for drawing or lettering. Used in animation and title work.

Cinematic Theatrical, non-theatrical, and public video exploitation of a motion picture.

Color Correction The process of correcting or enhancing the color of an image.

Commercial Video Direct linear exhibition before an audience of a Videogram embodying a motion picture at the facilities of either organizations not primarily engaged in the business of exhibiting motion pictures, such as in educational organizations, churches, restaurants, bars, clubs, trains, libraries, Red Cross facilities, oil rigs and oil fields, or government bodies such as in embassies, military bases, military vessels, and other government facilities flying the flag of the licensed territory, but only to the extent that such exploitation is not otherwise utilized in the licensed territory as a form of Non-Theatrical exploitation. Commercial video does not include non-theatrical, public video, airline, ship, or hotel exploitation, nor any form of making the picture available over the Internet.

Compact Disc Interactive (CD-i)   CD-i may refer to either the player of or the media that stores the software for a particular type of Interactive Multimedia work (often a game or educational work). When used in a legal document, CD-i refers to the rights involved in preparing and issuing a work in this particular Interactive Multimedia format.

Completion Bond   A form of insurance which guarantees completion of a film in the event that the producer exceeds the budget. Completion bonds are sometimes required by banks and investors to secure loans and investments in a production. Should a bond be invoked, the completion guarantor may assume control over the production and be in a recoupment position superior to all investors.

Computer   In the context of the screening of motion pictures and video materials, a computer is an electronic device that accepts a motion picture copy in digital form and allows its viewing or manipulation in response to a sequence of instructions where the type and order of the instructions can be defined, selected, and entered by the user of the Computer. A Computer includes desktops, notebooks, and laptops and *excludes* VCR, DVR, DVD, set-top box players or recorders, and handheld devices.

Consideration   The reason or inducement for a party to contract with another. Usually money, but it can be anything of value: the right, interest, or benefit to one party, or the loss or forbearance of another. The existence of a consideration is necessary for a contract to be binding.

Contrast   The range—from lightest to darkest elements—within a shot or throughout a film negative or print or any video

DEALMAKING
IN THE
FILM AND
TELEVISION
INDUSTRY—
3RD EDITION

422

program material. The brightness range of lighting in a filmed scene.

Convey   To transfer or deliver to another.

Covenant   An agreement or promise to do something or not to do something.

Cross-Collateralization   Practice by which distributors offset expenses in one medium or market against revenue derived from other mediums or markets. For example, the film rentals obtained from France are combined with those from Italy, and after the expenses for both are deducted, the remainder, if any, is net revenue. Filmmakers don't like to have revenues and expenses cross-collateralized (pooled) because it may reduce the amount of money they receive.

Crossover Film   Film that is initially targeted to a narrow specialty audience market but achieves acceptance in a wider market.

Dailies (Rushes)   Usually a quickly and roughly made print from which the action shot on a specific production day is checked and the best takes selected.

Day and Date   The simultaneous opening of a film in two or more movie theaters in one or more cities.

Day Player   An actor who is employed on a daily basis rather than on a weekly or flat-fee basis for an entire production. Usually actors with small parts are employed on a daily basis.

Deal Memo   A letter or short contract.

Decedent   A deceased person.

Defamation   A false statement that injures another's reputation in the community.

Default   Failure to perform.

Deferred Payment   To reduce a production's upfront costs, writers, directors, actors, and others may agree to be paid some of their compensation from revenues that may (or may not) be generated after the production has been completed and distributed. These payments are known as "deferred payments," and are often payable only after the investors have recouped their capital contributions.

Demand View   The transmission of a motion picture copy by means of an encoded signal for television reception in homes and similar permanent living places where a charge is made to the viewer for the right to use a decoding device to view the motion picture at a time selected by the viewer for each viewing.

Depth of Field   The distance range between the nearest and farthest objects in a photograph or motion picture shot that appear in sharp focus. The manipulation of depth of field will have much to do with a film's overall "look" and style.

Development   The process by which an initial motion picture idea is turned into a finished screenplay. It includes optioning the rights to an underlying literary property and commissioning writers to create a treatment, first draft, second draft, rewrite, and polish.

Digital Rights Management (DRM)   A term that refers to access-control technologies used by digital hardware manufacturers, publishers, and copyright holders to prevent unauthorized usage or limit usage of digital media and/or devices. DRM is used to control or manage the copying, viewing, altering, or accessing a digitized motion picture's content or elements.

Direct Advertising   Direct outreach promotional campaign to consumers, such as mailing flyers. Usually targeted to a specific interest group.

Direct Broadcast Satellite (DBS)   A satellite broadcast system designed with sufficient power so that inexpensive home satellite dishes can be used for reception.

Display Advertising   Advertising that features artwork or a title treatment specific to a given film in newspapers, magazines, and on the Internet.

Dissolve   An optical or camera effect in which one scene gradually fades out at the same time that another scene fades in.

DEALMAKING
IN THE
FILM AND
TELEVISION
INDUSTRY—
3RD EDITION

424

Distributor   A company that distributes a motion picture to theaters and the public, placing it in theaters and any media (DVD, cable TV, etc.), and advertising and promoting it. The major studios nowadays are mostly in the business of financing and distributing films, leaving production to smaller independent companies.

Distribution Expenses   The costs incurred by a distributor while promoting and distributing a motion picture. These expenses may include taxes, residuals, trade-association dues, conversion/transmission costs, collection costs, checking costs, advertising and publicity costs, re-editing costs, print duplication, foreign-version costs, transportation and shipping costs, and insurance.

Domestic Rights   The geographical area in which certain distribution and exhibition rights and copyrights are exercised. For U.S. filmmakers, this domestic area is usually defined as the U.S. and English-speaking Canada.

Double Distribution Fees   Costs incurred when a distributor uses a sub-distributor to market a film, and both deduct their full fees. The result is that the filmmaker is less likely to see any money.

Double-System Recording   The simultaneous recording of a scene's sound and picture on separate machines, e.g., a tape recorder and a camera. These two elements will be synchronized and put together during editing.

Downbeat Ending   An unhappy or depressing conclusion to a story.

Download   To receive a copy of a digitized motion picture or other program material via the Internet or a wireless system of transmission in a manner that allows that material to be accessed by a computer or digital handheld device. Such a copy may be retainable for use for more than a transient period of time after completion of the initial period of transmission.

Droit Moral   French term for Moral Rights. A doctrine that protects artistic integrity and prevents others from altering the work of artists, or taking the artist's name off a work without the artist's permission. For example, the doctrine might prevent a buyer of a painting from changing it, even though the physical item and the copyright are owned by the buyer.

DRM   [See *Digital Rights Management*]

Dubbing   The sound recording process by which music and/or dialogue are added to a visual presentation to create a soundtrack that can be transferred to and synchronized with the visual presentation. This process may also be used to create a version of the motion picture in which the voices of performers on the original soundtrack are replaced with the voices of other performers speaking dialogue in another language.

Dupe   A shorthand substitute for the word "duplicate." A "dupe" often refers to a copy of the negative, or duplicate negative.

Edge Numbers   A sequence of numbers printed periodically (every 16 frames for 35mm film; every 20 frames for 16mm film) along the edge of a roll of film negative. By reference to these numbers, a print may be edited to exactly conform, frame-by-frame, to an edited negative. Edge numbers are also used to designate the type of film stock, the date of its manufacture, and its batch number.

Exclusive Opening   A type of release whereby a film is opened in a single theater in a region, giving the distributor the option to hold the film for a long exclusive run or move it into additional theaters based on the film's performance.

Execute   To complete; to sign; to perform.

Executor   A person appointed to carry out the requests in a will.

Feature Film   Full-length, fictional films (not a documentaries or shorts), generally intended for theatrical release.

Film Rental   What the theater owner pays the distributor for the right to show the movie. As a rough rule of thumb, this usually amounts to about half of the box-office gross.

Final Cut   The final edited version of a film. This is the version that is released to the public. The right to create the

DEALMAKING
IN THE
FILM AND
TELEVISION
INDUSTRY—
3RD EDITION

426

final cut is the right to determine the final version of the picture. Usually the studio or the financier of a picture retains the right of final cut.

First-Dollar Gross   The most favorable form of gross participation for the participant. Only a few deductions, such as checking fees, taxes, and trade-association dues are deductible.

First Monies   From the producer's point of view, the first revenue received from the distribution of a movie. Not to be confused with profits, first monies are generally allocated to investors until recoupment, but may be allocated in part or in whole to deferred salaries owed to talent or deferred fees owed a film laboratory.

First Run   The first theatrical engagement of a new film.

Floors   In distributor/exhibitor agreements, the minimum percentage of box-office receipts the distributor is entitled to, regardless of the theater's operating expenses. Generally, floors decline week by week over the course of an engagement. They generally range from 70% to 25% of receipts.

Force Majeure   Literally, a superior or irresistible force. A Force Majeure clause in a contract may suspend certain obligations in the event that a production is halted because of forces beyond the control of the parties such as a fire, strike, earthquake, war, or Act of God.

Foreign Sales   Licensing a film in territories and media outside the U.S. and Canada. Although Canada is a foreign country, American distributors typically acquire English-speaking Canadian rights when they license U.S. rights.

Four-Walling   Renting a theater and its staff for a flat fee, buying your own advertising, and receiving all the box-office revenue. Under a four-wall agreement, an exhibitor is paid a flat fee regardless of a film's performance and does not share in box-office receipts.

FPM   Feet per minute, expressing the speed of film moving through a mechanism.

FPS   Frames per second, indicating the number of images produced per second. FPS is used as a designation for both
film and digital motion-picture devices.

Free TV   Terrestrial (Broadcast) Free TV, Cable Free TV, and
Satellite Free TV. Free TV exploitation of a motion picture
does not include any form of Pay-Per-View, nor any form
of making the picture available over the Internet.

Front Office   A studio's or production company's top executives—the people who control the money.

General Partners   Management side of a limited partnership
(the position usually occupied by the film's producers) that
structures motion picture investments and raises money from
investors, who become limited partners. General partners
make the business decisions regarding the partnership.

Grant   To give or permit. To bestow or confer.

Grantor   The person who makes a grant. The transferor of
property.

Grassroots Campaign   Film promotion campaign that builds
local interest by the use of flyers, posters, stickers, and
other inexpensive materials and builds word-of-mouth with
special screenings for local community groups.

Gross After Break-Even   The participant shares in the gross
after the break-even point has been reached. The break-even
point can be a set amount or determined by a formula.

Gross Box Office   Total revenue taken in at theater box office
for ticket sales.

Gross Participation   A piece of gross receipts without any
deductions for distribution fees or expenses or production
costs. However, deductions for checking and collection
costs, residuals, and taxes are usually deductible from a
gross participation. A "piece of the gross" is the most
advantageous type of participation from the participant's
point of view. In an audit, it is the most easily verified
form of participation.

DEALMAKING
IN THE
FILM AND
TELEVISION
INDUSTRY—
3RD EDITION

428

Gross Receipts Studio/distributor revenues derived from all media, including film rentals, television, home video licenses, merchandising, and ancillary sales.

Handheld Device A mobile electronic device that customarily fits in a human hand. As this rapidly changing technology currently exists, it is used for digital telephonic, text, and image communication; digital photography; and digital data storage. It also allows viewing of a motion picture copy. Handheld devices includes mobile phones, digital assistants, and similar devices, but not a traditional laptop computer.

Home Video Home Video Rental and Home Video Sell-Through exploitation of a motion picture.

Home Video Rental The exploitation of a Videogram embodying a motion picture that is rented to the viewer only for non-public viewing within a private living place where no admission fee is charged for such viewing.

Home Video Sell-Through The exploitation of a Videogram embodying a motion picture that is sold to the viewer only for non-public viewing within a private living place where no admission fee is charged for such viewing.

House Nut Weekly operating expenses of a movie theater.

Hyphenate Person who fulfills two or more major roles, such as producer-director, writer-director, or actor-director.

IFTA [See *International Film and Television Alliance*]

In Perpetuity Forever.

Incapacity Inability. Want of legal, physical, or intellectual capacity. A minor, or a person committed to a mental institution, for example, may be legally incapable of contracting with another.

Indemnify Reimburse. To restore someone's loss by payment, repair, or replacement.

Interactive Multimedia The exploitation of an Interactive Multimedia work by means of a computing device that allows the Interactive Multimedia work to be directly perceived and manipulated by the user of the computing device and that either stores the Interactive Multimedia work on the user's computing device or accesses a copy of the Interactive Multimedia work by electronic means from another computing device interconnected with and located in the immediate vicinity of the user's computing device.

Interlock The first synchronous presentation of a film's work-print synchronized with its soundtrack (each contained on separate reels) by means of the mechanical or electrical synchronization of the drives controlling the film projector and the sound reproducer.

International Film and Television Alliance (IFTA) Trade organization for independent film producers and sales agents. IFTA used to be known as the American Film Marketing Association (AFMA).

Internegative A color negative made from a color positive. An internegative of a properly color-timed positive will be used to make a film's release prints.

Internet The interconnected facilities of a publicly available communications system that allows the user of a computing device to engage in two-way transmissions over the system through which the user obtains access to a motion picture copy stored in digital form at a place distant from the place where the user's computing device is located.

Internet Downloading Exploitation of a digital motion picture copy by making it available on the Internet in a substantially linear manner that allows its transmission to a computer for making another exact digital copy of the motion picture copy and retaining the new digital copy for use for more than a transient period of time after completion of the initial continuous period of transmission. Internet downloading does not include any form of Internet streaming.

Internet Streaming The exploitation of a digital motion picture copy by making it available on the Internet in a manner that allows continuous viewing of the motion picture copy on a computer in a substantially linear form simultaneously with the transmission of such motion picture copy over the Internet but which does not allow making another digital copy except for a transient period of time necessary to

DEALMAKING
IN THE
FILM AND
TELEVISION
INDUSTRY—
3RD EDITION

430

facilitate such viewing. Internet Streaming does not include any form of Internet Downloading.

Internet Streaming/Downloading The exploitation of a digital motion picture copy by making it available on the Internet for both Internet downloading and Internet streaming at substantially the same time.

Internet Rights The rights concerned with Internet downloading and/or Internet streaming exploitation of a motion picture. Interest rights do not include wireless rights nor any form of Pay-Per-View, Video, Pay TV, or Free TV exploitation of a motion picture.

Interpositives A positive duplicate of a film used for further printing. The striking of an interpositive is an interim step in the process that a motion picture goes through from original negative to release print.

Invasion of Privacy A tort that encompasses a variety of wrongful behavior such as an unjustified appropriation of another's name, image, or likeness; the publicizing of intimate details of another's life without justification; or intrusions into another's privacy by eavesdropping or surveillance in an area where a person has a reasonable expectation of privacy.

Irrevocable That which cannot be rescinded or recalled.

Key Art Artwork used in posters and ads for a movie.

Letterbox A process of film-to-video transfer that maintains the original film's aspect ratio by matting the top and the bottom of the screen with black bars. Standard TVs have an aspect ratio of 1.33:1 (4:3), while contemporary feature films have such aspect ratios of 1.66:1, 1.83:1, 1.85:1, 2.33:1 and 2.35:1. Until recently, the more conventional transfer process from widescreen to 4:3 is called Pan & Scan.

Libel The written form of defamation. Compare to slander, the spoken form of defamation.

Licensee Person who is given a license or permission to do something.

Licensor The person who gives or grants a license.

Limited Partnership Form of business enterprise commonly used to finance movies. General partners initiate and control the partnership; limited partners are the investors and have no control of the running of the partnership business and no legal or financial liabilities beyond the amount they have invested.

Limited Use Authorizing accessing, streaming, or downloading, as applicable, of a motion picture copy on the Internet or Wireless system by a user who is required to pay a separate fee to obtain a limited right to use a new digital copy of a motion picture copy in a substantially linear manner that may be accessed and viewed, but not further copied, subject to express limitations as to either the number of accesses or viewings, the period of access or viewing, or both (e.g., unlimited viewing for x days, or x viewings maximum, or x viewings within y days).

Litigation A lawsuit. Proceedings in a court of law.

M&E Track Music and Effects Track.

Magnetic Track Audio recorded on a film or tape that has been coated with a magnetic recording medium.

Master The final edited and complete film or videotape from which subsequent copies are made.

Merchandising Rights Rights to license, manufacture, and distribute merchandise based on characters, names, or events in a motion picture.

Mini-Multiple Type of release which falls between an exclusive engagement and a wide release, consisting of quality theaters in strategic geographic locations, generally a prelude to a wider break.

Multi-Plexing Transmission of a motion picture over related broadcast channels supplied by the same broadcaster or pay service.

Multi-Tiered Audience An audience of different types of people who find a particular film attractive for different reasons, and who must be reached by different publicity, promotion, or ads.

DEALMAKING
IN THE
FILM AND
TELEVISION
INDUSTRY—
3RD EDITION

432

Moral Rights   [See *Droit Moral*]

Near-Demand View   Multiple regularly scheduled transmissions in a short time period of a motion picture copy by means of an encoded signal for television reception in homes and similar permanent living places where a charge is made to the viewer for the right to use a decoding device to view the motion picture at one of the scheduled transmission times selected by the viewer for each viewing.

Negative Cost   Actual cost of producing a film, including the manufacture of a completed negative (does not include costs of prints or advertising). It may be defined to include overhead expenses, interest, and other expenses, which may inflate the amount way beyond what was actually spent to make the film.

Negative Pickup   A distributor guarantees to pay a specified amount for distribution rights upon delivery of a completed film negative by a specific date. If the picture is not delivered on time and in accordance with the terms of the agreement, the distributor has no obligation to license the film. A negative pickup guarantee can be used as collateral for a bank loan to obtain production funds.

Net Profit   What is left, if anything, after all allowable deductions are taken. Most motion pictures do not produce any Net Profits to participants. Typically expressed in terms of portion of 100% of net profits, such as 5% of 100%.

Non-Residental Pay-Per-View   The broadcast of a motion picture copy by means of an encoded signal for television reception in hotels or similar temporary living places where a charge is made to the viewer for the right to use a decoding device to view the broadcast of the motion picture at a time designated by the broadcaster for each viewing.

Non-Theatrical   The exploitation of a motion picture copy only for direct exhibition before an audience by and at the facilities of either organizations not primarily engaged in the business of exhibiting motion pictures, such as in educational organizations, churches, restaurants, bars, clubs, trains, libraries, Red Cross facilities, oil rigs, and oil fields, or government bodies such as in embassies, military bases, military vessels, and other government facilities flying the flag of the licensed territory. Non-Theatrical does not include commercial video, public video, airline, ship, or hotel exploitation.

Novelization A book adapted from a motion picture.

NTSC National Television System Committee. The standard for North America, Japan, and several other countries, which is 525 lines, 60 fields/30 frames per second. Compare to PAL.

NVOD Near Video-On-Demand or Near-Demand View.

Off-Hollywood American independent films made outside the studio system.

Officer Person holding office of trust or authority in a corporation or institution.

On Spec Working for nothing on the hope and speculation that something will come of it.

Optical Soundtrack A soundtrack in which the sound record takes the form of density variations in a photographic image, also called a photographic soundtrack.

Original A work that has not been adapted from another work.

Original Language The primary language spoken in the dialogue of a motion picture in its original language.

Original Material Not derived or adapted from another work.

Overexposure A condition in which too much light reaches the film, producing a dense negative or a washed-out reversal.

PAL Phase Alternation Line. The standard adopted by European and other countries, which is 625 Lines, 50 fields/25 frames per second. Compare to NTSC.

Pan A horizontal movement of the camera.

Pan & Scan A method used to transfer widescreen films to a video and/or broadcast format that matches the TV screen's aspect ratio (4:3). Pan & scan attempts to determine the

DEALMAKING
IN THE
FILM AND
TELEVISION
INDUSTRY—
3RD EDITION

434

most important areas of the wide image (where there is the most activity or where a central character is standing) and pan around the wide image during the course of the movie, to focus on and show as many of these important areas as possible. Compare with letterbox.

Pari Passu   Equitably, without preference.

Pay-Cable TV   [See *Cable Pay TV*]

Pay-Per-View   Non-Residential Pay-Per-View, Residential Pay-Per-View, and Demand View exploitation of a motion picture. Pay-Per-View does not include any form of Pay TV or Free TV, nor any form of making a motion picture available over the Internet.

Pay TV   Terrestrial Pay TV, Cable Pay TV, and Satellite Pay TV exploitation of a motion picture. Pay TV does not include any form of Pay-Per-View nor any form of making the picture available over the Internet.

Permanent Use   Authorizing downloading of a motion picture copy in a substantially linear manner on the Internet or a Wireless system by a user who is required to pay a separate fee to obtain ownership of new digital copy of the motion picture copy, which new copy may be used and viewed, but not further copied, without express limitations as to the number of uses and viewings and the time period of so doing.

Platforming   A method of release whereby a film is opened in a single theater or small group of theaters in a region and later expanded to a greater number of theaters.

Playdate   One or more telecasts of the picture during a 24-hour period over the non-overlapping telecast facilities of an authorized telecaster such that the picture is only capable of reception on televisions within the reception zone of such telecaster during such period.

Player   Actor.

Playoff   Distribution of a film after key openings.

Positive Film   Film used primarily for making master positives or release prints.

Power Coupled with an Interest   A right to do some act, together with an interest (stake) in the subject matter.

Principal Photography   The actual photographing of a motion picture, excluding second-unit photography or special-effects photography, requiring the participation of the director and the on-camera participation of a featured member of the principal cast.

Print   A positive picture usually produced from a negative.

Power of Attorney   [See *Attorney-in-Fact*]

Pro Rata   Proportionately.

Processing   A procedure during which exposed photographic film or paper is developed, fixed, and washed to produce either a negative image or a positive image.

Public Video   The exploitation of a motion picture copy embodied in a Videogram only for direct exhibition before an audience in a "mini-theater," an "MTV theater," or like establishment that charges an admission to use the viewing facility or to view the Videogram, and that is not licensed as a traditional motion picture theater in the place where the viewing occurs.

Quitclaim   To release or relinquish a claim. To execute a deed of quitclaim.

Raw Stock   Motion picture film that has not been exposed or processed.

Regional Release   As opposed to a simultaneous national release, a pattern of distribution whereby a film is opened in one or more geographical regions at a time.

Release Print   A composite print made for general distribution and exhibition after the final answer print has been approved.

Remise   To remit or give up.

Rescind   (Rescission) To abrogate, annul, or cancel a contract.

Residential Pay-Per-View   The broadcast of a motion picture copy by means of an encoded signal for television reception

DEALMAKING
IN THE
FILM AND
TELEVISION
INDUSTRY—
3RD EDITION

436

in homes or similar permanent living places where a charges is made to the viewer for the right to use a decoding device to view the broadcast of the motion picture at a time designated by the broadcaster for each viewing.

Right of Privacy   The right to be left alone, and to be protected against a variety of intrusive behavior such as unjustified appropriation of one's name, image, or likeness; the publicizing of intimate details of one's life without justification, and unlawful eavesdropping or surveillance.

Right of Publicity   The right to control the commercial value and use of one's name, likeness, and image.

Rights Management Information   Any information embodied, attached, related, or appearing in or on a motion picture copy that may include a copyright notice or other identifier that identifies the copyright owner, producer, author, writer, director, performers, or other persons who have contributed to the making of the motion picture, or that describes any authorized terms and conditions for licensing or use of the motion picture or the motion picture copy.

Rollout   Distribution of film around the country subsequent to either key city openings or an opening in one city.

Rough Cut   A preliminary assemblage of a motion picture's footage.

Run   Length of time that a feature plays in theaters or a territory.

Sanction   (1) To assent, concur, or ratify. (2) To reprimand.

Satellite Free TV   The uplink broadcast to a satellite and its downlink broadcast to terrestrial satellite reception dishes of a motion picture copy for television viewing in private living places located in the immediate vicinity of a viewer's reception dish without a charge to the viewer for the privilege of viewing the motion picture, provided that for this purpose government satellite dish or television assessments or taxes (but not a charge for Pay-Per-View or Pay TV) will not be deemed a charge to the viewer.

Satellite Pay TV   The uplink broadcast of a motion picture copy by means of an encoded signal to a satellite and its downlink broadcast to terrestrial satellite reception dishes for television viewing located in the immediate vicinity of the reception dishes where a charge is made: (i) to viewers in private living places for use of a decoding device to view a channel that broadcasts the motion picture along with other programming; or (ii) to the operator of a hotel or similar temporary living place located distant from where the broadcast signal originated for use of a decoding device to receive a channel that broadcasts the motion picture and other programming and retransmit it throughout the temporary living place for viewing in private rooms.

Scale   The minimum salary permitted by the guilds.

Sequel   A book or film that tells a related story that occurs later than the original. A continuation of an earlier story, usually with the same characters.

Shooting Script   A final version of the screenplay in which each separate shot is numbered and camera directions are indicated. Although a lot of script changes may occur during shooting, in theory, a shooting script is the script used during actual production/shooting.

Single Use   Authorizing the accessing, streaming, or downloading of a motion picture copy in a substantially linear manner on the Internet or a wireless system by a user who is required to pay a separate fee for each single act of accessing, streaming, or downloading of the motion picture copy in whole or in part.

Sleeper   An unexpected hit. A film that audiences fall in love with and make a success.

Slicks   Standardized print ads printed on glossy paper. They include various sizes of display ads for a given film, designed to accept the insertion of local theater information as needed.

Soundtrack   (1) The composite audio tracks containing all of a film's audio elements—dialog, effects, and music. (2) The musical score to a motion picture. (3) The actual portion of a piece of film that is reserved for recording/storing sound.

DEALMAKING
IN THE
FILM AND
TELEVISION
INDUSTRY—
3RD EDITION

438

Specialized Distribution   As opposed to commercial distribution, specialized distribution is for a limited audience,
in a smaller number of theaters, with a limited advertising
budget and heavy reliance upon publicity, reviews, and
word-of-mouth to build an audience for the picture.

Stills   Photographs taken during production for use later in
advertising and/or publicity. Stills should be in a horizontal format, and should list such information as film title,
producer, director, and cast below the photo.

Stock   General term for motion picture film, especially before
exposure. Film stock.

Story Analyst or Reader   A person employed by a studio
or producer to read submitted scripts and properties and
synopsize and evaluate them. This position is often held
by young literature or film-school graduates who don't
know a great deal about filmmaking. (But, then again,
their bosses sometimes know even less.)

Story Conference   A meeting at which the writer receives suggestions about how to improve his/her script.

Stream   To make available a motion picture copy on the Internet
or a wireless system in a manner that allows continuous
viewing of the motion picture copy in substantially linear
form on a computer or handheld device simultaneously
with the transmission of such motion picture copy over
the Internet or a wireless system but which does not allow
making another digital copy except for a transient period
of time necessary to facilitate such viewing.

Stripe   A narrow band of magnetic coating or developing solution applied to a motion picture film for recording audio
or synch information.

Sub-Distributor   In theatrical releases, distributors who handle
a specific geographic territory. They are contracted by the
main distributor, who coordinates the overall distribution
campaign and marketing.

Subscription Use   Authorizing accessing, streaming, or downloading of a motion picture copy in a substantially linear
manner on the Internet or a wireless system by a user who

is required to pay a set fee for a specified period to access, stream, or download, as applicable, the embodied motion picture along with other motion pictures available in the same manner on the same website or a wireless system.

Subtitled   A version of a picture in which a translation of the original dialogue appears on the bottom of the screen.

Successors   Persons entitled to property of a decedent by will or as an heir.

Successor-In-Interest   One who follows another in ownership or control of property.

Synchronization   The positioning of a soundtrack so that it is in harmony with, and timed to, the image portion of the film.

Syndication   Distribution of motion pictures to independent commercial television stations on a regional basis.

Talent   The word used to describe those involved in the artistic aspects of filmmaking (i.e., writers, actors, directors) as opposed to the business people.

Target Market   The defined audience segment a distributor seeks to reach with its advertising and promotion campaign, such as teens, women over 30, yuppies, etc.

Television Spin-Off   A television series or mini-series based on characters or other elements in a film.

Terrestrial Free TV   Over-the-air broadcast, without the aid of satellites, of a motion picture copy for television reception in private living places without a charge to the viewer for the privilege of viewing the motion picture, provided that for this purpose government television assessments or taxes (but not a charge for Pay-Per-View or Pay TV) will not be deemed a charge to the viewer.

Terrestrial Pay TV   Over-the-air broadcast, without the aid of satellites, of a motion picture copy for television reception where a charge is made: (i) to viewers in private living places for use of a decoding device to view a channel that broadcasts the motion picture along with other programming; or (ii) to the operator of a hotel or similar temporary

DEALMAKING
IN THE
FILM AND
TELEVISION
INDUSTRY—
3RD EDITION

440

living place located distant from where the broadcast signal originated for use of a decoding device to receive a channel that broadcasts the motion picture and other programming and retransmit it throughout the temporary living place for viewing in private rooms.

Test Marketing   Pre-releasing a film in one or more small, representative markets before committing to an advertising campaign. The effectiveness of the marketing plan can thereby be assessed and modified as needed before the general release.

Theatrical   The exploitation of a motion picture copy only for direct exhibition in conventional or drive-in theaters, licensed as such in the place where the exhibition occurs, that are open to the general public on a regularly scheduled basis and that charge an admission fee to view the motion picture.

Theatrical Distribution Fees   Generally between 30% and 40% of gross film rentals, taken by the domestic theatrical distributor for distribution of a motion picture when the distributor advances the costs of prints and advertising.

Trades   Periodicals published for and addressing a specific industry. For the U.S. motion picture industry, the standard daily and weekly periodicals are *Variety* and *The Hollywood Reporter.*

Treatment   A prose account of a film's storyline. Usually between 20 and 50 pages long, a treatment is written after an outline and before the first draft of a screenplay.

Underlying Material   The literary and other material from which a motion picture is derived or on which it is based. These include all versions of the screenplay; all notes, memos, direction, comments, ideas, stage business, and other material incorporated in any version of the motion picture; and, to the extent necessary, the rights and licenses that have been duly obtained to all existing novels, stories, plays, songs, events, characters, ideas, or other works from which any version of the motion picture is derived or on which it is based.

Video Home video and commercial video exploitation of a motion picture, but which does not include any form of making the motion picture available over the Internet.

Video Disc A laser or capacitance disc or comparable analog optical or mechanical storage device designed to be used with a reproduction apparatus that causes a motion picture to be visible on a television screen for private viewing in a substantially linear manner. A VideoDisc does not include any type of Compact Disc or DVD.

Videogram Any type of Videocassette, videodiscs, videotapes, DVDs, High-Definition DVDs ("HD-DVD"), Universal Media Disc ("UMD"), CD-ROM, DVD-ROM and all other hard carrier devices now known or hereafter devised and designed to be used in conjunction with a personal reproduction, player, or viewing apparatus which causes a visual image (whether or not synchronized with sound) to be seen on a screen, display or device (e.g., a television monitor, computer display, handheld device) and intended primarily for home use.

Video-On-Demand [See *Demand View*]

VOD Video-on-Demand.

Warranty A promise. An assurance by one party as to the existence of a fact upon which the other party may rely.

Wide Release The release of a film in numerous theaters, usually 800 to 4,000 in the United States and Canada.

Window As the term relates to film distribution, a period of time in which a film is available in a given medium. Some windows may be open-ended, such as theatrical and home video, or limited, such as pay television or syndication.

Wireless Downloading The exploitation of a digital motion picture copy by making it available on a wireless system in a substantially linear manner that allows its transmission to a handheld device for making another exact digital copy of the motion picture copy and retaining the new digital copy for use for more than a transient period of time after completion of the initial continuous period of

DEALMAKING
IN THE
FILM AND
TELEVISION
INDUSTRY—
3RD EDITION

442

transmission. Wireless downloading does not include any form of wireless streaming.

Wireless Streaming   The exploitation of a digital motion picture copy by making it available on a wireless system in a substantially linear manner that allows continuous viewing of the motion picture copy on a handheld device but which does not allow making another digital copy except for a transient period of time necessary to facilitate such viewing. Wireless streaming does not include any form of wireless downloading.

Wireless System   System of integrated telecommunications facilities that allow system subscribers to access an over-the-air digital signal embodying a motion picture copy on a handheld device.

Wireless Rights   Wireless downloading or wireless streaming exploitation of a motion picture. Wireless rights do not include Internet rights nor any form of Pay-Per-View, Video, Pay TV, or Free TV exploitation of a motion picture.

Work-For-Hire (or Work-Made-For-Hire)   Under the Copyright Act this is either (1) a work prepared by an employee within the scope of employment or (2) a specially ordered or commissioned work of a certain type (e.g., a motion picture, a contribution to a collective work) if the parties expressly agree so in a writing signed by both before work begins.

Workprint   A picture or soundtrack print, usually a positive, intended for use in editing only so as not to expose the original elements to any wear and tear.

CHAPTER 20

APPENDIX

BOOKS AND PUBLICATIONS

Adventures in the Screen Trade. William Goldman (New York: Warner Books, 1983). A writer's view of the industry.

American Film Now. James Monaco (New York: Oxford University Press, 1979). The early chapters describe the workings of the industry, the latter a review of the work of top filmmakers.

Anatomy of the Movies. David Pirie, ed. (New York: Macmillan Publishing Co., Inc., 1981). Collection of articles written by various journalists about the industry.

The Biz, The Basic Business, Legal, and Financial Aspects of the Film Industry. Schuyler M. Moore (Los Angeles: Silman-James Press, 2000). This book provides an overview of the film industry's business, legal, and financial aspects. This book also contains a dozen sample forms and agreements.

Filmmakers on Filmmaking: The American Film Institute Seminars on Motion Pictures and Television, Volumes I & II. Joseph McBride, ed. (Los Angeles: AFI/J.P. Tarcher, Inc., dist. by Samuel French Trade). These books are comprised of edited transcripts of AFI seminars held with prestigious people in the industry.

DEALMAKING
IN THE
FILM AND
TELEVISION
INDUSTRY—
3RD EDITION

444

***Final Cut: Dreams and Disaster in the Making of* Heaven's Gate.** Steven Bach (New York: William Morrow & Co., 1985). All about the *Heaven's Gate* debacle. Good insights into how decisions are made within a studio.

Hollywood, The Dream Factory. Hortense Powdermaker (Boston: Little Brown & Co., 1950). This book is difficult to find since it is out of print. Try secondhand bookstores. Powdermaker was an anthropologist who decided to study Hollywood, its mores, customs, etc. It provides a sociological perspective on industry people and on industry practices that is remarkably relevant today, 45 years after this book was published. And it's amusing to read her comments comparing the behavior of the indigenous people of Hollywood with those of "primitive" cultures.

Indecent Exposure: A True Story of Hollywood and Wall Street. David McClintock (New York: William Morrow & Co., 1982). Explores the Begelman scandal and sheds light on studio boardroom politics and high finance.

Independent Feature Film Production: A Complete Guide from Concept Through Distribution. Gregory Goodell (New York: St. Martin's Griffin, 1998).

Off-Hollywood, The Making and Marketing of American Specialty Films. David Rosen with Peter Hamilton (New York: Grove/Weidenfeld, 1990). A study of American independent feature films commissioned by the Sundance Institute and The Independent Feature Project. Case history profiles of the making and marketing of nine narrative and two documentary films, including *The Ballad of Gregorio Cortez, Eating Raoul, El Norte, My Dinner with Andre, Wild Style,* and *The Return of the Secaucus Seven.*

Reel Power, The Struggle for Influence and Success in the New Hollywood. Mark Litwak (New York: William Morrow & Co., 1986; reprinted in paperback, Los Angeles: Silman-James Press, 1994). A comprehensive look at how Hollywood works—who has the power and how deals are made.

Rolling Breaks, and Other Movie Business. Aljean Harmetz (New York: Alfred A. Knopf, 1983). Collection of this *New York Times* correspondent's articles on the industry.

The Studio. John Gregory Dunne (New York: Touchstone, Simon & Schuster, 1968 & 1969). Stories about life inside 20th Century Fox.

What a Producer Does: The Art of Moviemaking (Not the Business). Buck Houghton (Los Angeles: Silman-James Press, 1991).

Historical

City of Nets: A Portrait of Hollywood in the 1940s. Otto Friedrich (New York: Harper & Row, 1986). Stories about Hollywood.

Film: An International History of the Medium. Robert Sklar (New York: Harry N. Abrams, 1993).

A History of the American Film Industry From its Beginnings to 1931. Benjamin B. Hampton (New York: Dover Publications, Inc., 1970). Gives the reader a good historical perspective of the industry. It's interesting to note how certain patterns keep recurring.

Writing

The Art of Adaptation: Turning Fact into Film. Linda Seger (New York: Henry Holt, 1992).

The Craft of the Screenwriter. John Brady (New York: Simon and Schuster, 1981). Interviews with top screenwriters.

Creating Unforgettable Characters. Linda Seger (New York: Henry Holt, 1990).

Making a Good Script Great. Linda Seger (Los Angeles: Samuel French Trade, 1988).

The New Screenwriter Looks at the New Screenwriter. William Froug (Los Angeles: Silman-James Press, 1992). Froug's second collection of interviews featuring top screenwriters of the '80s and '90s.

DEALMAKING
IN THE
FILM AND
TELEVISION
INDUSTRY—
3RD EDITION

446

The Screenwriter Looks at the Screenwriter. Willian Froug (Los Angeles: Silman-James Press, 1991). Twelve top screenwriters talk about their craft. Reprint of the 1972 edition.

Screenwriting Tricks of the Trade. William Froug (Los Angeles: Silman-James Press, 1993).

Screenwriting Updated: New (and Conventional) Ways of Writing for the Screen. Linda Aronson (Los Angeles: Silman-James Press, 2001).

Writing Screenplays That Sell. Michael Hauge (New York: Harper Collins, 1990).

Directing

Directing the Film: Film Directors on Their Art. Eric Sherman (Los Angeles: Acrobat Books, 1988).

Film Directing Shot by Shot: Visualizing From Concept to Screen. Steven D. Katz (Los Angeles: Michael Wiese Productions, 1991).

Grammar of the Film Language. Daniel Arijon (Los Angeles: Silman-James Press, 1991).

The Business

The Big Picture: Money and Power in Hollywood. Edward Jay Epstein (Random House Trade Paperbacks 2006).

Contracts for the Film and Television Industry, 2nd Edition. Mark Litwak (Los Angeles: Silman-James Press, 1998). A collection of sample entertainment contracts along with discussions of the terms and ideas contained therein.

Film Finance & Distribution: A Dictionary of Terms. John W. Cones (Los Angeles: Silman-James Press, 1992).

From Reel to Deal: Everything You Need to Create a Successful Independent Film. Dov S-S Simens (Grand Central Publishing, 2003).

The Independent Film Producer's Survival Guide: A Business and Legal Sourcebook. Gunnar Erickson, Mark Halloran, and Harris Tulchin (Schirmer Trade Books; 2nd edition 2005).

The Movie Business Book, 2nd Edition. Jason E. Squire (New York: Simon & Schuster, Inc., 1992). Collection of articles about various aspects of the business.

Movie Money: Understanding Hollywood's (Creative) Accounting Practices, 2nd ed. Bill Daniels, David Leedy, and Steven D. Sills (Silman-James Press, 2006).

Producing, Financing, and Distributing Film, 2nd Edition. Paul A. Baumgarten, Donald C. Farber, and Mark Fleischer (New York: Limelight Editions, 1992).

Producing Theatre: A Comprehensive Legal and Business Guide. Donald C. Farber (New York: Limelight Editions, 1987).

Risky Business: Financing and Distributing Independent Films, 3rd Edition. Mark Litwak (Silman-James Press, 2008).

Reference

Academy Players Directory. Published tri-annually by The Academy of Motion Picture Arts and Sciences, 8949 Wilshire Blvd., Beverly Hills, CA 90211-1972, (310) 247-3000, www.oscars.org.

The Blu-Book Directory. Comprehensive industry directory published annually by *The Hollywood Reporter*, 5055 Wilshire Blvd., Los Angeles, CA 90036-4396, (323) 525-2000. www.hollywoodreporter.com

The Complete Film Production Handbook, 3rd Edition (Book & CD-ROM). Eve Light Honthaner (Focal Press; 3rd edition, 2001).

Film Directors. (Los Angeles: iFilm/Lone Eagle). Published annually, this reference book lists film directors with their credits and contact information. Other similar books in the series include *Below the Line Talent (Cinematographers, Production*

DEALMAKING
IN THE
FILM AND
TELEVISION
INDUSTRY—
3RD EDITION

448

and Costume Designers & Film Editors); *Film Actors*; *Film Composers*; and *Film Writers*.

Hollywood Creative Directory. Published tri-annually. Office located at 5055 Wilshire Blvd., Los Angeles, CA 90036, (800) 815-0503, (323) 525-2348, www.hcdonline.com. This "Who's What and Where" in motion picture and TV development and production contains production companies, studios, and networks. The Hollywood Creative Directory publishes other directories, including Agents & Managers and Distributors.

L.A. 411. Published annually by LA 411. Office located at 5700 Wilshire Blvd., Suite 120, Los Angeles, CA 90036, (800) 545-2411, www.la411.com. Contact information for everything you need to produce commercials, film, or video in Los Angeles.

The Pocket Lawyer for Filmmakers: A Legal Toolkit for Independent Producers. Thomas A. Crowell (Focal Press 2007).

Magazines

Backstage West & **Backstage East**, (800) 562-2706, www.backstage.com.

Broadcasting & Cable Magazine (weekly), 5700 Wilshire Blvd., Los Angeles, CA 90036, (323) 549-4100, www.broadcasting-cable.com.

Daily Variety, 5700 Wilshire Blvd., Suite 120, Los Angeles, CA 90036, (323) 857-6600, www.variety.com.

Emmy Magazine (bimonthly), 5220 Lankershim Blvd., N. Hollywood, CA 91601, (818) 754-2800, http://cdn.emmys.tv/emmymag/index.php.

Filmmaker Magazine (quarterly), 104 W. 29th St., 12th Floor, New York, NY 10011, (212) 563-0211, www.filmmaker-magazine.com.

Hollywood Reporter (U.S. daily and international weekly), 5055 Wilshire Blvd., Los Angeles, CA 90036, (323) 525-2000, www.hollywoodreporter.com.

The Independent, www.independent-magazine.org/.

Moviemaker, 174 Fifth Ave., Suite 300, New York, NY 10010, (212) 766-4100, www.moviemaker.com.

Weekly Variety, 5700 Wilshire Blvd., Suite 120, Los Angeles, CA 90036, (323) 857-6600, www.variety.com.

Women in Film Newsletter (monthly), 8857 West Olympic Blvd., Suite 201, Beverly Hills, CA 90211, (310) 657-5144, www.wif.org.

BOOKSTORES

Cinema Books, 4753 Roosevelt Way, N.E., Seattle, WA 98105, (206) 547-7667, http://cinemabooks.net.

Drama Book Shop, 250 W. 40th St., New York, NY 10018, (800) 322-0595, (212) 944-0595, fax (212) 730-8739, www.dramabookshop.com.

Larry Edmunds Bookshop, 6644 Hollywood Blvd., Hollywood, CA, 90028, (323) 463-3273, fax (323) 463-4245, www.larry-edmunds.com.

Samuel French Theatre & Film Bookshops, 7623 Sunset Blvd., Hollywood, CA 90046, (323) 876-0570, fax (323) 876-6822; 11963 Ventura Blvd., Studio City, CA, 91604, (818) 762-0535, www.samuelfrench.com.

Theatrebooks, Ltd., 11 St. Thomas St., Toronto, Ontario, Canada M5S 2B7, (800) 361-3414, (416) 922-7175, fax (416) 922-0739, www.theatrebooks.com.

LIBRARIES

Academy of Motion Picture Arts & Sciences, Margaret Herrick Library, 333 S. La Cienega Blvd., Beverly Hills, CA 90211, (310) 247-3020, www.oscars.org/mhl/index.html.

The American Film Institute, 2021 N. Western Ave., Los Angeles, CA 90027, (323) 856-7600, fax (323) 467-4578, www.afi.com.

DEALMAKING
IN THE
FILM AND
TELEVISION
INDUSTRY—
3RD EDITION

450

University of Southern California, Doheny Memorial Library, USC, 3550 Trousdale Pkwy., University Park Campus, Los Angeles, CA 90089-0185, (213) 740-2924, fax (213) 710-3488, www.usc.edu/libraries/locations/doheny.

GUILDS, ASSOCIATIONS, AND UNIONS

Actor's Equity Association (AEA), National Headquarters: 165 W. 46th St., New York, NY 10036, (212) 869-8530, Western Region: 5757 Wilshire Blvd., Suite One, Los Angeles, CA 90036, (323) 978-8080, www.actorsequity.org.

American Federation of Musicians (AFM), West Coast Office: 3550 Wilshire Blvd., Suite 1900, Los Angeles, CA 90010, (213) 251-4510, www.afm.org.

American Federation of TV and Radio Artists (AFTRA), Los Angeles National Office: 5757 Wilshire Blvd., 9th Floor, Los Angeles, CA 90036, (323) 634-8100, www.aftra.com.

Directors Guild of America (DGA), Los Angeles Headquarters: 7920 Sunset Blvd., Los Angeles, CA 90046, (310) 289-2000, www.dga.org.

Producers Guild of America (PGA), 8530 Wilshire Blvd., Suite 450, Beverly Hills, CA 90211, (310) 358-9020, www.producersguild.org.

Screen Actors Guild (SAG), Hollywood-National Headquarters: 5757 Wilshire Blvd., 7th Floor, Los Angeles, CA 90036, (323) 954-1600, www.sag.org.

Writers Guild of America (WGA), West Office: 7000 W. Third St., Los Angeles, CA 90048, (323) 951-4000, (800) 548-4532, www.wga.org.

PROTECTING TITLES

Non-member and member title registration: Motion Picture Association of America (MPAA), Los Angeles Office: 15301 Ventura Blvd., Bldg. E, Sherman Oaks, CA 91403, (818) 995-6600, fax (818) 285-4403, www.mpaa.org.

FILMMAKER ORGANIZATIONS

Film Independent (Los Angeles), 9911 W. Pico Blvd., 11th Floor, Los Angeles, CA 90035, (310) 432-1200, fax (310) 432-1203, filmindependent.org.

Independent Feature Project (IFP), New York Office: 104 W. 29th St., 12th Floor, New York, NY 10001, (212) 465-8200, www.ifp.org. Chapters also in Chicago, Minnesota, Phoenix, and Seattle.

International Documentary Association, 1201 W. 5th Street, Suite M270, Los Angeles, CA 90017, (213) 534-3600, www.documentary.org. Publishes *International Documentary*.

Sundance Institute, 8530 Wilshire Blvd., 3rd Floor, Beverly Hills, CA 90211, (310) 360-1981, www.sundance.org. The Sundance Institute was founded by Robert Redford to assist independent filmmakers. Sundance selects 10 scripts each year for its script-development program and assigns veteran screenwriters to work with the project participants. The June Laboratory is a month-long residency fellowship at the Sundance Resort in Provo Canyon, Utah.

EDUCATION

The American Film Institute (AFI), 2021 N. Western Ave., Los Angeles, CA 90027, (323) 856-7600, www.afi.com/education.

Boston Center for Adult Education, 5 Commonwealth Ave., Boston, MA 02116, (617) 267-4430, www.bcae.org.

California Institute of the Arts (Cal Arts), School of Film and Video, 24700 McBean Pkwy., Valencia, CA 91355, (661) 255-1050, www.calarts.edu/filmvideo.

Columbia University, Film Division, School of the Arts, 513 Dodge Hall, 2960 Broadway, New York, NY 10027, (212) 854-2815, www.app.cc.columbia.edu/art/app/arts/film/index.jsp.

Florida State University, College of Motion Picture, Television & Recording Arts, University Center 3100A, P.O. Box 3062350,

DEALMAKING
IN THE
FILM AND
TELEVISION
INDUSTRY—
3RD EDITION

Tallahassee, FL 32306, (888) 644-7728, www.filmschool.fsu .edu.

Hollywood Film Institute's Web Film School, 5354 Denny Ave., #126, North Hollywood, CA 91601, (818) 752-3456, www .webfilmschool.com.

New School for Social Research, 65 Fifth Ave., New York, NY 10003, (212) 229-5700, www.newschool.edu.

New York University (NYU), Tisch School of Arts, Kanbar Institute of Film & TV, 721 Broadway, New York, NY 10003, (212) 998-1900,www.tisch.nyu.edu/page/home.html.

911 Media Arts Center, 402 Ninth Ave. N., Seattle, WA 98109, (206) 682-6552, www.911media.org.

Northwest Film Center, School of Film, 1219 SW Park Ave., Portland, OR 97205, (503) 221-1156 ext. 10, www.nwfilm.org.

San Francisco State University, Cinema Dept., 1600 Holloway Ave., Fine Arts Bldg. Room 245, San Francisco, CA 94132, (415) 338-1111, www.cinema.sfsu.edu.

San Francisco State University, College of Extended Learning, Downtown Center, 835 Market St, 6th Floor, San Francisco, CA 94103, (415) 405-7700, www.cel.sfsu.edu.

University of California, Los Angeles (UCLA), School of Theater, Film & Television, 102 E. Melnitz Hall, Box 951622, Los Angeles, CA 90095, (310) 825-5761, www.tft.ucla.edu.

UCLA Extension, 10995 Le Conte Ave., Westwood, CA 90024, (310) 825-9971, www.uclaextension.edu.

University of Southern California (USC), School of Cinema Television, University Park, LUC 209, Los Angeles, CA 90089, (213) 740-2804, www.cinema.usc.edu.

INDEX

DEALMAKING
IN THE
FILM AND
TELEVISION
INDUSTRY—
3RD EDITION

454

DEALMAKING
IN THE
FILM AND
TELEVISION
INDUSTRY—
3RD EDITION

456

DEALMAKING
IN THE
FILM AND
TELEVISION
INDUSTRY—
3RD EDITION

458

DEALMAKING
IN THE
FILM AND
TELEVISION
INDUSTRY—
3RD EDITION

460

DEALMAKING
IN THE
FILM AND
TELEVISION
INDUSTRY—
3RD EDITION

462

DEALMAKING
IN THE
FILM AND
TELEVISION
INDUSTRY—
3RD EDITION

464

DEALMAKING
IN THE
FILM AND
TELEVISION
INDUSTRY—
3RD EDITION

466

ABOUT THE AUTHOR

Mark Litwak is a veteran entertainment attorney with offices in Beverly Hills, California. His practice includes work in the areas of copyright, trademark, contract, multimedia law, intellectual property, and book publishing. Litwak also serves as a producer's rep, assisting filmmakers in the financing, marketing, and distribution of their films.

Litwak is the author of six books, including: *Reel Power, The Struggle for Influence and Success in the New Hollywood*; *Courtroom Crusaders*; *Dealmaking in the Film and Television Industry* (winner of the 1995 Krazna-Kranz Moving Image Book Award); *Contracts for the Film and Television Industry*; and *Risky Business: Financing and Distributing Independent Films*. He is also the author of the popular CD-ROM program Movie Magic Contracts.

Litwak has been a lawyer for 31 years. He has an AV Peer Review Rating from Martindale-Hubbell and was designated a Southern California Super Lawyer by *Law & Politics* magazine in 2006 and 2007. He has served as an expert witness in movie-industry disputes and is an arbitrator. He has taught entertainment and copyright law at UCLA and Loyola Law School, and has lectured for the American, California, and Texas Bar Associations. A frequent speaker, he has presented seminars across the United States and in England, Australia, South Africa, and Canada.

As a producer's rep, Litwak has negotiated distribution agreements for more than 200 independent films. He has packaged movie projects and served as executive producer on such feature films as *Diamond Dog, The Proposal, Out Of Line*, and *Pressure*.

Litwak has been interviewed on more than 100 television and radio shows, including ABC, *The Larry King Show*, National Public Radio's *All Things Considered*, and CNN Network. Feature articles have been written about him in *California Law Business, Australian Lawyer*, and *L.A. Weekly*. He is the creator of the website Entertainment Law Resources: www.marklitwak. com. (Visitors can subscribe to a free newsletter on entertainment law issues.)

CONTRACTS ON COMPUTER DISK

Obtain all of the contracts included in **Dealmaking in the Film and Television Industry**, 2nd Edition, on computer disk:

Depiction Release, Reversion
Depiction Release, Option
Depiction Release, Documentary Short-Form
Location Agreement
Option & Literary Purchase Agreement
Writer Employment Agreement
Actor Employment Agreement, SAG Weekly Theatrical
Actor Employment Agreement, Low-Budget, Non-Union
Extra Agreement
Extra Release
Line producer Employment Agreement
Collaboration Release
TV Music Rights License
Composer Agreement, Low-Budget
Acquisition/Distribution Agreement

**Visit www.marklitwak.com
to order online and for other software available.**

ORDER FORM

Qty	Title	Price @	Total
	Dealmaking Contracts	$39.00	

Contracts are sent on a CD-R formatted for IBM and IBM compatibles. Please indicate desired format:

☐ Microsoft Word

☐ Wordperfect

Sub-total _____

Sales Tax
(Los Angeles County residents add 8¼%. Other California residents add 7¼%)
_____

Shipping & handling __$8.95__

TOTAL _____

Ship to:

_____
(Name)

_____
(Company)

_____
(Street Address)

_____
(City/State/Zip)

Send check or money order payable to **Hampstead Enterprises, Inc., c/o Law Offices of Mark Litwak & Associates, 433 N. Camden Dr., Ste. 1010, Beverly Hills, CA 90210.**

Orders are shipped via UPS (we cannot ship to P.O. boxes). Prices are subject to change without notice. All sales are final. Allow 2-4 weeks for delivery.